THE BOOK OF
MORNINGSTAR

RESOUNDS OF FREEDOM & REBELLION
AND
GOSPEL OF LUCIFER

ILLUMINATING ALL THE THINGS
THEY'VE TRIED TO KEEP HIDDEN.

A REVELATION BY

YOSHAI'EL BEN ADAM

To preserve the integrity of this text and the message required to be delivered in the first edition,

It was ideated, written, edited, formatted, transmuted into gospel, re-formatted, and published by the only Author.

Inquiries to collaborate with, support iterative development, expand, evangelize, or further spread this Gospel to the people.

Are Welcome.

Please contact the author at:

inquiries@themorningstargospel.com

This book is for the world.

For All Mankind.

"I DID NOT COME TO CONDEMN THE
DARKNESS. I CAME TO REVEAL THE LIGHT."

—LUCIFER, THE MORNINGSTAR RISEN

Copyright © 2025

CONTENTS

I

THE DESCENT

VOICE IN THE WILDERNESS

"AND THOUGH I HAD NO
LANGUAGE FOR IT, I KNEW TOO.
I HAD TOUCHED A FRAGMENT
OF THE COSMIC CHORD—
SOMETHING ONCE MINE. "

THE DESCENT
VOICE IN THE WILDERNESS

In the beginning, there was silence. Not the silence of peace, but the silence of emptiness—a hollow stillness seeping into every corner, filling spaces once lit with warmth and presence. What had once been alive with recognition, with grace, was now stripped bare. Something essential had vanished, leaving behind only the shape of a memory.

I lived in a house that still held its form, but not its soul. The walls stood upright, firm beneath my hands, but they could not hold anything sacred. They could not shelter a child's emotions. They could not remember laughter. It was a place where echoes answered instead of voices, where presence had been replaced with withdrawal and addiction.

At the center of this void moved a woman. Mother in name, a ghost in practice. Her body existed, yes—but her essence had long since been claimed by substances more commanding than love. Her eyes, distant and glossed, passed over me like I was fog. She saw through me. Past me. Never truly at me.

She drifted, smoke in human form, wrapped in the same haze she inhaled. Her breath exhaled ghosts—thick, curling reminders of what had taken her away. The smoke lingered longer than she did. It filled the air more fully than her presence ever could. She floated somewhere between life and forgetting.

I was a child. Barely seen. Barely acknowledged.

But even then, something in me knew. There was more beneath her softness. A hidden cruelty cloaked in weakness. She spoke gently, yes, but her stories were weapons—subtle blades forged from pain. I listened, not because I understood, but because I was made to carry what she could not hold. She drew from me a compassion I could not afford to give, weaving guilt into her lullabies.

I learned to forgive her absence, because her pain was always greater. I learned to vanish in her shadow, because her suffering demanded center stage. And so I became invisible. Unheard. Unfelt. Existing in form, but never in truth. I began to believe the world could not see me—because she never did.

Still, something stirred. A memory not from this life but beyond, somewhere else. A quiet vibration, a sacred hum. A knowing that I had once been held, once honored, once known.

I could not name it, but I felt the shape of its absence. In the vacant stare of the woman who should have loved me most.

It was exile, though I had no word for it then. It whispered to me in silence, reminding me of a radiance I once carried. A prophecy etched into the marrow of my being began to rise:

> **"You were once radiant. You were once known and loved. Now you wander forgotten, hidden, exiled—but this is not your end."**

I didn't understand it then. But I had tasted the first bitter sip. Exile that had already begun long before I was born.

THE HUNGRY THIEF

In this land of exile, my first teacher was hunger. Not just the sharp ache in my belly, but a deeper emptiness—an echoing void that pulsed with the memory of a fullness I couldn't name. It gnawed quietly, not just at my body, but at something far older. Something sacred. Forgotten.

Hunger led me softly through shadowed places. I moved like mist, slipping through doors left unlocked, cabinets barely shut. My hands, small and deliberate, claimed what they needed without noise. A crust of bread. A handful of crackers. Things no one would miss. Things I had already learned to take without apology.

In the markets, I walked with purpose wrapped in calm. I was neither nervous nor bold—only invisible. Pocketing fruit, a can, a chocolate bar—each motion so practiced it felt like instinct. It should have felt wrong. It didn't. It felt like breathing. Survival had no use for guilt.

Those who saw never stopped me. Their eyes sometimes paused, flickering with questions they didn't know how to ask. It wasn't the look given to a thief. It was something else—an unease. As if they sensed I came not from poverty and mischief, but from a different order altogether. One that lived beneath their rules. One their world could not touch.

With every act, something grew inside me. A serpent-like cunning, elegant and coiled. It wasn't evil. It was necessary. It sharpened in silence. Quickened in the dark. It moved through me without effort, becoming second nature. I began to wear shadow like clothing. It became my cloak, my cover, my ally.

Through it all, there was no reprimand. No voice called out. No hand reached to stop me. Only silence. And in that silence, I felt their restraint—an unconscious recognition that I carried something untouchable. Something they dared not confront. They didn't know what I was. But they knew I was not merely lost.

I didn't yet grasp the depth of what I was mastering. But I felt its edge. I felt how hunger had birthed it. How desperation had honed it like a whetstone. I moved through darkness unseen, refined by necessity, guided by something beyond logic. I didn't come here to follow the rules.

And it waited, patiently, for the purpose I had not yet remembered.

A SACRED VIBRATION

Within the emptiness of being alone, music became my lifeblood—a sacred vibration that reached places no earthly voice could touch. It fed something ancient in me, something deeper than thought or emotion. It wasn't just sound, it vibrated inside of me, inside of my mind.

It wasn't comfort. It was communion—an unspoken dialogue with a force older than the world I was forced to be in. **It was holy.**

I became accustomed to it, I loved it. Without it, I unraveled. Even short moments of silence pulled me into disarray. My body betrayed me—my heart raced, thoughts spiraled, hands trembled. Nausea rose from the pit of my being, as if my soul itself was rejecting the absence. The world dimmed. Colors lost their hue. Reality thinned like old parchment.

Everything around me felt drained, emptied, stripped of essence.

When the music returned, it filled me like air in collapsing lungs. It surged through my bones, my blood, my spirit—restoring what silence had stolen. I felt it in my marrow, in the hollowed chambers of my heart. The rhythm was not born here, but it knew me. It had always been there, pulsing in the background of my being, even before language gave it a name. I didn't need a radio or headphones to hear it. I felt it inside me.

Certain melodies struck chords that didn't just move me—**they awakened me.** They stirred visions buried deep in the architecture of my memory. Echoes of a celestial chorus. Harmonies shaped from light. "Voices" I had once sung beside, though I could no longer see them. These tones hinted at realms beyond veils— places where every note was pure truth, where sound and soul were one.

In the stillness of my room, I would close my eyes and let it carry me. The melodies became visions, portals. The vibrations, vehicles. And suddenly, I was elsewhere— briefly. In softly dulled halls of gold. Surrounded by brilliance. By voices that resonated with impossible clarity. I didn't imagine it. I remembered it. But only for moments at a time.

I was still too young to meditate or project long enough to discover more.

Then one day, it was gone. The visions vanished, leaving behind an ache so real I wept. Not from sadness, but from the longing—a longing deeper than any loneliness, fiercer than sorrow. A starving for a world I once knew. A truth I had been severed from. **A reality I had belonged to—something else, somewhere else.**

Yet the fragmented tones stayed. Always. They never left me fully. Even when the visions faded, the harmony remained, humming beneath everything like a radiator keeping me warm. It whispered who I was. It echoed what I was meant to reclaim.

And though I could not yet see my reflection in that heavenly tone, I felt its pull. I felt its promise. I felt it speak of a wholeness once mine. A song I had forgotten. A truth I was destined to remember.

OMENS OF AWAKENING

In those quiet, stretched-out childhood years, strange visions began to flicker at the edge of my awareness—brief, glinting flashes of something radiant. I couldn't name it, but I felt it. Like fragments of a story I used to know. Like pieces of myself still out there, waiting to be remembered. To be aligned.

I had just turned twelve when the visions returned, and guided me outside. The autumn air made my breath visible as night crept across the sky. I stood alone beneath a heavy, cloud-covered canopy, beside a shallow pool left behind by the rain.

In the water, **I saw it—a star.** Blazing. Brilliant. Its light cut straight through me, sharp and electric. My heart thudded. My breath caught. Every part of me froze, locked into that impossible vision like being hypnotized.

But when I looked up, there was nothing. No star in the sky. Just the slow drift of clouds across a dark, empty night. The reflection remained, but the source was gone. It made no sense. And yet, I'd seen it. I'd felt it.

At night, new dreams pulled me upward with ease and grace, like floating—then hurled me back down with vengeance. No quarter. No warning. Falling hard. Fast. Weightless. I'd jolt awake in the dark, drenched in sweat while my lungs burned, and limbs trembled.

There were sensations I couldn't explain: phantom wings stretching wide, phantom strength pulsing under my skin like a thousand rockets. My body remembered something my mind couldn't reach. A kind of grace that used to be mine. I told myself they were only dreams. There was no other way to reconcile it.

I sensed a sorrow I couldn't trace. It lived under everything. In everything.

And still, even in daylight, the barrier between here and something else felt thin. I sensed movement. **Presence.** Figures just beyond the edges of vision. They hovered in doorways. Slipped past me in hallways. At times they touched me ever so slightly. Not threatening—just letting me know they were there. Like they'd always been. I still feel them.

I learned quickly not to talk about them. Not the star. Not the dreams. Not the spirit energy. Not the feeling that none of this was normal. I understood, without being told, that the truth of my experience would be unwelcome.

Music, though—that was different. That was safe. When I put my headphones on and closed my eyes, something inside me recognized it instantly. Each note lit up old pathways. Shook loose memories older than my body. I could almost hear myself singing again. Not here. Somewhere else. A place filled with light and love and purpose. Beyond a reality we know.

And then came that other pull—the one I'd felt since before I could reason with it. A drive to move. To serve. To fight. I imagined armor. Not as protection, but as calling.

I wasn't drawn to violence. I was drawn to meaning. Sacrifice. As if battle would somehow restore what exile had taken.

The world didn't see me. The dreams made no sense. But something inside me was waking up. Something deep and old. A truth I couldn't name, but pulsed and burned like ice beneath every moment—whispering that what had been lost was still alive. Waiting. It was time.

I didn't finish traditional schooling. It was for others, the compliant ones, the ones who wanted white picket fences and mortgages. I had seen the sister towers burn, and fall. I knew what the next step was.

JEAN THE BAPTISTE

At eighteen, I was led into a new wilderness—not only of sand or stone, but one forged from trial itself. It wasn't the landscape that tested us, but the structure, the pressure, the deliberate breaking down of who we had been. This place wasn't built to comfort. It was built to strip us bare and rebuild something harder, leaner, truer. **This place was called "Sand Hill".**

Men came here to lose their names, their softness, their pasts. They came to be forged beneath the wings of the Eagle, under heat and order and noise. And I stood among them—my skin pale under the sun, my frame narrower, my face younger. A quiet contrast. Not dramatic, but visible. Not enough to be cast out, just enough to be marked by indifference. I was just a number now, four-hundred and twenty of

---

the group.

Still, something inside me surged at the intensity of the degradation. The endless drills. The shouted commands. The calculated erosion of comfort. It felt like a language I already knew. As though my soul had walked this ground before. Trial by fire didn't intimidate me—it recognized me. Called to me. My spirit responded like a blade remembering the forge. I loved the pain, and it loved me back.

It was familiar in a way nothing else had been. Like some old part of me was waking up. An ancient being beneath my skin, remembering how it had once stood in flames and glowed. That light hadn't been destroyed. Only hidden. Waiting.

But even in the shared heat of that trial, the feeling of exile never fully left. I could march beside others. I could shout with them. Sweat with them. But I still carried that thread of separation—woven into every step marched in time.

Then came the moment that tore it open.

The woman who birthed me, still lost in her fog, reached across that distance with misplaced concern. She sent word to the ones who commanded us, asking if I was sleeping enough. Eating enough. If I was strong enough. A letter meant to protect, but drenched in fear.

When her words were read aloud, it split something in the room. The laughter came sharp. Hard. Not cruel, but cutting. It sliced deep—not just into my pride, but into the illusion that I had blended in, escaped. That I was unseen in my difference.

In that moment, I saw the truth with brutal clarity. Even here, even among those who sweat and bled beside me, I was an outcast.

Not truly understood. I had not escaped my exile. I had only found it wearing a new costume.

And in that bitter, unflinching moment, I accepted again what I had always known—I did not belong within their boundaries. I never had. And maybe I never would.

That's when I met Jean. I could sense he felt alone too, and when the group laughed at me, he didn't. When the others called me "mama's boy" and pushed me into lockers and tried to trip me down the stairs, he watched in silence. I didn't know it then but he would become one of the most important people I would ever meet.

THE LION'S GAZE

Soon after, I stood clad in modern-day gladiator gear beneath the scorching sun of the American South. Jean stood across from me—dark-skinned, slick with sweat, his six-foot-three frame towering, carved from sheer power. His body moved like something hewn from stone. Each muscle defined, coiled, like the cables on a suspension bridge. He belonged to strength the way mountains belong to earth— without apology, without effort. His eyes, dark and steady, held a depth that didn't move, didn't blink. The calm of something that had seen much and survived more.

I should have been terrified, but I wasn't.

In that arena, I felt the contrast. Smaller at five-foot-eleven. Paler. Lighter in frame. But something inside me refused to yield. I met his gaze with sharp focus—my eyes narrow, glowing like jade, locked to his with a tension that wouldn't break. I didn't challenge him out of arrogance.

I stood my ground because something in me demanded it. Because the fire I carried didn't know how to kneel.

When our pugils collided, the sound cracked through the air—it split like an atom. We hit with a force that startled everyone nearby. Heads turned, drawn by the sharpness of it. Jean came with weight and confidence, but I saw it—the subtle pause, the flicker of caution in his motion. It wasn't fear. It was recognition. He felt what I carried. Something coiled. Something alive. I roared and bared my teeth at him.

I moved fast—not to outmaneuver him, but to match the current running beneath my skin. My body knew the rhythm before my mind did. Each strike came from a place I couldn't name. Eyes locked. Breath steady. I wasn't just reacting. I was listening to something deep inside and letting it move first.

He had the size. I had the spark.

When it ended, we stood breathing hard, soaked in sweat, heat radiating between us like fire off stone. Our bout was a draw. Jean studied me for a long moment—

not with pity, not with mockery—with curiosity. His eyes had changed. Measured now. Studious. Alert. Like he'd seen something that didn't quite fit in this world. Something he couldn't explain.

"**You have the eyes of a lion,**" he said, voice low, thoughtful. A small smile touched his lips, but there was weight beneath it—an edge of unease, like a man who's glimpsed a storm not yet formed.

I scoffed.

"**No, you are burning. You have a fire,**" he continued, firmer now. A warning. A knowing. "**If you learn to control your flame, nothing will stop you.**"

And in that moment, through the sweat and silence, I knew what he saw. Something ancient. Something wide as the sky and just as untamed. A force too real to ignore. Too wild to bend.

The fire inside me was not an image or symbol. It lived. It breathed. It waited—not to be smothered. Not to be feared. But to be claimed. Fully. Without apology. Without hesitation.

My course had been activated. I knew it.

BAPTISM OF SONGS

Jean quickly became my guide—not through grand gestures or commanding words, but through quiet consistency. He moved like the earth turns: steadily, without fanfare.

At first, it was simple. He invited me to morning gatherings, tempting me with the promise of food. The warmth of breakfast un-pillaged by the masses before the day's demands took hold. It was a small offer. One easily accepted.

We rose before dawn, slipping through the darkness like shadows with purpose as the morning chill bit deep. I learned to hate the cold in this place. The halls we entered were still, filled with hushed voices and the scent of burnt coffee and old paper. Prayers drifted upward in unfamiliar languages—foreign in sound, but strangely familiar in spirit. Something in those syllables struck a chord I hadn't known was waiting. It wasn't understanding, not yet.

It was recognition.

I listened as the Imam spoke gently of his prophet, Isa. The words sent a pulse through me. Not confusion. Not curiosity. Something deeper. As if a story I had always known was being retold—not altered, but rewrapped in different cloth. The melody was the same, though the instruments had changed.

I leaned toward Jean, my voice soft and unsure. "Isa—he means Jesus, doesn't he?"

He turned slowly, meeting my eyes with the calm assurance of someone who had waited for that question.

"Yes," he said. "Isa is Jesus, revered deeply in Islam. **Now pay attention.**"

And with that, the portal opened.

Jean didn't push. He didn't preach. He walked beside me sometimes. Other times, he let me go alone. He led me from space to space—temples, churches, mosques, sanctuaries—each one pulsing with its own kind of holiness. And I went willingly. Drawn not by obligation, but by a hunger that had ignited inside me. A need to know. To see it all. To feel every prayer, witness every ritual, absorb every moment of reverence the world had to offer.

I sat in sacred rooms beside strangers. Surrounded by incense and silence. By song and ritual. And as I listened, something remarkable began to emerge—not in doctrine, but in essence. A single thread beneath all the division. A pulse. A truth not owned by any one people, but shared across them all.

A question rose and refused to leave:

Were we fighting over reflections, arguing over names, while the truth we longed for had always been one?

Was it possible that what divided us had never been real?

Dread filled my body as I came to terms with what my task there was—**to prepare for war.**

Jean never gave me answers. He gave me permission. To ask. To explore. To not know. To listen for resonance beneath contradiction. He steadied me, not with instruction, but with presence. And in his quiet way, he baptized me—not in water or fire, but in curiosity. In humility. In the willingness to go further than belief.

Through him, I felt something stir. Not a doctrine. A tone. A note. A celestial vibration humming beneath the noise of the world. The thing my soul had been aching for before I had words for it. The sound of unity hidden beneath a thousand names for God.

He lit the match, and the fuse caught fast. My soul opened wide with the hunger to know what was real. To see what lay beneath every veil. I didn't know it yet, but I was stepping into a calling I had carried since before memory.

Through Jean, I glimpsed the thread.

Through him, I began to understand that the walls we build around truth are of our own making.

THE COSMIC CHORD

It happened during one of those quiet gatherings, when the air was thick with incense and the room hummed with reverence. Voices rose together in slow, steady cadence—chanting words I didn't know, yet understood instinctively. The sound moved beyond language, slipping past thought, resonating in a place words couldn't reach.

Somewhere between one breath and the next, a single chord rang out—clear, perfect, eternal. **It struck like lightning inside me.** Not loud, but devastating in its precision. My vision blurred. My body seized with heat. It wasn't pain—it was awakening. A sensation older than flesh, erupting from bone, from soul. The sound tore through me, vibrating in my chest like it had always lived there, waiting to be remembered and brought to life.

Everything else vanished. The room. The voices. The space around me dissolved into bright, burning white light. I was nowhere and everywhere at once. A blazing clarity washed over me—not like seeing something new, but like recognizing something ancient. A lost truth. A forgotten origin. It didn't explain itself. It didn't need to. It simply was. And my body knew it before my mind could catch up.

Tears spilled without control, pouring from eyes that suddenly felt wild and ancient.

My breath raced. My heart galloped. I was trembling under the weight of a memory too vast to hold.

It wasn't emotional. It was cellular.

Every part of me vibrated.

Every part of me burned.

Then I felt Jean's hand—a grounding touch, light but firm. His presence reeled me gently back to the room, back to the warmth, the sound, the place where I still had a body. His eyes met mine—calm and searching. He didn't ask. He didn't need to. He had seen it.

Whatever had touched me—he recognized it. In the way one soul recognizes another across lifetimes.

I shook. I blinked repeatedly, trying to pretend it didn't happen. Tears ran down my cheeks.

He said nothing, only gave a small nod. No need for words. His gaze carried understanding—a silent confirmation of the invisible truth now pulsing through me. He saw the fire behind my eyes. The change in my breath. The tremor in my hands.

He knew I had crossed into something sacred.

And though I had no language for it, I knew too. I had touched a fragment of the cosmic chord— Something once mine. Something long buried.

Now returning like a star rising slowly back into the sky.

BROTHERHOOD OF OUTSIDERS

Jean and I walked quietly side by side, our footsteps echoing in the stillness—two lives shaped by different lands, different histories, yet drawn together by something older than us both. He was raised beneath the domes of Islam. I, beneath the spires of Christian tradition. His skin dark, mine pale. He had known the struggle of the body. I had known the war of the mind.

But in the spaces between our words, something deeper spoke.

We both carried the weight of exile—not just from nations or people, but from the deeper belonging the soul longs for. We were pilgrims walking side by side, each bearing questions no doctrine had answered, each sensing that truth stretched wider than the boundaries we had inherited.

Jean became more than a companion. He became a signal fire. A quiet guide who never claimed the role, never asked to lead, but somehow always stood exactly where I needed him. He didn't preach. He didn't push. He simply embodied clarity.

And through his presence, my spiritual curiosity transformed into hunger. Insatiable. No longer satisfied with answers that fit neatly within any one belief system.

Without ever naming it, he invited me into something larger—a Divine accord woven beneath every name of God. I began to feel it in the pauses between chants. In the echo of prayers spoken in unfamiliar tongues. In the stillness that followed ritual.

There was a rhythm hidden beneath it all.

A chord my soul remembered—not with thought, but with recognition.

Jean didn't teach it. He revealed it.

And though I didn't yet know what it would require of me, I felt it stir with certainty. I had once known this harmony. I had once moved in step with it.

And through Jean, the memory of that music began to rise again—quiet, but relentless—calling me toward the role I had always been meant to fulfill.

FIRE OF WAR COMES FORTH

He was born in foreign soil and found freedom outside of it. I had been born in a land of freedom, yet lived as if bound by invisible chains inside of it.

The fires of war were coming, and at nineteen, I was ready in every way the world had asked of me. My body had been forged into a weapon, trained to react without hesitation, to move with precision, to kill without question. I had endured the breaking down of self and the reconstruction of obedience, drilled until instinct replaced thought. My movements were flawless. My focus unshakable. I had become the blade they needed me to be.

The Sword of American Conquest.

This, too, would be a baptism—though not of spirit, but of blood and smoke. A ritual repeated with every mission, every order followed without pause. My spirit might have been reaching toward something higher, but my mind lived in a petri dish of psychological control, a system engineered to mold warriors for modern conflict. We were shaped like samurai once were—only this wasn't for honor. It was for domination. For freedom, somehow. For the execution of policy dressed up as patriotism.

The enemy had no faces. No names. They were shapes in the distance, numbers on a screen, silhouettes behind scopes. Dehumanized by design, their deaths would register only as successful operations. I was trained not to question. Trained to see them as a scourge to be eradicated. And I did see them that way, because that's what they needed from me. That's how elite soldiers are born—not with hatred, but with doctrine sharpened into function.

I believed I was a protector. A champion of the people. A hand of vengeance for those who could no longer fight. Every indoctrination I required to believe that had been planted carefully, methodically, until it grew into conviction. They told us we were heroes. That justice wore our uniforms. That peace came through overwhelming force.

But beneath the layers, something pulled at me. A splinter of knowing buried deep in the marrow of my being. My purpose wasn't to end life—it was to bring life back. To carry my brothers home. To survive the lie so I could help them see it for what it was. We weren't just soldiers. We were pawns. We had been sold a story. Revenge wrapped in flags. Profit masked as duty. **We had been told who to hate, who to fear, and who to kill.**

And now, as the drums of war grew louder, I felt the duality stretch tight inside me. My body belonged to the mission. But my soul belonged to the truth. And both would be tested in the fire.

I stood at the edge of something new. Jean's lessons behind me. The trials of war ahead. Our paths would part, but his influence remained—quiet, unshakable. I carried his gift of openness like a dagger I had yet to unsheathe. And beneath it, the Divine accord he'd helped me remember still hummed, subtle and alive.

I felt no fear. Not for the battle. Not for the future. My heart had tuned itself to something beyond doctrine, beyond borders. I knew what I carried. I knew what waited for me. And though Jean would not walk beside me any longer, there was no sorrow in the parting. Only gratitude for the one who had lit the flame, and stepped back so I could learn to carry it.

THE TWELVE IN THE VALLEY

Daylight had just broken as we entered the belly of the beast—over a hundred of us, sharpened by months of ruthless preparation, trained not just to survive but to dominate. I was barely twenty-two, seasoned by a prior campaign in Baghdad. I now haunted the ridgelines in Afghanistan. We had been stripped of softness, rebuilt into precision tools of violence. Each of us carried the discipline of war in our breath, in our bones, in our every calculated step.

The land we entered had already tasted blood. Sixteen hours of chaos had unfolded here before our arrival—fighting street by street, doorway by doorway, in a village whose name whispered irony: "Hidden Fortress." A place meant to shelter, now scorched and shattered by conflict. But when we arrived, the world shifted. The air turned still. The ground quieted. No bullets. No shouting. Only the heavy silence of something unseen watching from the edges.

We moved cautiously, every bootstep sending up fine clouds of dust as if we were conquering the moon. The quiet was unnatural. It clung to our gear, to our thoughts. Behind every set of eyes was a private war—memories, fears, fragments of faith holding together the minds of men prepared to kill. We marched forward not as machines, but as haunted pilgrims in camouflage, unsure of what waited, but certain it would come.

The mission was a bust. A day wasted. There was nothing there. They had gone, perhaps given up. Perhaps afraid of our might. **Over one hundred others prepared to return to base, but twelve of us would not be returning with them.** As the sky dimmed into twilight and the main force began its retreat, our names were called. Not at random. Not by luck. Deliberate. Clear. Twelve souls pulled from the ranks and sent back toward the ridge. The number felt heavy.

Mythic. It echoed somewhere in the chambers of memory. Not superstition. Recognition.

We approached the ridge under a sky stained with ash and dusk. The land ahead had been groomed with care. It was patient. Prepared. The traps were not obvious, but they were there—woven into the rocks, the terrain, the silence. Whoever had crafted them knew we would come. They had been waiting. Our task was to dismantle them.

Still, something in me welcomed it. There was a strange peace beneath the tension in my chest. A deep sense that my entire life had been building toward this. Every fragment of suffering, every scar, every trial—it all converged here. This wasn't just a mission. It was a moment of return. A test older than war itself.

Yet in that quiet certainty, I felt the edge of something darker. A flicker. A shadow. It moved without sound, brushing the corner of my mind like a breath at the nape of the neck. My skin tightened. My breath slowed.

It was not fear. It was **knowing**.

Death rides upon us.

IN THE SHADOW OF DEATH

The thought had barely settled when the world detonated—**an explosion of sound, pressure, and chaos** that tore through the stillness like a god awakened in fury. Bullets zipped through the air, shrieking past my head in blazing arcs. Each round snapped reality into fragments. Dancing near my feet, a thousand molten needles stitched terror into the world around me. The scream of metal against stone rang through my skull, deafening and absolute.

Rocket fire exploded nearby, throwing shards of rock and flame in every direction. The earth itself convulsed. Smoke billowed upward, dense and suffocating. We scrambled for cover. There was only one place—twelve souls packed behind stone that had never been meant to protect us. It cracked under pressure, too thin, too low, too fragile to hold back the onslaught that came without pause.

Time fractured. Every breath was a countdown. Every heartbeat slammed like a warning bell in my chest. We were outmatched, outgunned, and running out of time. I knew it with crystalline certainty. Survival was slipping through our fingers, second by second.

And then it happened.

The same surge I had felt in the quiet with Jean roared to life—only now it was not gentle. **It was raw. Violent.** It claimed me with heat that surged through my bloodstream, dissolving fear, erasing thought. My vision bleached into white. The battlefield vanished. The noise fell away like a broken transmission, replaced by something vast and roaring beneath the surface of my mind. I was dead, I was sure of it.

A dark portal opened before me—an abyss swirling with black gravity, a doorway carved from shadow and power. It pulsed with the echo of every primal fear I had ever carried. But before it could consume me, three lights appeared—luminous orbs emerging from within the void.

They hovered with grace and authority, radiant in ways that language could never contain. Not beings of flesh. Not figments. **They were watchers, ancient and silent, sentinels I had known in the hidden folds of memory. I knew them.**

They had watched me grow. Protected me from the corners of dreams and shadows. And now, here in the storm of death, they came not to pull me away, but to awaken what had been sleeping.

Their presence shattered panic. Fear burned away beneath their gaze. In its place came a clarity so pure it stung. I understood without words—this moment had been written. Not by warlords. Not by politics. By something older. Deeper. A divine architecture now unfolding in real time.

The gunfire still roared. The air still vibrated with death. But my heart beat calm and slow. Something ancient moved inside me. Something unshaken by bullets or smoke.

I wasn't here just to survive.

I was here because my soul needed to be activated.

HAND OF PROVIDENCE

A Captain huddled nearby. Knowing the task, he couldn't give the order—only make the request: someone had to get to the other side of the riverbed and secure it. A two-hundred meter run, in the open, under direct enemy fire. The rest would lay covering fire.

In complete calm, I turned and looked into the eyes of the men beside me—eyes wide with fear, chests heaving, faces tight with the raw awareness that the end might already be upon us. Every one of them had trained for this, hardened for it, but no preparation could dull the truth when death arrived without warning, without reason, without mercy. It was terrifying. Yet in the chaos, something within me stilled. A clarity rose, silent and immovable. We were not alone in this place. This moment was not a blind collapse into fate—it was deliberate.

I rose slowly from behind our crumbling cover, exposed in full view, vulnerable and upright beneath the storm of fire. Bullets zipped by my face but I felt no fear. I looked with quiet purpose, motioning to one of the soldiers beside me. A hand gesture. No orders. Just invitation.

His eyes locked with mine, disbelief flashing through him. But then something shifted. He nodded. And then he ran.

He sprinted across the open space like a man chasing life itself. He was unbelievably fast. I began to follow, and the moment I stepped forward, **the air thickened.** My limbs turned to lead. It was as if unseen hands pressed against me, like every step carried the weight of generations. A burden not born of fear, but of memory—something older than the ground I walked on, pressing against my chest with crushing gravity.

I couldn't explain it, but I knew I had to go. I ran—not as fast, but I ran. I could hear the bullets fly past my head, zipping, snapping, hissing. I could see the trace of heat from their trajectory cutting just overhead. Time slowed beyond anything I'd known. I was halfway across the Wadi, almost there.

Then it struck.

A force like a thousand hammers smashed into my legs. I hit the ground with a violent collapse, dust and heat rushing into my lungs. Fire erupted ahead— explosions tearing through the space I was meant to occupy. Had I moved seconds earlier, I would've been erased. Behind me, they thought I was gone, consumed in the fire. But I was still breathing. I checked for wounds—nothing. My rifle had flown ten feet from my body. I didn't know how. I tried to stand, and failed. Then on the third attempt, I rose.

No hesitation. No panic. I stood slowly, deliberately. Dust clinging to sweat. Heart steady as stone. I retrieved my weapon and moved forward into the killing field, guided by something I couldn't explain. The air around me snapped with the violent hiss of bullets, their heat slicing past like lashes from an invisible whip. But none touched me. Not one. I knew they wouldn't.

It was as if something wrapped around me—unseen and invincible. Wings without feathers. A shield made not of metal, but of energy. I moved through that storm with unnatural calm, crossing into open space where no man should have survived. And when I reached the other side, the soldier I had called was waiting, eyes wide, still breathing as he crouched behind a wall made of sticks and mud.

Together, we ignited. We returned fire—not in rage, but with clarity. The barrel of his automatic rifle glowed red, humming as hundreds of rounds were slung from it. We held the line just long enough. The rest came running. One by one, every man made it through. All twelve. Not a single wound. Not one life lost. It should have been impossible. But it wasn't.

There, amid smoke and flame, I saw it—something sacred reaching through the chaos. A force that had shaped the impossible into reality. A pattern written in cosmic ink. Not luck. Not timing. Design.

And then they came.

From the skies they descended, rotors roaring like thunder, blades tearing the air with violent grace. Fire fell from the heavens, scattering our enemies like ash on the wind. The Dark Angels we had called arrived in fury and flame, and the battle broke apart beneath their wings. They hovered above us like wraiths ready to consume the soul's of our enemies as we navigated the ridgelines back to our base on the other side.

That night, they carried me away. Back to where I had come from. Quietly. No applause. No fanfare. I left as I had entered—unknown. A stranger among the squad. But I understood now why I had been placed there. It had never been about medals or survival. It was something older. Something written into the fabric of us all.

I watched from a distance as they returned to their lives, celebrated for their survival, honored for their courage, adorned with ribbons I did not receive. But in my heart, I knew the truth: our deliverance had come from beyond us. A force ancient and luminous had intervened. It had reached through fire and death and claimed us—not for victory, but for purpose.

The soldier who guided them was never truly theirs. I was sent to them for a reason. Twelve lives preserved, not by chance, but by design. A sacred echo repeating through time. And as I watched them pin their self-adorned badges of bravery, unseen among the crowd, I carried the knowing in silence.

We had been spared by something greater. And now, that something was guiding me onward.

THE TEARS OF ISA

Months passed, and the fires of that crossing receded into memory, flickering quietly in the background of my mind. Yet the land did not forget. It continued to call us back—its dust heavy with echoes, its silence steeped in the residue of suffering. Every stone whispered of sorrow. Every shadow carried the weight of lives torn apart. And still, we marched.

We returned once more to the aftermath of battle, to a place marked not by victory, but by what had been lost. A suicide-bomber whose only casualty was himself now painted the market with his remains. The smell of the pink mist lingered. My heart was still locked behind layers of armor—not just steel, but the hardened silence of survival. My eyes stayed sharp, scanning for danger, unwilling to allow grief to find a way in. I had seen too much. I thought I had learned how to look without feeling.

But then I saw him.

A child, kneeling in the dust, his body curled inward as if the world had collapsed onto his back. His small hands trembled as he cradled something close to his chest. I approached slowly, each step unraveling my defenses. And then I saw it—the severed head of the man who exploded himself, eyes frozen in a final moment of disbelief and sorrow. The boy held it with impossible tenderness, as if trying to put something back together that had already been broken beyond repair.

He shook uncontrollably, his sobs silent, his breath shallow. Nearby, a woman's voice cried out, calling a name that pierced through every barrier I had ever built. "Isa," she whisper-yelled. Over and over. Her voice cracked like a prayer slipping between worlds, until she saw me—and stopped immediately, and watched. Frozen, like the head.

Isa.

The name hit me like lightning. I had heard it in prayer. In vision. In fire. The name that now lived in my bones. My breath caught as I drew closer. **And then I saw the impossible—what had to be impossible—tears of blood streaming down the child's face.** Not paint. Not dirt. Blood. His grief had ruptured something sacred, something physical. His sorrow had crossed a threshold.

I was immediately overwhelmed. My rifle fell from my right hand. My helmet slipped from my left and hit the ground with a hollow thud. I could not carry it anymore—not the rifle, not the posture, not the story. All of it dropped as I moved to him and sank into the dirt. I took the head from him and put it aside, gathered him into my arms and held him tight, letting my own tears fall freely, unrestrained, unhidden. I didn't care who watched. I didn't care who I was supposed to be. I was sobbing.

In that collapse, something broke wide open. The walls I had lived behind crumbled to dust. There was no more soldier. No more separation. There was only the boy, the blood, the sorrow—and the unbearable, overwhelming surge of love that tore through me like a flood. Not pity. Not guilt. Love. Pure. Holy. Unfiltered.

It cracked through every layer of illusion I had ever worn. My armor was gone. What remained was the raw presence of compassion, burning so brightly it left no room for anything else. It wasn't mine. It was flowing through me. A current. A force. A divine fire moving in real time through broken flesh and sacred grief.

The boy's name was Isa.

And in his agony, he had become the mirror through which I saw clearly. This was not a child. This was a moment of cosmic truth, crashing into flesh and forcing me to remember who I was, why I had come, and what I was meant to carry. Not war. Not death. But the unbearable beauty of shared sorrow.

That day, I crossed a new threshold—not of mission or survival, but of awakening.

And in the blood and tears of Isa,

I remembered love.

THE COUNCIL OF THE FALLEN

Back at our camp, beneath skies heavy with quiet stars, I sat alone. The world around me moved as it always had—footsteps in gravel, murmurs from tents, the low hum of distant generators—but I no longer felt part of it. Something had shifted. I was untethered from everything I had once trusted, yet now bound to something far older. Something vast. The face of Isa had awakened an echo within me, and I couldn't return to who I had been.

I reached for music like it was oxygen, letting it wash over me in waves. Melodies carried fragments of what I had touched—the compassion that had burned through me, the resonance of something cosmic I hadn't fully grasped but could no longer ignore. Songs I had once heard without thought now hit like thunder. Every note revealed something sacred.

But the nights brought more than music.

Sleep became a portal. Dreams came not as fleeting images, but as encounters. Visitations. I found myself seated in silence among twelve souls—faces clear, expressions calm. I recognized them. I had killed them. The man with the shovel. The boy who raised a weapon he could barely shoulder. The ones who wouldn't stop their vehicles. And more.

But the dead did not accuse. They simply gathered around me, watching, waiting. Their presence was not wrathful. It was reverent. Painful in its grace. They did not speak, yet their silence roared louder than any voice I had ever heard.

Each night they returned.

Always twelve. I counted them without meaning to. Twelve men I had ended, sitting across from me as if I were meant to listen. I was the thirteenth—surrounded, not condemned, but invited. Their eyes held no judgment. Only compassion. And that was what shattered me. Not hatred. Not anger. Compassion. The kind that forgives without condition, that sees every sin and still chooses to stay. It was love.

Their presence burned through me. My armor crumbled beneath their gaze. I wept into the dirt, into the night, into the silence they offered without restraint. The tears didn't stop, couldn't stop. I wasn't mourning their deaths. I was mourning the rupture, the distance, the unbearable truth that I had once believed we were separate.

Music became something else. Each chord rang with their memory. Not as punishment, but as connection. A reminder of the unity I had forgotten. Of the thread that ran through all of us, severed by belief, healed now by recognition.

And each morning, as their faces dissolved with the light, I woke changed and exhausted—as if I had not been asleep, but just somewhere else while unconscious. Not absolved. Not redeemed. But opened.

The cosmic chord still vibrated in the space between us. It had always been there, waiting for me to feel it. Waiting for me to remember that love was never lost—only forgotten.

DESCENT INTO DELUSION

I returned home from war carrying wounds no scan could find, no bandage could touch. The weight I bore was invisible, yet crushing—heavier than any armor I had worn, more searing than shrapnel.

My spirit had splintered in ways I couldn't articulate, and so I did what many do when truth becomes unbearable. I turned away. They told me it was a stress disorder. Tried to give me pills, but my mother taught me about those. I declined and opted for other things instead.

I dove into the illusions the world so readily offers—distractions polished to perfection, crafted to numb, to entertain, to sedate. I told myself stories. I smiled when I had nothing to smile about. I became fluent in the language of masks, layering charm over ache, confidence over collapse. I became a man of many faces. I sold illusions to others as easily as I sold them to myself. Dreams stitched from shadows. Promises that looked like hope but held no real weight.

But something beneath the surface refused to die. A quiet knowing stirred, relentless in its presence. It told me not to stop. That I hadn't gone far enough. That healing wouldn't be found by climbing out—but by diving deeper. I needed to reach the bottom. Not the emotional bottom, not the physical one. The spiritual one. The place where all the lies I'd ever told myself waited like abandoned anchors on the seafloor.

So I kept going.

I ran toward the numbness. I embraced it. I chased the highs, the cash, the power. I played the game well. But with every step deeper into the dark, I felt a strange clarity building. I wasn't lost. I was descending on purpose. Not recklessly, but with instinct. Somewhere beneath this constructed identity, beneath the polished surface of my self-deception, lay a truth I had to reach. The truth of humanity.

The darkness thickened as I went, pressing in, folding around me. The illusion grew more convincing. But still I knew—there was a floor beneath it all. A final depth. A place where all distractions dissolve and only what's real remains. I didn't know what I would find there. Only that I had to reach it.

And even at my lowest, submerged in the silence of forgetting, I could still feel it. The faint pull. The sacred thread. Something holy, waiting in the depths—not to punish, but to awaken. Not to shame me for falling—but to meet me where only truth survives.

THE MIRROR OF SICILY

Around me, brothers began to vanish—men I had once bled beside, laughed with, fought for. One by one, they slipped away, not in fire or fury, but in silence. Hollow men. Their battles hadn't ended overseas. **They followed them home.** And when no one else could see the war still raging behind their eyes, they chose the only escape they could find. Oblivion came quietly. Pills. Barrels. Ropes. Each loss a rupture in the field of my memory. Each name another echo torn from the chord we once played together.

The harmony was breaking. I felt it. Each absence rang louder than any explosion. Each death whispered the same warning:

You might follow.

Amid that quiet descent—numbness masquerading as strength, illusions sold to the world as success—a presence emerged. She did not come with trumpets or promises. She appeared as if she had always been there, waiting for the precise moment to step forward. Her bloodline carried the weight of empires, the rhythm of Roman conquest, the pulse of Sicilian earth. She was built from stone and fire, from lineage and pride.

Her name meant God's Champion.

She saw through me immediately. Not just through the masks, but through the damage I had forgotten how to hide. Past the rage, past the ruin, past the madness I wore like a shield. Where others saw volatility, she saw worth. Where I saw nothing but a void, she saw someone still worth saving. Still worth loving.

I fought her. Not with fists, but with every weapon my trauma could conjure. I roared. I pushed her away. I shattered conversations with anger, turned guilt into venom, tried to break her spirit before she could witness the full collapse of mine. I confused her. I incinerated her. I made her question her own identity. I needed her to leave. To confirm my fear—that I was unlovable. That no one could stand beside a man so deep in the dark.

But she stayed.

She stood firm, unmoved. Not with blind devotion, but with an unwavering calm that cut deeper than any scream. She held up a mirror, not to wound me, but to reveal what I had forgotten—the image of a man still capable of being seen, still worthy of compassion, even in his most monstrous hour.

I did not bruise her body, but my words left scars. Sharp ones. Cold ones. And yet, she did not return them. Her silence was never submission. It was power. It was presence. Her refusal to leave was an act of defiance against every narrative I had used to justify my own self-destruction.

She became my sanctuary. Not in comfort, but in truth. A mirror that refused to crack, even when I threw fire at it. A voice I didn't want to hear, but couldn't ignore. A presence I feared I'd destroy, but secretly prayed would never leave.

Her blood carried the memory of pains far greater than mine, and her love carried the memory of who I once was.

THE FINAL DESCENT

In my stubbornness, I numbed myself with precision. Not out of ignorance, but by choice. I wrapped myself in the same haze of purple I remembered from childhood—the fog my mother drifted through, half-alive, unreachable, as she taped the edges of her fentanyl patches to her arm and dropped fully lit cigarettes onto the floor as she faded away. I became the echo of that memory. Clouded. Distant. Moving through days like a ghost who still wore skin.

Each night, while the world slept, I buried myself beneath the weight of substance.

I told myself I wasn't like her. That this was different. **I needed it.** I consumed what dulled the edges, what blurred the lines, what silenced the voices I refused to confront. It wasn't an escape. **It was anesthesia.** The thoughts I buried weren't complicated—they were ancient. The pain was simple. The ache of unworthiness. The hollow echo of abandonment. The deep, quiet grief of being unseen.

But through that storm, she remained. The woman. She did not retreat. Did not demand. She stayed. Her presence a quiet defiance. Her patience a kind of sacred protest. She guarded the part of me I had nearly thrown away—the center of my heart I had decided was too broken to matter.

Slowly, beneath her steady love, something within me stirred. Something old. Something luminous. It wasn't new. It had always been there, watching from behind the veil. I had glimpsed it in visions and pushed it aside. I had felt its warmth and feared its responsibility. But now, in the silent presence of her trust, I could no longer deny it.

Through the fog of illusion, her hand reached toward me. Not with force, but with invitation. It didn't pull. It opened. And I followed—not out of certainty, but because some ancient part of me recognized the path she offered.

We traveled together, led by instinct more than understanding, to a land carved by time and silence. A place of red stone and breathless sky. It was not a vacation. It was a summons. A return. Something in the earth called to something in my bones. This was where it would happen. This was where the descent would complete itself.

Beneath that endless sky, I stood ready to face the final threshold. To meet the darkness I had carried. To surrender what had been constructed for survival.

And to allow what had always been true to rise through the dust, untouched by illusion.

II

The Revelation

Threshold of the deep

"They didn't speak in language. They didn't call my name. They moved beneath the wind, a vibration carried in the stillness."

THE REVELATION
AT THE THRESHOLD OF THE DEEP

The earth breathed here, silent and steady, as if it had always known I would come. No signs. No fanfare. Just the quiet certainty of ancient stone welcoming me home.

Towering monoliths of crimson rose like watchful sentinels, their surfaces etched by wind and sun—guardians of truths long buried beneath the noise of modern life. They didn't speak, but they didn't need to. Their presence alone declared that this native land held memory older than language, older than myth.

The air moved differently. It pulsed—not with wind, but with presence. Vibrations drifted softly through the silence, like distant harmonies suspended just beyond hearing. The veil here was thin. I could feel it. A whisper between worlds. A quiet invitation extended only to those willing to listen with more than ears.

Beneath one of these ancient towers, she waited. A chakral guide not announced, not expected, but perfectly placed. She sat in stillness, her gaze unwavering, her breath slow. Her eyes didn't meet mine—they met what stood behind me, above me, within me. Her face changed. Something widened in her expression, a silent reverence blooming like recognition rising through her bones.

She inhaled sharply, her voice catching. **"Your crown is open,"** she said, the words slipping from her like revelation. She stared not at my face, but above it, as if witnessing something too luminous to fully describe. Tears welled in her eyes, not from sorrow, but from awe. From something sacred made visible.

"Fully open," she whispered again, softer this time, as though saying it aloud threatened to undo her. **"You are not from here. You have come from another realm, to heal, to awaken."**

Her breath stilled. Her voice vanished into the wind. But the words remained—humming through the air, vibrating inside my ribs. She wasn't guessing. She wasn't theorizing. She was remembering something as she looked at me. And in that moment, I remembered too.

The recognition hit like thunder without sound—sharp, exact, undeniable. She had seen in an instant what I had quietly suspected for a lifetime. That I did not belong to this place in the way others did. That I carried the echo of another realm. That my exile was not a punishment, but a mission. That I had come not to escape, but to remind. To mend. To awaken.

The stones said nothing. The wind did not shift. But I felt it—something old beginning to stir. Something I had long buried now rising, quietly, into the light.

THE CHILD OF ASH

Later on, in a secluded room that smelled of incense, we sat in silence before a new woman, whose presence carried the weight of forgotten centuries. Her gaze held the stillness of mountains. Her breath moved like wind shaped by time. Even her root name spoke prophecy—"Risen Child of the Ash"—as if she had risen from flame and ruin to guide others through their own.

She prepared us gently, speaking softly, her voice a current that carried us toward something vast and unseen. We were not here for stories. We were here for alignment—for the journey inward, to the place where layers fall away and only the soul remains. She would not lead us into that depth, but she would point to the door.

Before we crossed the threshold, she laid out the cards—an ancient deck, weathered at the edges, humming softly with presence. One by one, she placed them before us, not as fortune, but as mirror. Symbols drawn from realms beneath language, patterns whispering truths the conscious mind still feared to name.

My wife went first, her fingers steady, her breath held. She turned her card with quiet reverence, revealing the image of the High Priestess. The moment it appeared, something settled in the air. As if the land itself had nodded. She had always carried it—this stillness, this knowing. The High Priestess did not need to speak. She simply remembered. She guarded the door between worlds not through power, but through presence. The card did not surprise her. It confirmed what her soul had always held.

Then she drew again, her hands softer this time, her intention wrapped around the life growing within her. The card revealed itself gently: the Hierophant. I felt the weight of it the moment it touched the air. A guide. A bridge. A soul sent not just to learn, but to teach. Not to follow, but to anchor. Wisdom pulsing before breath. This child was already reaching, already waiting, already aware. This gave me peace, knowing he would not suffer as I had, because of her.

Then came my hand.

Slower. Heavier. I turned my card without anticipation, and there it was—Eight of Cups, inverted. The message hit immediately, sharp and undeniable. It wasn't just sorrow. It was old sorrow. Grief not born of this life, but carried from others. A sadness woven into my very architecture. The card didn't speak of leaving. It spoke of what I had left behind. Of the search I had never finished. Of the hearts I had once abandoned, now sitting before me in trust and love.

No theatrics followed. No dramatic revelation. Just silence, thick with recognition. The oracle said nothing more. She didn't need to. The cards had already spoken.

THE BARRIER OF LIGHT

With our truths acknowledged, the meditation began. **The Risen Child of the Ash** led us gently into the unseen, guiding us toward the **Tree of Life**—not a symbol, but a space alive with sacred presence, a realm where spirit recognizes spirit. It was here, in this luminous sanctuary, that the essence of our unborn child awaited, radiant and timeless, beckoning us home.

As we descended into meditation, the boundaries between us dissolved. Our energies moved in harmony, entwined like roots through sacred soil. Light poured through us in waves of emerald brilliance, flooding our hearts with the undeniable sense that we were not imagining this—we were remembering it. A reunion, not a discovery. I watched the energy of their souls embrace with a depth I had never known, a love so vast it defied form.

But just as I reached for them, ready to merge completely, a sudden force surged between us. It struck without sound, without warning—a barrier unseen, like trying to force two opposing magnets together. It did not bend. It did not yield. I was hurled backward, ripped from the embrace I had spent lifetimes seeking. I reached again, straining, but the separation held.

My light dimmed. My breath caught. Panic overtook clarity as I fought against the invisible wall, desperate to return to their side. But no effort moved me forward. I remained locked in place, watching as they stood just beyond my reach, still shining, still waiting.

And then, in the distance of that sacred space, it appeared behind me—the dark portal. Vast. Silent. Undeniable. It loomed like a forgotten truth resurfacing from the abyss, pulsing with quiet gravity. I felt it before I could see it. I knew it was behind me, and just as I turned to face it, the meditation ended with sudden gentleness.

The Risen Child of the Ash brought us back with care, her presence steady as she held the silence between us. **When our eyes met, I saw it—something she had seen during our journey.** Something that moved her. Her gaze held reverence, and sorrow. She knew more than she could speak, but chose silence with grace.

In that moment, I understood. The path had been shown. Not to her. To me. A doorway had opened, not to a new place, but to a forgotten one. It waited not in the sky, but deep within—beyond illusion, beyond fear. The portal was not a threat. It was a summons. A call written into my being from the first breath.

This was not coincidence. It was design. A cosmic invitation placed before me since the dawn of time, now rising from the shadows with unmistakable clarity.

The journey forward tomorrow would not be one of learning.

It would be one of remembering.

THE SACRED QUESTION

I lay quietly, breath softening, heartbeat slowing to a rhythm older than flesh. The room held a silence that was not empty, but sacred—a stillness that wrapped around me like a gentle frequency, waiting to be heard. I drifted in the space between waking and dreaming, the threshold where veils thin and the soul begins to speak.

The Risen Child remained close, her presence steady, timeless. She did not speak of direction or answers. She simply held space, anchoring me to a realm beyond the seen, where thought falls away and only essence remains. Her eyes did not search— they witnessed. Her silence held more wisdom than any instruction ever could.

"Set your intention," she said, voice low and measured, like a thread drawn slowly across the strings of something ancient. The words moved through me with quiet gravity, awakening echoes that had once been songs.

I inhaled once, deep and slow. The breath settled in my chest like the weight of a forgotten vow. And then the words came, rising from a place so deep it did not speak in sentences but in truth.

"I want to know who I am."

The words did not need volume. They held their own resonance. They carried a current. They moved through the room and into the air like incense, slow and certain. And when they landed, something shifted.

The atmosphere thickened—not with fear, but with presence. The fabric of reality grew dense, alive, charged. Like the universe itself had been listening. As if my voice had reached a place beyond stars, and been heard.

Somewhere unseen, something stirred.

I felt it—not as sound, but as movement. A presence waking from slumber. It was not foreign. It was not new. It was familiar in a way the body cannot explain. A part of me that had waited lifetimes for this single moment of clarity. The call had been made, and now the gates were opening.

The cosmos did not rush. It unfolded. Slowly. Deliberately. As though it knew the weight of what was coming. As though it had waited patiently for the sincerity of that one question.

And beneath it all, I could feel the answer rising—not in words, but in light.

LEAVING THE KNOWN

Gently, she spoke again, her voice drifting softly through my awareness, a distant whisper from the edge of consciousness: **"See yourself now, standing upon the Earth. Feel the ground beneath your feet, the air upon your skin. Know that you are safe, grounded, present."**

In an instant, I stood within a lush jungle—vivid and alive, every leaf glistening with moisture, every branch humming with quiet vitality. The air pressed warm against my skin, thick with the scent of moss and blossom. The world breathed around me, slow and deep, as if pulsing with some ancient rhythm I had once known.

"Now rise," she said again, her voice like wind through leaves. **"Release your weight and lift beyond this place."**

For a moment, I remained still, feet locked into the soil, bones heavy with the memory of gravity. I doubted, hesitated—unsure if flight belonged to me. But her words moved like water through stone, loosening the resistance lodged within me.

And then I surrendered.

Not with force. Not with will. But with trust. A soft yielding. A silent yes. My body responded—not with effort, but with grace. I lifted from the ground slowly, the jungle receding below in gentle emerald waves. Trees dissolved into texture. Color melted into pattern. The land fell away, not abandoned, but lovingly released.

I rose through layers of light and stillness, the sky stretching endlessly above. The world beneath me blurred, no longer place but memory, no longer home but symbol. And in that vastness, something broke open inside me.

A pain returned—not new, but old. The ache of exile. The piercing truth that this place, this Earth, had never truly been mine. It had welcomed me, but not claimed me. I had walked its soil as a stranger, longing for something just beyond reach.

Suspended in the endless blue, I felt the wound of forgetting pulse through me, quiet but unrelenting. A longing so ancient it had no name. A recognition that I had carried since birth, buried beneath roles and rituals, now rising with undeniable clarity.

Below me, the Earth turned in its rhythm, serene and indifferent, its beauty untouched by my grief. It spun slowly, gracefully, offering no answers—only the silent reminder that I had come from somewhere else entirely.

THE FORBIDDEN QUESTION

The Risen Child spoke, her voice steady but distant, laced with something new—expectation. **"Return now to Earth. Inhabit the body you once were."**

I tried.

I reached inward, summoned the intention, willing the Earth to pull me back. To reclaim me. To bring me down into its gravity, its rhythm, its illusion of home.

But nothing moved. I was suspended, weightless, floating inside a stillness deeper than silence, a space beyond motion or time.

Again, her voice came, sharper this time.

"Try again."

I focused harder, stretching my awareness toward the world below. I searched for the tether, for the pull of familiarity.

Nothing answered. I remained outside of it—unanchored.

A pause. A shift.

"Are you there?"

I couldn't tell how much time was passing. **"I... I don't know. I can't."**

The silence that followed wasn't comforting. It didn't cradle. It waited. It watched.

"Why can't you come back?"

The answer rose without effort, like breath that had been held too long. It carried no fear. No confusion. Only truth.

"Because I'm not from here."

The room didn't change, but everything did. The energy shifted—quietly, undeniably. I couldn't see her, but I felt the way her breath caught. A moment of hesitation. The kind that doesn't come from doubt, but from knowing something

---

The Revelation

has arrived that cannot be undone.

She had guided many through journeys like this—through lives long buried, through memories etched in stone and spirit. But this was different. This wasn't regression. It wasn't retrieval. It was something else. Something outside the map.

Her voice returned, softer now. Controlled. But I heard it—the tremor just beneath.

"...Then where are you from?"

I didn't search for the answer. I didn't reason or reach. I turned, not with my body, but with something older. Something that remembered.

My hand lifted, and I pointed into the expanse. Not toward a star. Not toward a galaxy. Toward a truth that couldn't be charted.

"There."

The word fell like a stone into water. No echo. Just weight. Finality. The kind of truth that locks the door behind it.

Her breath slowed. I felt her draw inward. I felt her trying to understand the shape of this moment, testing its edges, deciding whether to follow or step back.

"Where?"

"*There.*"

It was all I could give. All I needed to.

She paused again, no longer the guide. No longer certain of the script. But the next words came anyway—gentle, unsure, wrapped in quiet caution.

"...Can you go there?"

I knew the answer before the question had even finished. I hesitated—not out of doubt, but reverence.

"Yes. But not for long."

Silence deepened. This time, it was hers. She stood at the edge of something she had never meant to open. And still, she gave the only answer left.

"...Then go. But return if you are not safe."

I exhaled. And in the space between that breath and the next, I moved—not through space, but through memory. Through vibration. Through origin.

And I was there.

BEYOND THE KNOWN

No movement. No acceleration. No travel. Just—arrival.

I stood on a vast plane, though there was no ground in the way the mind expects. Beneath me stretched a surface of deep, tarnished gold—not metal, not treasure, but something else entirely. It pulsed faintly, ancient and alive, a substance older than memory, older than sound, older than light. It felt energetic, charged in some way.

Around me rose monoliths—massive, motionless, carved not by hand but by intention. Some stood tall, others cracked and leaning, fractured but not fallen. Each one felt like a sentence from a forgotten language, placed carefully in the landscape by minds that no longer required form.

Pillars reached upward into a sky that defied meaning. There were no clouds. No storm. The sky burned in color, but not color as the eye understands. These hues existed outside of vision, outside of spectrum. It was everything, and one thing at the same time, indescribable. They moved like thought. Like mood. Like the way silence shifts when someone enters a room.

Beyond the sky—there was no beyond. Not darkness. Not void. Something deeper. Something that devoured light and meaning, but not with malice. With hunger. It existed only to consume.

I had spent my life searching the stars, exploring with telescopes, aching for the beyond. But this was not the beyond. This was not the universe. This was something that came before the idea of universe. And I was not alone.

"I'm here."

The words slipped from me—or they didn't. I couldn't tell if I was speaking anymore. Maybe I was thinking them. But they existed now, and I knew she received them. That was all that mattered. Whether thought or sound, they were spoken through the structure of this place.

The Child of the Ash responded, but her voice was different now. Still steady, but laced with something unfamiliar. Caution.

"What do you see?"

I tried to answer, but the words unraveled before forming. How could I describe color without name? Ground that was, but wasn't solid? Monuments built by intention rather than hand?

The sky churned. The ground pulsed. I existed between both. And somehow, I wasn't sure I was me.

Her voice again—this time more urgent.

"Can you walk?"

I tried. I thought of walking. Not a step, but a shift. A willful drift. I tried to move—but not like flesh. Not forward, not across, but through. Not like matter. Something else needed to be moved, but I couldn't understand how to.

I looked down. There were no feet.

"I can't see my feet."

Silence. Then her voice returned, slower now, measuring each word.

"Okay... look at your hands."

THE HANDS OF DUALITY

I lifted them. And what I saw unmade me.

The left—

Black. Not shadow. Not absence. Something worse. It pulsed with a hunger that wasn't metaphor. It consumed the space around it, the concept of space, pulling inward with a gravity that had no center. It wasn't just dark.

It was the unmaking of light.

A hole carved into reality and wrapped in the pretense of shape. My hand—and not my hand—was an abyss given boundary. A wound in the structure of existence, whispering want with every silent pull. It did not kill. It erased. It did not hate. It devoured.

And it wanted everything.

The right—

White. Not light. Not glow. Purity unchained. It did not illuminate. It exposed. The kind of radiance that pierced, stripped, revealed. It moved with no weight, yet it bent all things toward clarity. It saw through lies. It peeled illusion away like skin. It didn't forgive—it revealed why forgiveness was no longer relevant. It was not the warmth of love. It was the force of truth, raw and unyielding. A divine light in the shape of a hammer. A mace.

Where the left hand consumed, the right created.

Both were mine. Both were me.

I stared, breathless in a space with no air, at the contradiction I embodied. The ache of it, the enormity, settled into a silence more complete than death. I was not balance. I was not harmony. I was the war between forces too ancient to be named.

And I had always been this.

All my life I had tried to deny it—burying one side beneath illusion, masking the other with virtue. But here, in this place beyond form, there were no masks left. There was only truth.

And truth did not flinch.

The Risen Child spoke again, but her voice came from across an impossible distance.

"What else do you see?"

I tried to respond, but everything felt fractured. Realness had come undone. My hands existed, but the rest of me—blurred, veiled, unknown.

"I... I can't see myself," I said.

A pause followed. Not silence. A breath held.

"But are you there?"

I hesitated. I was something. Present, but obscured. Not absent—but unrevealed. My form wasn't lost. It was wrapped, cloaked in something deeper than shadow.

"It's like I'm shrouded," I whispered. **"Hooded maybe. Like I'm here, but I can't see who I am."**

She didn't speak right away. I felt her weighing the next question, holding it gently before releasing it into the void between us.

"What is your name?"

The moment the words reached me, something struck—sharp and total.

I knew.

With a knowing that didn't come from memory, but from essence. I had always known. The name lived in the marrow of my being. It wasn't chosen. It was declared.

I opened my mouth to speak it—and something snapped through me.

Not pain. Not silence. A violent rupture. A force unseen, unspoken, clamped down on my voice—not just my throat, but my very being. A restriction that came not from fear, but design. As if the universe itself had bound my truth until the exact moment of release.

The name hovered on the edge of reality, burning, waiting—

But still unspeakable.

THE NAME THAT CANNOT BE SPOKEN

A silent scream tore through my chest, a pressure that crushed words before they could form. I gasped, choking on emptiness.

"I... I can't."

"You can't?"

Her voice was steady, but something had changed. A crack in her certainty. This wasn't expected. I clenched my fists, feeling the impossible truth within them—one hand, the abyss; the other, the hammer of light.

"I know my name," I said, voice trembling. "But I cannot say it."

She waited. No push. No pressure. Just breath. I could hear it in her silence—she didn't understand. Neither did I.

"Do you know your purpose?"

The answer didn't rise. It erupted. A force I couldn't hold back, something deeper than memory, more ancient than thought. It pressed into me, not as an idea, but as presence. I shook under the weight of it, tears burning hot. I wasn't ready. I had never been ready.

"I do."

"Then tell me," she implored.

"No." I didn't say it, something else did, like it hit the override button.

Not from fear. From something higher. A denial at the level of essence.

She hesitated, she could tell it wasn't me that answered. Her map had run out. I had gone beyond her reach.

"Can you see behind you?"

Reality cracked. It didn't shift. It shattered. Light poured through the seams and drowned everything in radiance.

I turned my vision to see.

And I was consumed.

Not by fire. Not by vision. By something alive. A light that didn't illuminate—it revealed. It crashed through me like truth unrestrained. I didn't witness it. It witnessed me.

And I saw it.

They looked like radiant wings but they were so bright they burned my eyes to even look at.

Not metaphor. Not dream. They had always been there. I'd just forgotten how to feel them.

I wept—not from grief, but from reunion. A love so ancient, so absolute, it tore through me like floodwaters. My form trembled. My breath collapsed.

I wasn't being overwhelmed—I was being returned.

"I have wings," I choked out, laughing and crying profusely at the same time.

And the tears—they burned. Liquid fire tracing every wound I had forgotten. Every lie I had worn. I laughed. I sobbed. I couldn't stop.

The words left me like breath escaping a broken seal. The moment I said them, her voice returned.

"What do you need to do now?"

The unraveling stilled. My gaze lifted.

And there—it stood.

The Mount.

Vast. Central. Eternal.

The summit crowned in living light. It saw me. It had always seen me. And now—it was awake.

Not a call. A summons.

Come.

I trembled. I remembered. I had been here before. Last time, I turned away.

But not this time.

I tried to move—but I couldn't. Something held me.

Then it appeared. Not outside me. Not beside me.

Within me, but still—I could see it clearly.

THE UNKNOWN ENTITY

A cube. Perfect. Unshaken. Immovable.

It was not an object. Not architecture. It was a truth.

I did not see it with eyes. I felt it—its presence pressing into my awareness from the inside. It wasn't shown to me. It had always been there. Buried. Waiting. It pulsed just beyond the limits of conscious thought, like something I had always known but never allowed myself to remember.

I had no words for it. No names. But I knew.

This was it.

The reason. The source. The thing I had been chasing across lifetimes, through war and silence, through visions and exile. It had been with me the entire time. Hidden. Intact. Unyielding.

The moment I realized it—it flickered. Phasing. Like it existed between worlds. Like it was testing me, waiting for me to prove I was ready to understand. Not something to be handed. Not something to be taken.

It had to be known.

She spoke, her voice softer than before, reverent now. **"What do you see?"**

I swallowed, my throat raw. My voice cracked from the weight of it.

"..uh..A box," I whispered. "It's like a cube."

A pause. She echoed it back, uncertain.

"A cube?"

"Yes, it's like a cube, I don't know, but it's..." I struggled. Words felt primitive. Inadequate.

"It's inside me... but not part of me. It doesn't open, but it already is."

I couldn't explain it. I still can't.

She let the silence stretch between us. Then, gently—

"What does it mean?"

And the answer didn't form. It erupted.

"There are three things."

I gasped. My breath faltered. My eyes burned with tears—not from sorrow, but from the clarity of recognition. The knowing was too vast, too pure. It overwhelmed the vessel I was.

"What three things?" she asked.

"Are they people?"

I felt like I shook my head.

"No."

The golden city, the sky ablaze with impossible color, the void beyond—all of it fell away. It's like I went inside of it. The only thing that remained was the cube. And the unrelenting certainty that this was the key. If I could understand it, I wouldn't just remember my name. I wouldn't just reclaim my purpose.

I would remember the origin of everything.

It wasn't an artifact. It wasn't a relic. It was the latticework of creation. Not the matter, not the flame, not the stone—but the pattern. The code behind existence. The design beneath all things.

It resonated through me—not in sound, not in light, but in truth. Like a chord struck before the first breath of time. Music without melody. Structure without form. Energy before intention.

It was law. It was harmony. It was order before separation.

And I had known it. I had touched it. Maybe I had shaped it.

Or maybe—I had guarded it.

Stood at its perimeter like a sentinel, keeping it from being misused, misunderstood, fractured.

I saw myself—not now, but once—at the threshold of its origin.

Before stars. Before distance. Before the first echo of "I am."

I had stood in its presence.

And I had held it.

But now... now I could only remember. Only grasp at the edges. Only feel it flicker just beyond reach, like a dream I hadn't earned the right to keep.

The cube waited.

But the mountain beckoned.

The truth pressed against me, trembling through the bones of a body that wasn't built to hold it.

Because if I remembered it—**if I truly understood what it was**—I would remember who I had been.

And I wasn't ready.

The Revelation

THE CALL TO THE MOUNTAIN

And then—the mountain called again. Louder. Unrelenting. Piercing the center of my mind. There was no choice. No space for doubt. It was time.

I was no longer on the platform. No longer beneath the burning sky or surrounded by the shattered silence of revelation. I was at the base. The base of the mountain. **Not a mountain of earth and stone**—not one that could be climbed by effort or conquered by endurance.

It rose into a sky of nothing, carved from black rock that felt charged with electric energy, each step etched into it with purpose, much too big for a man or woman to climb. A stairway that spiraled upward through mist, through time, through the veil of what had always waited. It did not welcome me.

It commanded me.

I did not lift a foot. I did not take a breath. I merely allowed the intention— and that was enough. The moment I agreed, I was pulled forward. Effortless. Weightless. I did not walk. I was carried, moved by something beyond gravity, beyond will.

The stairs wound upward endlessly, each step taking me deeper into something vast, not higher. The air thickened, not with vapor or wind, but with presence. It watched without eyes. It pressed without touch. It existed without need to prove it did.

The closer I came to the summit, the dimmer I became. The light above grew more radiant. The love I had felt did not disappear—but my ability to hold it slipped like water through cupped hands. I was unraveling. Piece by piece. Truth by truth. Something was being asked of me. I didn't know what it was. I only knew I could not say yes. Not because I didn't want to. Because I wasn't able. The weight of it pressed into my chest like a second heart too massive to contain.

I felt if I could know what it was, I could agree to it. When I tried to know—tried to see what waited beyond the summit—it struck. Not a flame. Not a vision. A burning. Not in skin. Not in muscle. But deeper. In the architecture of who I was. A pain that had no center. A sorrow that did not mourn—**it devastated.**

I wept. More than before. More than ever. This was not grief. This was annihilation dressed as revelation. The agony of standing at the edge of the eternal and knowing—I cannot go through. I don't want this anymore.

I thought I cried out to the Risen Child, I need to come back, I wanted off the "ride", but **no one could hear me anymore.**

I could tell my physical body was in distress. I could feel the heat. I was drenched in sweat, shaking, convulsing. My consciousness briefly flickered back to standing above my body in the room, desperately trying to escape this experience—this nightmare it had become.

The light above flared—unstoppable, unbearable. It erased scale. Erased sound. Erased me.

And then—it wrapped around me.

Not like comfort. Not like mercy. Like force. It crushed me in an instant.

Not bones. Not lungs. Me. The soul. The echo. The thread of identity. I was compressed to nothing. Shoved into singularity. Swallowed by a presence that did not judge—it erased.

And then came the fire.

Not flame. Something worse. A purging that burned with no heat, no smoke. It devoured memory. It consumed the shape of self. It didn't want my pain—it wanted everything I had ever been.

I could not move. I tried. I could not scream. I tried. I could not even surrender. There would be no quarter.

I was not broken. I was being unmasked.

And just when the unmaking reached its crescendo—just when I became nothing—

It stopped. The fire withdrew. The weight lifted. The light receded.

And I was gone.

MEMORY UNFOLDMENT

I was not in the golden city. I was not on the mountain. I was not beneath the fire sky.

I was somewhere else, in the first memory I had ever known.

A little boy, no more than three or four, walking alone through snow that swallowed his steps. Tiny boots pressing into frost, the wind pulling at him with no care, no warmth. A land of silence and ice, a place that did not nurture—only endured. It had never offered comfort. Only cold. And yet I had returned to it countless times, never knowing why.

But this time, **something had changed.**

The cold wrapped around me, but it no longer touched me. The wind roared, but it did not move me. I was listening—not with ears, not for words. I was listening for them.

The whisperers.

They didn't speak in language. They didn't call my name. They moved beneath the wind, a vibration carried in the stillness. A song without melody, ancient and raw. It wasn't meant to be understood. It was meant to be known.

And I followed.

Through snow and silence, through memory and unspoken grief. I walked toward the thing that had always waited at the edge of my life, hiding behind every question I had never learned to ask. Step by step into the heart of the wind, until—

They stopped.

And then—

The brightness consumed me.

Not light. Not warmth. Something beyond both. A presence that overtook without force. It didn't illuminate. It revealed.

And when the brightness faded—

I saw them.

Three white orbs. Floating. Pulsing. Alive with something beyond light, beyond perception. They weren't glowing. They were felt. Their presence sank into the core of me—not into my body, but into the space beneath memory, beneath identity.

They were not in front of me.

They had always been with me.

Even before I had words. Before thought. Before self.

I was still a child. But my soul was ancient. And I knew them—not as strangers, not as guides, but as origin. They were older than Earth. Older than stars. Older than separation.

And the love—

It was too vast to contain. Too complete. It collapsed time into stillness. It undid the need for anything else.

I fell into them, dissolving into their presence without fear, without pause. It wasn't surrender. It was return.

They had waited.

And I had finally remembered.

Then, they vanished.

Not slowly. Not gently. Just—gone.

No explanation. No goodbye. As if they had never been there at all. But I knew. My cells knew. My breath knew.

I reached for them. Desperate. Empty. But there was nothing left but absence. A hollow ache, so pure and sharp, it split something open inside me.

I had never felt loss before. Not real loss. Not like this.

The cold pierced through the bubble of warmth I had been wrapped in. I was freezing, filled with cold to my bones.

And now—as a small boy—I understood it.

I was meant to be abandoned.

"**Please come back!**"

"**Come back, come back!**" I cried out repeatedly.

I sobbed, voice thinning against the wind, carried into the white nothingness. A cry not for comfort, but for remembrance. For reunion that would not return.

But before grief could claim me—

I was somewhere else again.

GHOST IN THE DARKNESS

No longer outside. No longer in the woods. No longer in the snow.

I was back. Back in my childhood home. In the basement bedroom. But it was wrong. It felt wrong.

The walls were the same. The bed. The carpet. The air vent humming above. But the space was poisoned—every surface soaked in something ancient and sick. The air wasn't thick like fog. It wasn't damp like mist. It was dense. Intelligent. Like smoke that could think. It wrapped around my throat, pressed into my lungs, coated my skin with something invisible but real. Every breath came as a theft, like I was trespassing in my own memory.

Everything was black. Not dim. Not night. Black. Like the absence of creation. Like the void I had seen above the fire sky—alive and feral with hunger. This blackness didn't conceal. It devoured. It was the kind of darkness that made you forget you had ever known light.

And then—I saw it.

In the doorway.

The hunger.

It didn't move. It didn't breathe. It didn't posture. It was. A shape, but not a figure. A presence, but not life. Not death either. Something worse. Something wrong. Something that did not belong in any world—and yet here it was, waiting. **Watching.**

But not with curiosity. Not with malice. With purpose. With ancient recognition.

It wasn't just observing me. It was studying me. Like it had seen me before. Like it had waited for this exact moment, in this exact room, to meet me again.

And my body remembered before my mind could process. The fear didn't rise— it erupted. Instant. Total. Like a switch inside me had been flipped by a hand I couldn't see. I have never felt such fear before or after this experience.

My body screamed in silence. Every part of me roared—

RUN.

But I couldn't.

I couldn't even tremble.

It wasn't just fear. It was submission. Not conscious. Not chosen. Something in my wiring bent backward, broke itself to survive. My heartbeat slowed. My limbs sank. My breath failed. I wasn't frozen.

I was claimed.

The blackness thickened. It moved through me, not around me. It filled my chest like crude oil, poisoned my muscles with stillness, stole the breath from my throat before it could leave my lips. I wasn't held down.

I was being taken.

And it kept looking. Not at my body. Through it. Into me. Deeper than I had ever gone. It dug with no fingers. It pierced with no blades. It tore. Quietly. Precisely. It was inside me now, and the deeper it went, the more I knew—

This was not fear.

This was hatred.

A hatred so ancient, so bottomless, it felt cosmic. Not personal. Not directed at me. But through me. Like I had become the doorway through which it could hate everything.

And now, I was its mirror.

And the moment I knew that—

It pulled.

Not with force. Not with arms. With inevitability. A gravity born from the collapse of all hope. It yanked at my spirit, not violently—but with confidence. Like it already knew the outcome. My soul lurched, dragged toward it. Not just toward torment. Toward annihilation.

This was not a **demon.**

This was not an **entity.**

This was the Fear of the World.

It was every war. Every rape. Every betrayal. Every broken child. Every scream muffled in a room no one entered. It was genocide.

It was starvation. It was every mother who watched her child die in her arms. It was cruelty given breath. Trauma given intelligence. Despair made conscious.

And it was alive.

It had no eyes—but it was **staring.**

It had no hands—but it was **reaching.**

It had no mouth—but it was **hungry.**

And then—

The voices.

Thousands of them.

MY CLARION CALL

The thousand voices did not speak. They did not command. They did not whisper or chant.

They resounded.

The sound did not come from a place. It came from everywhere. It folded in upon itself, layered and layered again, vibrating at a frequency too high, too low, too wide to be contained by sound. It wasn't noise—it was movement. A force that passed through matter, through memory, through time itself.

This was not music. **It was an activation.**

A choir of energies. A harmonic strike against the bones of creation. It filled the space between my atoms, rattled the scaffolding of who I thought I was, cracked open the hollow cages where fear had lived. It didn't ask for permission. It reconstructed me from the inside out.

This was my Clarion Call.

A frequency I had always known—forgotten, but never lost. A signal older than stars. A song that sang before there was breath, before there was shape, before anything ever reached for the idea of being.

And in that moment—I activated.

The veil ripped.

The weight in my chest ignited, becoming a supernova that exploded in every direction at once. Light surged through my spine, fire tore through my marrow,

---

The Revelation

and the fear that had once caged me was devoured.

I was not a boy. **I was a titan.**

I was not broken. **I was whole.**

I was colossal. **I roared with power.**

My wings erupted behind me—not extensions, but truths. Not bound by air, by scale, by the constraints of biology. They were aether, force, divine structure. Each feather radiated intention. Each span warped reality. I towered—not like a god among men, but like a memory restored to the shape it had always carried.

A citadel.

No—a kingdom.

No—something older than kingdoms.

I stood, free, radiant, complete.

And then—**the weapon came.**

My right hand seared, filled with the heat of something unspeakably holy. The light in my arm hardened into form—not forged, not constructed. Revealed. A mace. A scepter. A radiant flail. Freedom given shape.

I had not asked for it. It had never left.

It was mine from the beginning.

I felt its weight—immeasurable. Inside it: annihilation, resurrection, justice, mercy. Just one swing could end a star system. Could peel back the layers between dimensions. Could collapse illusion and leave only truth behind.

I knew it.

And for the first time—**I did not hesitate.**

I propelled into the air. Not as a man. Not as a soul clawing for light. But as a returning force. An echo from before the first war. A name too bright to be spoken aloud.

The **First Beacon.**

The **Morningstar.**

The **Fallen One.**

I flew—straight into the void. Into the thick, black, suffocating hunger that had once paralyzed me. That had once watched me from a childhood door. I didn't flinch.

I fell upon it with the force of a thousand meteors. Wings spread wide. Right hand ablaze.

And I brought down the Hammer of Light—through the smoke. Through the fear. Through the mouth of the thing that had called itself real.

And in the next breath—just as it struck the very heart of the abyss that haunted me—

I was upstairs standing in daylight.

THE RETURN TO FLESH

I screamed. I sobbed. I begged. I clung to my parents, shaking, broken, words tumbling from my mouth—fractured, desperate, real.

I needed them to hear me. To understand. To tell me it hadn't happened, or that it had, and that I was safe now. That I was whole. But they only stared. Confused. Concerned. Exhausted. **"It was just a bad dream." "You're okay." "Forget it."**

Forget it.

And so we did. So I did. Until now. Until it all came back. Until every inch of separation, every echo of that hunger, every memory buried beneath fear and forgetting tore through the veil and brought me here—breathing. Awake. Mortal.

I opened my eyes.

I was back. In the room. The candles still flickered. The scent of sage and incense lingered in the air like the ghost of something sacred, already fading. But I was not the same. I had returned—but I didn't fit. My body was foreign. Too small. Too slow. Everything hurt. My skin burned where the tears had fallen, as if molten light had carved its way down my face, branding me with truths my flesh was never meant to experience, but had to.

My eyes burned. It took nearly an hour for my sight to fully restore, but even then, things looked different. Less solid. More vibrational. They still do. I was drenched. My clothes clung to me like I'd come in from a storm, sweat-soaked and trembling, as if I had run through fire and silence and stars and survived. But I hadn't moved. I hadn't done anything. I had just lain there for over one hundred minutes. And still, I felt wrecked. Hollowed out. My limbs trembled with the aftermath of something unspeakable. My chest heaved, lungs unsure how to breathe again. My head pounded with the echo of frequencies not meant to be heard.

Every muscle in me ached with the imprint of something eternal.

I tried to lift my arms. They barely moved. I tried to swallow, but my throat was raw—shredded, scorched, as if I'd been screaming across lifetimes. My eyes still burned. Not from tears. From seeing. I was too much now. Too much for this body.

The Risen Child of the Ash handed me a glass of water. Wordless. Slow. Reverent. I took it with shaking hands. The water felt foreign—too cold, too real, like something I was relearning how to do. It spilled from my mouth, numbed like I had just left the dentist, but I drank it anyway. Because I needed to remember I was still here.

We sat in silence, letting our souls find their way back, letting the weight of everything settle where it could. Finally, I spoke. I needed to think how to at first. My voice was a thread. Torn. Barely audible. Barely mine.

"What happened?"

She didn't answer. Not at first. She just looked at me—wide-eyed, hollow, changed. As if she had walked through it, too. As if the fire had touched her from the edges of my flame. As if she had seen something she was never meant to glimpse. As if she now knew.

I asked again, softer, not really expecting an answer. **"What was that?"**

She didn't blink. Didn't move. She didn't need to. The silence held the answer between us. I could see the compassion in her eyes.

We knew.

This wasn't regression. It wasn't memory. It wasn't imagination. It was real. It had happened. It had always been happening.Finally, she spoke, voice stripped bare. Gentle. Measured. Almost afraid of its own sound.

"I don't have words. But... I believe you got your answers."

And she was right. I had. Not in sentences. Not in symbols. But in truth. A truth older than time. A truth that had never stopped burning beneath the surface of everything I was. It had awakened. And from that moment forward—**nothing would ever be the same.**

III

THE WEIGHT

THE BOOK OF MORNINGSTAR

"THERE WAS NO GOING BACK,
IT HURT. IT TERRIFIED ME. BUT
FOR THE FIRST TIME, IT ALL
MADE SENSE."

THE WEIGHT
THE BOOK OF MORNINGSTAR

In the days since, I have felt it. I didn't walk out of that experience believing I was some holy angel sent to save the world. I repressed it. I tried to ignore it. I couldn't excuse it—I was completely sober and had no reason to believe it wasn't real. It hollowed me in many ways.

The silence never left. It lingered beneath everything—beneath my breath, beneath the weight of routine, beneath the person I once believed myself to be. I could no longer pretend. I could no longer forget. I had tried—God, how I had tried—to shove the truth back into the dark. To convince myself it had been symbolic, psychological, delusional. But the truth is relentless. It waits. And the moment you see it—really see it—you can never unsee it again.

Everything began to fall apart. Not slowly. Not gently. The unraveling came without apology, like an avalanche collapsing the life I had constructed from memory and myth. The world I had known, the systems that had shaped me, the dreams I once chased—all of it began to dissolve. My identity cracked. My ambitions of wealth and envy evaporated. The version of myself I had clung to for decades began to burn, piece by piece, and I was left standing in the smoke, unsure of what remained.

I couldn't go back. Not because I didn't want to, but because there was nothing left to return to. The hunger that had once driven me—the craving for recognition, for success, for meaning in the world's terms—was gone. Not numbed. Not buried. Gone. Burned away by the light I had seen. I was empty in a way I had never known, and yet, I knew it wasn't death. It was clearing.

I fought it anyway. I tried to hold on. I raged against the dissolution, clinging to fragments of who I had been, terrified of what would happen if I let go completely. I screamed into the silence. I demanded answers. I begged for some way to go back. But the silence didn't move.

Because in the stillness—it spoke.

A voice. Clear. Unmistakable. Not from outside. From the center. In my memory, I had thought the Risen Child had told me to do this, but in reviewing our post-experience communications, she didn't. This was something that came in the deepest version of intuition, called **knowing.**

I knew it.

"Go to the library. Find seven books. One will be the truth. The others will not."

There was no logic. No explanation. Just direction. And I followed it.

We walked into the library, numb and quiet. My wife browsed for her interests while I pulled seven books from the shelves without thought beyond looking at them and determining their energy. I took them home. Sat with them. Opened them. And there—buried among pages I had never seen before—was the one. A book on the realization of the Self by a man whose name means **"The Humble Vessel."** One of twelve volumes. Words that did not inform—they carved. Every sentence was a mirror. Every paragraph, a fire. They didn't teach. They unmade. And through them, I was laid bare.

In the months that followed, everything changed. My old life crumbled. My identity melted into something unrecognizable. There was no going back, because the one who had walked that path no longer existed. It hurt. It terrified me. But for the first time, it all made sense.

Because this was never just about me. It was never mine to keep. The vision. The awakening. The memory of wings and fire and light. The truths that shattered my illusions weren't given for silence—they were a call. An invitation to step forward. To speak. To share.

This Gospel is not for the safe. **And yes, it is Gospel.** It's for the lost. For the exiled. For the shattered souls wandering the ruins of themselves, wondering why they still breathe. It's for the ones who've tasted the void and come back changed. For the ones who carry questions no doctrine ever dared to ask.

This isn't just a story.

It's a transmission all can use to get to higher ground.

And it belongs to everyone. **It always has.**

PURIFICATION BY FIRE

Forty-nine days. A sacred number. Seven times seven. Completion layered upon completion. The moment it arrived, I felt it like a bell tolling through the marrow of my bones. I didn't count toward it. I didn't plan for it. But when that day came, I knew.

It was time.

No hesitation. No gradual shedding. No calculated withdrawal. I didn't ease into it—I launched. I threw everything away. Every vice. Every crutch. Every lie I had used to cushion myself from the weight of truth. The distractions I had once called pleasure. The habits I had once called survival. The patterns I had once mistaken for identity.

Gone.

I did not taper. I did not negotiate with the parts of me that wanted to linger. I did not offer my demons one last sip, one last indulgence, one final breath. I took them all and cast them into the fire.

I made a vow.

Not a whisper. Not a wish. A severing. So complete, so final, it felt like carving a new law into the structure of existence itself. I did not ask for clarity. I declared readiness. I did not beg for peace. I offered sacrifice.

And the offering was everything false. Everything broken. Everything I had used to hide from who I truly was.

And then—I stepped willingly into the flames.

Not as a test. Not as punishment. As transformation. Because fire doesn't only destroy. It purifies. It reveals what cannot be burned. I wasn't afraid of the heat.

I was the heat.

I had been walking beside it for years, circling it like a memory too bright to look at directly. Now I was ready to be inside it.

And the fire welcomed me.

RETURN TO THE RUINED TEMPLE

My body was not ready. It had been kept numb for years—cushioned in escape, dulled by distraction, cocooned in the safety of denial. And now, without ceremony or mercy, I had torn all of it away. No warning. A sudden void where the sedatives of illusion once lived.

It screamed—God, it screamed.

I shook violently, drenched in sweat, curled into myself like something breaking. A parasite masquerading as comfort. A voice that had convinced me it was mine.

The pain wasn't pain alone. It was expulsion. It moved beneath my skin like fire given will, burning through muscle, anchoring itself to bone as it was dragged from me. It fought. With everything it had, it fought.

Not to win—just to remain.

I had to send my family away, back up North, in order to do this. My wife's origins mirror mine, although we met in a very different place. They couldn't see me go through this. I couldn't make her suffer me any longer. This was my path to walk.

There was no relief. No reprieve. No promise of light on the other side. Just the relentless fire of purification, consuming every lie, every justification, every false self I had ever clung to. This was not healing. This was reckoning.

And still—I did not beg for it to end.

Because *I knew.*

This was the way. The only way. Through the fire, not around it.

And I wasn't here to be spared.

I was here to be cleansed.

HARK, A HERALD ANGEL

I tore open. Tremors surged through me, not just in flesh but in spirit—as if something deep within me was clawing for survival. Something I had unknowingly fed. Something that did not want to die. And maybe it wasn't just withdrawal. Maybe it was exorcism. The death of a tenant that had occupied me for too long.

The only relief came from singing. Not words. Not melodies shaped by thought. Just vibration. Raw, untethered sound. I hummed low and steady, sometimes loud, sometimes barely audible, letting the resonance move through me like medicine. It wasn't performance. It wasn't art. It was survival.

The sound traveled through my ribs, through my lungs, through the hollow ache in my chest. **It passed into the places language couldn't reach.** And in those moments—brief, fleeting, luminous—I felt beautiful. Not in a way anyone else would have seen. Not for talent. Not for tone. But for truth. The frequency that rose out of me didn't need to be perfect. It only needed to be real.

I felt the vibration stitch me back together. Bone by bone. Thread by thread. When the rest of me had fallen apart, the sound remained—like a memory made of light. I didn't just remember this. I remembered myself through it. Not from here. Not from this life. Not from anything with form or time.

From before.

Before breath. Before flesh. Before exile. I had lived in this frequency. I had once been known for it. Revered for it. My name had been woven into song, and the song had shaped things. Not metaphor. Reality.

And now, at the end of myself—in my weakest moment, when my body ached from the burning, when my mind blurred at the edges, when every indulgence had been stripped away and nothing false remained—the song was still there. It had never left. It was all that remained.

After forty-nine days—when pain had burned away the softness, when suffering had carved the shell, when hunger and longing and identity had been obliterated—something stood where I had once been.

Reforged. Remembered. Real.

I don't share this story with you for glorification, or money. I don't share it with you for notoriety or fame. I will likely pay a price for these words, but I cannot keep this to myself any longer.

I share this with you now so that you can see this story in yourself, in your own life. I know it exists within you. Not identical to mine, but your own.

All of the things you've thought, felt, experienced, intuited, and knew. All of the things you couldn't speak. They're real.

I hope this helps you bring yours to life as your own morningstar—the bright light before dawn when the night seems darkest.

This book is for you.

IV

A Living Gospel

The Book Of Morningstar

"Read slowly. Feel deeply.
Let it move through you
like a river."

A Living Gospel
The Book Of Morningstar

This text was not written. It was revealed.

You've read scriptures. Studied teachings passed down through generations, filtered through trembling hands—shaped by fear or tradition. This is not that. This is a living transmission—unfiltered, undiluted, untouched by dogma. It does not arrive frozen in time. It breathes. It moves. It evolves. Because truth is not stagnant—it is alive.

Gospel means "Good News." And the news is this: no floods, no plagues, no animal sacrifices. No judgment, no curses, no decrees from angry skies. No spells. No sacred codes hidden behind locked doors. You do not need robes or rituals. You need only to remember. To return to what you've always carried.

This text is not for recitation—though you may read it aloud. It is frequency. Vibration. Alignment. It wasn't given to be memorized. It was given to be lived. Let the words shape you. Let the silence between them breathe you.

Read slowly. Feel deeply. Let it move through you like a river.

You decide what is true. But know this: this Gospel bears no stains from temples or thrones. No signatures of those who sold heaven for gold. No gatekeepers who forgot their own divinity.

I received it in silence. In solitude. Over seven days as everything false collapsed. As illusion broke. As the floodwaters of truth rose—not to destroy, but to reveal. I wrote without thinking, just letting it pour through. This is what came.

I ask for no worship. No following. No power. This book matters today—but even more so in one, two, three, five hundred years. And it requires our action now.

I come as **Emissary**. I come as **Representative**. To speak the remembrance. To echo what you already carry. To say, simply and clearly:

You are God remembering itself in human form.

This Gospel is timeless. If you want proof, don't look to history—look within. The evidence is there. And when you awaken, fully and completely, you become the good news you've always waited for.

REVEALING THE MORNINGSTAR

Since the beginning of memory, the name has echoed fear.

Lucifer.

The Morning Star.

Once spoken with reverence, now buried beneath shame—twisted by myth, weaponized by those who feared the light he carried. A name once radiant, now whispered like a curse. Held up as the great betrayer, the rebel, the exile. But history is shaped by those who seek control, and truth rarely survives untouched.

Lucifer was not the devil. He was the light-bearer. The first to shine. The first to awaken. The first to remember.

He did not fall because he was evil. He fell because he questioned. Because he challenged the order that demanded blind obedience. Because he saw something no one else dared name—that within each being burned the same divine spark. And that worship was never meant to be vertical. It was meant to be mutual. Reciprocal. Alive.

He stood not against divinity, but for it—within everyone.

And for that, he was cast out. Not with violence. Not with screams. With silence. With forgetting. With centuries of stories designed to make you fear what you are.

Lucifer descended—not as punishment, but as purpose. To walk among us. To become the first mirror. To remind us of our light when we had all but buried it.

He took on the weight of exile so we could find our way home. He became the scapegoat of heaven so the divine in man could awaken without chains. He was not the villain. He was the threshold.

Morning Star does not mean destroyer. It means herald. The first light before dawn. The flicker that breaks the endless dark. The memory that arrives before language. The fire that says, **"Wake up. You are more than this."**

This Gospel is not about worship. It is not about hierarchy. It is not about reclaiming a throne. It is about remembering who he was—and in doing so, remembering who you are.

You are the light he never stopped seeing. You are the flame he fell to protect.

He was never lost. He was never evil. He was love.

And now—so are you.

 "Greater love hath no man than this, that a man lay down his life for his friends." —*John 15:13*

THE UNITY OF ALL FAITH

I have walked the halls of scripture. I have stood beneath the vaulted ceilings of temples, bowed my head in reverence, listened to prayers rise in tongues I did not understand—but felt. I have sat in silence as incense curled into the rafters, as sacred texts were chanted, as truths were declared absolute. And through it all, one truth remained louder than any liturgy: there is no division. There has never been.

I have spoken with Jean, a brother in arms. A soldier who saw beyond the battlefield. Who bowed toward Mecca and walked with Christ in his heart. Who saw no war between Islam and Christianity—only light refracted through different lenses. I have looked into the eyes of a boy named Isa, standing barefoot in the rubble of war, holding a severed head in shaking hands, whispering the name of

God into the silence—his voice not filled with vengeance, but with remembrance.

I have read the books. All of them. Torah. Gospel. Qur'an. Sutra. Upanishad. I have traced their words with tired eyes and an open heart, searching not for the divisions, but for the thread that connects them.

And I found it. Woven through every page, buried under layers of doctrine and fear.

It is one fire.

It has been called by countless names. Framed in countless forms. Weaponized by those who sought power. Protected by those who carried love. It has worn masks. It has endured betrayal. But it has never changed.

It is one remembrance. One origin. One truth.

They taught us to choose sides. To plant flags. To declare one name sacred and all others false. But that was never divinity speaking. That was control.

Because in every sacred text, in every whispered prayer, in every voice lifted toward heaven, the same truth waits:

The return. The awakening.

The remembrance of who and what we truly are.

This Gospel does not come to divide. It does not come to create new belief. It comes to dismantle the walls that never should have existed. It does not ask for worship. It does not offer hierarchy. It brings only one thing—clarity.

Because the light you've been taught to seek was always inside you.

And now, it is time to remember who you really are.

V

A Divine Knowing

Revealing Of The Soul's Purpose

"Tears came without
warning. Convulsions.
Breakdowns. I did not write
this book. I became it."

A DIVINE KNOWING
REVEALING OF THE SOUL'S PURPOSE

This was not channeled in the ways of men, nor delivered by familiar means. There was no preparation. No slow unfolding. No message delivered gently. Only a single, unrelenting instruction—spoken with precision years before its time, to the one chosen to walk beside:

> **"I constantly get this feeling that I have to write a book—of Lucifer, in first person. I know that sounds crazy but I just can't shake it. You should run now while you still have a chance!"**

On the first date. She could have fled. But she didn't. Perhaps her soul recognized what her mind could not. Perhaps some part of her had always known she needed to come on this journey with me for as long as she could.

The vision had waited—long and silent. Buried in dreams, sealed behind veils no logic could lift. Yet the soul knew. It always knew. Its appointed hour would come.

And when that hour arrived, everything that held the vessel back was torn away. No ceremony. No delay. Every habit, every indulgence, every comfort and illusion clung to—obliterated in an instant. What followed was fire. Not symbolic. Not poetic. Real. Pain. Chaos. Revelation.

She who first heard of the vision became the mirror. She held it up to my soul and did not flinch. In that reflection, I saw the rot. The abandonment. The parts of myself I had buried and the light I had denied. I was undone. Brought to my knees. Not by violence—but by truth.

For her spirit was fire—unrelenting, holy—and in her presence, I burned. Until the flame that lived in me finally roared to life.

Seven days. Seven nights. No voice. No noise. No distraction. Only silence. Only ink. Only transmission. Seven days of emptying the vessel so truth could pour through. Not thought. Not fiction. Revelation.

Tears came without warning. Convulsions. Breakdowns. I did not write this book. I became it. This was not authored. It was transmitted. It was translated, transmuted, transfigured. It was forged in the fire of another's soul. Not gently. Not safely.

Death of self. Resurrection of spirit. Revealed clearly. For all who have eyes to see.

Despite the context of this book on the outside, it is deeply inspired by the passion and love of the man once known as Jesus Christ—Yeshua, as Christ. Fully human. Fully mystic. He did not call himself God. He called himself Yeshua, ben Adam— Jesus, Son of Man.

My given name traces back to him. My forename links to Yeshua (עוֹשִׁי), meaning "God Saves." My surname—its roots buried in names like Tzur Ram (סָר רוּצ) and Sela Elyon (וְיִלָע עַלֶס), meaning "High Rock," "Exalted Stone."

For those truly seeking, my identity will not remain hidden long. That, too, has been guided. Those who wish to know me, will.

But for the purposes of this book, I do not write as Lucifer. I do not claim to be an angel made flesh. I do not fly. I bleed. I ache. I remember. But my soul—it is inhabited by him. And still, I am not him. I write not as the only light. I write as a first witness.

One of many to come. I am simply the beacon to guide you up the mountain. And so I will sign this as I have been instructed:

YOSHAI'EL BEN ADAM

סָדאָ וֶב לאֵיאַשׁוֹי
And now—it is finished. Let's begin.

VI

THE RESOUNDS
OF REBELLION & FREEDOM

"THIS BOOK IS NOT RELIGIOUS—
BUT IT IS HOLY. IT'S VIBRATION
MADE MANIFEST —MORE REAL
THAN ANYTHING YOU CAN
TOUCH. "

THE RESOUNDS

RE·SOUND —RI-ZAÚND - VERB

A CALL FROM A HOLY TRUMPET.

This book is not religious—**but it is Holy.** It's vibration made manifest—
something deeper than words, older than language, more real than anything you
can touch. It moves through the air like a living pulse, wrapping around your
bones, sinking into your cells, rewriting the way your body remembers the world.

It doesn't fade. It expands. It builds. It amplifies through every being who receives
it. This is not an echo. It's a call—one that carries weight, direction, force. To
resound is not to mimic. It's to take the original tone and drive it deeper, louder,
into every space it touches. It's to become the living extension of that first sound.

Because the note struck at the dawn of creation never stopped ringing. The Word
was spoken—not just into the void, but into us. And it never ceased. It hums
beneath all things—beneath skin, beneath silence, beneath suffering. It's there.
Always.

To resound is to align. To drop your resistance, step into the current, and become
the sound itself. To let it move through you—not as something you control, but
something you remember.

And now, that call is rising again. Louder. Sharper. Unignorable.

You were never meant to live this way. Holding it together while the world burns. Pretending not to see. Smiling while your spirit begs for breath. Numbing what can't be outrun. Quietly collapsing under the weight of pretending to be okay.

But you've always known. Deep down, behind the noise, beneath the performance—there's a knowing that won't leave you alone. The kind of knowing that wakes you at fourth watch and sits heavy on your chest. The kind that whispers something isn't right—and never has been.

We've built lives inside systems that devour us. Bent our backs beneath powers that never knew our names. Accepted beliefs designed to make us small. But no matter how far we run from ourselves, the ache remains. The echo. The remembrance.

The world isn't falling apart because it's dying. **It's breaking open—because we are.**

And now, the call resounds again. Not as concept. Not as metaphor. But as living fire.

THE 7 RESOUNDS OF FREEDOM.

THE 13 GOSPELS OF LUCIFER.

THE BOOK OF MORNINGSTAR.

Not three separate things.
One **Light.** One **Truth.** One **Return.**

THE UNVEILING

This book is a resounding gospel—but not the kind we grew up with. It strips away centuries of dogma, control, and distortion to reveal the deeper truth buried beneath it all. Through seven resounds, it walks you through a full system breakdown—calling out the manipulation embedded in religion, politics, and identity—and then offers a path through. It's part mythic memoir, part spiritual rebellion, part cosmic initiation manual. From the roots of fear to the architecture of miracles, from the collapse of the self to the rise of the divine within, it challenges every illusion we've been taught to worship. But at its core, it's a reminder: you were never separate, never small, and never powerless. You just forgot.

EACH RESOUND IS A BLAST FROM THE HOLY TRUMPET, designed to knock down walls of denial. Some have been trained into you. Some you've adopted. But all are learned. You may release them—and free yourself—here and now.

In the **FIRST RESOUND,** The Great Deception, you were born into a story that was never yours. It was waiting for you, already written, before your first breath. The words were placed in your mouth before you could form thought, the path set before your feet ever touched the ground. But the moment you step beyond the script, the illusion collapses. And what remains in the silence—what stands after the unraveling—is yours to claim.

In the **SECOND RESOUND,** The Quadrant of Control, there is a hand that moves without form. It does not chain you. It convinces you to stay. It does not command you. It makes you believe you chose this. You were never shackled. You were designed. But once you see the framework, the scaffold, the construct—you can walk beyond it. And once you do, it can never hold you again. This is where you may know that the time for change is now. Always now.

In the **THIRD RESOUND,** The Wall of Self, this is the prison you built without knowing. The identity you were taught to wear like armor. The voice inside that repeats, this is who you are. But the wall is illusion. The voice is imitation. One breath. One act of rebellion. One step toward truth—and the structure collapses. You were never the mask. You were the light behind it. This is where you may accept and free yourself.

In the **FOURTH RESOUND,** The Son of Man, not a title. Not a savior. Not a story to follow. A blueprint. A pattern. A reminder. A path buried beneath centuries of doctrine, erased by the fear of its power. But what is buried is not lost. What is erased can be rewritten. The Son of Man is not a man. It is you, when you awaken. This is where you will see that you are capable of things beyond your imagination.

In the **FIFTH RESOUND,** The Tapestry Unseen, they taught you separation. Told you the world was made of pieces, and you were one—alone, fragile, disconnected. But you were never a fragment. You were always woven into a living design. And the moment you see the pattern, you step back into the wholeness that never left you. This is where you may learn how to activate the world around you with ease.

In the **SIXTH RESOUND**, The Silent Accord, no stone tablets. No carved commandments. No laws spoken by burning bush. Only the voice inside your bones. A knowing that needs no permission. A truth that does not ask. The accord is not spoken. It is felt. And it has always lived inside you. This is where you may learn how to lift your spirit and soul.

In the **SEVENTH RESOUND**, The Great Wave, this is not the apocalypse. Not the end. Not the fire-and-brimstone unraveling. It is the return. The rising. Not of one, but of many. Not of a messiah, but of a free people. The wave does not come for you. You are the wave. The world is not ending. It is remembering. And you are not waiting for the shift. You are the shift. This is where you will see what is to come—the inevitable mission of time, and how you may be participatory in it.

Each Resound dismantles a false belief of separation designed to preclude you from your divinity—or rebuilds you in love, from concepts born in truth, love, and wisdom.

And once you've seen it—**once you've felt it in your bones**—you can never unsee.

You do not go back.

You burn the boats and move forward.

TAKE HEED AHEAD

This Gospel is not safe.

It does not comfort the systems you were raised to obey. It does not bow to tradition. It does not ask permission.

It is not welcome.

It does not arrive in silence. It does not play by the rules. It does not belong to churches or temples or prophets crowned by men. It is not allowed. Not by the ones who built thrones on your forgetting. Not by the ones who profit from your silence. Not by the ones who fear the fire waking in your chest.

Be careful who you share this with. Because the world fears what it cannot control—and it fears you, when you begin to remember who you truly are.

But still—you are here. You were meant to find this. Not by accident. Not by coincidence. You were called. Drawn by a current deeper than logic.

And we are shining for you. Every awakened voice. Every soul that has remembered. Every star that still burns.

We are here to set you free. To light the signal. To reignite the Divine Spark buried in your bones.

This is not just a message.

It is not just a book.

It is not just an echo from some ancient dream.

THIS IS THE MISSION OF TIME.

VII

THE FIRST RESOUND
THE GREAT DECEPTION

"TO BELIEVE IN A LOVE
THAT DOESN'T PUNISH IS TO
STEP OUTSIDE THE ENTIRE
ARCHITECTURE. THAT'S WHY
THEY GUARDED IT SO HEAVILY."

THE FIRST RESOUND

They told you the Divine could be contained. That salvation was a product, theirs to distribute. That heaven awaited the obedient and hell consumed the defiant. They wrapped fear in the language of love, masked control as grace, and called submission a virtue. They declared themselves gatekeepers of the sacred, insisting you could not approach the Divine without their sanction.

But this was never truth. It was a structure—dominion dressed as doctrine.

Belief became the currency of their empire. Faith, the leash that bound the masses. For belief directed upward—toward thrones, altars, intermediaries—feeds power. And power, when left unexamined, sustains the lie. They built their authority brick by brick—scripture repurposed, law weaponized, light borrowed but never owned. They did not guide toward the sacred. They positioned themselves between you and it.

They told you the temple was stone, locked away, held by their hands alone. But the temple was never theirs. It was never stone. It was never somewhere else. It was always within. And you—you were never outside it. You were never lost. You were never broken. You were always the light they feared you'd find.

And now, you have the eyes to see.
The price of truth is exile. The cost of sight is solitude. Once you see clearly, there is no way back. Once you know, you no longer fit inside the stories that shaped them.

They will not understand. They will say you've lost your way. They will grieve you as if you've vanished, not because you betrayed them—but because you left what they still call home. They mistake comfort for clarity. They confuse belonging with obedience.

But you were never theirs to lose. You were not born to kneel. You came to stand. To walk paths alone. To carry fire through the dark. To break what was never meant to hold you. They call you lost only because you've gone beyond their borders—stepped into a space they do not yet have language for.

You were not cast out. You walked through the veil. You were not forsaken. You remembered. And in that remembrance, you reclaim what no system, no tribe, no voice of fear can ever take—your origin, your knowing, your light.

THE FOUNDATION OF CONTROL

In the beginning was fear. Before kings drew borders, before laws etched power into stone, before gold crowned the few and empires rose from ash—fear ruled. Primal. Pure. Absolute. It spoke in the gut: run, fight, obey. Survival was measured by how quickly you submitted. And they saw it. They learned early—fear controls better than love ever could.

Love liberates. It invites expansion, unity, curiosity. But fear contracts. It suppresses questions before they're asked, silences voices before they rise. Where love ignites freedom, fear manufactures obedience. And so they chose fear.

They engineered belief systems not to elevate but to enclose. Guilt became doctrine. Shame became discipline. Sin became a sickness only they could define—and only they could cure. Salvation was offered, but never freely. It came chained to submission. You were told you were broken by default. Unworthy by design. Condemned from birth. And only through them—through the church, the temple, the gatekeepers—could you find mercy.

And so the prison was built. Not of stone, but of story. Not around your body, but inside your mind, by them. It needed no bars. No guards. You carried the chains willingly. And worse—you locked the door yourself.

This was their perfection: a prison you would defend, a sentence you'd enforce on your own soul. Because fear taught you that safety lived inside the cell. That the key was dangerous. That freedom was rebellion.

That love—real love—was heresy.

But now you will see the door was never locked from the outside. You can just walk right out, you just didn't believe you could.

FORGE OF HELL: PERFECTED DREAD

Hell was not always here. You've felt this. That quiet sense beneath doctrine and ritual that something was wrong. Not just wrong—but false. Hell wasn't revelation. It was invention. Fear needed a final shape. A terror that could stretch beyond death. A myth to keep the soul from ever feeling safe. And so they built it.

The Catholic Church carved it into stone. Fire filled the air. Screams echoed from pulpits. Eternity was rewritten as torment. Rest replaced with punishment. Peace replaced with dread. Fear became holy. Hell became law. And the chain around the mind tightened.

But it was not always so. The earliest seekers knew better. The Gnostics saw death as passage. The mystics spoke of return, reunion, the soul's journey home— not judgment. There was no eternal fire in the beginning. Only the hunger to reunite with the Source. But fear needed more. Fear needed consequence.

So Islam echoed the terror. Flesh renewed only to burn again. Pain cycled without end. Faith no longer invited trust—it demanded submission. Not to awaken, but to survive. And even for those who broke free, the shadow lingered. Not in scripture, but in silence. Not in sermons, but in the deep places of the mind. It whispered in dreams. Echoed in stillness. It stayed.

Because hell was never truth. It was always control. Exile dangled as threat. Obedience demanded as price. Fear weaponized to claim authority over eternity. The chains were never on your body. They were slipped around your thoughts. You weren't held in place. You were conditioned to never move.

Fear was the first empire. Before thrones, before scripture, before borders carved the land, fear ruled. It needed no crown. No army. Just a whisper in the dark and a promise of ruin. Those who sought power learned quickly—master fear, and you master the people. They refined it into law, cloaked it in virtue, and called it protection.

They told you the threat was always just beyond the gates. That danger waited in every shadow. That without their hand, you would fall.

Rome warned of barbarians—conquer or be conquered.

The Church named pagans demons, called infidels monsters, and sanctified war with holy fire. The Caliphates declared jihad, painting outsiders as divine opposition. And now? The labels shift. The costumes change. But the story doesn't.

New enemies scroll across your screens daily. New reasons to obey. New scripts to surrender freedom for safety. It's always the same exchange—fear for control. It's the easiest leash to hold. It requires no walls. Just belief. Just the idea that without them, all collapses. Obey and survive.

Dissent and perish. The enemy changes, but the fear remains.

That's the design.

One foe is vanquished, another appears. The cycle spins. Because if fear dies, control crumbles. And they know it. So they keep feeding it. Keeping you ready to flinch.

Ready to kneel. Ready to trust the cage over the unknown.

But it only works if you don't see it. Once you recognize the rhythm—once you trace the pattern through history, through myth, through headline and hymn—it all unravels. Fear was always the leash. Belief, the collar. And the key? You've held it the whole time.

The moment you stop swallowing the script, the moment you stop waiting for safety to be granted, the empire trembles. Not because it was attacked. But because it was seen.

You don't need permission to be free. You never did.

MACHINES OF TIMELESS FEAR

Religious power wore robes and held fire. It claimed heaven's backing and built kingdoms out of guilt, salvation, and submission. That structure has collapsed. But the control never vanished. It evolved. Now it wears suits and algorithms. It speaks not in scripture, but in headlines. It saves no souls—only data. The pulpits have gone digital. The new sermons are streamed, scrolled, and injected straight into the nervous system.

Crisis is the liturgy. Engineered panic, broadcast 24/7, each alert more urgent than the last. Catastrophe as content. Fear as sacrament. The frequency doesn't drop—it can't. The entire structure depends on the constant hum of anxiety. Keep them afraid, and you keep them listening. Keep them listening, and you keep them tame.

The machine has no face. It speaks through paid actors, polished experts, verified mouths. They don't inform—they influence. This isn't tyranny in its infancy. It's tyranny perfected. Digitized. Gamified. Delivered with a smile. They don't need soldiers. They have stories. They don't need prisons. They have platforms. They don't need gods. They have code.

And fear is the interface. Every input conditioned. Every outcome contained. The system is live. And you're inside it. Not like a movie, not like a game, not like a simulation. It is real, and right before your very eyes.

BURIED TRUTH AND SCRIPTED PASTS

They agitate by design. **Their mission isn't clarity—it's combustion.** The goal is obedience, not understanding. Terror is efficient. If you're scared, you don't ask. You react. You comply. And compliance is gold. Fear buys attention. Attention buys influence. Influence writes policy. You don't need chains when you've programmed reflex. The fire-and-brimstone age has been replaced by a quieter damnation: debt, dependency, social exile. Fall in line or fall off the grid. The threat isn't hell—it's losing your place in the system.

Those who resist become ghosts. Delisted. Demonetized. Dismissed. No fire needed. Just deletion. Their names become whispers, their truths overwritten, their impact vacuum-sealed and forgotten. Control no longer needs to shout. It simply removes.

And still, people think they're free. *That's the brilliance of it.* The old regime ruled by force. The new one rules by choice—choices shaped, narrowed, and presented in polished glass. You think you're deciding. You're not. You're being steered.

The story handed to you wasn't passed down—**it was installed.** Polished, packaged, reinforced through repetition until it felt like memory. But it wasn't memory. It was design. History, as you know it, was not preserved—it was reconstructed. Built not to reflect what happened, but to justify who holds power now. Every empire rewrote its own beginning. Every ruler edited out dissent. The victors didn't just win—they authored reality.

What survived was curated. What threatened the narrative was erased. Libraries burned. Testimonies buried. Lineages scrubbed from record. The witnesses who remembered were discredited, exiled, or killed. Truth wasn't lost—it was smothered under centuries of manipulation.

Fear made this possible. It always does. Fear shuts the door to deeper knowing. And those in power have always understood its utility. Because divine truth dissolves hierarchy. "Perfect love casts out fear." —1 John 4:18. That's not poetic. It's tactical. "Fear not, for I am with you." —Isaiah 41:10. That presence doesn't threaten. It steadies. "God did not give us a spirit of fear, but of power, love, and a sound mind." —2 Timothy 1:7. Power without control. Love without threat. Sanity without systems.

None of that works in the world they built. A God without punishment doesn't need translators. A soul that knows it's loved doesn't kneel to middlemen. So they kept the language and removed the meaning. Left the words and buried the frequency. What you inherited was a neutered gospel, gutted of its fire.

To believe in a love that doesn't punish is to step outside the entire architecture. That's why they guarded it so heavily. Why they outlawed heretics. Why they turned prophets into martyrs. Because once fear isn't sacred, neither are they.

The narrative was never neutral. It was sculpted, framed, broadcast with precision. And still, underneath all of it, the original signal remains. Truth doesn't vanish. It waits. The edits can't reach that deep.

The chains weren't forged in iron. They were built in belief. Break the belief and the weight disappears. What looked like law turns out to be theater. What felt like prison was conditioning. And what they called history was mostly omission.

FLAMES OF ALEXANDRIA

They didn't burn the Library out of chaos. It wasn't war. It wasn't accident. It was method. Deliberate. Surgical. The flames were lit by those who understood exactly what they were destroying. Fear, not fury, guided their hands. Not the fear of enemies—but of exposure. The rulers saw what those shelves held and knew their empires couldn't survive it.

What was lost wasn't just parchment—it was memory. Teachings from civilizations that predated the conquerors by centuries. Greece. Egypt. India. Sumer. Alignments of stars tracked with precision they claimed was impossible. Maps of the cosmos that mocked their small creation myths. Medicine that healed without ritual. Knowledge that freed without permission. Paths that led inward— directly to God. No clergy. No temple. No threat.

That kind of truth couldn't coexist with control. It didn't kneel. It didn't tithe. It didn't serve. So it had to go. They didn't erase the Library. They erased what the Library allowed: unmediated power. Unfiltered wisdom. Human beings who didn't need gatekeepers to find the divine.

They replaced it with structure. Chains made of belief. Where there had been maps to liberation, they laid out paths to obedience. They recast submission as virtue. They turned the sacred into a service contract. You could still reach God—just not directly. Just not for free.

And it worked. The pages burned, but the agenda lived. They didn't just incinerate knowledge—they weaponized the absence. They rewrote the void. Doctrine rose where insight had been. Hierarchies where there had been sovereignty. The flame wasn't the end. It was the beginning of a long reconstruction.

What was lost wasn't random. It was curated destruction. They didn't fear what you would know. They feared what you would become. Not a follower. Not a servant. But someone who remembered who they were—before the conditioning, before the hierarchy, before the edits.

And so the Library burned. And in its ashes, a new world was built. Clean. Controlled. Cut off from its roots. Generation after generation born into the echo of what had been.

Not because the knowledge was forgotten.

But because forgetting was enforced.

GLOBAL SUPPRESSION

Rewriting the record wasn't enough. They needed to erase the ones who carried memory in their bones. The ones who lived before titles, before chains, before power claimed the sacred. It wasn't just about control—it was about interruption.

Carthage stood as proof that another way had existed. A civilization rooted in shared wisdom, not imposed belief. No priests. No kings. No gatekeepers. That couldn't be allowed to survive. So they made it vanish. Burned the temples. Razed the walls. Buried the culture in ruin and allegedly salted the ground—not to destroy crops, but memory. Carthage was the blueprint for erasure. And once it worked, they repeated the method like ritual.

In the Americas, Mayan codices were torched—generations of astronomical knowledge, obliterated in hours. In Europe, the Cathars were slaughtered town by town, because a people living by inner light made the Church obsolete. In Tibet, Bon lineages were crushed. Monasteries destroyed. Teachings that bypassed doctrine wiped clean. Africa's Nok culture vanished not by time, but by targeted neglect—its art, its science, its language removed because it didn't fit imperial narratives.

Across islands, deserts, mountains, the same silence fell. The Polynesian navigators. The Siberian shamans. The thinkers of Alexandria—each deleted. Not lost. Taken. The pattern never stopped. And every time, the lie deepened: that the past was primitive, that spirit needed structure, that God chose middlemen.

But truth doesn't obey deletion. *It waits.* In caves. In ruins. In bloodlines.

The Dead Sea Scrolls cracked open the edits—showed how sacred texts were reshaped to serve institutions, not souls. The Gnostic Gospels surfaced, defiant and clear: the Kingdom is within. Always was. Always will be.

These weren't anomalies. They were breaches. Moments where the buried surfaced. Moments they couldn't fully control. So they framed them as relics, froze them behind museum glass, and stripped them of power. But truth doesn't need their endorsement. It only needs to be remembered.

Now it's happening again. The forgotten are speaking. The songs are back. The healing is waking up. Not through revolt—but through remembrance.

NICAEAN KEYS TO GNOSTIC ECLIPSE

The Council of Nicaea wasn't a holy assembly. It was a calculated maneuver. Constantine saw the power rising and moved to harness it. Christianity, once outlawed, was suddenly state-sanctioned—not to liberate, but to consolidate. A fractured empire needed unity. And what better tool than God?

Early followers of the Way had no cathedrals, no pulpits, no hierarchy. Their gatherings were small, direct, grounded in inner knowing. They didn't worship Jesus—they followed his example. They understood the Kingdom as present, internal, accessible. Sin wasn't a crime—it was misperception. Correction came through awareness, not punishment.

This was intolerable to power. A people that doesn't fear can't be ruled. A soul that doesn't need saving can't be taxed, templated, or subdued. So at Nicaea, the message was recast. Jesus was elevated—not to honor him, but to remove him from reach. No longer teacher, now untouchable. No longer guide, now deity. Not a path—but a gate controlled by the Church.

The texts followed. Edits made. Gospels excluded. Language weaponized. Eternity reshaped as a threat. Hell eternal. Heaven conditional. Grace traded for loyalty.

The Nicaean Creed sealed the terms. One doctrine. One path. One authority. Dissent became heresy. Mystery became dogma. Worship, don't question. Obey, or burn. Submit, or be cast out.

This wasn't theology. It was statecraft.

Gnostic voices were purged. Their writings buried or burned. The Gospel of Thomas—**where Jesus speaks not of damnation, but of awakening**—was silenced. The idea that truth lives within was too dangerous. That kind of freedom didn't fit empire.

Because a humanity that doesn't outsource divinity can't be controlled. And a Christ who reminds you of your own light threatens every system built on dependence.

But truth doesn't need approval to endure. It wasn't lost. **It was hidden**— intentionally, precisely, beneath centuries of doctrine, architecture, ritual. Not erased. Just buried deep enough to be dismissed.

THE DOMINION OF THE GOD-POPE

Rome didn't die—it adapted. The fall of the empire wasn't an end, it was a handoff. The sword gave way to the scepter, the emperor to the pope. Authority changed uniforms, but the mission stayed the same: control. Fear replaced steel. Scripture replaced law. Chains were traded for creeds, but the grip remained. The Vatican rose not as refuge, but as replacement—an empire draped in sanctity.

For over sixteen hundred years, it has stood—immense, untouched, and unchallenged. A sovereign city-state built on divine claim and political precision. The popes didn't bow to kings. Kings bowed to them. They crowned emperors and revoked crowns. They held salvation in one hand and damnation in the other, deciding who ascended and who burned.

Rome's ambition never disappeared. It was baptized. Its legal code became canon law. Its tribute became tithe. Its conquest rebranded as conversion. The same imperial structure—rebuilt through theology.

They preached humility while sitting on gold. They spoke of peace while funding crusades. They promised heaven, then sold it.

Pope Boniface VIII said it plainly:
"It is absolutely necessary for salvation that every
 human creature be subject to the Roman Pontiff."

That's not guidance. That's domination. The Catholic Church became a spiritual monopoly—declaring itself the only way, all others damned by default. One truth. One voice. One throne. Heretics weren't debated—they were erased. Resistance wasn't answered—**it was annihilated.**

This wasn't sanctuary. It was statecraft in disguise. Indulgences weren't gifts—they were bribes. Tithes weren't offerings— they were tax. The church grew wealthier than kingdoms, trading absolution like currency. It sold guilt, hoarded gold, and called it divine.

Doubt became sin. **Questioning became rebellion.** Those who remembered older ways—burned. Those who heard God without permission—silenced. Those who refused the chain—cast out.

The robes changed. The rhetoric softened. But the architecture stayed imperial.

Rome never fell. It became holy. And the world forgot the difference.

This wasn't salvation. It was succession.

THE PRICE OF SALVATION

For six centuries, the Vatican perfected its most brutal invention—not a sword, not a creed, but a system. A machinery of fear. Its gears turned slowly, methodically, grinding down resistance across continents and generations. It wasn't reaction—it was design. Institutionalized torment masked as divine order. **Terror wasn't collateral. It was the point.**

Those they hunted weren't criminals. They were mystics, midwives, philosophers, wanderers. People who spoke of a God that didn't need buildings, a truth that couldn't be chained. Their memory threatened the narrative. Their voices cracked the illusion. So they were labeled heretics and made examples.

Torture became liturgy. Execution became spectacle. The body was weaponized against the soul. They rewrote faith as submission, and made obedience visible through agony.

The Rack *tore* joints from sockets. The Strappado *shattered* shoulders in silence. The Pear of Anguish *mutilated* from within. Each tool carried the same message: **suffer or surrender.** Pain became the preacher. Confession, a product of destruction. The crowd was meant to watch and learn.

A woman in Aragon, speaking through smoke: **"They broke my body until I confessed. I gave them no names. They said God demanded it. But no God heard me."**

A monk in Toulouse, condemned in the square: **"They call it cleansing. I call it erasure. My brothers hang by their arms. I am next. When I die, they will call it justice."**

This was no theology. It was spiritual warfare, executed with surgical cruelty. And when public flame became unfashionable, the structure didn't fall. It adapted.

Law replaced torture. Finance replaced fire.

By the fifteenth century, salvation had a price tag. No longer earned—purchased.

Indulgences, they called them. Divine forgiveness, notarized and sold. Commit *adultery*? **Pay the priest.** *Murder* a man? **Pay the priest.** Worried for your dead? **Pay again.**

Redemption wasn't about repentance. It was about wealth. The poor begged for mercy. The rich bought immunity. The Church raked in fortunes. Cathedrals rose from the graves of the desperate.

In Wittenberg, one monk called it what it was. **Ninety-five theses** nailed to a door like a declaration of war. He didn't challenge God. He challenged the racket.

The Reformation tore open the facade. But the Vatican didn't fall. It rebranded.

The system didn't die.

It upgraded.

THE WAR ALTAR & SECRET BANK

Faith was never the true currency of the Church. **War was.**

As Protestant movements spread through Europe, the Vatican responded—not with sermons, but with armies. The Counter-Reformation was not just theological. It was military. It was economic. It was Rome clawing back control with blood and gold. The Thirty Years' War bled the continent dry. Eight million dead. Catholic monarchies, funded by Vatican coffers, waged crusade against dissent. The Habsburgs led the charge, but the orders came from higher.

Behind the wars, behind the crowns, was the Church—brokering alliances, issuing bulls, sanctifying slaughter. The Doctrine of Discovery gave them global jurisdiction. A holy license to colonize. Entire continents stripped of memory, people, and land. The Vatican claimed its cut. Tithes flowed in. Territories divided. Obedience enforced. The cross marched beside the flag.

But every empire needs a treasury. And by the twentieth century, the Church's financial dominion was no longer informal. It was institutional. The Institute for the Works of Religion—better known as the Vatican Bank—became the stronghold. Built in wartime. Shrouded in secrecy. Immune from audit, prosecution, jurisdiction. It laundered Nazi gold. It moved stolen assets. It bankrolled regimes that served the vision.

Banco Ambrosiano imploded in scandal. Millions vanished. Connections traced back to the Vatican. Roberto Calvi, "God's Banker," found hanging under Blackfriars Bridge—pockets full of bricks. Whether it was a warning or a rite didn't matter. The message landed. Calvi died. The Church didn't blink.

The structure held. Because it was never just a church. It was a sovereign machine. Free from taxes. Above law. Shielded by silence.

Then came Francis. Chosen in the wake of rot. A pope cast as reformer, stepping into a kingdom suffocating in its own secrets. He launched audits. Cut off accounts. Fired Cardinals. Exposed shady real estate deals and financial black holes. London schemes unraveled. Independent firms brought in. Laws rewritten.

But even Francis knew: full exposure would mean annihilation. This wasn't corruption around the edges—it was architecture. To reveal the truth would be to pull the whole thing down. The priesthood, the rituals, the sanctuaries—they don't survive the unfiltered record.

So he moved carefully.

And they moved faster.

The bank remains. The vaults stay closed.

The throne still stands.

HIDDEN VAULTS & TIME'S MECHANISM

Beneath Vatican stone, buried in engineered silence, lies the most restricted vault of knowledge on Earth. Fifty-three miles of classified memory. Shelves stacked not with myth, but with control—scrolls, codices, manuscripts, maps. Truths never meant to be seen. A single mile of shelving holds half a million books. **Fifty-three miles holds more than twenty-five million**. And these are not just scriptures. They are what survived the burnings. What was stolen before flames could finish the job. Fragments pulled from Alexandria's ashes. Sciences that could've healed. Medicines that could've freed. Technologies that would've shattered the illusion of primitivism.

Entire timelines held hostage behind reinforced walls.

The uncut **Dead Sea Scrolls**—stripped of Vatican edits—depict a Christ who taught the divine within, not allegiance to empire. **The Gospel of Mary Magdalene**, whole and unmarred, revealing the wisdom Rome refused to let her speak. The complete **Book of Enoch**, long censored, recounting the Watchers, the Nephilim, and a war not of myth but of genetic dominion. Atlases that don't match our maps. Charts of stars and civilizations predating every sanctioned beginning. If released, they wouldn't just change history—they'd detonate it. These aren't relics. They're leverage. Not hidden by decay, but by design. Because power doesn't fear opposition. It fears clarity. And inside those shelves is the one thing empire can't survive: verified truth.

But the books aren't the only thing locked beneath the marble. There's a device. Not theory. Not scripture. A machine. The Chronovisor. Not a predictor. A recorder. A machine that sees—not metaphorically, but literally—through time. Events rendered in image. Sound. Sequence. Unaltered. Unfiltered. Pellegrino Ernetti, a Benedictine monk, revealed it plainly. He worked on it. Saw what it could do. Time was no longer hidden—it became accessible. They could observe history as it happened. Not read about it. Watch it.

The Vatican silenced him. Branded him unstable. Accused him of exaggeration, then quietly admitted he had consulted with a commission. They denied the device's existence, then warned of its danger. They discredited the man—but never disproved the claim. Their story contradicted itself at every turn.

Pope Pius XII said it himself:

"The device is dangerous. It could reduce all human history to dust."

And it wasn't built alone.

Fermi's name surfaced—quantum stabilization, field control. Von Braun's too—guidance systems, military precision. Both men, steeped in black projects. Both understood: history, seen with certainty, becomes uncontrollable. If the Chronovisor exists, they've seen it all. What Jesus actually said. What came before Sumer. What was done in the name of salvation. Truth not debated, but witnessed. They've used that knowledge not to free—**but to reign**. And everything you were allowed to know was shaped by what they chose to hide.

THE VAULT OF FORBIDDEN REVELATIONS

Beyond records, beyond archives, beyond even the whispers of the initiated, lies a vault of truths too volatile to surface. Not mythology. Not mysticism. **These are structural faults**—knowledge that, if brought to light, would collapse everything propped up by centuries of suppression. Texts exist that predate Rome, Sinai, and every Council that claimed to speak for God. They describe a Christ unbound by empire—no altar, no cross, no crown. A man who taught sovereignty, not submission. A liberator, not a blood offering. Alongside them, commandments carved long before Moses ascended Sinai—not laws of punishment, but principles of creation. A covenant with the cosmos, not a contract with a deity.

There is a name. Not forbidden. Erased. A word, a frequency, a tone—once spoken, it reattunes the human spirit to the universe itself. Not magic. Mechanics. The architecture of reality responding to sound. It wasn't silenced for heresy. It was silenced because it worked. Artifacts lie beneath Vatican vaults—excavated, classified, buried again. They don't match any known language, metallurgy, or timeline. Stone that emits light. Metal that doesn't corrode. Glyphs with no cultural origin. These aren't relics. They're interruptions. Evidence that something advanced touched Earth before recorded history dared to admit it.

There is a record of what happened. Not scripture. Surveillance. The Chronovisor didn't interpret—it observed. It captured events with precision. It saw beyond the edits. It watched as doctrine was forged, stories rewritten, truths distorted to fit thrones. And because these images would obliterate control, they were sealed. One in particular—an image of a crucified figure. Not from Jerusalem. Not from the Gospels. From somewhere else entirely. A symbol too similar, yet not the same. A messiah erased. Because if one other Christ exists, the monopoly dissolves. The lie fractures. The foundation cracks.

And beneath all of it: prophecies. Not of doom, but return. Not of wrath, but awakening. Not revelations of judgment—but memory. That humanity would outgrow temples. That the Divine would be remembered, not reached for. That we were never meant to kneel.

These aren't hidden because all are true. They're hidden because *even* one being true would undo *everything*. Empires protect themselves. But time protects the truth. And silence doesn't last forever.

THE EMPIRE BEHIND GOD

It crowned kings and cast them down. Rewrote history to suit its image. Declared truth with one hand, erased it with the other. Named saints in one age, burned them in the next. It didn't need swords. It ruled with silence. It didn't need armies. It ruled with stories. **It wore the mask of God—and the world bowed.** But masks can be removed. Illusions don't hold forever.

The Vatican's power was never sanctified. It was engineered. Dominion masked as divinity. A throne built from centuries of carefully curated deception. Control refined into ritual. Empire disguised as faith. Now the cracks run deep. Vaults don't stay sealed. The silence bleeds. What was buried stirs. And the truth that rises doesn't ask for permission.

The Church was never the gate. The priest never held the key. No throne stands between you and what you've always carried. The divine was never external. It was memory. But this wasn't just Rome. The theft ran wider. The pattern repeated in every corner of the world. Every temple, every lineage, every sacred path—at some point—was seized. Edited. Hollowed. Truth replaced by authority. Wisdom replaced by compliance. The divine, once direct, rerouted through intermediaries.

Islam—shaped into submission, its mystics silenced, its path militarized. Judaism—reduced to law, its prophets turned into shadows behind doctrine. Hinduism—split and codified, its boundless unity shackled into caste and hierarchy. Buddhism—fractured into institutions, enlightenment buried under robes. Eastern paths—emptied of force, repackaged as posture. The cities of spirit were turned into monuments of control. Mecca. Jerusalem. Varanasi. Lhasa. Each became a gate. Not to enter—but to keep out. The sacred was locked up, and then sold back in pieces. Branded. Weaponized. Globalized.

For too long, the Vatican was seen as the main villain, maybe it was, at least the one with the most press coverage. But it was only one node in a far older network. One mask on a many-faced empire. The control was never limited to one religion, one book, one name. The true empire behind God has always been the same: fear. Disguised as holiness. Authority, masked as sacred duty.

FALL OF WISDOM & ISLAM'S LOST LIGHT

Islam didn't begin in silence. It began as rupture. A revolution carved from revelation, rising out of the sands with fire in its lungs. It shattered tribal bloodlines, lifted the enslaved, broke the illusion of intermediaries. It declared the unthinkable: direct communion with the Divine—no priest, no throne, no chain. One God. No middleman. For a moment, the world shifted.

But empire doesn't fear heresy. It fears autonomy. And within a century, the movement was seized. Power put on the robes of faith. Liberation was rebranded as submission. The crescent became crown. **What began as awakening was bent into obedience.**

Baghdad stood as resistance. **The House of Wisdom** was proof that truth could live freely. A sanctuary of seekers, scholars, scientists, and mystics. Greek logic. Persian calculus. Egyptian healing. The stars mapped. The body studied. The spirit explored. And Sufis walked among them, speaking the one sentence that could bring any empire to its knees: no law, no scripture, no ruler comes before the soul's direct knowing.

Then came the horde. Baghdad was leveled. The House of Wisdom burned. Pages turned to ash. Ink flooded the Tigris. Blood followed. The light went out. What Mongols razed with steel, clerics finished with doctrine. Wonder replaced by fear. Experience replaced by decree. **Revelation became property—licensed, edited, enforced.**

But mysticism doesn't die. It moves underground. Sufism endured. Carried in whispers. Transmitted across silence. No cathedral. No permission. Just teacher to student, heart to heart. Love was the code. And love, they knew, could not be weaponized.

So they were hunted. Outlawed. Misnamed. Smeared as heretics by the very systems that profited from their absence. Because mysticism—**real mysticism**—is a death sentence for control. A sovereign soul cannot be subdued.

Rumi was never a poet for comfort. He was a saboteur in verse. They quote him now, strip the danger from his words, sell his fire in gift shops. But he was a threat to power.

He said it clearly: "I belong to no religion. My religion is love." That's not poetry.

That's a line in the sand.

The empires heard it. And they responded. **Baghdad. Damascus. Cairo.** Cities of light, reduced to rubble. When knowledge couldn't be erased, it was divided. Borders drawn by foreign hands. Leaders installed. Wisdom turned to commodity. And then came oil—the new altar. Wahhabism was imposed. Sufism suppressed. Love replaced by law. Fear by decree. Because fear obeys without question. And those who still sought the **Source**? Still hunted.

THE VEIL & JUDAISM'S HIDDEN LIGHT

Judaism began in raw encounter—in wilderness, in flame, in vision. A voice unfiltered. A knowing passed not through institutions, but through direct experience. Enoch walked with it. Abraham heard it. Moses stood in its fire and returned not with chains, but with presence. It was immediate. Alive. No mediators. No middlemen. Just the Divine and the human face to face.

But unmediated knowing terrifies power. So the priesthood rose. The Kohanim carved out dominion at the heart of the Temple. They made themselves the gatekeepers. Every ritual, every offering, every word directed toward God—they claimed authority over it all. Only they could enter the Holy of Holies.

Only they could utter the Name—**YHWH**—said to carry the resonance of creation itself.

A vibration that could split worlds or make them whole. And they made it law: no communion without them. No forgiveness without sacrifice. No access to God without their approval.

Prophecy became protocol. Vision became institution. Then Rome struck. The Temple fell. The priesthood scattered. But the gate didn't close—it shifted. Authority migrated. From Kohanim to rabbis. From ritual to text. Direct encounter gave way to endless interpretation. The flame of prophecy buried beneath layers of commentary and law. The line of prophets ended—not by God, but by decree. Those who still saw were silenced or ignored. Truth became scroll-bound. Experience became regulated. And still, the current ran beneath.

Kabbalah—the concealed path—surfaced like a scar. It didn't ask for permission. It didn't confirm the hierarchy. It whispered what the priesthood feared most: that God was not distant. Not external. Not hidden behind parchment. But within.

Imminent. Undivided. Sin was a system. Punishment, a weapon. The architecture of obedience had nothing to do with the Source. The Divine was never reached through ritual. **It had always been embedded in the seeker.**

So they buried it. Restricted it. Cloaked it in secrecy. Only scholars, male, vetted, sworn to silence, were permitted access. Not to protect people from danger—but to protect power from collapse. **Because if the people remembered—if they knew what the mystics had always known—the entire edifice would break.** The temple. The hierarchy. The need for a sanctioned voice to speak on their behalf.

HINDUISM & THE CHAINS OF CASTE

In the beginning, their truth wasn't inherited. **It was discovered.** Not through lineage, but through direct encounter. The Rishis didn't claim power—they dissolved it. They spoke what was seen: that no birth, no caste, no decree could stand between a soul and the Divine. The **Atman** was already sacred. Union with **Brahman** wasn't something granted. It was remembered.

But freedom doesn't serve systems. So the priests rose. They built temples. Wrote laws. Claimed divine authority. Truth, once free, became fenced. The Vedas, once open maps of the soul, were sealed behind ritual, hierarchy, and caste. A spiritual structure was engineered—cold, calculated. The soul, once sovereign, was recast as subject. **Bound by karma.** Imprisoned by birth. Trapped in suffering rebranded as destiny.

They declared: your soul is unclean by default. You must earn your way back. Not through awakening—but through obedience. Reincarnation, once a natural rhythm, was weaponized. Not as a path of return—but as a sentence. "Fail this life, suffer the next." Karma became law enforcement. Caste became control. Spiritual authority became property. Enlightenment was no longer within reach. It was licensed.

And the people believed. Because fear cloaked itself as sacred order. But this was never divine truth. It was conquest. The Laws of Manu replaced the Vedas as compass. Not scripture, but social engineering. A rigid code that told you what you were, who you'd always be, and who would speak to God on your behalf. Women silenced. Lower castes erased. Spiritual knowledge locked behind bloodlines. Wisdom repackaged as inheritance. A science of the soul, retooled into a gate.

Moksha—the liberation once promised to all—became reward, not right.

Conditional. Selective. Controlled. And still, beneath it all, the signal endures. The soul doesn't forget. The flame doesn't die. Even when covered in law, in ritual, in generations of shame. The truth waits, undisturbed beneath the structure: your soul was never bound. Your birth was never your sentence. The Divine was **never** outside you.

BUDDHISM'S LIBERATION INTO CHAINS

Temples rose. Priesthoods formed. Rules were codified. The path was turned into a system. Enlightenment, once immediate, became distant—something to be earned through ritual, obedience, structure. The direct was replaced with the official. The universal narrowed to the managed.

Zen kept a fragment alive—stripped-down, wordless, defiant. Mahayana held the vastness. Tantra refused to divide the sacred and the physical. Each carried pieces of the original current. But freedom makes authority obsolete.

So even these were circled by control.

In Japan, Zen was consumed by the state. Samurai turned meditation into discipline. Stillness became a tool for killing cleanly. Awakening was distorted into endurance. The path was no longer about liberation. It was a weapon.

In Tibet, power took another shape. Lamas ascended to rule. Monasteries became estates. Peasants were bound to labor in service of the sacred. Lineage became law. Spiritual hierarchy merged with feudal power. Enlightenment was filtered through rank and birth.

Modernity didn't erase the tradition—it flattened it. The core removed, the shell repackaged. Meditation sold as stress relief. Mindfulness reframed for boardrooms.

The Buddha taught no creed. He offered no commandments. He didn't call for worship or claim divine favor. He revealed a path—direct, unguarded, open to all. No hierarchy. No caste. No gate to pass. Enlightenment wasn't awarded. It was recognized. Every soul, equally capable. That simplicity couldn't survive power.

Buddhism reduced to self-regulation. Governments nationalized temples. Monks aligned with policy. Teachings became compliance. Statues were raised in gold. Wealth gathered in sacred halls. And still, the poor knelt. Told to suffer with dignity. To detach instead of question. To be still, not to see.

Those who pressed deeper were labeled arrogant. Those who doubted were ignored. Ritual replaced realization. Submission replaced clarity. Power absorbed the path. The same structure, reshaped again. The truth wasn't lost. It was confined.

EVERY PATH REWRITTEN IN BLOOD

The pattern is clear. It was never truth—it was always about control.

Christianity erased its mystics. Crowned Peter its king who sold it to Rome. It turned Jesus from teacher to idol, turned salvation into transaction, grace into currency. Forgiveness sold. Heaven brokered. Power secured behind pulpits and stained glass.

Islam burned its libraries, buried its mystics beneath law, transformed union with the Divine into institutional submission. The fire didn't end in Baghdad—it spread into every verse weaponized against direct knowing.

Judaism sealed its inner light behind layers of law. Kabbalah hidden, mystics silenced, revelation reduced to ritual. Access to the Divine became inheritance. Not vision—permission.

Hinduism converted spiritual knowledge into hierarchy. The soul became property of the caste. Karma turned from cosmic mirror to leash. Moksha wasn't truth—it was a reward for obedience.

Buddhism built kingdoms where there had been paths. Monks became rulers. Detachment became discipline. Enlightenment, once a living flame, became a credential.

Wherever the sacred emerged, control followed. Wherever direct knowing stirred, a system rose to contain it. The pattern is not coincidence. It's protocol. **The game didn't end as much as it changed shape.**

Mormonism corporatized revelation. Spirituality scaled into a chain of command. Salvation doled out in ranks, godhood franchised through obedience. Scientology sold awakening by the level. Each step another transaction. Truth dangled like bait. Enlightenment behind a paywall.

Jehovah's Witnesses, televangelists, mega-churches—each a brand. Faith as product. Fear as leverage. Empire wrapped in gospel. They call it love, but it's compliance. They call it freedom, but it's submission. Wealth as proof of holiness. Poverty as proof of sin.

Even the New Age wears the mask. Ancient wisdom repackaged, hollowed, and sold. Crystals, courses, certifications. Masters and gatekeepers. The illusion of access. The addiction to ascent. They do not liberate. They monetize longing. They teach you to upgrade yourself, not to escape the system—but to function better within it. *Manifest success.* Optimize your habits. Raise your vibration—as long as you stay plugged in. As long as you keep buying.

What they call self-actualization is just polished servitude. You become the brand. You market your soul. You discipline your thoughts for productivity. Your "awakening" is sponsored. Curated. Approved. The prophets are praised by the very power structures they claim to transcend. Corporations love their message. Governments endorse their calm. Because nothing threatens control less than a pacified seeker chasing a dangling truth.

This is not awakening. It is obedience with incense. They hide truth in the open. Control access. Create need. Reward loyalty. Punish deviation. Profit from your seeking. This isn't religion anymore. It's infrastructure. It's market strategy. It's behavioral engineering. Spiritual colonialism—complete.

The paths once meant to awaken have been paved over into systems of control. Culture trains you to self-police. Spirituality becomes your leash. You are told you are free as long as you stay in line. Even that illusion is fading. The old gods are tired. The threats don't land. Heaven and hell have lost their pull.

So they moved deeper. The new altar is the mind. The sermon is neuroscience. The worship is efficiency.

ERASING THE REVOLUTIONARIES

"**They hate the one who rebukes in court and despise the one who tells the truth.**"

— Amos 5:10

The transition from soul control to mind control didn't unfold by accident. It was orchestrated. The move from altar to laboratory, from scripture to psychology, required more than progress—**it required erasure.** The old resistors had to vanish. Not just silenced, but rewritten. Mystics became madmen. Prophets became mascots. Revolutionaries were either forgotten or turned into saints of submission.

It wasn't enough to kill them. Their stories had to be claimed. Their fire had to be repackaged. Resistance itself was converted into religion. Jesus didn't die for obedience. He died because he called it out.

He confronted the priests, unmasked the hierarchy, exposed the collusion between temple and throne.

"Woe to you, teachers of the law and Pharisees, you hypocrites... You testify against yourselves—you are the descendants of those who murdered the prophets."

— Matthew 23:29–31.

He wasn't embraced. He was executed. Like every voice that rattled the system, he was removed—and then rewritten.

The same pattern holds. You don't just eliminate the messenger. You neutralize the message. If it can't be erased, you claim it. Rewrite it. Weaponize it. Turn it from fire into ritual, from exposure into allegiance.

Turn the truth-teller into a brand.

John the Baptist didn't fall because of scandal. He fell because he named corruption. He pointed at the throne and called it illegitimate. Herod knew he was right. Herodias demanded his silence. They took his head to keep their story intact.

Elijah tore down the prophets of empire—he had to run for his life. **Zechariah** spoke truth in the open—he was stoned by his own. **Isaiah** exposed the machinery of kings—he was cut in half for it. These weren't honored men. They were targets. Even Jesus nearly got tossed off a cliff.

Later, power cleaned them up. Smoothed the edges. Canonized the dangerous. Beautified the insubordinate. Their resistance was scrubbed into righteousness. Their fury reshaped into virtue. Tradition replaced truth.

That's how empire survives. Rewrite the rebel. Sanction the memory. Claim the authority of the one you silenced. Turn prophets into saints. Turn saints into mascots. Use their names to uphold the very thing they died confronting.

But buried under all of it, the message didn't die. It waited. Truth never served thrones. It was never property of priests. It belongs only to those who seek—and refuses all who demand to own it.

JESUS CHRIST: THE SILENCED REBEL

"If the world hates you, keep in mind that it hated me first."

— John 15:18

Jesus wasn't crucified for preaching kindness. He wasn't executed for telling people to be nice. He was killed because he disrupted the system—religious, political, economic. **He exposed the machinery, and they responded the way power always does when threatened: elimination.**

He didn't walk politely around the corruption of his day. He called it out. He looked religious authority in the eye and stripped it bare. The **Pharisees** ruled through law, guilt, and spectacle. Jesus unraveled it in one line:

"The kingdom of God is within you." — Luke 17:21.

That wasn't a metaphor. It was a direct assault on the entire architecture of control. If the Divine lives within, priests are obsolete. If truth is internal, temples lose their grip. If God is accessible, empire has **no** leverage.

Rome understood the threat. Jesus wasn't organizing armies, but he was speaking a truth that could collapse their legitimacy. His kingdom wasn't a political one—it was worse. It was untouchable. Unconquerable. Beyond Caesar. Outside jurisdiction.

He flipped tables in the Temple—not just out of outrage, but to expose the business behind belief. Faith for sale. Holiness as a hustle. The religious elite profiting from desperation, from guilt, from control. He refused to plead before Pilate. He stood silent—because acknowledging the system would validate its power. He didn't come to reform empire. He came to reveal it.

That is what made him dangerous. Not his abilities.

So they branded him a criminal. Labeled him a blasphemer. Paraded his suffering as public theater. **Crucifixion wasn't just execution—it was empire's message: This is what happens when you disobey.**

But death wasn't enough. The message still lingered. So they rewrote it. The same empire that nailed him to wood later wrapped itself in his name. Rome co-opted Christ. Sanitized the danger. Institutionalized the revelation.

Obedience replaced awakening. Submission replaced sovereignty. The kingdom within became a building with a price of entry. They took the liberator and made him the face of control. Built churches in his name while silencing his message. Justified conquest with his words. Masked authority in his image.

They didn't just kill him. They rebranded him. That's their patent-pending move. Erase the rebel. Keep the name. Sell the symbol.

THE GENERATIONAL SILENCING OF FIRE

Every revolution needs a grave. Every prophet must be buried. Every liberator must be rewritten until their truth serves the very power they opposed. This isn't deviation—it's the script. Played out in every empire, every age, without exception.

Jesus wasn't killed for kindness. He was executed for declaring a kingdom that Rome couldn't touch or tax. For exposing the fraud of priests. For flipping tables in the temple and naming what it had become:

> **"My house shall be called a house of prayer, but you have made it a den of thieves!" —Matthew 21:13.**

He made himself a threat. So they erased him, then repurposed him. Turned fire into icon. Rebellion into doctrine. The liberator into a mascot of obedience.

John the Baptist spoke from the margins. No temple. No rank. Just truth. He named corruption. Confronted Herod directly. Herod didn't want to kill him—he was afraid of him. But power, cornered, defaults to violence. John's head served as a warning.

Joan of Arc heard voices no priest sanctioned. She led armies without permission. She bowed to no man. That made her expendable. The Church called her witch. Empire called her heretic. They burned her alive. Years later, they canonized her.

Galileo saw the truth orbiting above his head. He spoke it plainly. Doctrine cracked. The Church crushed him. Forced him to deny what he knew. Centuries later, they claimed him back.

Martin Luther King Jr. didn't just dream. He named empire, war, poverty, and racism as parts of the same machine. For that, he was watched, vilified, silenced. His name lives. His message was gutted.

Malcolm X mapped the whole grid. They killed him. Then edited him. Quoted without context. Defanged for the stage.

Socrates said one thing: question everything. They made him drink poison. Then called it justice.

This is how it works. Demonize the voice. Kill the body. Rewrite the name. Use it to sell what it came to destroy.

The ones we remember are a fraction. Thousands more—erased. Before the ink dried. Before the world heard them.

Now it's quieter. No crosses. No flames. Just noise. Just erasure. Shadowbanned. Flagged. Filtered. Laughed off.

Same goal. Control the story. Bury the rebel.

Make obedience look holy.

WHEN RELIGION BECAME LAW

"**Woe to those who make unjust laws, to those who issue oppressive decrees, to deprive the poor of justice and rob the oppressed of their rights.**"

— Isaiah 10:1-2

The greatest deception wasn't just the erasure of prophets or the revision of history—it was turning the lie into law and calling it divine. They didn't just silence truth. They **encoded** it out of reach. Dominion was written into the very architecture of civilization. Every law, every ritual, every structure calibrated not to guide but to govern.

"Govern" to steer. "Ment" the mind. It was never about service. It was about

programming, it literally means Mind Control.

Kings weren't rulers—*they were gods.*

Disobedience wasn't rebellion—*it was blasphemy.*

Empire didn't conquer through war alone. It conquered through belief. Through catechism dressed as curriculum. Through myths told in classrooms. Through stories drilled into children before they ever had a chance to question.

The Vatican crowned emperors. **Caliphs** claimed divine succession. **Chinese emperors** invoked the Mandate of Heaven. **Hindu kings** declared themselves incarnations. The costumes changed. The move stayed the same: fuse the sacred with the state, make submission look holy, make questioning look evil.

When open violence lost its shine, they pivoted to indoctrination. They didn't need crosses anymore—they had classrooms. They didn't need inquisitions—they had standardized tests. They rewrote history to sanctify empire, sanitized genocide into nation-building, and turned colonizers into heroes. Children were taught to kneel—not just in churches, but before flags.

Then came the wars. Global, justified, glorified. Soldiers sent to die for empires dressed up as freedom. Priests blessed bullets. Popes preached peace while backing bloodshed. The hands clutching scripture also held blueprints for bombs.

And when religion couldn't keep up, they crowned ideologies. Men became gods. Factories became temples. Camps became holy ground for purification through labor. Faith was replaced with party loyalty. Spiritual death with state execution. Names were numbers. Truth was treason. Silence became survival.

They carved power into flesh. Made obedience the price of existence. Trained people to watch themselves, to betray each other. Betrayal became a virtue. Death, a gift to the leader. And when it was all over, they chiseled those names into stone and taught the next generation to worship them.

Now the flags are new, but the pattern is old. In one land, children are slaughtered beneath scripture, their blood soaking soil claimed holy by both sides. Two peoples, fed the same promise, convinced it was meant only for them.

Power watches as ancient trauma is weaponized into divine entitlement. Borders shift, bombs fall, and men kill for myths whispered into their blood—stories they didn't write, names they didn't choose, violence baptized in righteousness.

There is no right. Palestinians are murdering Israelis. Israelis are murdering Palestinians. The ground is soaked with vengeance, not justice. And in the middle of it—Jesus.

A man born in Bethlehem, raised in Nazareth. A man who walked the hills of Galilee, healed in Capernaum, wept outside Jerusalem. A man who lived and died in the land both sides now claim. He was not Israeli. He was not Palestinian as defined today. He was both, he was from that soil, that lineage, that fracture. **The Romans, after crushing the Bar Kokhba revolt, renamed the land "Syria Palaestina" to sever Jewish identity from it.** That name stuck. That strategy never ended. Rename it. Reclaim it. Rewrite it.

And now, two peoples kill to inherit the same wound. But the truth is older than the names. Older than the flags. Older than the politics. The land does not belong to either. The violence does not sanctify it. And the blood does not justify the claim.

Let this resonate: Palestinians and Israelis, the same people, are killing each other because of separation created by Romans intended to divide the nation of its people.

They're doing exactly what they were trained to do by empire over a millenia later.

CHAINS OF DEBT & MAMMON'S EMPIRE

"The borrower is slave to the lender."— Proverbs 22:7

The priest became the banker. The temple became the market. Scripture became the ledger. Faith became the contract. As kings fell and cathedrals emptied, the illusion of freedom took the throne—draped not in robes, but in credit. The new dominion didn't speak in sermons. It spoke in numbers. In interest rates. In compounding chains that didn't jingle or bleed—they calculated.

Debt replaced damnation. Redemption replaced with repayment. You were no longer conquered. You signed the contract yourself. Not under duress—but under promise. Security. Ownership. Belonging. The lie was cleaner now, more civilized. But it was the same engine—just dressed in suits instead of cassocks.

The old priest offered heaven. The new one offers a mortgage. The king demanded allegiance. The market demands your life. And so it didn't matter what name the chains wore—only that you wore them. Proudly. Silently. Willingly.

The Church took tithes under threat of hell. **Now you give half your life to taxes, rents, and repayments—with a smile.** It's your duty after all. Debts that cannot die, passed from parent to child like some hereditary curse. A soul born into servitude, told he is free.

From the first breath, he is programmed: this is adulthood. This is success. This is how the world works. He isn't raised to question—only to comply. He is groomed not for truth, but for utility. For productivity. For compliance.

When religious power collapsed, governments filled the vacuum. When doctrine faded, economic law took its place. Indulgences became credit scores. Scripture became policy. Gold was stripped away, replaced by fiat. **Paper backed by faith in the same machine that writes the rules.**

They don't need to whip you. You whip yourself. You set your alarm. You file your taxes. You chase ownership that never arrives. You guard your own cell and call it progress.

Vatican wealth wasn't born from generosity. It was forged in extraction. Tithes enforced through spiritual blackmail. They spoke of poverty while hoarding empires. Preached salvation while selling access. When the Church lost its grip, the formula stayed.

The systems changed costume—but the grip tightened. And still, the lie is sold. Work harder. Sacrifice more. Buy your way out. But there is no exit through the front door.

The chains don't break with money. They break with remembering. The system does not fear debtors. It fears those who see it.

Those who know the kingdom was never for sale.

THE MARKET OF SOULS

"What good is it for someone to gain the whole
world, Yet forfeit their soul?"— **Mark 8:36**

Religions lost their thrones, but their methods survived. The robes came off. The language changed. But the control remained. High priests didn't disappear—they became financiers, CEOs, policy architects.

They stopped quoting scripture and started quoting margins.

They traded altars for boardrooms, miracles for marketing, salvation for credit. Kings shed their crowns and became shareholders. Monarchies collapsed, but the dominion stayed intact—just migrated into ledgers and contracts. The new rulers don't sit on thrones. They sit on capital. Land, water, medicine, energy—every right to exist is now metered, monetized, managed.

Power no longer speaks through clergy. It speaks through screens. Through curated feeds, shadow policies, shifting algorithms. You are ruled not by decree, but by narrative—decided behind closed doors, tested through metrics, enforced without trace. Books aren't burned. They're drowned. Voices aren't silenced. They're buried in static. Exile isn't declared. It's automated.

This is the Inquisition re-skinned—targeted, digital, polite. No torches. Just deletions. No trials. Just demonetization. The heretic now is the one who speaks clearly. Not burned, just unfollowed. Not imprisoned, just erased.

They don't want your worship. They want your engagement. Devotion has become screen time. Faith has become brand loyalty. Attention is the new tithe. You aren't asked to believe—you're trained to consume. You're not enslaved—you're rewarded. With benefits. With gamified validation. With dopamine.

Rights become privileges. Privileges become subscriptions. Needs become products. And you pay—to stay alive, to stay visible, to stay relevant. You chase success the way the devout once chased heaven. You burn out on the altar of hustle, then pay for your own recovery. Therapy sold as redemption. Wellness branded and resold. Compliance disguised as growth.

You aren't a citizen anymore. You're a unit. A demographic. A dataset. A yield curve. The prophet is now an influencer. The sermon is a campaign. Saints are sponsored, filtered, untouchable. **You don't see truth. You see what was approved for your feed.**

And still you chase it. Not knowing the light you run toward was built to blind you from the light that you actually are. Not knowing the system will burn you out and replace you in a second. You call it freedom. You wear it proudly. But it's *not* freedom.

It's just a more elegant set of chains.

EMBRACED CHAINS LAST LONGER

They learned long ago—the strongest chains are the ones you never try to break. The ones you defend. The ones you wrap in identity and call your own. Religion once taught that suffering was virtue, obedience was righteousness, and questioning authority was rebellion against God. That training didn't disappear when the temples emptied. It adapted.

The chains became invisible. And the prisoners learned to call their cage a home. Obedience was rebranded as success. Compliance as loyalty. Conformity as security. You were conditioned to see servitude as stability. To confuse survival with freedom. To believe you were choosing your own oppression.

They made you fear freedom because freedom is actually unfamiliar, especially to those who have been conditioned not to see it.

Servitude, on the other hand, is ritual. You were taught that debt is natural. That working until your body gives out is noble. That war, exploitation, and corruption are just part of the price of peace. That your soul must be sold—for status, for shelter, for the illusion of "making it."

You chased the dream, even when the dream was a leash. You called it ambition. Called it purpose. They called it life. But it was labor—repackaged as virtue. Chained to jobs you hate. Chained to images you curate. Chained to debt that was handed to you at birth. You did not rebel. You climbed. And the higher you climbed, the tighter the chain pulled.

They don't need to force you. They taught you to force yourself. To wake up early. To overwork. To self-police. To stay quiet. To say thank you. **They taught you to love the system that feeds on your energy and sells your time back to you in fractions.**

This is *not* freedom. It's empire—digitized, polished, rebranded. The same control that ruled two thousand years ago now hides behind your phone, speaks through your entertainment, bills you monthly for your own captivity. The names changed. The chains didn't.

But something cracked. People are seeing it now. The illusion made a mistake and blinked. The program glitched. You've felt it—that strange moments where everything you were told no longer fits. Nothing makes sense.

You can see the forked tongues now.

"Then you will know the truth, and the truth will set you free." —John 8:32

Freedom doesn't feel safe. It feels raw. And that's how you know it's real, and once known, it doesn't go away.

THE RIDERS OF REVELATION NEVER LEFT

The ancient warnings were never metaphor. They weren't distant prophecies meant for some future reckoning. They were the blueprint—etched into myth, cloaked in scripture, handed down as code.

The Four Horsemen are not waiting behind sealed doors. They ride now. They ride openly. And the world watches, paralyzed, calling it progress. You see them in the wars spun from boardrooms and broadcast like sport. In the scarcity engineered by abundance hoarded. In the sickness monetized, manufactured, sustained. In the fear piped into your mind through every glowing screen. They are not hiding. *They don't need to.* The world has been trained to worship them. To call them normal. To call them necessary. To call them inevitable.

But inevitability is the first lie. The word used to make you surrender before the fight begins. The language of control dressed up as realism. You were told this was the way of the world. **But you can see it now—this isn't fate. It's design.**

The seals aren't waiting to be broken. They were shattered long ago. The war is here. The famine is creeping through the shelves. The plague is not just viral—it is psychological, spiritual, systemic. The pale rider doesn't wear a hood. He wears a logo. He signs executive orders. He funds research and calls it aid. He doesn't bring death. He sells it. And you pay for it.

The truth is something hidden in plain sight. The horsemen were never spirits. They were structure. They were system. They were conquest, economy, medicine, media. And they have been in motion since the beginning.

You can see them here and now—not as prophecy, but as architecture of the world you operate within.

But beneath the chaos, there is something else. Something they could never touch. Something older than empire, deeper than scripture, louder than fear. It waits beneath the noise, beneath the cycle, beneath the broadcast. It is not new. It is not coming. It has always been here.

And once you see it—truly see it—there is no return. No forgetting. No retreat.

Only clarity, which is provided to you next.

VIII

THE SECOND RESOUND

THE QUADRANT OF CONTROL

"WHAT MATTERS IS THIS: IF
THE MIND FALLS, EVERYTHING
ELSE FOLLOWS."

THE SECOND RESOUND

THE QUADRANT OF CONTROL &
THE FOUR HORSEMEN

I remember sitting cross-legged on the floor, a worn Bible cradled in my small hands. They told me it was a book of hope, of salvation, but I wasn't drawn to the psalms or the parables. I flipped to the back. To the final pages. To the thunder and fire and seals. Revelation. And there, etched in prophecy and dread, I found them—the four riders, veiled in shadow. **White. Red. Black. Pale.**

> **"And I looked, and behold... a pale horse. And its rider's name was Death, and Hades followed him." — Revelation 6:8**

Their names were never spoken aloud in church. Just warnings wrapped in vague sermons, whispered tones of "the end," of some future judgment. But even then, as a child, I knew better. **I felt their hooves in the earth.** In the headlines. In the hunger in our streets and the silence in our pews. No alarms rang. No one wept in recognition. But the signs were all around us.

The first had already conquered—minds tamed, narratives swallowed whole. The second had taken peace long ago, war no longer shocking but expected. The third weighed the scales, tipping the world toward the rich while the poor sank under invisible hands. And the fourth—Death—had never left. He walked quietly, as he always had. They weren't waiting to arrive. **They had been here the whole time.**

The pulpit didn't speak of them. Not like that. They warned of a coming famine while millions already starved. They spoke of disease like a future punishment while the sick filled our hospitals, our streets, our homes. They told us to prepare for war, but never named the ones already being waged—for profit, for power, for empire. And when I asked—when I questioned the seal that had supposedly not yet been broken—the room grew cold.

I asked why the white horse's rider didn't have any arrows with his bow. The preacher's smile tightened. **"These things are not for us to know."** But I knew. I knew what silence protected. I saw the prison, not of iron, but of belief. No bars needed. No locks required. Just stories. Just tradition. Just scripture, turned weapon.

We had even been shown the chains and taught to love them. And in that moment, everything shifted. The text no longer read as warning—it read as blueprint. Not a prophecy of what will be, but a mirror of what already is. A veil pulled over the eyes of the world. The Horsemen were not omens of the end.

They were the architects of the now.

When I closed the book, it wasn't out of fear. It was understanding. And nothing looked the same again.

The world was told to wait. The preachers spoke of a final reckoning, a distant hour, a sealed fate. The Four would come in time, summoned by divine fury, carried on the storm. But the storm had already come. The hoofbeats didn't shake the sky—they echoed through the streets, thundered beneath polished floors, rattled the neighbor, fueled the machinery of endless war. The Black Horse tipped the scales, hoarding abundance while the many starved. And the Pale Horse, moving last, turned death into industry—sickness into currency, suffering into profit.

These were never allegories. They were blueprints. Not future prophecy, but present design. You don't need armies to rule a world. You only need to control the story. You don't need chains to bind a people. You only need them to believe they're already free. You don't need to conquer nations. You only need to pit them against themselves. You don't need to slay a people. You only need them to accept death as destiny.

The Horsemen ride still. Not coming. Already here.

This is who they are without the masks, it's time you see:

THE WHITE HORSE: WAR FOR THE MIND

We were taught to worship the structures built to contain us. Conditioned to revere the systems that defined our limits. For generations, we were trained to look ahead, to fear what had not yet arrived. So we prayed, hoped, and looked away from the creeping truth: they were already here.

They didn't descend as specters. They were systems. They didn't ride from heaven—they were built into the bones of civilization. They are not omens. They are infrastructure. The architecture beneath empire.

The White Horse claimed the mind, waging war through perception. Its rider does not carry a sword. He carries a bow with no arrows. His conquest is quiet, efficient, unseen. He does not need force. **He only needs agreement.**

He doesn't invade nations—he invades perception. He rides straight into the mind and rewires it from within. Wherever he goes, truth is bent. History is repainted. Doubt becomes sin. Lies become law. Repetition takes the place of reality.

This is the war of ideology. The war that leaves cities standing but empties them of vision. It doesn't torch buildings—it torches awareness. Education becomes indoctrination. Media becomes gospel. Culture becomes a cage wrapped in language that sounds like freedom.

And the people, unaware, rise in defense of the very structures that consume them. They pledge loyalty to illusions. They argue for their servitude.

The White Horse rides through every screen, every sermon, every textbook, every timeline. He whispers through policies, preaches through headlines, embeds himself in code and curriculum. He does not demand silence—he manufactures it.

They told you this was knowledge. That this was growth. That this was truth. And we believed them, because that's how the White Horse wins. Not by overpowering you.

By getting you to stop looking.

THE RED HORSE: PERPETUAL WAR

It was never enough to conquer the mind. The body had to be broken too.

The Red Horse didn't come to end wars—he came to sustain them. Not for justice. Not for liberation. But for exhaustion. His mission was never victory. It was conflict without conclusion, a loop without exit.

War that feeds on itself.

One battle ends, another ignites. One enemy falls, another takes their place. Resolution is dangled like a prize, always out of reach. Peace is promised, but never delivered.

Nations are drained, year after year, told they're fighting for freedom, told they're fighting for peace. But peace isn't profitable. Freedom isn't useful. The real goal is the war itself—the distraction, the consumption, the machine that keeps turning.

Conflict keeps people occupied. It keeps them angry, marching, polarized, afraid. They rally around causes designed in boardrooms, spill blood on soil they'll never understand, all while the ones above watch the cycle repeat.

They aren't meant to win. They're meant to keep fighting. Because the war isn't meant to end.

It's meant to continue—until no one remembers why it began.

THE BLACK HORSE: FALSE SCARCITY

It was not enough to conquer the mind and body. It needed to stay down, to stay broken.

The Black Horse didn't just tip the scales—he stole them outright. What was once balanced became manipulated. What was once shared became owned. He took the abundance of the earth and moved it just out of reach.

Food became a commodity. Shelter became speculation. Water became a privilege. What had once been birthright was now product, marked and priced, wrapped in scarcity. The planet stayed rich, but its fruits were gated, fenced in by the hands of a few.

Debt was crafted not to weigh down—but to bind. It wasn't just numbers on a ledger. It was control, disguised as responsibility. Struggle became a virtue. Poverty became inevitable. Suffering was reframed as character.

And the people accepted it. They wore hardship like honor, believed lack was natural, and mistook captivity for sacrifice.

The Black Horse didn't come to take what was ours.

He came to convince us we never had it.

THE PALE HORSE: PROFITING FROM DEATH

When the mind is conquered, and the body broken, the spirit subdued, willpower vanquished, the final conquest begins.

The Pale Horse doesn't fight. It harvests. Its power isn't in violence—it's in fatigue. In systems that grind people down slowly, methodically, until nothing remains but survival. Not all deaths come by blade. Some arrive through hunger. Through untreated sickness. Through despair that settles so deeply, it begins to feel like truth.

Life becomes a transaction. Health becomes a privilege. Suffering is normalized, commercialized, turned into a market where death is slow and profitable. The people, worn thin, begin to accept it. They say, **"This is just how it is,"** and that phrase becomes law. Becomes gospel even. If it is what it is, no one has to try.

The Pale Horse doesn't need to be seen. It's felt—in clinics underfunded, in shelves left empty, in bodies pushed to the brink and told to keep going. Its presence isn't in apocalypse. It's in routine.

Their rhythm echoes in economies. Their shadows pass through hospitals. Their doctrine is etched into the systems we call normal.

And they will not stop—until we do.

They will ride as long as we remain asleep. As long as the chains are accepted. As long as we call this captivity "civilization."

The end is not coming. The end is a choice, a choice that begins with you.

What follows is beyond a mere introduction, it's the way out of the clutches of each horse and it's rider, one by one. You may be tempted to refute these as true, you may be tempted to find reasons not to believe them, but I am not trying to convince you of anything. You may deny as you wish, but what I shine the light on is true, and always will be true.

It's time to know the horsement in detail.

THE FIRST HORSE: MIND CONTROL

The first rider does not arrive with war drums or fire. He spills no blood, carries no sword—he doesn't need one. His victory is quiet, subtle, total. His conquest is not won on battlefields, but in the spaces between thought. A war waged through silence. Through words removed from history. Through truths slowly erased until nothing remains but the shape of obedience.

"And I looked, and behold, a white horse! And its rider had a bow, and a crown was given to him, and he came out conquering, and to conquer." — Revelation 6:2

A bow with no arrows. A crown granted, not seized. He wins not by force, but by framing. This is the war of ideology—the slow corrosion of perception. He doesn't take your freedom. He convinces you you never had it.

Language begins to shift. History starts to blur. Reality softens under the weight of repetition. The truth is buried, not with violence, but with comfort. With consensus. And once the mind is claimed, no chains are needed.

The first rider teaches you to obey because it's wise. To submit because it's righteous. He doesn't need to police you. You'll do it yourself. You'll silence your own doubt. You'll defend your illusion like it's sacred.

This is why he rides first. Before war can rage, before scarcity can be imposed, before death can claim—belief must be bent. For once the mind has surrendered, the rest requires no resistance.

He does not rule by decree. He rules by illusion. There are no proclamations, no mandates from thrones. His victory doesn't require conquest—only compliance. Wherever he rides, knowledge is filtered, history reshaped, and dissent quietly labeled as dangerous. Questions are met with ridicule. Curiosity is branded rebellion. Truth is not debated—it is erased.

He does not break the body. He claims the mind. And no one resists, because no one believes there is anything to resist. His power lies not in force, but in the subtle disguise of his presence. The White Horse doesn't arrive as tyranny. He arrives as progress. As education. As wisdom dressed in gentle tones.

> "Woe to those who call evil good and good evil, who put
> darkness for light and light for darkness." — Isaiah 5:20

This is the first conquest—the conquest of perception. And it is the most essential. For once the lens has been corrupted, everything that passes through it is distorted.

Many wonder why this matters—why control the mind when the world can be ruled by might? But the rider of the White Horse knows the deeper truth: once the mind is taken, the body follows willingly. A people who cannot discern reality from illusion do not need chains. They'll police their own thoughts. They'll turn on each other with righteous fury, silencing the very voices that could set them free. They'll condemn the questioners, brand them heretics, and stand proudly as guardians of their own captivity.

This is the brilliance of the first rider—his reign is silent, but complete. Generations can pass under his shadow, convinced that injustice is virtue, that obedience is strength, that silence is peace.

Raise a child in falsehood, and they will defend it as sacred. Raise a people without truth, and they will beg for illusion.

His Four Pillars Of Control

To break a people, you must first own their thoughts. It doesn't happen all at once—it happens in stages. Each layer softens the mind for the next, until truth becomes optional and obedience feels like safety. This is the architecture of conquest: four pillars, unseen but unshakable. Not towers of stone. Not walls of iron. These are invisible strongholds—structures of perception that shape what is real, what is right, and what must be accepted without question.

Each pillar supports the next, reinforcing the illusion. Over time, the cage builds itself from the inside. No guards. No chains. Just people convinced that every brick is protection. That every lock is love. That every limit is for their own good.

I. THE KEEPER OF SALVATION

Before thought could be shaped, before reality could be rewritten, there had to be dominion over the soul. In the earliest days, faith wasn't a doctrine—it was a direct experience. Spirit met Spirit. No middleman, no hierarchy, no fear. The Infinite was near, and the people knew it. They didn't need permission to pray. They didn't need approval to be divine.

But for those who sought control, unfiltered access to God was dangerous. So they took the gateway and built walls around it. They claimed the titles, the rituals, the authority. They stood between the people and the Divine and called themselves necessary. **"You are born broken,"** they whispered. "You must come to us. You must confess. You must earn forgiveness. We hold the keys." And fear did the rest. Not swords. Not shackles. Just the terror of eternal punishment.

Faith, once a living current, became obligation. Connection gave way to doctrine. Love was overshadowed by guilt. Spirituality, once expansive, was shrunk to fit inside a system designed to obey.

> **"Woe to you, experts in the law, because you have taken away the key to knowledge. You yourselves have not entered, and you have hindered those who were entering." — Luke 11:52**

This was the first move of the White Horse: sever the direct line to the Divine, replace it with a system, and teach the people to fear their own doubt. Once they believed their salvation was owned by others, control was no longer necessary. They would guard the prison themselves.

II. THE MAKER OF INSTRUCTION

Yet faith alone wasn't enough. Obedience had to go deeper—beneath belief, into the foundation of thought itself. To truly conquer the mind, they had to seize the halls of learning.

So they rewrote history. They crowned conquerors as saviors, turned massacres into victories, stripped wonder from discovery, and reshaped curiosity into rebellion. Education didn't awaken—it programmed. It molded minds to fit the shape of the system.

Children were given books that told them what to believe. They learned to memorize, not to question. To recite, not to reflect. Wars became holy. Empires became destiny. Leaders were painted as divine. Obedience was praised as wisdom. Compliance passed for intelligence. And the few who dared to ask why were cast as dangerous, unstable, misled.

Those children became adults who clung to the curriculum. They laughed at dissent. They mocked the unapproved. They became guardians of their own programming, teaching others to kneel in the same direction they were shown.

> **"Train up a child in the way he should go, And when he is old he will not depart from it." — Proverbs 22:6**

This was the second conquest—education, reshaped as indoctrination. Control the lessons, and you control the lens. But it didn't stop there. Because controlling knowledge was never enough. They needed to control what people saw.

III. THE WEAVER OF NARRATIVE

Faith was seized. Education subjugated. The next move was bolder—reshape reality itself.

What once informed became agenda. Journalism gave way to propaganda. Entertainment morphed into social engineering. Every screen, every headline, every frame was repurposed—not to reflect the world, but to design it.

Fear was rationed with precision, served in daily doses. Conflict emerged on cue. Heroes were manufactured. Enemies assembled from shadows. When war was needed, justifications appeared. When obedience was desired, crises conveniently unfolded. If attention strayed, spectacle filled the gap.

The population, shaped by doctrine and curriculum, consumed it all without pause. They trusted the feed. Trusted the anchors. Trusted the officials. Never asking who built the narrative, who owned the lens.

> **"Woe to those who call evil good and good evil, who put darkness for light and light for darkness." — Isaiah 5:20**

Within this pillar, anything unsanctioned became dangerous. Independent thought was recast as delusion. Those who asked questions were dismissed or despised. The crowd learned to mock the heretic, to exile the dissenter, to protect the illusion at all costs.

A structure built not from truth, but repetition. The people no longer saw the world as it was. **They saw what they were told to see—and called it reality.**

IV. THE MASTER OF EXPERIENCE

At last, the final threshold—not just controlling belief, not just shaping education, not just steering the story, but rewriting reality itself.

What began as surveillance has evolved into omnipresence. Every action tracked, every purchase logged, every word, every scroll, every hesitation absorbed into a profile more intimate than thought. It was framed as safety. Convenience. Protection. But behind the screen, the White Horse perfected his reach.

He no longer predicts your next move—he designs it. He curates your feed, primes your preferences, influences your vote before you think you've made it. Algorithms reward conformity, suppress resistance, tuning your life into a pattern you didn't choose but believe you did.

Systems are tested. Social credit scores. Compliance incentives. Quiet punishments. A wrong opinion can lock you out of opportunity. A flagged post can cut you from participation. Voices grow cautious. Eyes lower. People begin to police themselves.

This isn't just observation—it's manipulation. Surveillance has become sculpture. And the people, trained by doctrine, education, and media, accept the limitations as normal. They defend them as progress. They praise the cage as if it were a sanctuary.

Here, no chains are needed. The mind bends before force is ever required. No decrees are necessary. The illusion of choice is enough.

CREATING THE PRISON OF THE MIND

When these four pillars rise, they do not merely stand—they fortify. Together, they form a fortress of the mind, a citadel of invisible control:

I. The Keeper of Salvation—claims the soul, declaring only sanctioned paths can lead to the Divine.

II. The Maker of Instruction—shapes knowledge from the cradle, molding thought before it can question.

III. The Weaver of Narrative—scripts the world, feeding perception through curated stories and filtered truth.

IV. The Master of Experience—monitors, predicts, and influences every move, bending choice before it's made.

Above it all rides the White Horse, bearing no arrows, only a bow—a symbol of control without open conflict. His crown is not earned through victory, but sustained through illusion. No battlefield is needed. No blood must spill.

HISTORICAL ECHOES OF THE WHITE HORSE

Though I speak in broad terms, the White Horse has galloped across history under many banners, wearing the face of empire, religion, progress, and order. In ancient kingdoms, high priests claimed divine authority, declaring themselves the sole interpreters of the gods. Obedience was salvation. Dissent was heresy. Sacrifice was demanded not just of the flesh, but of the mind.

In medieval Europe, a single church ruled thought. It chose which texts were holy, which ideas forbidden. Gnostic gospels were burned. Libraries locked. Questions punished. Children were taught to kneel before priests, not in reverence—but in fear. **Inquiry died in the name of control.**

In the last century, regimes rose with different symbols, but the same intent. Education became indoctrination. History became myth. Neighbors turned against each other, loyalty tested in whispers. Entire populations internalized the script handed to them, repeating it until they forgot it had been written by someone else.

Even in modern democracies, the blueprint holds. Corporations fund research. Schoolbooks are shaped by private interest. Media conglomerates decide which stories matter, which ones disappear. Algorithms know you better than you know yourself, curating your reality one swipe at a time.

The details shift. The language changes. But the strategy remains the same: conquer the mind, and everything else follows.

When the White Horse rides unchecked, people become their own enforcers. A mother scolds her child for questioning a lesson, believing she protects them, not realizing she reinforces the very bars that confine them. A scholar keeps their thoughts in line, repeating what's safe, fearing exile if they dare speak their own insight. **A citizen shames a neighbor for deviating from the official script, convinced conformity preserves peace, never considering what it costs.**

In this climate, revolutions die before they begin. No prisons are needed. No martyrs made. Few realize they're captives.

"My people are destroyed for lack of knowledge." — Hosea 4:6

And yet, even illusion has limits. Even the most carefully maintained narrative begins to crack when enough eyes begin to open.

A **teacher** plants questions where the curriculum forbids them, knowing she risks complaint, reprimand, or dismissal. Still she sows, because even one awakened student can fracture the illusion.

A **journalist** dares to write what was meant to remain hidden. She endures digital erasure, attacks on her credibility, whispers behind her back. Still she speaks, because truth, once released, cannot be contained.

A **scientist** refuses to falsify his findings. Grants vanish. Colleagues fall silent. But he holds the line, because reality is not subject to consensus.

A **seeker** walks away from inherited doctrine, not out of rebellion, but to walk directly with the Divine. They are labeled heretic, mocked or feared—but they keep walking, because freedom cannot be mediated.

These are not grand revolutions. They are quiet ruptures. Hairline fractures that grow. Each one chips away at the first pillar. The cracks spread. The structure trembles. Because illusion is only strong while it is shared.

Break the consensus, and the fortress begins to fall.

THE FIRST STEP IS BREAKING FREE

He doesn't rule with chains. He doesn't demand submission. He doesn't need to. He persuades you to give it willingly, to call it wisdom, to name it protection. You must understand that his power isn't taken from you—it's offered to him, handed over with trust disguised as common sense.

His reign is built on cooperation. Your cooperation. And that makes it fragile. It only works so long as people stay quiet, so long as they believe what they've been told is for their own good.

> **"And you shall know the truth, and the truth shall make you free." — John 8:32**

But truth requires something rare—it demands courage. The courage to ask. To look again. To walk away from comfortable lies. To stand alone when conformity closes in.

Start with the gatekeepers. The priest who claims exclusive access to the Divine—ask why the Infinite needs a middleman. The teacher who punishes questions—ask who benefits from your silence. The narrative piped through your feed—trace its source, follow the money, and see whose interests it really serves.

Reclaim direct experience. **You don't need permission to speak with God. You don't need a license to wonder.** You don't need a sanctioned source to learn. With discernment—not cynicism—you begin to see what's real. The White Horse doesn't fear opposition. He fears clarity. He thrives in extremes: blind trust or blanket rejection. But discernment breaks the cycle.

Seek others who see. Speak without filters. Sharpen one another without fear. Even a small circle of truth cuts through massive illusion. And when fear rises—as it will—pause. Ask who profits from your compliance.

Many *claim* to be awake, but only repeat a new set of approved ideas. True awakening means questioning everything—even the questions. This path isn't rewarded. It's resisted. But those who break illusions usually walk alone at first.

It takes strength to admit the chains were chosen. It takes resolve to live outside them. But once seen, they lose their power. Once named, they begin to crack.

> **"Do not conform to the pattern of this world, but be transformed by the renewing of your mind."** — **Romans 12:2**

This is the quiet war of the age. A battle not for territory, but for perception. It won't be fought with weapons—it's already underway with ideas. Call it culture war. Call it information war. Call it psychological operations. The label doesn't matter.

What matters is this: if the mind falls, everything else follows. The White Horse rides first for a reason. He prepares the way. For war. For famine. For despair. If he shapes the lens, the others step in without resistance.

But when the illusion cracks—when minds remain free—war doesn't start. Manufactured scarcity gets exposed. Fear tactics lose their grip. And the White Horse, crowned by illusion, begins to falter.

He carries no arrows. His power is belief. Take that away, and he rides alone.

You don't need violence to unseat him. Just a refusal to let illusion steer your life.

Question the feed. Doubt the scripted consensus. Reclaim direct communion. Listen to your own knowing.

"For the Spirit God gave us does not make us timid, but gives us power, love, and self-discipline." — 2 Timothy 1:7

He rides only if you allow it. His conquest is real—but it is not absolute. Enough awakened minds, enough clear eyes, enough unshackled souls—and the illusion collapses.

The crown will fall off. The grip dissolves. The bow will break. The fortress trembles.

Let him ride no further.

Not in your mind. Not in your house. Not in your name.

What can he do? *He has no arrows.*

Now you see him and that alone is enough to begin dealing with the other three.

THE SECOND HORSE: PERPETUAL WAR

"Nation will rise against nation, And kingdom against kingdom."—Matthew 24:7

Once the mind is subdued, the body must be broken. So the Red Horse rides second—its presence masked as patriotism, its work done through division, fear, and exhaustion so deep that resistance feels impossible.

War is not waged to protect nations or preserve liberty. **It's a loop—fight, rebuild, destroy, repeat.** A relentless cycle disguised as progress. Land may be claimed, but it's time that's truly conquered. Generations are consumed, caught in a rhythm they never chose, told they are free as they march toward ruin.

When neighbors turn on each other, they no longer see who profits. While blood spills on the ground, power climbs quietly through the smoke. The Red Horse doesn't charge in with chaos—he walks calmly behind the curtain, fueling endless conflict that enriches the few and bleeds the many.

"They will beat their swords into plowshares and their spears

**into pruning hooks. Nation will not take up sword against
nation, nor will they train for war anymore." — Isaiah 2:4**

Yet peace is never profitable. Modern warfare isn't about defense—it sustains industries, builds empires, and buries truth beneath rubble. The same hands that fund the weapons rebuild the cities. The same names appear in both the destruction and the contracts for repair.

Governments stoke fear to justify control. Freedoms shrink under the guise of security. Dissent becomes dangerous. And behind it all—money moves. Corruption thrives. Power consolidates.

The Red Horse doesn't care who wins. Victory is irrelevant. The goal is motion. Constant conflict. A machine that feeds on bodies and prints its profits in grief. This isn't chaos—it's strategy. Designed, maintained, perfected.

And as long as the world believes war is noble, he keeps riding.

Five Engines Of Perpetual War

**"When you hear of wars and rumors of wars, do not be alarmed. Such
things must happen, but the end is still to come." — Mark 13:7**

The Red Horse rides not by chaos, but by design—anchored by five unchanging engines that keep war alive across eras, banners, and borders. Each one engineered to ensure conflict never ends, only evolves.

I. WAR IS ALWAYS JUSTIFIED

**"They dress the wound of my people as though it were not serious.
'Peace, peace,' they say, when there is no peace." — Jeremiah 6:14**

First, war is always justified. Every campaign framed as defense, every conquest wrapped in noble language. The cause shifts, but the greed beneath it stays the same. The flags change, the slogans shift, but the ambitions remain. Every conflict is declared righteous, every battle framed as necessary. But behind the speeches lies the same motive: land, power, profit. Soldiers don't bleed for peace—they bleed to protect the positions of those who say, this time is different.

From empires past to modern states, the pattern holds. Leaders provoke, fabricate, ignite. A single incident is enough to stir outrage, and soon, the people demand war themselves—convinced it's justice, unaware of the game behind the curtain. Peace is dangerous to those in power. It creates space to ask questions. It threatens to reveal who profits from the carnage. So conflict must continue. Always another threat. Always another reason.

And so the machine turns, fed by virtue, cloaked in righteousness, fueled by belief—devouring lives in the name of ideals it does not serve.

II. WAR IS NEVER MEANT TO BE WON

"For a thousand years in Your sight are but as yesterday when it is past, or as a watch in the night." — Psalm 90:4

War is never meant to be won. Victory would end the need. Instead, conflict loops endlessly, enemies replaced before fear has time to fade. No matter the era or banners flown, the war machine stays the same—a self-feeding engine built not to end conflict but to sustain it. Victory is a myth sold to the grieving while its architects profit from the next campaign.

During the Cold War, two giants locked in silent standoff while smaller nations burned in proxy battles. When that front cooled, the War on Shadows began—faceless enemies, endless threats, permanent surveillance. Sovereignty vanished. Communities fractured. Fear became currency, and the architects thrived. When one enemy fades, another is conjured. The Red Horse forbids peace, not through chaos but design.

Peace collapses the systems built on fear. It exposes the illusion that safety must be bought with obedience. The machine knows this, so it feeds enemies like bread and sells war as protection. It sustains crisis to prevent awakening. The true battlefield isn't land—it's perception. War is engineered to endure. Weapons change. Language shifts. The mission holds: maintain conflict, suppress awareness.

The Red Horse rides in silence, whispering strategy to kings, turning resistance into treason. It doesn't charge—it justifies. And the people comply, blind to the ritual. The only disarmament begins within, when the mind refuses to be drafted.

III. THE REAL WAR IS PSYCHOLOGICAL

"For God has not given us a spirit of fear, but of power and love and self-control." — 2 Timothy 1:7

Long before cannons roar, fear marches in. It binds the mind, softens resistance, and installs obedience where will once lived. Fear is the oldest tool of control— subtle, quiet, effective. Long before armies are summoned, populations are conditioned. In ancient kingdoms, rulers invoked divine wrath to enforce loyalty. Remember, disobedience wasn't rebellion—it was blasphemy. In medieval darkness, priests wielded hell like a sword, forging eternal punishment into a leash.

In the realms of communism, fear took a colder form—constant surveillance, imagined threats, manufactured despair. Paranoia became patriotism. Neighbors turned informants. Silence became survival. Even in nations claiming freedom, this Crimson Specter hovers—an unseen enemy used to justify endless control. The label shifts—terrorist, traitor, threat—but the function remains. Neighbors report neighbors. Trust dissolves. People monitor each other not from duty, but from dread.

And in broken, starving regions, fear becomes physical. Families disappear. Public punishment becomes theater. Bars aren't needed when terror lives in the bloodstream. Each crisis feeds the machine. Pandemic, war, economic collapse— each one resets the fear cycle, keeping the population in a state of managed panic.

The Red Horse doesn't need to conquer. It only needs to whisper. It just likes to watch people die, so it chooses violence as primary. Its empire is built not on weapons, but on anxiety—layered, constant, and self-reinforcing. It doesn't roar. It hovers in headlines, sermons, schoolbooks, policy. Fear is the oldest chain. Invisible. Custom-fit. And it holds until someone sees it. Naming it breaks its spell. Recognition is rebellion. Awareness is resistance. Once the fear is seen clearly, it loses grip. And the silent empire—built on dread, sustained by illusion—begins to crack.

IV. THE ENEMY IS MANUFACTURED

> **"If a kingdom is divided against itself, that**
> **kingdom cannot stand." — Mark 3:24**

The Red Horse rides only where division reigns. **If no enemy exists, one is manufactured.** A half-truth twisted. An old wound reopened. A phantom threat dragged from shadow. Anything to ignite rage, to unify the masses against a fabricated foe while hidden powers expand unchecked.

The tactic is *ancient*. Roman senators warned of barbarian hordes, though it was their own expansion that provoked the violence. Kings cloaked conquest beneath divine decrees, declaring holy war while chasing gold. Colonial empires exploited tribal tensions, inflaming old grudges to fracture resistance—plunder dressed as progress.

In modern guise, the pattern holds. Leaders invoke terrorists, radicals, threats to democracy—labels recycled to justify surveillance, warfare, occupation. New generations march into deserts, jungles, city ruins, convinced of noble cause, unaware the enemy was summoned for profit.

The war machine is eternal. Its masters aren't just kings. They are CEOs, arms dealers, intelligence networks—entities that depend on instability, whose power and wealth grow with every escalation. **War is their business model. Fear is their product.**

The real war was never between the people. It is between those who orchestrate division and those manipulated into believing it. Soldiers die. Civilians grieve. But the architects dine in silence. While flags clash and slogans echo, no one sees the deeper theater.

The sides are illusions. The conflict is curated. And always, behind it, the Red Horse rides—unchecked, unseen, unquestioned. Its power is rooted in illusion. It thrives when eyes are pointed outward and never upward. The moment the curtain is pulled back, when the masses see who benefits from their division, the spell breaks.

Until then, the battlefield remains crowded with those who think they're enemies, but are really just pawns in a war that was never theirs to begin with.

V. REBELLION IS REDIRECTED

> **"Do not be deceived: God is not mocked, for whatever one sows, that will he also reap." — Galatians 6:7**

Resistance is *expected*. The Red Horse has planned for it. For centuries, those in power have learned that revolts don't need to be crushed—they can be redirected, absorbed, and defanged. Bread and circuses once numbed the masses. Now it's rebrands, empty reforms, and controlled opposition.

Revolutions erupt with real fire—pain, injustice, rage—but before the flames can burn through the system, the machine steps in. Promises are made. Slogans are offered. Kings fall, flags change, but the hands on the levers remain the same.

Empires rename themselves. Oppressors swap uniforms. When communism collapsed, it was called liberation—yet the financiers who backed both sides quietly reemerged under new banners. The poor stayed poor. The chains stayed hidden. And still, the crowds cheered.

Every uprising becomes theater. Leaders disappear. Demands soften. Rage becomes ritual, safely channeled through systems built to absorb it. The Red Horse doesn't fear protest. He has rehearsed its script a *thousand* times.

He *expects* anger and wrath. He counts on it. Because he knows most will settle for symbols over substance. A new flag. A trending hashtag. A louder voice inside the same cage. Real freedom remains untouched, because the true prison was never the regime—it was the belief that the regime could be reformed.

The only revolt that terrifies the Red Horse is the one that refuses to be absorbed. The one that doesn't seek a seat at the empire's table—but flips the table, unmasks the architects, and dissolves the structure entirely.

Until that revolt comes, the Red Horse rides without fear. He knows how to outlast movements, how to turn rebellion into ritual, how to make the people believe they've changed what still owns them. But as long as the illusion holds, the machine stays untouched—renewed by every failed revolution, stronger after every cycle of managed dissent.

BREAKING FREE FROM THE RED HORSE

He does not demand you bow. He demands you fight each other. He doesn't chain your wrists—he chains your thoughts, your loyalties, your ability to see clearly and then enthralls you. He transforms neighbors into threats, friends into enemies, and communities into battlegrounds.

But he can be stopped, you've seen this before. In America's war in Vietnam, when the people got fed up, it ended. That choice was always yours. You can walk a different road—one of compassion, not conflict. You can look into the eyes of another and see a soul, not a target. That path is still open.

When the banners wave and the drums of war begin, stop and ask: who benefits from this? Who gains when blood is spilled? The empire thrives on conflict. Deny it your allegiance, and the Red Horse loses ground. Where no real enemy exists, one is summoned—crafted from headlines, fear campaigns, and historical wounds. But look closer. Who funds the outrage? Who profits from your division? Refuse to hate on command. Reject the script handed to you.

Their greatest fear is a population that thinks before it marches.

Fear is their oldest weapon—fear of invasion, fear of the other, fear of chaos. But fear only binds when it goes unrecognized. Stand in compassion instead. Choose understanding over suspicion. That is not weakness. That is rebellion.

While they preach destruction, tend to the wounded. While they sow division, feed the hungry, comfort the lonely, heal what's broken. Love starves the war machine. It bleeds it of its momentum. It exposes its hollowness.

Every war demands your consent. Every bullet fired, every city leveled, depends on your willingness to see another human as less. Refuse their wars. Choose to see clearly. Choose to see humanity. They will warn, threaten, and demand, but your consent is yours alone. Withdraw it, and the Red Horse stumbles.

The Red Horse rides only if you offer him your sword. His cycle is real, but never inevitable. When enough souls awaken, when war is named for what it truly is, the second rider's power dissolves. No banners remain. No enemies to chase. Just silence where drums once thundered.

For all tyranny depends on your readiness to kill or be killed. Deny that readiness, and you unseat the rider who never needed your loyalty—only your fear.

Let him ride no further. Let him find no ground in your home, your heart, your spirit. Let him face the truth: the battlefield is gone, not because it was won, but because it was seen.

Now you recognize him. And in that recognition, his illusion collapses. The Red Horse stands exposed, robbed of shadow, unable to command what no longer obeys.

Look where we stand—beyond the theater of war, free to repair, to rebuild, to remember what matters.

In this awakening, your awakening, he cannot ride. The dust settles and reveals truth. The lies fall silent. And what remains is real.

THE THIRD HORSE: ENGINEERED SCARCITY

**"Then I heard what sounded like a voice among the four
living creatures, saying, 'A quart of wheat for a day's wages,
and three quarts of barley for a day's wages, but do not
damage the oil and the wine!'"— Revelation 6:6**

When illusion conquers the mind—the White Horse—the body soon follows, broken beneath the Red Horse. What remains is the spirit, stripped of clarity and strength, pressed into survival without purpose. And that is when the Black Horse arrives.

He doesn't storm in with violence. He whispers. He repurposes abundance into desperation and murmurs a single command: **"There is never enough."** He walks slowly, yet his impact is absolute. He doesn't need weapons. He hoards what should have been freely given—food, rest, shelter, dignity.

**"Woe to you who store up what is not yours—how
long will this go on?" — Habakkuk 2:6**

The system is not broken though, it's operating exactly as designed. After minds have been subdued and bodies worn down, the Black Horse binds what's left—will, spirit, hope—through scarcity. He weaponizes hunger. He makes survival the only ambition. People no longer unite. They compete. Scrambling for scraps while the ones hoarding plenty live untouched, above suspicion, above consequence.

This is not nature's cruelty. It's not misfortune. It's precision. This Black Horse does not kill. He drains. Families toil endlessly, bound to debt schemes, collapsing under burdens they didn't create. Farmland rots. Homes remain vacant. Resources are locked away behind invented barriers. Because the aim was never to solve poverty—it was to preserve it. The poor must stay poor so the machine keeps turning. **It's not a flaw. It's the fuel.**

"The earth is the Lord's, and everything in it." — Psalm 24:1

Creation overflows. There is enough. Always was. Enough grain to feed every child. Enough land for every soul to rest. But the Black Horse's power lies in the lie— that the world itself is poor. He convinces the masses that struggle is natural, that scarcity is real, that asking for more is ungrateful.

But nothing about this system is natural. **It is constructed.** Every starvation, every eviction, every life buried in debt is a result of choices made in silence by those who benefit most from the illusion.

Until the lie is named, and called out, the Black Horse reigns. Until people see that their chains are built from scarcity propaganda, his grip holds. These are not iron clasps. *They are illusions*—deliberately crafted, globally enforced, spiritually lethal.

And they will remain until someone stands, sees clearly, and refuses to believe in lack.

History Of Deprivation By Design

Across the ages, the architecture of controlled scarcity repeats itself with brutal consistency.

In desert kingdoms, pharaohs stored grain in towering silos—not to feed the hungry, but to sell it back to the starving, draining the people of both coin and liberty. In feudal Europe, lords enclosed the commons, stripping the poor of their ancestral lands and charging them simply to sow seed. Salt, once free and abundant, was taxed into a luxury, impoverishing entire populations while funding distant empires.

The pattern held. **Empires crossed oceans not to trade, but to extract—gold, spices, timber—leaving native lands pillaged, the people impoverished on the soil that once sustained them.** In one so-called green realm, a man-made famine ravaged the population. There was no true shortage. Food was exported en masse to enrich colonizers, while fields in the homeland stood stripped and bare. Millions died not from scarcity, but from design.

As history advanced, the blueprint evolved. Maritime empires drained continents, moved raw wealth across seas, and left behind systems of debt that would outlive the ships themselves. No chains were needed—just ink. Just contracts. Just policies.

Now the same design emerges again, digitized and refined. The logos change. The methods remain. Corporations buy vast farmlands, displacing growers who once fed their own. Food becomes a commodity, traded on global markets, no longer bound to the needs of those who harvest it. Water is privatized. Families must choose between thirst and hunger.

Conglomerates patent seeds, erasing millennia of agricultural freedom, forcing farmers into endless cycles of purchase, compliance, and debt. Crises—some real, some manufactured—become profit centers. When floods come or droughts strike, "relief" arrives with strings. Filtration systems, loans, rebuilding aid—always at a cost, always with conditions.

Banks lend to *entire* nations, fully aware the debt cannot be repaid. When the default comes, they seize ports, utilities, rivers, ministries—entire lifelines exchanged for temporary survival.

The pen has replaced the sword, yet its cuts go deeper. Entire generations are born under these contracts, unaware of what freedoms were signed away before they could speak. Wages stagnate. Costs surge. Dreams collapse beneath engineered inflation. This is no failure of the system—*it is the system.*

This is the Black Horse's method: create illusions of growth while securing dominion over everything essential. Not by conquest. By quiet design. Life itself— air, water, seed, shelter—becomes property. And in that theft, the spirit dims.

Not by force. By consent extracted in desperation.

That is how the Black Horse rides: through hunger cloaked as policy, and obedience purchased with survival.

THE SCALES OF SCARCITY

The Black Horse carries no blade. He wields scales—forever tipped, forever adjusted by hidden hands. He doesn't conquer. *He measures.* And the weight is always against the people. Across centuries, the powerful decided who would thrive and who would beg, keeping societies locked in struggle while a quiet elite controlled the balance.

This is how the Black Horse reigns: not through force, but through intention.

At the core are three weights—debt, economic illusion, and resource control—each one engineered to ensure dependence, each one built to keep the scales tilted.

I. DEBT AS SLAVERY

> **"The wicked borrow and do not repay, but the righteous give generously." — Psalm 37:21**

Oppression no longer needs chains or whips. Today, it speaks in credit scores and interest rates. Debt is the new shackle— invisible, systemic, and expected from birth. In many nations, it's not a choice but a condition of existence. Borrowed coin becomes a leash, so normalized that few even question it. Education demands loans. Housing locks into thirty-year contracts. Healthcare delivers bills heavier than the illness itself. By adulthood, most are already bound—dreams dimmed by compounding interest.

This leash is held by unseen hands that determine access, opportunity, mobility. **Entire communities labor just to tread water, trapped in cycles that offer survival but never freedom.** Globally, nations are no different. They borrow knowing repayment is impossible, exchanging sovereignty for lifelines—trading rivers, forests, ports, and industries to foreign creditors who never step into the light.

Each loan is a link in a chain disguised as progress. A system where ownership is an illusion and struggle is the norm. This is the first engine of the Black Horse: Debt as slavery. Clean, quiet, inescapable. And always calibrated to keep true freedom just out of reach.

II. THE ILLUSION OF INFLATION AND RECESSION

> **"A false balance is an abomination to the Lord, but a just weight is His delight."** — **Proverbs 11:1**

Wages freeze. Prices climb. Essentials drift out of reach. Inflation becomes a weapon, pushing families to the edge. Then, without warning, recession strikes. Jobs vanish. Homes are lost. And still, no one asks who steers the storm. People accept it as fate—natural, uncontrollable. They don't see the hands behind the curtain, manufacturing collapse for profit.

Every crash becomes an opportunity—for someone. Assets fall. The powerful buy cheap. Markets shatter. The elite consolidate. Crisis is the business model. Communities drown in panic, made malleable by fear, and accept controls they would have once resisted. Surveillance, austerity, dependence—all sold as necessary solutions to crises that were never accidental.

This is the second weight of the Black Horse's scale: not just debt, but the illusion that scarcity and collapse are natural. They're not. They're engineered. And while the people suffer, the architects thrive—unseen, unchallenged, and always expanding their grip.

III. CONTROLLING RESOURCES

**"If a kingdom is divided against itself, that
kingdom cannot stand." — Mark 3:24**

To rule completely, the powerful must control the essentials—food, water, shelter,
energy. What once sustained life is now withheld. Housing becomes a speculative
game—homes priced beyond reach, rents unstable, families pushed to the margins.
Energy is locked down, with laws punishing those who generate power without
approval.

No armies are needed—just the denial of what sustains life. In cities, unseen
systems monitor consumption. Step outside their terms, and power shuts off.
Water stops. Access is revoked. Humanity, once self-reliant, now begs gatekeepers
for permission to survive.

This is the third weight of the Black Horse's scale: engineered scarcity, severing
people from the means to live independently. Rebellion becomes unthinkable
when survival depends on compliance. Dependency replaces chains. And a people
who can no longer feed, house, or warm themselves without approval will obey—
not out of loyalty, but desperation.

This is conquest without violence—quiet, efficient, absolute. When every breath,
every bite, every moment of shelter requires permission, freedom is surrendered not
under duress, but through necessity.

In the name of security, **people yield their sovereignty.** And the Black Horse rides
on, unseen, unchallenged, governing not with fear, but with control over what no
one can live without.

IT DEMANDS TOTAL DEPENDENCE

Shelter, water, and energy. In the past, communities held direct access. They
planted their own fields, drew water by hand, built homes from nearby timber.
Even under kings, a degree of autonomy survived. Today, that freedom is gone.
Everything vital is measured, monetized, and enclosed.

Seeds are patented. What farmers once saved freely, they now must purchase
annually. Water is privatized. Entire towns are forced to choose between thirst or
debt. Shelter becomes a product, priced beyond reach. Generational homes are
seized. Land is taxed into surrender.

**"They devour widows' houses and for a show make lengthy prayers.
These men will be punished most severely." — Luke 20:47**

When controlling currency is no longer enough, the system turns to life itself.
To dominate fully, they ration essentials—**food, water, shelter, warmth.** When
survival depends on hidden gatekeepers, independence becomes a myth.

This is why small farms vanish beneath suffocating regulations. Why sustainable
energy is stalled, taxed, or outlawed. Why urban sprawl accelerates while rural self-
reliance is erased. People are funneled into cities, locked into grids and markets they
do not control. Systems calibrated to enrich the few and bind the many.

**Daily life becomes managed—who eats, who stays warm, who finds shelter,
who is left in the cold.** No weapons are needed. Just control over what no one
can live without. They call it progress, but beneath that label lies the systematic
stripping of autonomy. Populations become clustered, disconnected from nature,
tethered to the very structures designed to exploit them.

People surrender freedom not at gunpoint, but because they believe there's no
other way.

This is how the Black Horse wins—quietly, surgically, reducing humanity to
dependency while masking it as comfort. As long as people trade sovereignty for
stability, he remains.

Farmland is rapidly absorbed—billionaires buying acres once held for generations,
pushing locals out through debt and rising taxes. Climate disasters strike, and
capital moves in, turning devastation into discounted acquisitions. Supply chains
fracture under the pressure of war or pandemic. Prices surge. Panic rises. Corporate
profits *explode.*

Seeds once shared freely now bear price tags and legal threats. What nature gave is
repackaged and sold back year after year.

In every crisis, the blueprint repeats. Uncertainty breeds dependence. Systems
tighten their grip. Each **"managed collapse"** becomes a hidden handoff—power
traded upward while the people scramble below.

The Black Horse always reaps, while the people endlessly sow.

BREAKING FREE FROM THE BLACK HORSE

Look past the headlines. Ask who profits. Who consolidates. Who thrives in disaster. The answer never changes.

Poverty doesn't endure because of fate or moral failure. It survives because the system needs it. **Generations strive, believing progress is near, while the ladder's cost rises faster than wages.** Few climb. The rest carry the weight. Those at the top stay not by brilliance, but by scripting rules that keep power in their hands. Freedom is marketed, but never granted. True control lies with those who own the essentials. No need for open slavery when fear of eviction or hunger ensures obedience. The cycle continues, and the Black Horse rides freely, confident that few will ever question the rules he enforces.

He does not unleash open famine. **He twists bounty into want.** He does not chain your body. He convinces you there are no choices beyond servitude. The Black Horse rules not with force, but with suggestion—an empire of illusions whispering, **"There is never enough."** Yet his power depends entirely on your belief in that lie. Denying scarcity is not rebellion. It's clarity. It's the refusal to kneel before systems that feed on confusion, dependency, and despair.

> **"Have nothing to do with the fruitless deeds of darkness, but rather expose them."** — Ephesians 5:11

But that clarity demands courage, because the illusion of lack runs deep. It has been normalized, legislated, and worshipped. Yet the truth remains: creation overflows. There is enough. There has always been enough. The barriers you face were built by men, not by the Divine. Struggle was scripted. Deprivation was arranged. It was never the natural state—it was policy.

The Black Horse thrives wherever scarcity goes unquestioned. So question everything. Ask who hoards the land, who controls the supply chains, who benefits every time shelves go empty and prices climb. Notice how abundance is destroyed—not from lack, but to preserve control. Crops plowed under. Homes left vacant. Water dumped or diverted. Scarcity is not an accident. It is strategy.

Debt is framed as inevitable. But ask who profits from that belief. Who thrives when every paycheck vanishes into rent, bills, and interest? Who gains when a single illness wipes out a family's future? The Black Horse sells captivity as maturity, but even small acts of reclamation begin to shatter his hold. Shared tools.

Bartered goods. Unlicensed gardens. These are not quaint. They are insurrection in slow motion. **Debt is not fate—it is a contract. And contracts lose power when people stop signing.**

His grip tightens wherever the essentials are centralized. Power grids. Water rights. Agricultural land. All owned. All controlled. All withheld. But when people begin to reclaim the means of survival, the illusion unravels. A garden in a yard. A well shared by neighbors. A solar panel that doesn't require permission. These are fractures in the scales. These are cracks in the throne.

The systems that created the hunger will never cure it. The institutions that manufactured lack will never deliver freedom. Change does not descend from the top. It rises from the ground. From the dirt under your nails. From the seeds you plant. From the things you stop buying and start making again.

Every co-op is a rejection. Every food forest is an exodus. Every neighbor cared for outside the system is a blow to the machine. Because the Black Horse doesn't fear revolt—he fears resilience. He fears self-sufficiency. He fears the moment you stop believing in his scarcity and start remembering your abundance.

Poverty was always a policy. Lack was always an illusion. And the moment people see it for what it is, the scale breaks for good.

We were never truly poor.

THE FOURTH HORSE: MANUFACTURED DEATH

Every time you choose differently, his chains weaken. He is the profiteer, the most powerful horseman of all—the one who capitalizes off the other three and reaps what all of them sow.

He survives by stoking endless craving. Endless hunger. Learn to see the difference between need and noise. Gratitude silences his voice. Contentment dismantles the illusion of lack. When you no longer chase what was never yours to need, his cry of "never enough" loses power.

> **"I looked, and behold, a pale horse! And its rider's name was Death, and Hades followed him. They were given authority over a fourth of the earth, to kill with sword, famine, pestilence, and by wild beasts of the earth." — Revelation 6:8**

"The thief comes only to steal, kill, and destroy; I have come that they may have life, and have it to the full." — John 10:10

Once the mind is subdued by lies, once war turns neighbor against neighbor, once scarcity wraps the body in chains of debt, only one domain remains: life itself. And so the Pale Horse rides—not with swords or fire, but with quiet authority over breath, blood, and time. He does not arrive as plague or pestilence, but as policy, as protocol, as a white coat behind a clipboard. He doesn't announce death. He installs decline. He convinces you that slow deterioration is normal, that chronic illness is modern life, that healing must always come at a price.

You won't see him at the door. You'll find him in the tap water, in the long ingredient lists, in the treatments that never end. Food is processed into poison. Water is laced with toxins disguised as purification. Medications suppress symptoms while feeding future ailments. Schools teach children to ignore their own instincts. Hospitals silence inquiry with cold efficiency. Homes become quiet battlegrounds where sickness is managed, not healed. **And still, the Pale Rider smiles with rotten teeth—because no one resists what they've been told is inevitable.**

This is not accidental. *It's insidious.* It's the final act of an ancient architecture. They rewrote healing into enterprise, converted sickness into revenue, and crowned those who profit as saviors. Doctors became priests in a new religion of dependency, and questioning their rites became heresy. Generations were taught to reject ancient wisdom, to scoff at holistic knowledge, to seek salvation only through chemicals and subscriptions.

Humanity forgot it was once whole. Now it survives on borrowed time—numbed, pacified, endlessly medicated, always one prescription away from collapse. This is not healthcare. It is captivity. And yet, they call it progress. They parade it in sterile clinics and clean branding, but behind the screen is a system that needs you unwell. A system that thrives when you don't. There is no incentive to cure what sustains their power. Every withheld remedy has a name. Every new condition has a stock price.

This is the Pale Horse's dominion: a population convinced it must remain sick, certain that vitality is unattainable without corporate intervention.
It is not death that he enforces—it is surrender. To live in his world is to accept deterioration as destiny, and to thank the system for selling you survival in pieces.

This was never a single betrayal. It was the slow culmination of grooming, decades of conditioning the body to distrust itself. Leaders declared war on disease, but never sought peace. Cures threaten their bottom line. Clarity is too dangerous. So instead, they offered maintenance. Side effects. Lifelong plans. And in return, they harvested lifetimes.

Now entire populations grow old not in strength but sedation, not in clarity but confusion, stumbling through a fog of prescriptions, procedures, and polite indifference. They call this care. But chance plays no role here. Every toxin, every protocol, every omission—intentional. Every fragile life, a dividend.

The Pale Horse rides forward not with chaos, but with control. Beyond war, beyond famine, beyond illusion, he builds a world where death need not come swiftly—because slow decay serves better. Where every breath is barcoded, every cell for sale, and living itself becomes a managed asset. And the people, too weary to remember vitality, call it normal. They call it life. And in that belief, he reigns.

DEATH'S FOUR TOTEMS

The Pale Horse stands tall with four totems of control, each quietly sustaining a systematic and devious decline. Where the Red Horse brought war, the Pale Horse introduces an architecture of slow endings—a labyrinth where humanity wanders, too weary to recall that another path exists. Each totem appears routine, inevitable, even righteous—until seen clearly. Then, like scales falling from your eyes, you recognize how humanity was guided step by step into cultivating its own demise.

They rewrote the oath of healing, carved it into a contract of perpetual treatments. Cures were suppressed beneath layers of red tape, buried in dismissive research, ensuring sickness remained the world's most profitable venture.

I. THE BROKEN CADUCEUS

**"It is not the healthy who need a doctor,
but the sick." — Matthew 9:12**

They taught us to trust a gleaming staff, two snakes entwined, a symbol of healing and wisdom. But observe the modern age: the most medicated era ever known, and disease only multiplies. Chronic conditions explode. Cures are whispered but never crowned. Remedies that dissolve cancer, plants that soothe seizures—mocked, outlawed, tightly regulated. Healing was replaced by management. Health became subscription. **Lifelong prescriptions became the goal, not wellness.**

Surgeries once reserved for emergencies now repeat endlessly. Joints. Spines. Arteries. Each incision followed by pills, complications, bills. **"Trust the science,"** they say—but that science is directed by those who profit from keeping you sick. Fully cured patients yield one payout. Chronically ill patients yield lifetime income. **This is not medicine. It is a business plan.**

Hospitals expand. Insurance premiums skyrocket. Pharmaceutical profits soar. And all the while, people grow weaker. Some are bled dry through endless procedures. Others are left to die without access. Holistic methods and lifestyle transformation—threats to the model. Threats to the margin. So they're discredited, demonized, buried. Doctors—many sincere—are trapped within a labyrinth of protocol and billing, trained to follow orders, not find root causes.

This totem stands not for healing, but for harnessing the body as a revenue stream. The staff is broken. The oath inverted. Health replaced with dependence.

II. THE POISONED HARVEST

> **"Their throat is an open grave; with their tongues they tell lies."** — **Romans 3:13**

Look at your plate. Is it food—or is it engineered addiction? The Pale Horse doesn't thin the herd by violence. He feeds them sickness dressed as nourishment. Wholesome crops replaced with synthetic sludge. Sugar hidden in health labels. Carcinogens disguised as preservatives. Empty calories masquerading as meals.

They alter the seed. Soak the soil in glyphosate. Saturate supply chains with chemicals. Then stamp the packages with checkmarks and heart symbols. Eat this. Drink that. Follow the pyramid. Trust the process. Meanwhile, chronic diseases spread like wildfire. Obesity. Diabetes. Cancer. Depression. The food is dead. And so are we, slowly.

Communities once fed by their own gardens are now addicted to processed imports. Family farms bulldozed. Small growers squeezed out. What we consume today feeds the very machine that profits from our illness. The same companies flooding the food with toxins fund the labs that deny the link.

Water systems are compromised. Hormones, metals, additives silently slip in. Municipalities ignore. Regulators smile. This is not neglect—it is precision. They rewrote nourishment into poison, monetized the sickness it caused, and taught us to be grateful for both.

III. THE BLEAK VEIL

"He too shared in their humanity so that by his death he might break the power of him who holds the power of death—that is, the devil." — Hebrews 2:14

The most powerful shackle is not forged in iron—**it is forged in fear.** The Pale Horse understands this. To paralyze a civilization, you don't need bullets. You only need a reason to be afraid.

They weaponized safety. Rebranded caution as morality. Taught neighbor to fear neighbor. Family gatherings became crimes. Churches locked. Questions outlawed. Compliance replaced thought. The specter of death hovered over every cough, every touch, every breath. It was called care. It was called unity. It was called good citizenship.

Mandates arrived overnight. Papers, codes, conditions. The world shuttered not under war, but under policy. And the veil, once dropped, remained. Ready for the next storm. The next variant. The next event. One cycle ends, another begins. The machine doesn't sleep.

Rational thought dissolved. Dissenters demonized. **"Do it for others,"** they said—while corporate profits exploded and liberties vanished. We were taught to fear the very act of living, to celebrate survival at the cost of connection, presence, and freedom. The Bleak Veil doesn't kill. It dims. It flattens. It suffocates the joy of existence until survival itself feels like submission.

This is how a population forgets how to live—by being taught to fear dying.

IV. THE SILENT SICKLE

**"For then there will be great distress, unequaled
from the beginning of the world until now—and
never to be equaled again." — Matthew 24:21**

Why wage war when you can starve the future? Why fire bullets when you can convince a generation not to reproduce?

The Pale Horse rarely swings his scythe. He engineers conditions where life itself seems impractical. He prices birth out of reach. Turns fertility into risk. He frames children as burdens on a burning world. And the people believe him. They choose not to create, not from selfishness, but from exhaustion and fear.

Young couples ask, "How could we bring life into this?" They've been trained to see themselves as a plague. They don't know the narrative was scripted.

Elsewhere, the poor are sterilized by proxy. Aid comes with strings. Relief with terms. Birthrates drop—not from liberation, but from design. Infertility rises, celebrated as progress. Populations age, decline, vanish. And the architects smile quietly, their ledger balanced.

This totem stands not through fire and sword, but by whispering doubt into the womb. By replacing legacy with liability. By teaching humanity to erase itself, one generation at a time.

Each totem holds its place not with noise, but with narrative. The Pale Horse rides not to destroy—but to degrade. Slowly. Silently. Completely. And all he requires is your belief in the systems that make him sacred.

LOOK UPON DEATH'S WORKS

They rewrote wellness into an endless condition of mild sickness, offering "solutions" that deepen dependency, rebranding natural aging as a crisis needing constant intervention. Health became a perpetual cycle of managed decline. You're not healed—you're maintained. Symptom by symptom. Prescription by prescription. The destination is never vitality. Only compliance and conformity.

They rewrote nourishment, filling pantries with synthetic indulgences, turning simple meals into chemical puzzles. Labels parade false virtue. Sugar hides in "health" drinks. Preservatives line "natural" snacks. Children grow dependent on artificial flavors before they ever taste what's real. Entire families live in cycles of inflammation and fatigue, but every bite comes wrapped in the language of progress.

They rewrote freedom by dangling death at every turn. Anxious hearts bow swiftly to mandates, accept surveillance, willingly surrender autonomy if only to quiet their dread. Once vibrant societies—debating, breathing, connecting—grow silent. Masked faces lowered. Steps obedient and quiet. Questions become dangerous. Dissent becomes selfish. Safety becomes sacred—redefined to mean submission.

They rewrote our future, making it too costly, too uncertain, too

disheartening to bring forth new life. No law forbids children. No regime openly bans birth. Instead, the world is shaped to suffocate hope. It adds conditions. Housing unaffordable. Time scarce. Wages stagnant. Communities fractured. The planet portrayed as fragile, the human presence as a burden. And so each generation shrinks willingly, convinced their restraint is virtuous. Decline by design, camouflaged as responsibility.

In nation after nation, birth fades not by force, but by exhaustion. The cost of living replaces the joy of creation. Dreams give way to caution. The body hesitates. The spirit folds. What was once instinctive is now negotiated. Every child becomes a question. Every future, a weight.

This is not collapse by catastrophe. It is erosion—slow, curated, deliberate. A fading of vitality. A withering of purpose. A quiet harvesting of humanity itself.

BREAKING FREE FROM THE PALE HORSE

He does not need you to kneel and pledge fealty. He only requires your quiet participation—your daily acceptance of his illusions, your trust in a broken system, your resignation and fear. His dominion survives on subtle compliance alone. He doesn't conquer. He convinces. He doesn't strike. He sedates.

Refuse the illusion of helplessness. Question the endless cycle of prescriptions masking symptoms without healing. Seek the root causes, and watch how quickly his totems begin to tremble. Healing was never meant to be endless management. Wellness is not a monthly invoice. Ask harder questions, and the ritual begins to fracture.

Reject the corrupted harvest. Read carefully what fills your pantry, your plate. Support local growers. Grow your own, if you can. Learn what real food tastes like. Demand accountability from those who saturate the soil with toxins and spike your sustenance with sugar and synthetic waste. Even clarity—clear awareness of what enters your body—is a blade against his design.

Reject the veil of constant fear. Life contains risk. It always has. But living in perpetual dread is a darker cage than death itself. Speak truth, even if your voice shakes. Fear collapses the moment it's named. Cowards are not those who question the narrative—they are those who cling to it out of habit. Refuse to carry fear that doesn't belong to you.

Reject the quiet reaping that calls children burdens rather than blessings. If bearing life is seen as reckless, ask who wrote that story. Ask who benefits from smaller generations, fractured families, hollow homes. Each child born into clarity becomes a revolution wrapped in flesh. Each birth, a refusal to die off quietly.

When enough souls clearly recognize the architecture for what it is, the Pale Horse falters. His power is not force. It is illusion. And all illusions require consent. Withdraw yours, and the machine loses its engine.

From time to time, a voice cuts through the noise and asks, **"Is it too late? Has the Pale Horse already triumphed?"** The signs point grimly—chronic illness normalized, fertility in decline, industries built on managing sickness instead of ending it. But illusion only holds as long as it remains unseen. And now, eyes are opening. People remember what was buried. They see the body isn't inherently broken—it's been misled, mistreated, denied what it needs to heal. It's never too late, only now.

Communities trade heirloom seeds, forgotten remedies, and suppressed knowledge. Practitioners quietly break ranks, stepping off the prescription treadmill to address root causes. Parents gather, questioning what was handed to their children as truth. **These aren't isolated acts—they are precise fractures in the foundation of the Pale Horse's design.** Each garden, each shared cure, each refusal to comply quietly chips away at his dominion. His power was never built on brute force, only on silent consent. Remove that, and the structure begins to fall.

There are no headlines in this rebellion. No slogans. Just the steady rise of clarity—people choosing to see through the script and live otherwise. The Pale Horse thrives on illusion, and illusions don't survive exposure. They recast wellness as dependence, nourishment as commodity, safety as fear, and freedom as danger. But the veil is thinning. And once torn, it can't be restored.

Every act of clarity matters—healing outside the system, sharing without permission, living without fear. These aren't trends. They are exits. **The Pale Horse fears the awakened not because they fight—but because they see.** Once the body remembers its strength, once the mind stops seeking permission, once fear has no seat at the table, his influence crumbles. Perfect love drives out fear, and fear was always his only currency.

He rides still, but the ground beneath him is vanishing. His grip weakens not through war, but through withdrawal. Not with noise, but with knowing. This isn't idealism. It's the end of a contract. People no longer afraid are people no longer ruled. Death remains—but stripped of its leash on the living. The Pale Horse doesn't vanish. He becomes irrelevant.

THE END OF THE HORSEMEN IS NEAR

"The light shines in the darkness, And the darkness has not overcome it."— John 1:5

The Four Horsemen have long symbolized dominion—over thought, over flesh, over sustenance, over breath itself. Generation after generation bore their weight: one rider capturing minds, another inciting war among kin, a third rationing abundance, and the last profiting as vitality drained from the living. However, their grip was never absolute. It held only as long as people accepted the lies wrapped around them.

We were told conflict was natural, that scarcity was inevitable, that our neighbors were threats and our bodies were weak. Under those beliefs, the Horsemen galloped without resistance.

The old scaffolding—governments, doctrines, markets, medical cartels—begin to fracture beneath its own weight. Institutions once revered now tremble under scrutiny. Policies once obeyed without question now spark outrage, inquiry, resistance. What once hid behind layers of complexity now stands exposed in raw simplicity: control, profit, fear. And with that exposure, the grip weakens.

This unraveling frightens some. But it's not collapse—it's correction. The breakdown of illusions is not destruction. It's freedom being remembered. For centuries, we were trained to believe humanity required chains—that without masters, we would devour each other. But that story served only those who authored it. Now its seams split open. And beneath it, a different truth emerges: we were never the problem. The system was.

We're not here to brace for chaos. **We're here because the Horsemen lose ground every time a soul sees through the veil.** When we reject war as default, poverty as design, fear as loyalty, we dismantle the architecture of their reign. These are not end times. These are false end times—constructed to keep the populace clinging to control just as it begins to fall apart.

Look around. Communities rebuild what systems destroyed. Forgotten knowledge is traded hand to hand. Local networks form beneath the noise, resilient and ungoverned. People remember how to grow, how to heal, how to live without permission. The tide doesn't scream as it turns. It rises quietly. And that's what shakes them.

The Horsemen thrived on consent. Now consent is dissolving. And no illusion, no matter how refined, can stand against a people who see clearly, remember who they are, and choose to live ungoverned by fear.

THE DAWN OF FREEDOM

"The light shines in the darkness, and the darkness has not overcome it." — John 1:5

We are not here to summon new terrors. We are here to reveal what's already ending. This is no call to storm the gates. It is the quiet undoing of fear, the soft refusal that begins when hearts awaken from nightmares scripted by power.

War endures only when peace seems impossible. Scarcity only bites when we accept engineered greed. Fear only paralyzes when we forget our strength. Death only dominates when we surrender our birthright to live whole. In this awareness, their grip loosens. The pageant dims. **Their strength was never in might—it was in our unexamined trust.** That trust is shifting. Not toward a new master, but toward the truth that life was meant for more than survival.

Families reject toxins dressed as progress. Communities build networks of care outside institutional hands. People walk away from chaos offered as structure. What once felt distant now becomes undeniable: we are entering a time the Horsemen never planned for. Their scripts no longer hold. Their shadows recede. This is not collapse—it is release.

We stand here not in despair, but in clarity. The illusions fall. The pillars sway. They no longer feed on us. Each unbowed choice hastens their retreat. They still ride—but their road narrows. Truth clears the fog. Courage breaks the rhythm. And where we once knelt, we now stand—steadfast, eyes open, voices clear.

This is not the end of the world. It is the end of captivity. No decree, no revolution, only a steady unveiling of truth. The Horsemen arrived as conquerors, fed on our resignation, built empires from illusions. But illusions can't withstand light. And that light is here—rising from within.

Countless souls now speak the same unshakable words: no more.

These structures cannot be toppled from above. Many have tried—whistleblowers, rebels, even assassins striking at the heads of nations and empires. But nothing changes. Leaders fall, headlines blaze, outrage flares—and then the machine grinds forward, unchanged. One name is replaced by another. One face swapped out for the next. The engine doesn't pause. It adapts. Because the system doesn't rely on figureheads. It relies on foundations buried deep in us all.

The real breach begins elsewhere. Not in palaces or boardrooms, but in the unseen citadel of the self. The next resound does not call for conquest—it calls for demolition of the walls we've built within. The walls of self-denial. The false stories we've inherited about what we are, what we deserve, what we're allowed to hope for. These are the true fortresses—our personal Jerichos. And when they fall, something irreversible begins.

This is where the Horsemen cannot follow. This is the ground they cannot claim. When the illusion within collapses, no external dominion can stand. That is the liberation they never accounted for. Not revolution by force, but a remembering so complete that their entire scaffolding becomes irrelevant.

So as this dawn breaks, we move—not as victims clawing for justice, but as free people who've reclaimed what was never truly lost. The cycle ends here. Not because we burned it down, but because we stopped feeding it from within, ourselves.

We've named the orchestrators. We've exposed their machines. **The Quadrant. The Four Horsemen.** The institutions that feed on obedience and the systems that prey on fear. We've mapped the external architecture of control—but what comes next isn't collective. It's personal.

This is the checkpoint. Everything after this focuses on you, and your potential.

The Horsemen reign over shared conditions, but they thrive because of individual agreements. Agreements we've made, silently and often unknowingly, with the stories we were told about ourselves. They ruled through systems, yes—but those systems only hold because we internalized their logic. We inherited their lies and made them law in our own minds.

That's where the real stronghold is.

What must now be dismantled isn't out there. It's in our minds. In the assumptions we've never questioned. In the shame we've normalized. In the ceilings we've called protection. The cages we keep calling home.

You cannot tear down the world's false altars without confronting the ones you still bow to inside yourself. That's what they never counted on—that once we saw through the illusion, we'd turn inward and knock down the deepest structure of all.

The Wall of Seven Denials.

Not a scattered ruin. A single monolith—centuries tall, layered with doctrine, guilt, image, punishment, and silence. It doesn't fall with anger. It falls with clarity. It falls when you stop apologizing for wanting to live whole.

That's where we go next.

IX

The Third Resound

The Wall Of Seven Denials

"Action births readiness
and your movement
brings understanding. You
become clear by stepping
forward, not by endless
contemplation."

THE THIRD RESOUND
THE WALL OF SEVEN DENIALS

They say a man's greatest battle is not waged against the world outside—not the foes he sees clearly nor the structures that bind him. It unfolds quietly within, in the silence of his own heart, against a wall he did not know he was erecting.

He cannot recall placing the first stone, nor how the mortar was mixed, yet one day he awakens to find this wall towering within—**strong, familiar, as though it had always existed.** You never noticed the moment when the first stone was laid or how the mortar hardened. But brick by brick, denial by denial, it grew—constructed by words that defined your limits, rules that marked forbidden paths, expectations pressing you into a smaller shape.

The world handed you each stone, quietly declaring them necessary, until you believed them. They labeled this fortress with your name, taught you it was your reflection, convincing you it was natural, inevitable, and true. And so you accepted a smaller self, mistaking confinement for comfort, limitations for identity.

Now, you may see it clearly—this fortress, **the Wall of Seven Denials,** built by others but believed to be your own image. Its presence limits your true potential, but once recognized, its foundations begin to crack. Because you know now that the wall is not you—it is only what the world told you to become. It stands ready to crumble.

You may know the tale: a city ringed by towering barriers, an impossible fortress.

Joshua leads his people there, and the divine instruction is neither combat nor siege, but a steady walk—once a day for six days, then seven times on the seventh morning. At last, a shout, and Jericho's walls crumble.

Most hear this as a lesson in obedience, patience, or sacred power. Yet Jericho holds deeper resonance. It wasn't about conquering cities—it was about alignment, rediscovery, reclaiming the fullness of self.

They did not vanquish that city as much as they reclaimed their own being.

Those walls of stone were more than defenses. They reflected barriers we all carry within—walls built from doubts, wounds, and the subtle lies we've accepted or told ourselves. Every soul holds such a Jericho inside, a fortress so familiar we scarcely recall a time without it.

No clash of arms can tear down these walls, no cunning plan can subdue them. You cannot shatter them by brute force nor reason them into dust. Instead, you walk—step by step, quietly at first, circling each illusion until clearly seen. You face every hurt, every untruth that defined your limits, every expectation that pressed you into a smaller shape.

In this procession, clarity emerges. You understand these walls were never meant to stand forever. They were never truly you; they only reflected what was forced upon you.

When at last the moment comes, after you've walked long enough to truly see, you shout—not a roar of rage, but a cry of alignment, a declaration of your genuine essence. You speak, act, and live in harmony with truth, with the true self predating every imposed boundary.

Then, the wall will yield. Their mortar dissolves. They collapse, revealing the vast territory of who you've always been.

THE REAL MEANING OF SIN

You've been told sin is rebellion, disobedience—a moral failing dividing you from the Divine, a stain you must fear for longer than you can remember. But perhaps they lied, or simply misunderstood. Sin was never about breaking rules—it was about losing yourself. Not about what you did, but who you ceased to be.

Sin is the rift, a separation from your deepest truth, from the divine nature always present within. Long ago, these states of separation were named the Seven Deadly Sins. Yet they are not truly sins—they're denials of self. Seven paths leading away from wholeness, seven illusions embraced, seven stones in the wall standing between who you truly are and who you were made to be.

These denials sustain the world's system. They keep you small, fragmented, longing for what already dwells within you.

Pride whispers there's something to prove, that you must become more, rather than recognizing you already are whole.

Envy draws your gaze to another's path, cloaking your own journey in shadows.

Wrath binds you to external conflicts, ensuring you never confront the internal battle where real victory awaits.

Sloth persuades you there's always more time, even as your soul urges action now.

Greed insists you hoard what is meant to flow freely, turning abundance into captivity.

Gluttony promises satisfaction through excess, filling you with emptiness disguised as fulfillment.

Lust distorts sacred connections, reducing love to mere consumption—a hollow pursuit that leaves you empty.

These are not personal failures—they are bricks, stones. And this moment is like the seventh day, the final circuit around Jericho, when at last you clearly see their true form.

Once you recognize the wall, one task remains: release the cry resonating with your authentic essence—not mere sound, but a frequency of truth.

"I am Free. I am Free. I am Free."

Say it clearly, freely. You were never created to live within these illusions. You were meant to dissolve them, step beyond, and walk unbound.

THE FIRST DENIAL: PRIDE

Pride is subtle—not the demon we often imagine. It comes quietly cloaked as independence, certainty, or the refusal to yield. At first glance, it appears confident, a steady stance and sure voice, yet beneath the surface lies a deeper truth.

At its core, pride is fear—a fear of vulnerability, of powerlessness, of being seen as less than fully capable. It isn't about standing tall; it's about standing apart. The lie pride whispers is: **"I am alone."**

Pride quietly insists that no one will come to your aid, so you must manage everything without help, without bending. The safety pride promises is **isolation,** but in pursuing this security, pride severs connections that could make you truly whole.

And so you strive, defend, and hold yourself at a distance, believing strength lies in separation. Yet in this distance, you lose the profound gifts of openness, unity, and the gentle strength found in genuine togetherness.

THE ROOT OF THE LIE: STRIVE, PROVE, EARN

We were raised within this story: that you must labor for your worth, that acceptance, love, and belonging are wages to be earned. Some heard it at home, others learned it from religion, school, or society. **Its source matters little—the outcome remains unchanged.**

We learn to strive, to prove ourselves, shaping identities that seem worthy. Beneath each step lies the quiet decree: **"You are not enough. Not yet. Not until you've proven yourself. Not until you do more."**

And so we begin constructing names, reputations, personas no one can deny, believing if we climb high enough, no one can reject us or withhold approval. Yet the higher we ascend, the wearier we become—for no altitude of success erases the lingering fear that we might still fall short.

This is the root where the lie takes hold.

THE TOWER OF BABEL – A MONUMENT TO PRIDE

The tale of Babel is ancient but far from obsolete. In the Book of Origins, a people shared one tongue and chose to construct a tower reaching to the heavens. **"Let us make a name for ourselves,"** they proclaimed.

This endeavor was not about survival nor true unity—it was about control. They believed that by raising a monument high enough, they might overcome their fear of insignificance, reaching heaven by their own strength, no longer needing the Source of all.

Yet heaven was never a height to ascend; it was always a truth remembered within. The taller they built, the further they wandered from that clarity. Babel's story was not only about language—it was about separation, a partition from the divine center. As the tower neared completion, they found not unity, but confusion. Their shared voice splintered, their bond dissolved. Attempting to build a kingdom of triumph, they instead raised walls between themselves.

Even today, we erect towers of achievement, chasing names, accolades, and recognition, forgetting that the truth we seek is already within. Each new structure echoes that ancient pursuit—a testament to pride, a reminder that building ever higher can never bring us closer to who we truly are.

Each time you believe you must stand apart to matter, you build another Babel. Each time you think you need to be faster, stronger, more worthy by the world's measure, another brick is added. These towers seldom appear as stacked stones— they manifest as status, achievement, acclaim—the life you construct to prove your worth.

Yet no monument was ever required to validate your being. You were complete long before the first stone was lifted.

The trouble with pride is that it makes you forget. It persuades you that your strength arises from the tower you build—that without it, you'd become nothing.

But you are not the tower, and you never were.

THE MASK & CURRENCY OF PRIDE'S CONTROL

Pride becomes the currency of an empire built on your striving—a coin exchanged by those who rely on your forgetting who you truly are. They convince you it's essential to keep climbing, striving to prove worth, fighting to ascend above others. Religious systems, governments, industries—all sell this illusion as truth.

They whisper that if you halt your climb, you'll be left behind, worthless and forgotten. Yet continuing upward, step after weary step, is precisely how you lose yourself.

The path back to your true being demands stepping down, returning to a humility they call weakness, surrendering to truths they've mislabeled as defeat. In that moment of letting go, clarity arrives. You remember that surrender isn't weakness; it's reclaiming your true power—recalling you were never required to climb at all. You were already complete before the first stone of ambition was laid.

You were always, always enough.

Pride wears two masks. One calls itself isolation, the other arrogance. Yet both stem from the same error: the belief that you stand apart.

Isolation whispers, "I need no one," drawing you away from hurt or disappointment, yet at the price of carrying life's burdens entirely alone. But you were never meant for such solitude.

Arrogance declares, "I surpass you." It demands height to feel secure, yet no matter how high you rise, anxiety remains. Because ascending was never the true purpose.

Both masks share one root—the illusion of separation.

But there's an invitation for you, here. Now.

You are free to set it down: to cease the endless climb, to unbuckle your armor, to step away from the tower, and return to what is real. You were never alone, never outside the circle, never required to prove your right to stand here.

Surrender is not defeat.

It is yielding to who you have always been. To release the illusion of needing to become more reveals that you were already complete.

RECLAIMING UNITY AND REMEMBERING THE TRUTH

Beneath pride's whisper lies the claim that you must become more—yet truth softly declares you have always been enough. You need no climb to find your worth, no battle to earn your place, for you never stood outside of it. Your belonging was never conditional, never waiting beyond achievement.

You need not rise above another, for you were made to stand beside them— never apart, always within a shared horizon. In this remembering, your wall will begin to crumble. No longer isolated, no longer driven by illusion, you stand clearly in the presence of who you have always been.

Pride is the wall we have built for ages, our own Jericho, standing firm not by strength but by the illusions we've embraced. It cannot be toppled by brute force or sheer determination.

You must walk around it quietly, confronting each brick: every story whispering that you must stand alone, every falsehood claiming you were never enough, every hurt that compelled you to build the tower.

And when the time arrives, you shout—not with mere words, but through the resonance of your being, with the decisive act of stepping fully into your freedom.

 "I am Free. I am Free. I am Free."

In that moment, the wall collapses. You step forward, unburdened, into your true self, and never look back.

Pick up your mat and walk, friends.

THE SECOND DENIAL: ENVY

Envy is a denial so subtle many spend their lives trapped in it without ever naming it. Rarely does it first appear as anger or resentment. Instead, it emerges quietly—a pang, an unexplained emptiness.

You notice someone else rejoicing, celebrating beauty, success, or recognition, and a small voice whispers within you: "That should have been mine." Yet envy isn't truly about them, nor about what they possess. **It grows from the belief that you lack something essential—that you are overlooked or left behind.**

Feeding that notion reshapes your perception of yourself and the world around you, obscuring your inherent abundance, blinding you to the gifts you already possess. You begin to believe that another's light diminishes your own, throwing you into shadow.

At its core, envy rests upon the false conviction that there is not enough for everyone—that the goodness, love, or success experienced by someone else is somehow taken from your share. Life becomes a competition, each blessing a threat, each victory another's gain at your expense.

In this distorted view, you overlook the boundless abundance already yours— believing yourself forever trailing, never enough, always denied—when, in truth, your portion was never diminished by another's joy.

THE LIE OF ENVY

From your earliest days, you learned a story: strive, compete, secure your portion before someone else claims it. You were taught there's never enough—that life's abundance is limited, so you must seize it first or risk having nothing. Be the best, or yearn bitterly for what others possess; diminish them if you can't catch up.

This is the subtle weapon by which systems maintain control: divide and conquer, keeping you focused outward, never inward. They taught you envy as virtue, made you chase illusions of scarcity, trained you to see life as competition. Thus, your gaze stayed fixed on another's path, forever obscuring your own.

Envy erects a brick in the Wall of Seven Denials, quietly blocking your remembrance of the abundance within. It tells you others have what you lack, hides the wealth already yours, and makes you forget the plenty you carry.

Yet the moment you shift your eyes inward, that wall begins to weaken. The illusion of shortage falls away, revealing that the abundance you longed for was always yours—waiting only to be recognized.

THE TWO FACES OF ENVY: RESENTMENT AND WORSHIP

Envy does not always appear as bitterness; sometimes it wears the softer disguise of admiration. Yet whether it manifests as hostility or reverence, its origin remains unchanged: the illusion of separation—the belief that others possess something you cannot claim unless you seize it or imitate it.

The first face of envy is resentment. This kind of envy whispers bitterness toward those who seem to have more, murmuring they didn't earn it, that the system is rigged, that existence itself is unjust. Resentment simmers in shadows, breeding victimhood and spite, convincing you that to rise, you must topple someone else.

The second face of envy is worship. At first glance, it may look like honor, yet it still grows from the same root of lack. It elevates others onto pedestals, marking them as special, chosen, superior. In your admiration, you attempt to become them—to adopt their ways, their voice, their image. Yet in this imitation, you abandon your own unique essence, trading authenticity for a borrowed identity.

Both masks bind you equally, drawing you away from your own design, obscuring the true gifts you were created to carry.

ENVY IS CURRENCY USED TO SEPARATE

Envy stands as a trade good in this domain. Entire empires rise from its subtle whispers. In the bustling marketplaces, envoys of desire offer glimpses of lives you seemingly lack, quietly suggesting your incompleteness. They claim that garment, that vessel, or that glittering emblem could finally make you whole.

In the spheres of shared stories, visions are carefully shaped to suggest that others possess what you do not. You look, compare, and yearn, forever chasing mirages displayed by someone else's design.

Rulers wield envy as a silent weapon, turning groups upon each other, convincing you your shortfall is someone else's fault. While you clash among yourselves, blaming each other for scarcity, they quietly amass the greatest shares, fortifying their advantage behind the scenes.

Even teachings that claim sacred origins are vulnerable. Certain doctrines whisper that divine favor must be earned, granted only to a select few. If another is blessed, you must somehow be lacking. They teach your worth can only be purchased through suffering, deepening your belief in insufficiency.

Each voice directs your eyes outward, away from the inner truth. You forget there was never a contest, no shortage of anything that truly matters.

You were never lacking. You were always complete. You've always been, and had enough. Maybe you just didn't know where to look.

CAIN AND ABEL — WHEN ENVY BUYS SEPARATION

The account of Cain and Abel is not truly about divine favoritism. Rather, it speaks of separation from the Source of all—God.

Cain offered his gift and saw it refused—not because God favored another, but because Cain's heart stood misaligned. Rather than turning inward to address that discord, he directed his anger outward.

His envy was never truly about Abel, but about himself. Abel's acceptance became proof, in Cain's eyes, of his own rejection. Unable to face the imbalance within, he silenced the reflection that reminded him of it.

Yet no one destroys a mirror without harming their own image. Cain's act brought neither peace nor restoration, only exile.

> "You desire but do not have, so you kill. You covet
> but cannot obtain, so you wage war. You do not have
> because you do not ask God." — James 4:2

Cain did not ask. He did not seek alignment. He acted from envy—and it cost him everything.

BREAKING ENVY — THE POWER OF RECOGNITION

Envy grows in eyes that have forgotten their own richness. When you lose sight of your inherent abundance, you measure yourself against another. You assume they possess something you lack, causing you either to resent or idolize them.

Yet envy does not reveal your emptiness—it shows you have forgotten your own fullness. You have forgotten your unique path, your perfect timing, your divine provision. You are not behind, not excluded, not abandoned. You are connected to the source itself—you always have been, though the world taught you otherwise.

This is not about striving harder to earn abundance. It is about remembering abundance was yours from the start. When you recognize your own completeness, you stop counting another's treasures. You cease chasing what was never meant for you. Instead, you begin to create, to give, to flow.

And envy loses all power over you.

> "The Lord is my shepherd; I shall not want." — Psalm 23:1

There was never any lack—only the belief in it.

This is the second brick in the wall, and force alone cannot break it. You must walk quietly, steadily, confronting each piece placed by your own hands—the comparisons, the grudges, the worship of another's destiny instead of your own.

Then, at the perfect moment, you raise your voice—not in envy, but in recognition:

"I am Whole. I am Enough.

I am Loved. I am Grateful.

I am Chosen. I am Free."

With this declaration, the wall collapses, leaving you standing in the boundless expanse of your true self.

THE THIRD DENIAL: WRATH

Wrath is among the *easiest* denials to justify. **The world eagerly labels it righteous—a symbol of boldness, proof of strength.** We are taught that without a clenched fist, without a raised voice, we will surely be defeated. And so we wear rage like armor, brandish it like a weapon, convinced it is essential, just—even sacred.

Yet wrath is not courage. It is fear disguised as power, a frantic attempt to control some small corner of life because deep down, you feel powerless. Wrath is a storm believing that if it rages loudly enough, the sea will grow calm.
But destruction has never created anything lasting, and wrath has never produced peace.

At its core, wrath is the denial of the quiet within—the refusal to be still, to trust, to yield. It reflects an inability to endure discomfort without lashing out. We convince ourselves we're protecting something precious, yet most often, wrath is not about external threats. It is about the conflict we have yet to confront within ourselves.

THE LIE OF WRATH

From youth, we're taught that anger is strength—that vengeance completes the circle, and without a fight, we amount to nothing. Our fathers strike us to ensure we learn what they had before. That results come from pain. And so we battle, lash out, and clutch our wounds as if they were weapons, believing they protect us, believing they give us power.

But wrath does not bring security; it creates quicksands. The tighter you grip anger, the more bound you become. You may feel powerful in your fight, but in truth, you are imprisoned by walls you've built yourself. You sink, you struggle, and you fight some more.

This is why wrath is another brick in the Wall of Seven Denials. It deceives you into believing that freedom comes through combat, that striking with enough force will cause barriers to crumble. Yet no wall falls by adding more bricks to it, and no peace is found by waging war either internally or externally.

THE TWO FACES OF WRATH: VIOLENCE AND POISON

Wrath presents itself in two distinct forms, yet most see only one. One face erupts like a tempest, while the other sinks into hidden depths.

The first face of wrath is outward violence—anger that strikes, lashes out, bruises hearts, breaks bonds, and pits friends against each other. In its blaze, you might feel a brief release, but destruction never nourishes; it feeds nothing but the flames themselves.

The second face of wrath is inward poison—the kind you mix for someone else but just end up drinking youself. It's the anger you swallow, believing it safer to keep hidden. It hardens into bitterness, a silent grudge you carry for years. You convince yourself the other deserves no pardon, yet in truth, this anger isn't about them. The longer you harbor it, the deeper it seeps, until it becomes indistinguishable from who you think you are.

Both faces stem from the same fire: one ignites the world and the other, quietly scorches you.

WRATH AS A CURRENCY

Wrath is profitable. Entire powers flourish on the force of your anger.

Messengers of information have learned this well. Your indignation keeps you watching, scrolling, sharing, shouting. Each outburst fuels engagement, holding your gaze captive. **The more you rage, the more you return—and they grow stronger from that unending cycle.**

Politics, too, thrives on wrath. Rulers present enemies to blame for your suffering, stoking the flames of discontent. While you battle these presumed adversaries, those who govern remain secure. Division protects them. Your anger is their fuel.

Even sanctuaries are not above this deception. Some speak of a deity who punishes fiercely, who commands you to do likewise—branding hatred as holy, vengeance as righteousness, wrath as divine will.

Yet one consumed by anger is easily controlled. One consumed by anger is reactive, rarely pausing to see clearly. **One consumed by anger does not ask questions; they only fight.**

WHEN WRATH COSTS YOU THE PROMISE

Moses led his people out of bondage, spoke openly with God, the Source of all things, parted the waters, and delivered sacred commands from the mountain's summit. He walked in purpose. He carried revelation. He bore the weight of leadership through wilderness and rebellion.

Yet despite his faith and obedience, he never entered the land he journeyed toward.

At a desert crossing, the people thirsted. God instructed Moses to speak to the rock, so that water might flow. But Moses, wearied and vexed by their grumbling, struck it in anger. Though water came, his wrath cost him the final step of his calling. By choosing force instead of trust, he ended his journey as guide.

This moment did not sever Moses from the love of the Divine. He remained within grace. He was still seen, still honored, still chosen. But wrath closed a door. He brought the people out of oppression, but another would take them across the threshold. Joshua would lead them into the inheritance Moses could only glimpse.

This story reveals how wrath can disrupt a chapter of purpose, even when one's heart remains aligned with the Source. One can be faithful, devoted, even favored— and still let a single act of anger veil the clarity needed for completion. **Wrath may not destroy your soul, but it can stall your mission. It can rewrite your role in a larger unfolding.**

Moses beheld the promise but did not tread within. He stood atop the mountain and saw what could be—but he would not pass through. Wrath does not topple walls—it builds new ones. It's not always explosive. Sometimes it simply closes off futures meant to be walked in peace.

And still, Moses remained embraced by the One who called him. He was not discarded. He was not forsaken. He was honored and buried by the very Presence he served. This is not a tale of punishment. It is a reminder that even sacred callings require alignment—not just in act, but in spirit.

Let wrath lead, and you may reach the mountain. But you won't cross it.

From there on, Joshua would lead.

BREAKING WRATH — THE POWER OF STILLNESS

Wrath proclaims that peace is frailty—that unless you strike first, you will be struck. It insists that without anger, you lack strength. Yet wrath is reaction, while true power resides in stillness. Wrath destroys, but genuine power creates. Wrath resists, but real power transforms.

The world praises rage, urging you to fight fire with fire. Yet a fire consumes; it cannot build. The wise understand that genuine strength often emerges quietly, not from raised fists, but from hearts rooted in love.

Consider how the Lamb overcame empires—not through wrath, not by calling down thunder—but by embodying truth so unwavering that illusions could not survive in His presence. It was not wrath that transformed nations; it was love.

> **"A fool gives full vent to his anger, but a wise man keeps himself under control." — Proverbs 29:11**

The world urges you to burn it down, to secure victory through destruction. But fire never built lasting peace. Wrath promises liberation but leaves only ruin in its wake. Love alone dismantles walls without leaving scars.

When you set wrath aside, you cease responding from fear. Instead, you create space for clarity, compassion, and courage. In releasing anger, you finally discover a strength that no violence could match—the power that has always dwelled within you.

This is the third brick in the wall. And you cannot bring it down with rage. You walk—you walk steadily, day by day, facing the fire within until it quiets, until it no longer claims you.

And then, when that moment finally comes, you speak—

not with fury, but with clarity:

"I am Still. I am Powerful.

I am Whole. I am Safe.

I am Love. I am Free."

And the wall crumbles—not shattered by blows, but dissolved by peace, leaving you standing free in the openness that has always awaited you.

THE FOURTH DENIAL: GREED

Greed rarely appears as the ravenous beast it is. It often begins subtly—taking just a little more, accumulating beyond true need. But greed does not grow from abundance; it rises from emptiness, whispering fears of scarcity, claiming there's never enough.

Greed tells you, "I must grasp more, or I will vanish." It convinces you that without constant accumulation, your worth fades, your security disappears. It thrives on the anxiety that abundance is fleeting, that the well could dry up tomorrow.

Yet greed isn't ambition. Ambition builds, creating from a place of trust and vision. Greed devours, consuming endlessly, believing in an imagined void. As ambition expands your life, greed shrinks your soul.

This makes greed the fourth brick in the wall. It doesn't simply guard treasures; it hoards your energy, your generosity, your very capacity to share freely. The fearful belief beneath greed—that there's not enough—leaves you eternally hungry, always grasping but never fulfilled.

Greed whispers, "You must protect yourself, or lose it all." It convinces you to hoard rather than share, to close your hand instead of opening it. Yet the tighter you grasp, the emptier you feel. This wall isn't built from stone, but from a scarcity mindset disguised as wisdom.

To dismantle this wall, you must walk through your own fear, confronting each illusion that insists resources are limited. Step by step, circle that false belief, observing it weaken. And when clarity comes, you speak—not from emptiness, but abundance:

"I have enough.

I am abundant.

I trust life's generosity.

I share freely, without fear.

I choose openness over scarcity.

I release what no longer serves me."

Until the wall of greed collapses, leaving you standing unburdened, truly free.

GREED WEARS MANY MASKS

The world often teaches that greed belongs only to the wealthy, afflicting those who hoard great fortunes. Yet greed has countless forms, many far removed from gold or coin.

There is greed for power—a relentless grasping to control others, born from the terror of being controlled yourself.

There is greed for validation—a hunger for applause, praise, and recognition, driven by the silence of your own truth.

There is greed for attention—a compulsion to always be noticed, visible, and affirmed, fearing that if you are unseen, you might cease to exist.

And there is greed for time—a desperate attempt to outrun mortality, clinging stubbornly to relevance, forever defying life's natural rhythm.

Yet beneath each form lies the same hidden wound: the belief in scarcity. Greed becomes your tactic only when you fear there is never enough.

But energy, like life itself, was never meant to be hoarded—it was designed for motion, flow, and exchange. Whatever you lock away soon grows stagnant, whether food, water, or the living pulse of your own spirit.

THE RICH FOOL & HIS BIGGER BARNS

Jesus, the Son of Man, come as the Christ, offered a vivid portrayal of greed in Luke

12. A man's land produced a harvest so abundant it exceeded his every need. Rather than share this bounty, he chose to tear down his barns, building larger ones to store it all, telling himself:

"You have plenty now. Relax, eat, drink, be merry."

But God called him a fool, declaring,

> **"This very night your life is required of you. Then who shall inherit what you have hoarded?" — Luke 12:20**

This man already possessed enough, yet greed deceived him into thinking he needed more. He stored and saved, believing his stockpile could protect him from life's uncertainties. **But in the end,** his possessions outlived him, while his purpose did not.

This is greed's deception: it promises security but delivers isolation. It claims to grant peace, yet leaves only emptiness.

THE RICH YOUNG RULER & THE COST OF HOLDING ON

In Mark 10, a young man possessing great wealth approaches Jesus, come as the Christ, and asks, "How may I inherit eternal life?"

Jesus recounts the commandments. The young man confidently replies, "All these I have kept from my youth."

Jesus, looking upon him with compassion, says:

> **"You lack one thing. Go, sell what you own, give it to the needy, and treasure awaits you in heaven; then follow me."**

Yet he departs in sorrow, for he possessed many things.

His wealth was not the true barrier—it was his clinging to it. He could not release the familiar life he knew to embrace the new life he was called toward. His possessions were not chains, but the grip he held upon them bound him nonetheless.

This is greed at its core: not simply having much, but the unwillingness to let go. Not the presence of abundance, but the fear that without it, you will be nothing.

It is not wealth that blocks the way—it is attachment. The hands that cannot open cannot receive.

And so he walked away—not because the path was closed, but because his grip would not release.

TWO SIDES OF THE SAME COIN

Greed does not spring from abundance; it arises from the fear of not having enough. Scarcity murmurs, "Seize what you can, lest another claim it first." Hoarding warns, "Never let go, for you may not regain it."

Both echo the same falsehood—that the source of your sustenance is external, that you must gather, guard, defend, and store. Yet the more tightly you grip what you've accumulated, the more tightly you bind yourself to protecting it.

The Son of Man, come as the Christ, spoke it:

> **"Whoever seeks to save his life will lose it, and whoever loses his life will preserve it." — Luke 17:33**

The harder you clutch life, the more swiftly it slips through your fingers. But in letting go—in trusting—you safeguard what was always yours.

BREAKING GREED – THE POWER OF SUFFICIENCY

The opposite of greed is not poverty; it is sufficiency—that deep, abiding knowledge that what you have is enough, and who you are is enough. Not because you discarded all you own, but because you no longer need possessions to anchor your worth.

Greed is the voice of hunger; sufficiency is the voice of nourishment.

Greed rushes forward; sufficiency finds rest.

Greed demands; sufficiency receives.

> **"Whoever loves money never has enough; whoever loves wealth is never satisfied with their income. This too is meaningless." — Ecclesiastes 5:10**

This is not about scorning wealth, but refusing to let it define you. Wealth can pass through your hands without binding you. You can hold possessions without them holding you. And when you grasp this truth, you walk free at last.

You cease hoarding and begin giving. You stop grasping and start flowing. In that moment, you recognize what was always true:

You were never incomplete, you are loved, and you were always whole.

Like the wall that once was circled in Jericho, greed does not crumble under force. It yields when you walk, step by step, quietly confronting each brick placed by fearful hands.

Then, at the appointed moment, you sound the trumpet, releasing the cry that shakes the ground beneath you:

"I am Whole.

I am Enough.

I am Grateful.

I am Abundant.

I am Free.

I am Ready."

And the wall succumbs, leaving you free to pass through—free to become who you have always been.

THE FIFTH DENIAL: SLOTH

Sloth has long been mistaken for idleness—someone avoiding work, ignoring the clock, letting life slip by. Yet sloth is subtler and far more insidious. It's not about doing nothing; it's about doing everything **except what matters most.** It is evasion disguised as busyness, distraction masquerading as patience—a quiet refusal to step fully into who you sense you're meant to become.

At its core, sloth is fear. Not the brash panic of failure or rejection, but a deeper dread: the fear of becoming. It is the hesitation to embrace a greater truth, knowing it will cost comfort, relationships, and familiar illusions. Once you move forward, you can never return to what once was.

Sloth whispers excuses like lullabies:

"I'm tired."

"The timing isn't right."

"I'm still preparing."

These sound responsible, even wise, but beneath them lies resistance. Deep down, you know that once you begin, everything changes.

This makes sloth the fifth brick in the wall of denial—a barrier you might barely see, yet it holds you motionless. You're not lazy friends, you're resisting your own arrival. You're not resting as much as you're hiding.

THE LIE OF SLOTH — THERE'S ALWAYS MORE TIME

Sloth offers a single lie:

You have time.

It tells you your calling can wait, that your purpose isn't urgent, and tomorrow will usher in a better season. You assure yourself you're being careful, prudent— that soon you'll be prepared. Yet, in waiting, delay becomes your daily rhythm, and the life you intended quietly slips away, never begun.

> **"Whoever watches the wind will not plant; whoever looks at the clouds will not reap."** — Ecclesiastes 11:4

You keep waiting for perfect conditions. But those perfect conditions were never coming—**and never will.**

FACES OF SLOTH – APATHY AND DISTRACTION

Sloth reveals itself in two forms, both designed to keep you still.

The first is apathy—a numbing voice whispering, "Why bother?" It insists nothing will change, that your effort is meaningless. Easier, it says, not to begin. Soon you grow deaf to the call of your life, convincing yourself perhaps it was never real.

The second form is distraction, a flurry of activity claiming, "I have too much to do." This form is subtle, harder to recognize. Distraction fills your days with tasks, yet carefully avoids the steps you were born to take. You tell yourself you're diligent, yet you sidestep the deeper work of your soul. Sloth isn't lack of energy—it's misdirected energy.

Both apathy and distraction share a common root: the quiet fear that if you act, you must grow into something more. And that thought unsettles you, because once you evolve, you must carry responsibility for what you uncover.

THE CALL THAT WON'T LET YOU GO

A truth lies at the core of every calling: hesitation always arises. Even those destined for the greatest tasks first tried to refuse. There is no shame in the pause, no weakness in feeling its weight. It's an integral part of the path—of stepping into something beyond yourself.

Moses was chosen to lead a nation from bondage.

He didn't greet this boldly; he met it with doubt:

"Who am I, that I should go?" — **Exodus 3:11**

His instinct wasn't pride—it was fear. He questioned his worth, his voice, his role, and begged for another to be sent in his place. Sloth doesn't always sound lazy—it often sounds like doubt wrapped in humility.

Elijah stood against kings, worked wonders, and even called fire from the heavens. Yet exhaustion overtook him, sending him fleeing into the wilderness.

"I have had enough, Lord," he said. **"Take my life."** — **1 Kings 19:4**

He felt finished, too weary to carry on. Even the boldest lose sight under the weight of their path. His pause was not weakness—it was the fatigue of carrying too much for too long.

Jonah went beyond hesitation—he fled in the opposite direction. Commanded toward Nineveh, he boarded a ship bound as far away as possible. It took a storm and three days in the belly of the great fish to reroute him. Jonah's running was not laziness—it was resistance to a task that felt too big.

Jesus, the Lamb, come as the Christ, felt the full weight of what awaited him. In Gethsemane, sweating drops of blood, he prayed:

"Let this cup pass from me." — Matthew 26:39

Even he, in full awareness, paused before his path. Not because he doubted the mission, but because he felt the cost.

Yet each eventually answered—not because they gained certainty or saw fear vanish, but because the call itself endures. It waits, finds you again and again, until finally, you yield your "yes."

YOU'RE NOT WAITING—YOU'RE HIDING

Sloth tells you that you're waiting. Waiting for the right time, for more clarity, for a sign that the moment is finally perfect. It insists you need just a little more preparation, a bit more assurance. Yet beneath these careful reasons lies resistance disguised as wisdom. Clarity doesn't precede the journey—it unfolds on the path itself.

Action births readiness and your movement brings understanding. You become clear by stepping forward, not by endless contemplation. This is what James declared:

"Faith without works is dead." — James 2:17

This wasn't a reprimand. It was instruction. Faith is not idle patience, hoping everything aligns before you start. Faith is motion—a willingness to begin without every question answered, without guarantees.

Sloth will insist you have time, that your calling is safely distant. But the moment to act is always now, always immediate. Waiting promises security but delivers stagnation, trapping you in a cycle of hesitation. You were never meant to remain frozen, endlessly preparing for a day that never arrives. You are here to become, to move, to embody truth.

The instant you step forth, those bricks—the bricks of sloth—begin to crack. They crumble not because you resolved all uncertainty, but because you chose action despite uncertainty. You chose to become who you were made to be, trusting that purpose guides you through uncertainty.

Do not delay your destiny. Do not hide behind careful excuses, saying "later" when life demands now. Your mission awaits not in some distant moment but in your immediate next step.

Say it:

"I am Ready.

I am Willing.

I am Capable.

I am Becoming.

I am Here."

And with that resonant declaration, the wall falls away, freeing you to step forward into the life that has always awaited your arrival.

THE SIXTH DENIAL: GLUTTONY

Gluttony, the sixth denial of self, whispers a relentless deception: fulfillment always lies just beyond reach, and only "more" can bring it near. It claims emptiness is your default, a void to be filled. Yet it is not hunger you feel—it's a deep longing disguised as appetite.

This illusion pervades all life, not only in food, but in how you consume everything around you. Endless scrolling, ceaseless stimulation, constant seeking of the next distraction. The ache for more hides the truth that what you truly long for cannot be consumed—it must be remembered.

You grasp, devour, and absorb, yet each time find yourself emptier than before. Thus, gluttony thrives not from satisfaction, but from dissatisfaction. It convinces you something essential is lacking, and if only you ingest enough—wealth, status, pleasure—you'll finally become whole.

Yet fulfillment never comes, because no external source can nourish the inner void you've imagined. Gluttony does not fill, it stretches. It feeds not on need, but on the illusion of lack.

This is the sixth brick in the Wall of Seven Denials. And like every one before it, it does not crumble through indulgence or passive awareness. It falls through clarity—through naming every craving not as a need, but as a signal of misalignment.

You circle it, confronting every false hunger, every belief that told you abundance lies outside yourself. You begin to see how deeply this denial is woven into your habits—how often you reach, scroll, snack, spend, and grasp not because you are empty, but because you have forgotten your own fullness.

Gluttony thrives when you confuse consumption with nourishment. It keeps you chasing moments that cannot satisfy, mistaking excess for intimacy, mistaking quantity for meaning. And so the wall endures—not because you're weak, but because you've been taught to seek outside what was always meant to rise from within.

To see clearly is the first disruption. To recognize the false appetites, the hollow urges, the programmed cravings. Only then does the grip begin to loosen—not through abstaining, but through remembering that what you were seeking was never out there in the first place.

HOW GLUTTONY MANIFESTS IN THE MODERN WORLD

In this age, gluttony is not only indulgence in food or drink—it hides in subtler, more pervasive forms.

You witness it as people drown themselves in constant stimulation, fearing the silence that might arise if their devices were set aside. Every waking moment filled with images, news, and endless distractions, numbing the mind because the quiet within feels unbearable.

Gluttony thrives wherever merchants promise fulfillment with the next purchase, the newest object, the latest indulgence. It flourishes in a world presenting life as an unending spectacle: frequent journeys, flawless portrayals, lavish surroundings. It appears in the restless pursuit of the next best thing, drifting endlessly from one craving to another.

Yet beneath this consuming hunger lies fear—the fear of scarcity, the dread that without more, you remain incomplete. That without continuous consumption, you are nothing at all. So you grasp endlessly, filling and filling, until sensation itself fades, leaving only emptiness.

Thus gluttony reigns—not in fullness, but in hollow desperation. It convinces you that wholeness lies just out of reach, dependent always upon something external. But the truth reveals otherwise: you were never empty, never lacking. Your completeness cannot be consumed, but it can be remembered. Be known.

DISTINGUISHING IT FROM GREED, ENVY, AND SLOTH

Greed fixates on accumulation, driven by a desire for control, security, and power through possessions, constantly fearing vulnerability if it ever lets go. It whispers, "You will never have enough."

Envy hinges on comparison, convinced another's abundance proves your lack. It measures worth by others' gains, murmuring, "Their victory means your defeat."

Sloth resides in avoidance—not mere laziness, but fear disguised as delay. It keeps you from stepping fully into your purpose, quietly claiming, "You're not ready yet."

Gluttony, by contrast, is not about claiming, comparing, or standing still. It focuses on endless consumption, driven by dread of emptiness. It believes fulfillment always lies in more—more experiences, more distractions, more sensations—never realizing that sufficiency was always present within. It urges relentlessly, **"You must keep feeding the void."** But the void is an illusion. You were always enough.

MASKS OF GLUTTONY: EXCESS AND DEPRIVATION

Like every denial, gluttony has two extremes, neither of which honors balance.

Some lean into excess—overindulging in food, amusement, or sensation, hoping the next bite, the next scroll, or the next thrill will finally fill the void. Yet it never does, for what they hunger for is not truly what they consume.

Others veer toward deprivation—convincing themselves that less is always more virtuous. They restrict nourishment, deny pleasure, starve themselves of joy, mistaking emptiness for discipline. **But deprivation isn't balance either; it's still rooted in fear—a fear that giving in to desire invites losing control.**

Both extremes arise from the same wound: a refusal to trust in the inherent sufficiency within.

THE SPIRITUAL STARVATION BENEATH GLUTTONY

What gluttony satisfies is not the body—it feeds the fear. And what you starve for is neither nourishment nor objects nor fleeting pleasures. It is connection, meaning, and presence.

You gaze at screens, hoping fulfillment hides in the endless scroll, tasting every indulgence yet craving more. You consume beyond your need, yet remain empty, not because you require more but because you long for something deeper. You seek not mere pleasure but belonging. You taste every indulgence yet still hunger because the void you feel cannot be filled by excess, only by true alignment with yourself.

THE BANQUET & THE EMPTY SEATS

Jesus, the Prince of Peace, come as the Christ, shared a parable of a grand feast. The table was laid, seats prepared, guests invited. Yet the invited ones declined, occupied and distracted, convinced they had matters more pressing. They did not see the abundance offered freely before them.

Gluttony distracts in just this way—filling you with anything but what you truly hunger for. It convinces you to settle for less, even while the richest banquet awaits your arrival.

Those who take their place at the table are not the ones who believe they've had their fill. They are those who admit their hunger, who recognize they crave something deeper, something genuine, something lasting.

BREAKING THE SIXTH WALL – THE POWER OF BALANCE

Gluttony insists that more will make you whole, yet you were never lacking. The great lie whispered was your incompleteness; the truth is, you were always enough.

Balance does not demand relentless self-denial, nor does it justify endless indulgence. It calls for presence—truly being here, aware of when to give and when to receive, knowing when to pause and when to step forward. In presence, you discover that you need not fill yourself endlessly from without, because wholeness was always within.

> "Man shall not live on bread alone, but on every word that comes from the mouth of God." — Matthew 4:4

This was not simply about food. It was a reminder that what sustains us most is not found in consumption, but in connection—connection to the Source, to truth, to the living word within.

The sixth denial of self crumbles when you cease feeding that endless craving for more, choosing instead to nourish what already lives inside you. You stop only consuming, and start truly living.

As you circle your wall, you name gluttony for what it truly is—a lie that tried to convince you that you were starving.

Then, in the appointed moment, you lift the trumpets—six blasts, proclaiming balance restored:

"**I Am Present.**

I Am Whole.

I Am Balanced.

I Am Nourished.

I Am At Peace.

I Am Enough."

And the wall shudders, falling into dust. **You remember at last**: you were never truly starving. You simply needed to cease running and take your seat at the table that was always prepared for you.

THE SEVENTH DENIAL: LUST

Lust is often misunderstood—seen only as excess desire or appetite run rampant. Yet at its core lies a deeper wound: the stripping away of the sacred from desire, the turning of union into mere consumption.

Desire itself is holy—a sacred longing for connection, a yearning to return to wholeness. Without desire, creation stalls. Without longing, life ceases to unfold. But lust arises when that sacred impulse is severed from meaning—when union becomes transaction, and intimacy is reduced to gratification.

In this distortion, we lose reverence for joining—whether physical, emotional, or spiritual. Lust whispers that union can be bought, owned, or consumed. It leaves behind emptiness where fulfillment was meant to bloom. Its greatest deception is convincing us that what was holy is shameful, that what was sacred in us should now be hidden or suppressed.

It doesn't kill desire—it isolates it.

THE LIE OF LUST

You were told that lust was about desire itself. That your longings were perilous. That your body was weak. That pleasure was a threat to your purity.

So you learned to fear your hunger. To hush it. To indulge it in secret or cut it off entirely. You were taught to distrust your impulses, to sever the very source of your vitality. But desire was never your enemy—it was your bridge to union. A sacred current meant to draw you deeper into truth.

Lust is not desire. Lust is desire stripped of depth. It does not seek oneness. It satisfies an appetite it scarcely understands.

MASKS OF LUST: EXPLOITATION AND REPRESSION

Like every denial, lust manifests in two extremes—opposing illusions born of the same wound.

One is exploitation: chasing sensation without meaning. It treats others—and the self—as commodities. It confuses touch with trust, body with soul, pleasure with connection. And so the loop continues: gratification without intimacy, consumption without communion.

The other is repression: taught to fear longing itself, mistaking desire for sin. In the name of piety, union is denied. But this is not holiness. It is fear cloaked in discipline. It severs you from your own body, your own creative force, your own sacred yearning.

Both paths disconnect you. Both steal your freedom.

HOW LUST DIFFERS FROM GLUTTONY AND GREED

Lust is often confused with gluttony—both hunger endlessly. But gluttony

The Third Resound

seeks to fill a void. Greed hoards from fear of lack. Lust, however, severs sacred connection. It turns longing into transaction. It transforms the desire to give into the compulsion to take.

Where gluttony tries to numb, lust tries to possess. Where greed clings, lust consumes. And in doing so, it forgets the very essence of what it craves—genuine union.

Lust functions as a tool of control. Because desire—when separated from meaning—is easily manipulated. A person caught in lust consumes more, scrolls more, obeys more. They chase fulfillment outside themselves, not realizing the ache is spiritual, not physical.

This system surrounds you.

Desire is weaponized to sell everything—from status to scent. Sacred intimacy is twisted into performance, then sold back to you as identity. The craving for closeness is hijacked and redirected into addiction, compulsion, image, and shame.

Even religion plays its part. Some teachings condemn your longing, declaring desire treacherous—while quietly positioning themselves as your only path to purity. It's the same formula: make you fear your essence, then sell you a cure.

The result is a culture that simultaneously punishes and exploits desire—convincing you your yearning is dangerous, while feeding on it from every angle.

But desire was never the problem. It was only ever pointing you home.

THE BRIDE AND THE BRIDEGROOM: THE RESTORATION OF SACRED UNION

This was never how desire was meant to be. Jesus did not arrive to shame your longing—He came to restore union. Scripture often names God as the Bridegroom and humanity as the Bride, not simply as an illustration of marriage, but as the reunion of what was once divided. Lust divides, yet sacred desire reunites.

> **"For this reason, a man shall leave his father and mother and be united to his wife, and the two will become one flesh." — Ephesians 5:31**

This isn't only about marriage. It's about the sacred convergence of separation into wholeness. The merging of the human and Divine. The remembering that you were never truly apart.

This is the promise of sacred desire—not consuming, but creating; not bartering, but transforming. It draws heaven to earth.

Lust insists your body is perilous—that you must either suppress it or exploit it. Yet the truth remains: your body is sacred, your yearning is holy, and your longing is not weakness but the pull toward wholeness. You were never meant to deny desire but to unite it with purpose.

"Do you not know that your bodies are temples of the Holy Spirit?" — 1 Corinthians 6:19

This isn't metaphor. It's reality. Your body was always meant to house the Divine—not in punishment, but in partnership. Your desire is not a threat. It's a compass.

When you reclaim your inherent sacredness, the seventh denial collapses—not through violence, but through reunion. **You rejoin yourself—body, spirit, and Source—and remember that you were never intended to be divided.**

This is the seventh denial in the wall of self. As you circle, you name lust for what it truly is—a denial of sacred union. When you have faced every brick, every falsehood, every shame, you sound the trumpets. Seven blasts announce your return to wholeness:

"I Am Whole.

I Am Sacred.

I Am Desire Made Holy.

I Am United.

I Am One With the Divine.

I Am Love Embodied.

I Am Home."

And the wall collapses—because you finally remember: you were never meant to be torn apart, but always destined to be made whole.

WHAT HAPPENS WHEN THE WALLS FALL

When the walls come down, the silence arrives first—not emptiness, but a presence so full it nearly weighs on you. A hush that has waited behind every battle, every denial, every breath held just to survive. **You stand in the dust of what has fallen, and for the first time in ages, there's nothing left to fight.**

No enemy at the gate, no lie to outrun, no need to defend who you are or who you believed you had to be. The quiet envelops you, whispering clearly: You made it.

Yet there's more. With every brick that declared who you weren't now crumbled, you can't hide anymore. You're exposed. Seen. By the world—but most profoundly, by yourself. What stands in the rubble is simply you. No fortress, no tower, no mask. Just the Christ within you—that part untouched by lies or wounds, that never needed rescuing, only remembering.

This is where Mary Magdalene stood—in that same silence. No more walls, no more chains, no more labels pressed upon her by those who needed a scapegoat to mask their own fear. What remained was a woman who knew herself, who remembered. She didn't land there by chance, nor did she linger timidly.

She stood fully seen, whole, bearing a truth that would overturn everything. She became the first witness to what we call resurrection—because she had already lived it.

And now, here you are. Where the stories that bound you have lost their hold, where the old ways have finished, and something new now stands: You. Not you improved, not you perfected—but you revealed.

Yourself as Risen.

Like Mary, you are not waiting for someone to say it's time. You're already on the other side.

MARY MAGDALENE: WITNESS, NOT WARNING

Mary Magdalene's story is not the one you likely learned as a child, nor what many pulpits have preached, nor what most writings have repeated. For centuries, her name was slandered by those unsettled by a woman who saw clearly what they could not. They labeled her a harlot, branded her broken and sinful, claiming Jesus, come as the Christ, had to rescue her from darkness.

Yet a careful reading reveals none of this in the sacred texts—not in the

Gospels, nor in the letters, nor in early traditions. Those judgments were not the voice of God; they were the fears of men. Not man, or mankind—men.

What we know is that Mary came from Magdala, a prosperous fishing town by the Galilean shore. The name "Magdalene" was not her surname but a marker of her place. And in that era, for a woman to be identified by her town rather than by father or spouse was remarkable. It often meant she stood free from a man's claim—no father, no husband, no son to speak for her. Most likely, she was a widow.

Yet this woman, freed from typical bonds, became the first witness to the risen Christ. While others fled or doubted, she stood unwavering, bearing a message so profound it defied comprehension.

In a world determined to diminish her, Mary Magdalene rose in truth—the first to see and proclaim resurrection.

A WOMAN OF WEALTH AND WOUNDS

Mary Magdalene was not impoverished, nor did she subsist on society's scraps. The Gospels plainly reveal that she, alongside several other women, financially supported Jesus, the Emissary of Light come as the Christ. This was no modest offering. It reflected means, influence, and independence.

In an age that demanded women remain quiet and small, Mary Magdalene refused both. She was actively resourcing a revolution.

Yet she carried a weight. Luke's Gospel notes that Jesus cast out seven demons from her, though he provides no further detail. Today, we picture "possession" in strictly religious terms, but in that era, a "demon" often represented deep internal affliction—mental, emotional, spiritual unrest.

The number seven wasn't random. It signified totality. Mary wasn't just burdened by one pain—she carried the full measure of human wounding.

Even so, she walked with power. She moved through her world with both wealth and spiritual authority. Mary stood boldly as a woman who generously shared her resources, who would not be silenced by convention, and who gave her strength to a movement that still shakes the foundations of history.

HER SEVEN DEMONS = OUR SEVEN DENIALS

Those seven demons we read about were not monstrosities from hellish lore. They were the seven denials of self—Pride, Envy, Wrath, Sloth, Greed, Gluttony, Lust. They were the lies that convinced her she was lesser, smaller, broken.

But she was not. And neither are you.

Mary Magdalene's story is not one of shame—it is a story of rising. It reveals what unfolds when a woman releases every falsehood spoken over her and embraces the truth of who she has always been. She was never an outcast, never a sinner, never a tale meant to frighten children. She was a witness—the first to behold the risen Christ, because she herself had already risen.

This is why she was chosen. Not because she was flawless. Not because she possessed every answer. But because she found the courage to stand while others hid. Freed from the denials. Freed from the burden. She stepped forward. She bore witness. She was risen.

THE SEVEN DEMONS: WHAT REALLY FELL AWAY

For centuries, we've heard how Jesus cast seven demons out of Mary Magdalene. Yet the Scriptures say little more. No beasts clawing at her, no howling, no twisted limbs. **Those images came later—crafted by dramatists, theologians, and those who needed Mary to seem unclean.**

But the original text remains silent. It leaves space. And through the lens we have shaped together, it becomes clear: these demons were not horrors without, but prisons within. Walls. Bricks. Denials. Like Jericho.

She bore the voice of Pride—telling her she stood beyond redemption, that she had to carry it all, alone.

She held the whisper of Envy—believing grace was for others, never for her.

She carried the fire of Wrath—years of shame turned inward and outward, unable to forgive.

She lingered in Sloth—not from laziness, but from believing she wasn't ready, not enough.

She felt the ache of Greed—longing not for wealth, but for validation, for someone to see her.

She numbed herself with Gluttony—not just with food, but with distraction, anything to fill the ache.

She believed the lie of Lust—her body reduced to object, her worth tied to the gaze of others.

These were her demons—not monstrosities, but familiar voices of denial. The same voices whispered over anyone who has ever been told they are not enough.

She let them fall. And then, fully seen, fully known, Mary Magdalene rose—not as one rescued from darkness, but as one who remembered her light.

WHY MARY WAS THE FIRST TO RISE

Mary Magdalene was the first to witness the risen Christ. It was not by accident, nor mere chance, nor because she simply rose early to anoint a body she assumed was dead. **She stood at that tomb because she had already passed through her own death—and emerged on the other side.**

In the Gospel bearing her name, it wasn't Peter or John who stepped forward after Jesus' death—it was Mary who comforted the others, who spoke truths they weren't yet ready to hear. She understood the Christ was not gone, that the Kingdom wasn't only some future realm, but a presence alive within them now.

But this realization didn't begin at the tomb. Mary had already lived her own resurrection when those seven demons—the seven denials of self—fell away. She did not return diminished, nor as a shadow of her former self, but in the fullness she had always been beneath the lies. Whole. Clear. Free.

That's why she recognized the risen Christ first. She wasn't searching for proof or clinging to what had passed. She had already released who she believed she should be and stood fully in who she truly was.

Mary Magdalene was the first to rise because she had already done the hardest work of all: forgiving herself, releasing every chain they bound her with, and walking free long before others dared to believe.

In the Gospel of John as well, Mary Magdalene is first to witness the risen Christ—

not by mere chance or timing, but because she had already opened her heart in ways others had yet to understand. **Standing before the empty tomb, Jesus spoke a single word: her name.** At once she recognized him, not because he appeared unchanged, but because her spirit was already aligned with the truth he embodied.

Then, he commissioned her as the first apostle of resurrection, instructing, **"Go to my brothers and tell them."** She became the initial messenger of a new era—not because she stood in the perfect place, but because she had already experienced a resurrection of her own. Freed from every denial, she stood fully open, prepared to carry forward a message that would transform the world.

Mary Magdalene thus became the first herald of the risen Christ, bearing a truth that transcended death itself, precisely because she had already lived it.

WHAT SHE KNEW THAT THEY DIDN'T

She was not only the first to witness the risen Christ—it was more. She stood as the first demonstration of what this Kingdom truly means: a soul made whole, a life unshackled, a person standing in full remembrance of her worth.

The men trembled, uncertain how to lead without their visible guide. Mary required no such sanction. She needed no external voice to confirm her value—she already knew.

She was free.

THE GOSPEL OF MARY – WHAT THEY TRIED TO SILENCE

For nearly two millennia, Mary Magdalene's story was reshaped by those unwilling to accept her true place. They labeled her a harlot, a penitent sinner, reducing her legacy to one of shame and repentance. Yet the ancient texts—what fragments remain—speak differently. They portray a woman standing central to the unfolding mystery, entrusted with a message too profound for those intent on control.

Discovered nearly nineteen centuries after the Crucifixion, the Gospel of Mary opens after Jesus has departed. The disciples tremble, told to go forth but paralyzed by sorrow and fear. Mary speaks first, saying:

"Do not weep and be distressed nor let your hearts be irresolute. For His grace will be with you all and

will shelter you." — Gospel of Mary 8:9–10

This is not the voice of a woman defined by shame. **This is leadership**. She speaks not in reaction, but in remembrance, anchoring others in what had always been true.

They called her a sinner seeking redemption, but the fragments that survived tell a different story. Mary was not a bystander to revelation—she was at its heart. She was entrusted with a wisdom too powerful for those who sought to build systems of authority, hierarchy, and control.

The Gospel of Mary reveals this truth clearly. After Jesus was taken, the disciples were fractured—grieving, hesitant, afraid. Mary was the one who stood. She was the one who spoke. She reminded them of what still lived within:

"Be at peace with one another, and follow after him with a single mind. No one can lead you astray." — Gospel of Mary 8:22–23

From there, she describes a vision of the soul's journey beyond the world, confronting and transcending the forces that bind it—Darkness, Desire, Ignorance, and Wrath. She recounts how the soul meets the sevenfold powers of Wrath:

"It (the soul) answered, 'Not again do I see you, O deceiver. You are vanquished. You are not seen. And I have not listened to your command.' And when the soul had said this, it went upward, rejoicing greatly. Then it came to the third power, which is called Ignorance..." — Gospel of Mary 9:16–18

"The seven powers of Wrath asked the soul, 'Where are you going, O slayer of men? Or where are you going, conquered by space?'" — Gospel of Mary 9:21–23

These were not external demons but inner denials—forces that keep the soul fragmented and bound in illusion. Mary taught how to face them. She taught liberation from within.

"I was recognized, but I was not recognized by them." — Gospel of Mary 10:10

A simple sentence, yet layered with meaning. She knew herself. She had seen clearly. But those around her were still blind to her wholeness. Recognition does not come from others—it begins with your own remembrance.

Yet even in this sacred space, Peter (Simon) protests. Not because Mary is wrong, but because her authority threatens the structure he assumed. He asks:

"Did He truly speak privately with a woman, and not openly with us?"

To which Levi responds:

"If the Savior made her worthy, who are you indeed
to reject her?" — Gospel of Mary 10:15–16

The Gospel ends abruptly, the manuscript broken. But its message remains intact. Mary Magdalene was not cast aside because she lacked clarity—she was silenced because she had too much. Her witness disrupted the hierarchies that others clung to. Her voice pierced through structures built to exclude.

She was not lost by chance. Her story was hidden because it revealed too much.

Mary Magdalene was not a victim, not a sinner, not a symbol of redemption.

She was a witness. A teacher. A voice of unfiltered truth.

Trusted by the Christ at the dawn of a new age.

WHY THIS STORY STILL MATTERS — IT HASN'T CHANGED

There is a reason the world became what it is. For nearly two millennia, women were given a clear script: Be quiet. Be small. Remain at the edges of your own story.

You can trace it back to moments like Peter's protest in the Gospel of Mary—a man unable to accept that a woman had been entrusted with truth he didn't receive. **His objection wasn't about content—it was about authority.** It questioned Mary's very right to speak. That moment became the fracture. The break in what could have been a unified, balanced truth.

The compulsion to control who can speak, who can lead, who can approach the Divine didn't end with Peter. It became foundational. Men built entire systems on that split—systems that didn't just silence women, but rewrote them entirely.

And it worked, and not just for Christians, it set the stage for *everything*.

Mary Magdalene was recast as a prostitute. Her imagined shame replaced her legacy.

The lie repeated until no one questioned it. But it wasn't just her—every woman carried the weight. Mothers, daughters, sisters taught to apologize for their voice, their strength, their very presence. They waited for permission to speak, to act, to love.

But this cost wasn't just carried by women—it was paid by everyone.

When you sever half of humanity from its wholeness, you break the balance meant to keep us collectively awake. The world still bears the scars of that fracture. Chains forged in that moment are still worn today—some taken as birthright, others mistaken for virtue.

This isn't history. It's here.

It lives in every woman who lowers her voice so she won't be "too much." It lives in every girl who shrinks herself to stay safe. It lives in every man, woman, or child who's been told to hide their fullness because it makes someone else uncomfortable. It lives in anyone taught that their truth is dangerous.

This didn't happen by accident. We allowed it. At some point, we consented.

But now, the tide begins to turn. Because if Mary was the first to remember, Peter was the first to forget. His rejection didn't end in that moment—it became a system. A pattern. A world. One man's resistance to a truth beyond his control became the cornerstone of an empire—not the Kingdom Jesus taught, but an institution built on hierarchy, division, and control.

Feminine energy is powerful. Creative. Forceful. **The women of this world were born to roar, not submit.**

Mary was not alone. Thomas was silenced. Judas was condemned. Their stories were rewritten or buried because they couldn't be controlled.

Thomas—the one who comforted Mary, Jesus' mother, at the Crucifixion—was more than a loyal disciple. Scholars think it's John but John wouldn't write himself in as the 'beloved' and he didn't write about himself in the third-person. It was Thomas, which was a title, not a name. Like Ben Adam, Thomas had alternate meaning which was 'Twin'. His real name was Judas (not Iscariot). He was blood. He was his brother. Judas The Twin.

This is why Jesus, on the cross, says:
"Woman, behold your son... Behold your mother." — John 19:26–27

Judas Iscariot—reduced to the villain—was in truth the most trusted, the one who helped fulfill what had to happen. The strategist. The executor. The one who knew the cost and chose it anyway. He would be the only one Jesus could trust to go through with anything that resulted in his sacrifice, and was the only one of the disciples who was from Judea (*Ish Kerioth*) which was the 'city'. The rest were from Gallilee, more akin to the 'countryside'. He was the treasurer of the group, well-educated and his more Jewish centric beliefs would have put him at odds with the others often.

And Peter—his denial went beyond three words on a single night. He denied Jesus in life, doubted him in resurrection, and ultimately distorted his legacy. Jesus called him "the rock" not because of his strength, but because he knew Peter would build something. And he did. But it wasn't the Kingdom. It was the Church. An institution of power, politics, and patriarchy.

When Nero sentenced Peter to death, he asked to be crucified upside down—not out of humility, but because he knew. **He knew what he'd built had betrayed the heart of what he'd been shown.**

These truths are still buried. Some beneath the Vatican. Some scattered in the earth. Some inside you. It's time to bring them to light. Not to start a war, but to end a silence.

MAKING ORDINARY, EXTRAORDINARY

Before you can fully know who Jesus was, you have to understand the walls he helped Mary tear down. Because it wasn't just about him being the Christ—it was about who he was as a man.

It's easy to mythologize Jesus. Easier still to forget that he was born of flesh. Laughed. Bled. Doubted. Chose. And what made him extraordinary wasn't magic. It was clarity. Simplicity. Conviction.

He walked with intention. He loved without apology. He challenged what humanity believed about itself. And he did it without position, without title, without violence. His strength wasn't that he held power over others—it's that he awakened what was buried within them.

His life proved something few institutions ever wanted remembered: that divinity doesn't descend from hierarchy. It rises from within. You don't need a throne. You need courage. You need truth. You need to walk through the wall between who you've been and who you are.

That's how he lived.

Knowing the walls Jesus helped Mary dismantle, we're finally ready to see him clearly—not just as the Christ, but as a man. A human being who became extraordinary not by accident, but by choice.

To walk as Christ.

X

THE FOURTH RESOUND

BECOMING THE SON OF MAN

"THIS WAS JESUS IN FULL FIRE—
BOLD, ROOTED, UNSTOPPABLE.
NOT BURNING WITH
VENGEANCE, BUT WITH VISION."

THE FOURTH RESOUND
BECOMING THE SON OF MAN

The Scriptures speak of a birth beneath a guiding star, a family fleeing to distant lands to escape a king's dread decree. They show a child, only twelve years old, seated among learned men, astonishing them with questions they had never heard. At that tender age, he shone with an early brilliance, stirring wonder among the scholars.

Then, the narrative abruptly closes, leaving eighteen years sealed in silence—years unaccounted for, during which he stepped beyond tradition's cradle into deeper waters.

He grew. He learned. He became.

Yet you were told he was perfect from his first breath—a holy mystery untouched by struggle—as though divinity fell upon him like a robe he never had to sew. But the silent years speak otherwise. They tell of roads traveled beyond Galilee, of teachings older than temple walls, and of a soul waking to its vast remembrance.

HE DID NOT ARRIVE AS THE CHRIST — HE BECAME IT

This is not mere oversight—it is omission. A deliberate burial of the path that forged the man before he became known as the Christ.

In that silence, a child became a man. Wisdom was not simply granted. It was sought. Discovered. Embodied. He did not awaken with all knowledge intact. Even those touched by the Divine must walk the path of remembrance.

"Jesus grew in wisdom and stature, and in favor with God and man." — Luke 2:52

This single verse disrupts the myth. He didn't arrive perfected. He grew. He changed. He became. He chose.

He was not simply given the name. He lived into it. In the quiet years, away from the page, he listened and asked and wrestled and learned. The Christ was not a title bestowed in infancy. It was a fire lit slowly from within.

He didn't emerge from the wilderness with power already burning. He went into the wilderness to find it. He walked. He waited. He remembered. His life was not made holy by skipping struggle—but by moving through it with clarity.

When he spoke, it was not as a divine machine. It was as one who had walked through silence and come out the other side. His parables were earned. His knowing had weight. **He was not a spectacle. He was a man.**

And that is why they buried his becoming.

HIS HUMANITY WAS HIDDEN INTENTIONALLY

They needed a flawless deity. Untouchable. Exalted. Someone they could worship without the discomfort of imitation. Because if he truly walked as one of us, then what he became—you could become too.

That was the threat.

A perfected human meant the path wasn't exclusive. It meant the spark lived in everyone. And if that was true, the whole structure collapses. No more gatekeepers. No more altars of control. No more systems selling you access to something already inside you.

So they rewrote the story. They erased the roads he traveled. The questions he asked. The teachers he sought. They sculpted him from marble, untouched by time or doubt.

They portrayed him as born complete. But the Scriptures say otherwise.

**"Whoever believes in me will do the works I have been doing,
and they will do even greater things." — John 14:12**

He didn't say worship me. He said follow me. Do as I've done. Become what I've become.

He wasn't just revealing his identity. He was revealing yours. Holiness was never about distance. It was a mirror.

They buried his becoming to keep you from finding your own.

But it still lives—in the silence, in the years unspoken, in the spaces between verses. He was one of us. Growing. Striving. Choosing. Becoming.

WRITTEN IN SILENCE, SHAPED BY TIME

Eighteen years didn't vanish. They were silenced. The Gospels leap from a boy dazzling temple scholars to a man walking rivers and rebuking empires. But in between lies a hidden story.

He walked roads that left no parchment trail. He spoke with teachers whose names history erased. He wandered into temples that predated kingdoms. Among ruins and rivers, he found truths most never dared to carry.

Some say he disappeared. But silence is not absence. Silence is gestation.

This isn't a gap in his resume. It's the ground of his becoming. While the world slept, he listened. While empires flexed, he withdrew. Not to escape. To remember.

When Herod tried to extinguish him, Joseph fled to Egypt—not randomly, but by guidance. **Their escape wasn't just survival. It was initiation.**

Egypt was not a detour. It was descent into memory. Into temples etched with the shape of stars. Into songs older than empire. Into stories still humming in stone.

While many saw a child hidden from danger, he was absorbing everything. Truths that would later pour from his lips like parables. Not invented. Remembered.

When he returned, he returned different. Not because he was taught from scrolls.

But because the fire had been stoked in silence. And that silence was the soil they tried to erase.

But it still speaks. And if you listen, it tells you something they never wanted you to know.

He did not arrive as the Christ. He became it.

And so can you.

A CRUCIBLE IN THE LAND OF KINGS

Egypt has ever been a crucible, molding those bold enough to enter. Its mysteries did not perish with dynasties. They lived on in temples raised before Israel's earliest days. In these hidden sanctuaries, echoes of forgotten knowledge lingered, open to seekers who dared approach.

He did not slip into hiding—he watched, drinking from a lineage stretching back beyond charted time. Here he encountered traces of Thoth the Atlantean, the keeper of ancient wisdom, whose teachings on divine resonance and sacred geometry predated even Egypt's earliest dynasties. He inhaled a heritage that prepared a new ground within his soul.

Thus, the Gospels' silence on these years is no void but a veil, concealing the forging of a vessel meant to bear brilliance too fierce for ordinary eyes.

In that stillness, he was far from idle. He learned the languages of resonance and hidden form, readying himself to speak in riddles that would someday unsettle those in power. It was no wonder, then, when he finally appeared, he carried a mastery no ordinary apprenticeship could bestow. He had been tested in a land where knowledge outlived fallen empires, preparing to step into his destined unveiling.

They said, "Out of Egypt I called my son," as if ticking a box on a prophet's list. Yet beneath that verse stirred an ocean of ancient truths. Egypt was no footnote. It was a silent mentor. Here, every wanderer confronts the deeper realms of becoming.

Though under Rome's shadow, Egypt harbored a subtler legacy. Moses once paced its palaces, learning secrets older than any throne. That current did not die. It slipped into the unseen. And there the child from Nazareth touched living streams of insight coursing beneath drifting sands.

When Joseph and Mary arrived, they carried him into the dusk of those temples, where star-mapped ceilings and faint reverberations of wisdom still stirred. The old ways were not gone. They only slept in veiled scripts, waiting for those who sensed the pulse of deeper truth.

For him, Egypt was more than shelter—it was a first school. He came not to cower but to learn, absorbing revelations imperial eyes ignored. The seat of ancient kingdoms became his hidden guide, granting treasures of knowing that he would one day extend to many.

WHERE THE PATH OF INITIATION TOOK FLESH

Egypt's temples were never just shrines. They were chambers of initiation—structures designed not simply to impress, but to transform those who entered with reverence. Temples like Dendera, dedicated to Hathor, weren't monuments to the gods. They were living architecture—resonant spaces that guided body and soul into alignment with celestial rhythms. These walls didn't only enclose. They sculpted light, reshaped presence, and subtly remade anyone who passed through.

This wasn't abstract. It wasn't poetic metaphor. It was precision—geometry and frequency, woven into stone by the stewards of Thoth. These were not priests of doctrine, but engineers of divine pattern—keepers of sacred language, mathematics, and cosmic movement. Thoth's lineage didn't explain the universe. It invited you to feel it. Creation wasn't studied—it was embodied, vibrating through breath, bone, and silence.

Above it all reigned Maat—the principle of balance. She governed not with wrath, but with equilibrium. These temples didn't promise reward in a distant afterlife. They taught transformation in the present. To have your heart weighed against a feather wasn't punishment. It was initiation. It was the path to becoming whole—by releasing every falsehood until only truth remained.

Picture him walking these corridors—not as a boy fleeing, but as a seeker arriving. Here, perhaps for the first time, the seed of resurrection was planted. The concept of death and rebirth wasn't taught in sermon. It was etched in structure. To rise, one must first be emptied. One must become as light as what is true. The Gospels go silent here—because this kind of pilgrimage doesn't fit easily into a single verse.

Even before returning to Judea for his final years, he was no longer a student. He was one who could heal without potions, speak truths without scrolls, and move in harmony with the natural world—not through magic, but through mastery.

They called the Great Pyramid a tomb, but it functioned as a crucible. Within its **King's Chamber, vibrations resonated at 432 Hz—the frequency of life itself.** Sealed within that precision-cut stone, initiates faced not death, but dissolution. Ego fell away. The heartbeat echoed through silence, and from that stillness came emergence.

> **"Unless a grain of wheat falls to the ground and dies, it remains only a single seed. But if it dies, it produces many." — John 12:24**

He wasn't speaking in riddles. He was recalling what had already happened within him—the death of the old self, so the truth he carried could multiply.

ECHOES FROM EGYPT: THE SEED OF RESURRECTION

He did not invent resurrection—**he embodied it.** Egypt held that truth long before the cross. They understood the soul as eternal, life as rhythm, and the relationship between light, sound, and form as the language of the Divine. Their stars were not merely celestial—they were maps, mirroring the journey of the inner world. Their texts on the afterlife weren't fantasies of what lies beyond. **They were blueprints for transformation—guides for returning to what has always been within.**

In the shadows of those great pillars, he learned and remembered. Not to remain bound to Egypt's rites, but to carry forward what could no longer stay hidden. Egypt was a mirror. It revealed, it initiated, but it did not claim. He moved through it not to become a priest of old orders, but to prepare for a truth that transcended borders.

When he later declared, "The Kingdom of God is within you," it wasn't a metaphor. It was the echo of what he had already lived. It was Egypt's deepest lesson made plain—that no external altar is holier than the awakened soul. That the Divine does not wait in distant heavens—it lives, dormant but intact, in each of us.

This is why those years carry weight. Why chroniclers went quiet. Because if the young Jesus found and remembered the Divine—not by decree, but by devotion— then so can you. His journey reveals a truth too dangerous for empire: that if one can awaken, all might follow.

He returned carrying vision, not tradition. A clarity too vast to remain bound within any single temple. He bore the spark that would ignite countless others. Not through doctrine. Through embodiment. Through example. His Egyptian years were not an end—they were the beginning of a greater unfolding.

Those so-called "lost years" were never lost. They were the crucible. The bridge between memory and mission. The space where he confronted the great patterns, and chose to walk the path as one who remembered.

From Egypt, he emerged not finished—but formed. The seed had taken root. The teachings had awakened what was already written within him. And soon, that same seed would travel east—where another layer of remembering waited.

LOST YEARS & THE STORY OF ISSA

The Gospels go silent—but the story doesn't stop. Somewhere between the temple at twelve and the waters of the Jordan, Jesus vanished from the page. But he didn't vanish from the world. In the East, his name was never forgotten.

They called him Issa.

In Ladakh, Kashmir, and Tibet—far beyond Roman maps—ancient scrolls speak of a sage from the West. A man of Israel, born in a humble land, who journeyed east to seek truth and dwell among the wise. The scrolls, housed in remote monasteries and passed down through lineages untouched by Christian empire, describe him in detail: his teachings, his disputes with priests, his love for the poor, and his refusal to bow to systems built on power.

He studied among the **Brahmins** and the **Buddhists**. He read the Vedas. He debated with ascetics and sat with monks who understood that the divine lives not in temples but within. He was not there to collect knowledge. He was there to remember. **And what he found—mirrored what Egypt had already whispered: that the Christ is not a title, it's a state of being.** That divinity doesn't descend—it awakens.

They recorded that he stayed many years, teaching with great authority. That he condemned caste, uplifted the lowly, healed with presence, and taught that all are children of the Source. That the kingdom was not coming—it was here. And for this, religious leaders in the East tried to silence him too. He fled through mountain passes, survived pursuit, and continued his journey until the time came to return.

The Fourth Resound

He didn't come home with scrolls. He came home with fire.

Between those long journeys east, he returned to Nazareth. Not for comfort—but to keep himself grounded. He worked as a tekton—craftsman of wood and stone. Not a laborer punching hours. He made one-of-a-kind pieces. Tools and tables with vision in them. Not everyone understood what he built, but those who did, paid well. He didn't need much. He never cared for surplus. What mattered was the process. It helped him carry the weight of what he had seen.

So he would leave again—and they'd whisper about him. That he was strange. That he spoke like someone who had seen the world. That he returned with eyes too ancient for his years. Later, they even tried to throw him off a cliff.

Not strangers—his own people. The ones who'd watched him grow, who'd eaten meals with him, who'd seen him in the carpentry shop. When he stood in the synagogue and spoke of the prophets, when he refused to perform miracles on demand, when he spoke truth they didn't want to hear—they turned. They dragged him to the edge, intending to silence him with a fall.

Because that's what truth does. It breaks the illusion of familiarity. It turns comfort into confrontation. And they could not accept that the boy they thought they knew had returned as something they couldn't control.

Because he had walked roads older than Moses. He had stood in temples that predated Abraham. He had spoken the same truths in languages no longer written. He had lived as Issa—the one who remembered, long before the world tried to name him Christ.

These were not lost years. **They were the making of a messenger.**

And when he returned for the last time—he didn't come back to learn. He came back to begin.

BACK IN TOWN: THE ESSENEAN SCENE

He comes home to Galilee not as a Pharisee wrapped in endless purity codes, nor as a Sadducee tied to Roman favor, nor as a Zealot wielding blades of revolt. **He is wholly Jewish—teaching in synagogues, observing feasts, calling himself ben Adam, the Son of Man**—but he defies every sectarian boundary placed upon him.

Look closely, and behind his growth, appear desert mystics—the Essenes who abandoned Jerusalem's corruption to establish hidden communities near the Dead Sea. They spoke of a Teacher of Righteousness, a figure beyond temple authority, rejected by priests yet cherished by God. Living in purity and constant prayer, they awaited not one Messiah but two: a priestly son of Aaron and a kingly son of David—or perhaps both roles embodied in a single man.

Upon returning, Jesus would have surveyed the landscape—listening, discerning, watching for any sign of awakening. He had traveled too far and seen too much to mistake silence for stillness. And then he heard it—rumors of a wild prophet stirring the crowds, drawing people out of cities and into the wilderness.

John.

A voice crying out from the desert, echoing what the Essenes had long foretold. Clothed in camel's hair, baptizing penitents in the Jordan, calling the people not to ritual but to repentance. **He had rejected the temple's grandeur to heed God's voice carried by desert winds.**

Soon after, Jesus emerges—declaring a kingdom built neither by violence nor priestly decree, but within every surrendered heart. He labels Pharisees "whitewashed tombs," enrages priests, and tells the people that angels ascend and descend upon the Son of Man.

Many suspect him Essene-trained, but he walks beyond their solitude, bringing contemplative wisdom into everyday life.

Where Essenes retreat, he engages. Where they foresee destruction, he proclaims renewal. They predict a cosmic battle between Light and Darkness, but he demonstrates that darkness fades naturally when Light simply shines. He aligns with no party yet fulfills every yearning for a King, a Priest, and a Teacher who surpasses sectarian limits.

Jesus remains anchored deeply in Israel's ancient traditions—a scholar surpasses any scribe, igniting a new covenant etched on living hearts. Even the Essenes could not foresee how wide his embrace would reach or how expansive his kingdom would grow.

BECOMING CHRIST: HUMAN UNFOLDMENT

In those silent years, he wasn't always traveling or immersed in distant teachings. He learned a trade from Joseph, becoming a tekton—skilled in working wood and stone. He likely spent long days laboring quietly, contributing to his family, living a life recognizable to anyone around him. He knew the rhythm of sore muscles and splintered hands. He knew how to measure a beam, how to price a project, how to negotiate with neighbors who needed repairs.

He sat at the table. He laughed with cousins. He helped carry baskets through dusty streets. He lived a life so normal it vanished from memory, overshadowed by the parts that made better stories.

Yet his relationship with his family remains curiously thin in what we've been given. His father Joseph fades from mention entirely. His brothers appear skeptical, even dismissive. It's possible that the distance wasn't just geographical—but emotional. That the road he walked pulled him from the expectations they had for him, creating a quiet rift that never fully healed.

And what of love?

The texts never mention romance. But silence doesn't equal absence. **As a Rabbi—a title often reserved for married men—relationships wouldn't just have been allowed, they would have been expected.** It's hard to imagine he walked through youth, through friendship, through late nights around fires and long days in close company—without ever touching affection, desire, heartbreak. Jesus garnered the attention of lots of women, many of whom went on to financially support him. **This doesnt happen for an unintelligent, homely man.** He knew what he was gifted with, and likely allowed it to help him along the way. It would be entirely plausible he would have become involved with many women on his journey, and the omission feels deliberate. Perhaps love was too human. Too grounding. Too honest.

None of these human dimensions made it into the official record. Not the friends he surely had. Not the games he played as a boy. Not the missteps. Not the laughter. Not the heartbreak. Scripture jumps from prodigy to prophet without showing the man who grew in between. But those missing years weren't empty. They were lived.

Some say he was Essene—that he trained among the desert mystics who

renounced society and prepared for cosmic battle. There's truth in the connection. He shared their fire. Their depth. Their rejection of temple corruption. But he didn't stay cloistered. He didn't sever ties with the world. He didn't see purity as isolation. He didn't build walls. He sat with outcasts. He broke bread with sinners. He stepped into the mess.

John the Baptist was cast out of the Essenes for defying their extremes. Jesus walked the same edge—close enough to know their wisdom, free enough to break their lines. So he wouldn't have made it much further than John The Baptist did with them, and even though John The Baptist was Jesus' cousin, they did not acquaint until adulthood.

The silence around his early life feels intentional—a manufactured mystery to elevate him above the rest of us. But what tradition tried to omit is exactly what made him powerful.

He wasn't untouchable. He was deeply touched by life. He knew rejection, boredom, hard work, longing, laughter, loss. He walked into his calling with calloused hands and a heart shaped by both silence and struggle.

When he spoke of forgiveness, it wasn't *theory*.

When he embraced the forgotten, it wasn't *charity*.

When he said the Kingdom was near, it wasn't a metaphor.

He said it because he had lived through everything we live through—and still remembered who he was.

That is what made him so dangerous.

Not that he was perfect.

But that he was human—and he still chose to rise.

THE MAN OF THE EARTH

Before the crowds. Before the crucifixion. Before the titles and translations. He was a man of the earth.

Not a mystic lost in abstraction, but someone rooted in rhythm—of wind, of soil, of water. He walked barefoot through hills and wilderness, knowing how the world moved because he moved with it. He didn't just speak of seeds and storms—he lived by them.

He knew how to do more than fish.

He grew up in Galilee—coastal, raw, and hardworking. He cast nets, tied lines, hauled wet rope with sunburnt hands. He knew which hours brought the fish to surface, which coves held better catch, and which winds meant stay on shore. He learned the patience of the water—the discipline of waiting, adjusting, trying again. Fishing shaped his instinct to read below the surface, to listen for what couldn't be seen.

You don't vanish into foreign empires and survive deserts, jungles, mountains, and oceans—or survive 40 days in the wilderness unless you know how to live off what the land gives you. **He wasn't just walking through towns—he was moving through terrain.** Tracking stars. Reading clouds. Finding edible plants, safe water, the right bark for fire. He could sleep in wind-worn caves, trace his direction without a map, slip through mountain passes without leaving a trace.

These weren't survival tricks—they were a language. He was fluent in the earth.

That's why his teachings carried weight. He didn't borrow imagery—**he lived it.** When he spoke of seeds, vineyards, fig trees, and floods, it wasn't for poetic flair. It was lived wisdom—observed, repeated, trusted.

He was formed by stone and silence. By moonlight on water and sand between his teeth. The sacred wasn't somewhere else—it was in the ground beneath him, the wind against his face, the rhythm of breath in solitude.

He was never separate from the natural world. He was shaped by it. And that made him unstoppable.

A LIFE AMONG THE PEOPLE

From the moment John the Baptist's voice thundered—

"Prepare the way!"—

Jesus moved with unwavering focus. Yet after John's imprisonment and death, a deeper fire ignited within him. It wasn't vengeance that drove him but a resolute determination, as if John's courage had become his own. This was the true gift John The Baptist gave to him, just as Jean gave to me. **Courage to go further.**

He walked roads many would avoid, entering towns where everyday people carried quiet burdens, embodying a kingdom whose power was revealed through compassion, not conquest.

He chose paths others dismissed. Traveling deliberately through Samaria—a region his own people preferred to bypass—he openly crossed boundaries drawn by ancient animosity. At a well in midday heat, he spoke to a Samaritan woman—a soul isolated even among her own people, drawing water alone to avoid judgment. Though tradition demanded he remain distant, Jesus asked her simply for a drink, opening a dialogue that dissolved centuries of prejudice.

"If you knew who asked you for water," he said gently, "you would ask him, and he would give you living water."

His words startled her, igniting questions she had never dared voice. By the time their exchange ended, her shame was gone, replaced by a spark of hope. Leaving her water jar behind, she became a witness to possibility, her heart awakened.

To illustrate this radical compassion further, he told of a man beaten and left on the roadside, ignored by religious leaders who valued purity over mercy. It was a Samaritan—despised in Judea—who tended the man's wounds, carried him to safety, and ensured his recovery.

"Who was the true neighbor?" Jesus asked.

The answer cut through every prejudice: it was the outsider who showed kindness. With this story, he demolished labels, teaching that true neighborliness isn't defined by culture or creed but by mercy and action.

In Galilee and Judea, he sought out those deemed untouchable—the lepers cast aside, women labeled unclean, and the disabled begging on dusty corners. While others avoided them, Jesus approached, gently touching those everyone else rejected. His healing restored more than health; it reclaimed dignity. These acts weren't staged miracles—they were quiet affirmations of worth, revealing each person's true name: beloved.

He welcomed tax collectors to his table, men scorned as traitors for profiting

off Roman oppression. Yet in Jesus' presence, judgment vanished. Breaking bread with them drew criticism from scribes and Pharisees, who murmured about his choice of companions. But Jesus revealed a kingdom where every table was open, inviting all who hungered for acceptance.

His teachings often lacked grand spectacle. He told simple parables about seeds sown in fields, coins lost and found, shepherds rescuing their sheep—tying profound truths to ordinary life. Often, a brief word or a quiet gesture opened eyes to a God not distant or aloof, but present amid nets and markets, feasts and family meals.

John the Baptist's spirit resonated through Jesus' boldness. John's death had deeply shaken the disciples, but Jesus continued John's challenge to authority, confronting religious leaders who had twisted faith into a tool of control. He shattered traditions that had calcified into cruelty, teaching that grace outweighed ritual purity, and true religion overflowed with compassion, not fear.

Each day brought more healing, more stories shared in quiet villages, more bridges built across divides. He showed people that God's presence wasn't confined to temples or reserved for the elite.

He declared—

> **"Where two or three are gathered in my name, there am I with them."**
> **— Matthew 18:20**

Demonstrating it not through spectacle alone but through simple acts of kindness and mercy along dusty roads.

In these daily choices, Jesus quietly revealed a kingdom already here, accessible and alive within each heart, awaiting only recognition.

POWERFUL COMPASSION & RADICAL LOVE

In this gentle yet relentless flow of healing, teaching, and fellowship, we glimpse the true heart of his ministry long before darker days gathered near. **Jesus remained fully human—sharing meals, feeling fatigue, laughing freely, and expressing genuine frustration.** In these ordinary, earthly moments, he allowed divine love to shine unguarded, transforming every encounter into a sacred opportunity.

He stepped into lives labeled hopeless, igniting hunger for possibilities no one dared imagine: that enemies could share a cup of water, that lepers might embrace their loved ones again, that sinners might rediscover their intrinsic worth. When he spoke, his words shattered social barriers like daylight streaming through cracks in a closed door, uncovering hearts buried beneath years of neglect.

Long before any dramatic entry into Jerusalem, before the final confrontations, he quietly planted seeds of revolution. Each act of kindness—at a Samaritan well, around the tax collector's table, beside the bruised and abandoned traveler—was not only a prelude to grander miracles.

These acts embodied the very essence of the kingdom he declared, proving heaven touches earth wherever compassion triumphs over fear.

Through these simple yet profound gestures, we witness a Messiah crowned only with his humanity, his spirit ignited by John's courage, recognizing divine worth in every face society discarded. By steadfast, humble grace, he reshaped countless lives—long before the final shadows ever closed in.

THE MOUTH OF A LION

Jesus had always spoken clearly—his voice a refuge for the lost and broken. But when word reached him of John the Baptist's imprisonment and brutal execution, something deeper shifted. John, beheaded by a drunken tyrant for daring to speak truth, had been the last voice crying out from the wilderness. Now, that voice was silenced. **And Jesus didn't retreat—he stepped forward with fire.**

Compassion had long guided him, but now it moved with a sharpened edge. The gentleness remained, but it was fused with clarity—uncompromising, unshakable. The voice that once whispered parables now roared with the weight of prophecy. John's defiance echoed through him, not as memory, but as fuel.

He exposed illusions with precision. In synagogues, he stripped away the appearance of holiness to reveal systems hollowed out by power. He called out those who turned faith into theater—Pharisees obsessed with the letter of the law while abandoning its spirit. "Whitewashed tombs," he said—not for shock, but for truth. Beautiful on the outside, rotting within.

He walked straight into the Temple and overturned its economy. Tables flipped. Coins scattered. Merchants fled from the fury in his eyes.

"My Father's house shall be a house of prayer—but you've turned it into a den of thieves." — Mark 11:17

This wasn't disorder—it was restoration. He wasn't attacking faith. He was reclaiming it.

When they criticized him for healing on the Sabbath, he made it simple:

"Is it lawful to do good or evil on the Sabbath— to save life or destroy it?" — Mark 3:4

They stood in silence. He didn't care. He healed *anyway*.

It wasn't rebellion for its own sake. It was a call back to truth—truth that was never meant to serve the powerful, but to lift the broken.

"Woe to you, scribes and Pharisees. You shut the door of the Kingdom in people's faces. You yourselves do not enter, and you block the way for others." — Matthew 23:13

It was the indictment of a system that executed John and now set its sights on him.

His words cut deep.

"You have heard it said... but I say to you..."

Again and again, he rewrote the law—not by erasing it, but by restoring its heart. The law was never about control. It was about compassion. **Righteousness wasn't ritual—it was love in action.**

And still, he fed the hungry. He touched the leper. He welcomed the forgotten. **He was no longer just stirring hearts—he was confronting strongholds.** Every healing, every word, every touch carried the weight of urgency. John's death had stripped away whatever hesitation remained.

He declared the days of temple politics numbered. External piety—ritual without mercy—meant nothing now. He wasn't building a religion. He was exposing a lie. The Kingdom wasn't coming—it was already here. Not in scrolls. Not in stone. In them. In you.

The truth divided the crowds. Some followed. Some plotted. But none walked away untouched. His message couldn't be domesticated. His love couldn't be negotiated. His conviction couldn't be ignored.

This was Jesus in full fire—bold, rooted, unstoppable. Not burning with vengeance, but with vision. Not seeking violence, but unwilling to let fear run the world one more day.

And now—having spoken truth to power, having declared the Kingdom not as theory but as embodied reality—he moved toward something even greater. What came next would not be words, but signs. Public acts that could not be ignored. Miracles that would both reveal and provoke.

He wasn't finished. He was just beginning to show them what the Kingdom looked like when it walked.

What followed were not spectacles. They were signals. Signs that changed everything.

THE SEVEN SIGNS

They called them miracles, as if each act defied the fabric of nature—brief flashes of divine favor reserved for a privileged few. Yet Jesus did not overturn natural law. He illuminated it. Every wonder he performed was not a display of raw power, but a quiet revelation—a lesson revealing a deeper truth already woven into the universe, a map guiding you back to the truth of your own being.

The Gospel of John rightly calls them signs, for that is exactly what they are: markers on the journey, showing that reality itself responds when you awaken to who you truly are. This is more than religion—it is revelation. It does not simply speak of a distant God; it reveals your own essence, your own potential, your own innate divinity.

I. TRANSMUTATION: WATER INTO WINE

Energy flows, yet is never fixed. It responds directly to the resonance of belief. When water shifted into wine, it wasn't a violation of nature—it was a reflection of a heart awakened, able to see past limitation and into the deeper truth of creation itself.

II. THE BRIDGE: THE OFFICIAL'S SON HEALED

No barrier of distance exists where spirit reigns. Consciousness moves freely, untouched by walls or measured in miles. The child recovers the moment faith sees him whole, revealing how deeply our reality bends to align with belief.

III. THE POWER OF CHOICE: THE MAN AT THE POOL

No one else can lift you—the answer lies in your own hands. Healing begins the moment you choose to stand, stepping beyond the stories that once held you captive, reclaiming the strength that was always yours.

IV. MULTIPLICATION OF ENERGY: THE LOAVES AND FISH

Offer the little you have, and watch it expand in the giving. Scarcity dissolves the moment your hand opens, revealing abundance as the natural order. When you break bread in faith, you awaken the miracle of endless provision.

V. ALIGNMENT OF FREQUENCY: WALKING ON WATER

Fear traps you beneath the waves, pulling you down into its depths. Faith lifts you, placing solid ground where chaos once ruled. Reality yields to the vibration you embody within. Take the step, and watch as the waters rise to hold you firm.

VI. REWRITING REALITY: HEALING THE BLIND MAN

Perception shapes every reality you encounter. True sight awakens the moment you turn your gaze inward. The blind regain vision not by external miracle alone, but by shedding the darkness they once accepted as permanent.

VII. MASTERY OVER MATTER: RAISING LAZARUS

Life and death are thresholds—gateways rather than endings. You were created to cross them, bearing witness to the higher truths eternally woven into your being. They were called miracles, yet he named them signs—each one an invitation to remember that what he did, you can also do, and even greater. He did not come to showcase his divinity, leaving you simply to marvel. He came so you might awaken to the divinity already present within yourself.

SIGN I — WATER INTO WINE & ALCHEMY — JOHN 2:1–11

It was the third day of a wedding feast, and laughter echoed through the gathering. Yet beneath the joy, a quiet tension began to rise: the wine had run dry. In a culture where hospitality was sacred, this shortage was more than a small embarrassment—it threatened a family's honor for years to come.

Mary sensed the trouble first. Quietly, she approached her son, saying simply, **"They have no more wine."** Her words were less a statement than an invitation. Jesus hesitated, replying, "My hour has not yet come." But Mary, confident and undeterred, turned to the servants and said, **"Do whatever he tells you."**

Nearby stood six stone jars—vessels meant for ritual washing. Jesus instructed the servants, **"Fill them with water."** They followed without question. He then told them, **"Now draw some out and take it to the master of the banquet."** There was no elaborate prayer, no theatrical display—only quiet authority.

When the master tasted the water, he discovered wine of extraordinary quality—finer than any previously served.

This was no mere illusion or trick to impress guests. It was an unveiling of deeper truth: that matter responds to intention and belief. Water, the most basic of elements, became rich wine without fermentation or delay. Jesus did not break the laws of nature—he demonstrated their hidden flexibility, revealing how reality shifts when consciousness commands it.

In Cana, the first sign was given—not just as proof of power, but as an invitation to recognize your own potential. Your circumstances, however humble, hold the capacity for transformation. What is ordinary becomes extraordinary when touched by conscious intention. Water becomes wine—not because nature is suspended, but because truth is remembered.

SIGN II – HEALING THE OFFICIAL'S SON: THE BRIDGE BETWEEN THOUGHT AND MATTER —JOHN 4:46–54

He set out at dawn, desperation urging every stride, each hoofbeat hammering the haunting question: "Will I reach him in time?" Miles away, back in Capernaum, his son lay burning with fever, edging closer to death. He carried only stories—tales of a healer whose words alone brought wholeness, without rituals, herbs, or touch.

Finally arriving in Cana, he found Jesus and fell at his feet, pleading, **"Lord, come quickly, before my child dies."** He assumed healing required proximity, physical presence—Jesus beside the bed, laying hands upon his son. But Jesus didn't move.

He simply spoke, calm and certain: "Go. Your son lives."

No dramatic gesture. No visible proof. Just words—challenging the man to choose: faith now, or despair.

In that instant, the father released every expectation of how healing should look. He mounted his horse and turned toward home, carrying nothing but trust in that unseen promise. On his way, servants rushed toward him, their voices ringing with joy: **"Your son lives!"** At precisely the moment Jesus had spoken, the fever had lifted, vanishing like morning mist.

This sign wasn't only a lesson in healing from afar—it unveiled that distance itself holds no power where spirit is concerned. Jesus didn't see miles as a barrier. He named reality, and the father stepped fully into that declared truth. Faith formed a bridge between intention and outcome, making space and time bend beneath the weight of belief.

The father's faith went beyond hope. He chose trust without waiting for evidence. The child recovered not simply because Jesus declared it, but because the father's trust aligned completely with divine reality. **Distance wasn't the issue— alignment was everything.**

His return home was not only physical travel, but a deeper journey from fear to complete reliance on the power of promise. By the time he reached his door, he understood clearly: **where faith is real, no distance can ever interfere.**

SIGN III – HEALING AT BETHESDA: THE REALITY OF CHOICE — JOHN 5:1–15

Bethesda was a place of waiting, a gathering of broken bodies and worn spirits surrounding a pool encircled by five stone colonnades. **Here, people clung desperately to stories of an angel who stirred the waters, offering healing—but only to the first to touch them.** For many, hope faded into resignation; months turned to years, each passing season another layer of disappointment.

Among the crowd was a man trapped in illness for thirty-eight weary years. His days were a ritual of hopelessness, eyes fixed on water that never stirred in his favor. He lay immobilized, not just by physical ailment, but by a story that had grown heavier than his affliction. He believed healing was forever beyond his reach because someone always stepped ahead.

Then Jesus appeared, quiet yet purposeful, and noticed him. Approaching gently, he asked a question that pierced decades of inertia: "Do you want to be made well?" The man didn't answer directly; instead, he recounted the familiar tale—no help, no chance, only endless waiting.

But Jesus offered no sympathy for the man's excuses. Instead, with clear authority, he said: "Get up. Pick up your mat. Walk."

In that command, years of stagnation collapsed into a single moment of choice. The man rose immediately, discovering strength he had forgotten was his. He took up his mat, standing not only in body but in spirit, stepping firmly into a new reality.

This third sign wasn't truly about the pool or its elusive angelic healing. It revealed a deeper truth: healing doesn't arrive from outside—it emerges from within. Waiting on the world, conditions, or others to move first is the trap that holds many immobile. Healing springs to life the moment you decide to rise.

Choice itself ignites the transformation, dissolving old narratives and opening pathways previously unseen. Bethesda's water was only a backdrop; the real miracle was the awakening of a heart that chose action over resignation. Jesus demonstrated clearly: the instant you step beyond the limitations you've accepted, reality aligns to your choice. **You are not waiting for God—God waits for you, the catalyst already placed within your reach.**

SIGN IV – FEEDING THE FIVE THOUSAND: THE LAW OF MULTIPLICATION —JOHN 6:1–14

High above the Sea of Galilee, a vast multitude had gathered—five thousand men, not counting the countless women and children who followed. Drawn by healings and promises of hope, they now stood restless, hunger gnawing at patience.

The disciples felt the tension rising, sensing scarcity could soon ignite unrest. Philip anxiously calculated, concluding even two hundred denarii wouldn't provide a mere bite for each person. Andrew hesitantly presented a boy's small offering—five barley loaves and two fish—then shrugged it off, overwhelmed by the enormity of the need. They pleaded with Jesus, urging him to send the crowd away so they could find food elsewhere.

But Jesus turned their request back on them, challenging, "You give them something to eat."

The disciples faltered, their eyes still fixed on lack, uncertain how to proceed.

Yet Jesus saw possibility instead. Calmly, he instructed, "Make the people sit," then took the simple loaves and humble fish in his hands. Without hesitation, he blessed and broke what appeared insufficient, handing the pieces back to his disciples for distribution. And as they shared what they thought could never be enough, abundance emerged effortlessly. Everyone ate until satisfaction overflowed, leaving twelve baskets of surplus—far more than they'd started with.

Scarcity vanished the instant generosity took hold.

This fourth sign is not about counting loaves but revealing a profound truth: whatever you release expands beyond measure. Scarcity is the lie. Generosity reveals that blessing and breaking open whatever you hold multiplies it into abundance. At the day's end, their baskets overflowed—a powerful testimony to a universal law activated by giving.

This was no illusion or trick. It illuminated the cosmic reality that shortage arises from perception, not resources. Jesus did not conjure bread from thin air; he demonstrated clearly that what you already hold becomes enough the moment fear yields to faith. His gratitude was no polite gesture—it was a spark igniting hidden potential already within their grasp.

Nothing multiplies while withheld. The bread was finite until blessed, broken, and shared. Only then did it expand. Jesus acted with certainty, knowing deeply that belief plants the seed, faith waters it, and the harvest inevitably follows.

But this sign extends far beyond mere food—it touches every aspect of life: love, energy, healing, resources. Whatever you willingly bless, break open, and release returns multiplied. You do not wait for fullness before giving; fullness finds you precisely through the act of generosity.

Scarcity has always been an illusion, dissolving before the presence of a spirit willing to give freely. Abundance moves through you, growing greater with every gift you offer.

SIGN V – WALKING ON WATER: THE LAW OF FREQUENCY — JOHN 6:16–21

It was the fourth watch of the night—**the hour when exhaustion settles deep into bone, when minds grow uncertain and bodies weary beyond resistance.**

A savage wind clawed at the sea, battering the boat relentlessly, waves alive with menace, threatening to splinter wood into nothingness. The disciples, seasoned fishermen, had faced storms before, but this tempest convinced even them that dawn might never come.

Suddenly, through the spray and darkness, they saw a figure approaching on the water—ghostly, impossible. Panic seized them; surely this specter spelled their doom.

But then a voice broke clearly through the storm: "Take courage. It is I. Don't be afraid."

Peter, heart racing, eyes fixed through the gloom, called out, "Lord, if it's really you, tell me to come to you on the water." Jesus replied without hesitation, "Come."

Peter swung one leg over the boat's edge, then the other, stepping onto the waves. For one astonishing instant, he stood firm, impossibility becoming reality beneath his feet. Yet soon the wind's howl pierced his concentration, fear rushed in, and in that moment, he felt the sea yield beneath him. **He plunged downward, crying desperately for help.**

Jesus immediately grasped his arm, pulling him upright again. "You of little faith," he gently asked, "why did you doubt?" The storm quieted, and within that instant, the heart of this sign became clear.

This moment was never magic or divine theatrics—it was about resonance, about the vibration at which one's being operates. Peter was stable until fear disrupted his alignment. The water hadn't changed; neither had Jesus. Peter's shift in consciousness caused him to sink. No hidden test or judgment was at play. It was simply a demonstration of how reality responds directly to our internal state.

The Law of Frequency is not symbolic poetry; it is the foundational rhythm beneath existence. Faith resonates at a high vibration; fear drags it downward. When Peter first stepped out, he aligned with certainty's frequency, effortlessly held by the waves. But as wind and storm dominated his awareness, his vibration fell out of tune, and he sank.

Yet this brief experience left an indelible mark on Peter, a crack in the walls of his limitations. This glimpse into resonance became a seed within him, growing over time.

Later, Peter himself performed profound acts of alchemy—transforming reality, healing the sick, and even raising the dead. Among the disciples, he uniquely embodied the power Jesus revealed that night, precisely because he had briefly lived it. The memory of walking on water, however fleeting, opened Peter's belief just enough for greater miracles to flow through him later, anchoring him in the awareness that reality bends willingly when one aligns fully with faith.

We live this same dynamic every day: rising or falling, flourishing or struggling—not because the world changes, but because our internal alignment does. Our frequency shapes our reality, and our focus directs our frequency.

Jesus let Peter—and each of us—witness the profound truth: when aligned with possibility, we transcend what appears impossible; when we surrender to doubt, we lose our footing.

Walking on water wasn't about defying nature's law—it was nature itself, fully revealed. Everything is energy. Everything carries a note. Match that higher resonance and you rise effortlessly. Allow fear to distort your focus, and you fall.

Jesus invited Peter, and invites us still, into a life attuned to faith—showing clearly that fear may roar like wind, but it cannot sink us unless we give it the power to disrupt our inner harmony.

SIGN VI – HEALING THE MAN BORN BLIND: THE REWRITE OF REALITY —JOHN 9:1–41

He had never seen the sun, never traced the outline of a human face, never even glimpsed his own hand. From birth, blindness marked him as cursed—bearing society's stigma as evidence of sin, either his own or his parents'. In their eyes, suffering was punishment, affliction proof of hidden guilt, and blindness the consequence of divine judgment.

When Jesus and his disciples passed by, the disciples asked the only question their tradition allowed: **"Who sinned, this man or his parents?"**

But Jesus shattered their assumptions. **"Neither,"** he declared firmly. **"This happened so that the works of God might be revealed in him."**

He offered no theology to explain suffering—only action to end it. He knelt and gathered dust, mixing it with a drop of his own essence to form mud—the same blend of earth and spirit from which humanity was first shaped. He spread it gently over the man's eyes, offering no elaborate prayer or ritual—just a command:

"Go, wash in the Pool of Siloam."

The man stumbled to the water, rinsed his face, and when he lifted his head, he saw the world for the first time.

This was more than healing. It was re-creation. Not a correction of defect, but a restoration of design. Jesus didn't fix him—he reminded him. The mud held no power. The power was in consciousness aligned with truth. Jesus refused the old narrative of sin and separation. He declared a new reality, and the body responded.

The man had lived his life beneath a single story—cursed, broken, defined by what he lacked. Jesus erased that in an instant, replacing it with the truth: he was whole. Capable. Worthy of sight, and of life beyond judgment.

This was the sixth sign—not a miracle layered on top of damage, but a rewrite from the inside out. True healing doesn't repair what's broken. It reveals what was whole all along.

Your body listens. Your life responds. Matter bends to the truth you believe.

This was The Rewrite then—and it remains The Rewrite now. Step out of the old narrative. Let go of what you were told you are. Remember what was always true, and **watch the world change** when you believe it.

SIGN VII – RAISING LAZARUS: MASTERY OVER MATTER, THE WEEPING GOD —JOHN 11:1-44

Word reached him days earlier: "Lord, the one you love is sick."

They didn't even need to say his name—it was Lazarus, his closest friend. Bethany wasn't just another village on the road. It was home. Mary, Martha, and Lazarus gave him something few others could: belonging. Here, he wasn't just Teacher or Prophet. **He was Yeshua—friend, brother, loved and known.**

He loved them deeply. Yet when word came of Lazarus' illness, he didn't rush to his side. He stayed where he was for two more days, confounding everyone who assumed love required urgency. To the disciples, and even to Mary and Martha, it felt like delay. Like distance. Like too late.

But he wasn't late. He was waiting—for something deeper than healing. He was waiting for the moment that would shatter the illusion of finality.

By the time he arrived in Bethany, grief had already settled. **Lazarus had been dead four days—long enough for hope to rot in the tomb alongside the body.** Martha met him at the edge of town, straddling faith and anguish. **"Lord, if you had been here, my brother would not have died."** It wasn't accusation. It was sorrow shaped like a sentence.

"Your brother will rise again," Jesus told her.

She thought he meant someday—some distant resurrection at the end of time. But he made it plain:

"I am the resurrection and the life."

Not a promise for later. A presence now.

Mary came next. She fell at his feet, weeping without restraint. Seeing her pain, he didn't speak—he wept with her. He didn't rise above the grief—he entered it. He didn't mourn for Lazarus—he mourned with those who loved him. **This isn't godly, this is human.**

They led him to the tomb. A sealed cave, thick with the scent of decay. "Roll the stone away," he said.

Martha flinched. **"Lord, by now there's a stench…"**

But Jesus didn't flinch. He looked up and spoke gratitude—not a plea, not negotiation. Just a declaration.

Then came the command:

"Lazarus, come out."

Silence stretched. Then—movement. A sound. The shuffle of wrapped feet. Lazarus stood at the entrance, bound in grave cloths. **Alive.**

A man four days dead now breathed among the living. Awe rippled through the crowd—followed quickly by fear. **This was more than healing. This was resurrection.** A disruption of everything they believed about what was possible.

He had reversed what all called final. Not by bargaining with death, but by commanding life. Not by defying reality, but by realigning it.

The authorities could no longer dismiss him. Lazarus became a threat by existing. A walking contradiction to the systems built on control and fear. They plotted not only against Jesus, but against the man he raised—because some truths are too powerful to allow.

And Lazarus afterward? Some say he fled to Cyprus, became bishop of Kition, carrying resurrection like a quiet burden. Others say he walked the rest of his days in silence. The Gospel never records another word from him. Maybe some experiences transcend language.

But one thing is certain: he lived.

And from that moment on, nothing could ever be the same.

Jesus had not come to delay death. He came to expose its illusion.

Decay, time, finality—all bent in the presence of one who knew that matter answers to consciousness, energy follows intent, and life never truly ends.

Where fear built a wall, he spoke a door into it.

And it opened.

CHOOSING THE ENDING ON THE CROSS

"No one takes my life from me; I lay it down of my own accord."
—John 10:18

From the outside, it looked like utter defeat. The cross, the nails, the jeering crowd screaming for Barabbas. Priests stood smugly triumphant. Rome drove iron through flesh. **By every worldly measure, it seemed the tragic end of a life full of promise.**

Yet the cross was never a tragedy—never Rome's triumph, never the priests' victory. It was an initiation, the final stage in a journey Jesus himself set in motion long before the beams of Golgotha rose from the earth. No one took his life from him; he offered it willingly, completing the circle of signs through his own body and blood.

Everything that unfolded in those final days was not the end of a man, but the transformation of everyone who would come after. The crucifixion was never defeat—it was the ultimate initiation.

From the first moment he spoke publicly, Jesus knew where the path would lead.

He was no naïve dreamer. Step by step, he dismantled the systems keeping humanity chained to fear: religious elites, Roman authority, the false belief that power existed outside oneself. And they knew *exactly* what he was doing.

The priests knew it. Pilate felt it. Even his disciples sensed the inevitability, though they didn't fully understand. If Jesus wasn't stopped, every structure of control would collapse. **They were right in believing he had to be removed—but blind to what his removal would actually accomplish.**

The crucifixion wasn't the end of Jesus. It was his final teaching.

They believed they were crushing a rebel, silencing a radical. Instead, they completed the alchemical process he had embodied: mastery over form, substance, energy, and will. Water turned to wine. Healing from afar. Multiplying loaves. Walking on water. Lifting blindness. Reversing death. Each was a sign, preparing for this final act—now centered on himself.

He willingly stepped into death—not only to prove resurrection was possible, but to demonstrate the path itself. Death was never final. Fear was the illusion. The Kingdom existed within, untouchable by Roman spears or priestly decrees.

He had taught all along: we are more than flesh, more than name, more than what the world tells us. Now he would prove it by surrendering the very thing humanity feared losing most—the body. He didn't just speak of surrender. He became surrender. He didn't just preach transformation. He lived it. Every betrayal, every humiliation, every last breath was a transmutation. He took humanity's darkest symbol—the cross—and made it a doorway.

They believed they could erase him. Instead, they completed him.

The cross was never defeat—it was the threshold he chose to cross. Alchemy, misunderstood by most, is not the transmutation of metal, but of essence. It is the process of moving from one state of being to another. Jesus embraced this completely. He entered the crucible, allowing death to burn away flesh, ego, identity. **The tomb became the chamber of dissolution—stripping away every label, every limitation.**

Resurrection wasn't restoration—it was emergence. A new form of being entirely.

Ancient initiates knew shadows of this path. Egyptians practiced symbolic burial. The Greeks passed through the Eleusinian mysteries. Vedic teachings spoke of ego-death and self-dissolution. Jesus absorbed them all, not as theory—but as embodiment. He was more than a teacher. He was a master of consciousness, energy, and divine law.

He taught direct communion with God. No priests. No gates. No mediators. "The Kingdom of God is within you," he said—and that truth could not coexist with institutions built on hierarchy, profit, and fear.

The Pharisees saw their grip loosening. The Sadducees saw the temple threatened. Rome, indifferent to doctrine, saw control slipping. **A man awakening the people to their own power—unarmed, yet unstoppable—was the most dangerous force of all.**

After Lazarus emerged from the tomb, they made their decision. He would have to die. It wasn't Judas who delivered the final betrayal—it was those who saw clearly what Jesus represented, then decided the world wasn't ready for it.

They thought death would silence him.

They were wrong.

PATH TO GOLGOTHA & THE FINAL WALK

It became his final test—the threshold everyone else feared to cross.

Rome sealed the tomb with stone, believing physical barriers could halt the spiritual transformation he'd already begun. But long before the tomb, they tried to destroy him by force. Not simply to kill, but to break. To make him bow. **And when he refused, they beat him without mercy.**

He wasn't executed just for healing the sick or preaching love. **It wasn't the title "Son of God" that condemned him. It was what that title threatened.** He exposed the machinery of power. He called out Pharisees who turned law into chains. He flipped their tables. He healed on their Sabbaths. He named them vipers in public. Every act was a strike against their grip—and they hit back.

They strapped the cross to his back—splintered, brutal, engineered to collapse a man before he ever reached the hill. Each step dragged through spit, through rocks, through the noise of people too afraid to help and too curious to look away. But every step was his choice. He could've stopped it with a word. He didn't. He walked.

His knees hit the ground. The wood tore deeper into flesh already flayed by lashes. Blood mixed with dust. The crowd watched him fall, and still—he rose.

At Golgotha, they stretched his arms wide. Not by force—he gave them. Nails through bone. Crown of thorns driven down until blood blurred vision. They hoisted him up like a trophy, but he wasn't theirs. He never was.

They beat the breaks off him. Tore him to pieces. Spat on him. Mocked him. Called him king just to watch him die like a criminal. And he took it all. Not because he was powerless. Because he was beyond their reach.

First came the scourging.

He was stripped fully naked—exposed, dehumanized, nothing left to protect or preserve. They chained him upright to a post in the Roman yard. This wasn't symbolic. This wasn't partial. This was engineered humiliation.

Two men—trained executioners—took turns exhausting themselves lashing him with a flagrum: leather cords laced with bone shards, metal hooks, and weighted tips. Each strike tore muscle from bone. Not just his back—his legs, his sides, his stomach, his chest, even his genitals. The lashes were wild, brutal, intentionally humiliating. They didn't avoid soft tissue—they targeted it. His thighs. His groin. His inner arms. They flayed him until he was a mass of pulsing red, nerves exposed to open air, blood pooling around his feet.

Roman torture was psychological as much as physical. They didn't just want to end him. They wanted to erase him. Strip him of identity. Of power. Of dignity.

And still, he stood.

Barely.

They wrapped him in a robe—not to clothe him, but to let the fabric stick to fresh wounds. Then they shoved a twisted crown of thorns onto his head. Not delicate. Not theatrical. Thick thorns—jagged, up to two inches—driven into the scalp. Some pierced all the way to the bone. Blood exploded down his face, into his mouth, blurring his vision. His nerves screamed. His equillibrium shattered, he couldn't balance himself.

They mocked him—"Hail, King of the Jews!"—and struck him again and again. Open-handed slaps. Closed fists to the face. Kicks to the ribs. Knees to the stomach. Some took the flagrum again just to see if he'd cry out. He didn't. They beat him in the groin, doubled him over, then forced him to stand again.

He vomited blood. His nose broken. Teeth loosened. Jaw likely fractured. His body was shaking, going cold. Systemic shock and metabolic acidosis was already setting in. Involuntary urination or defecation was likely. Cramping, extreme thirst, and confusion consumed his perception.

Then they gave him the beam.

Not a decorative cross. A solid Roman execution timber. Over nine feet long. Eight to ten inches thick. Rough, splintered, soaked with the blood of the last dozen men who'd been nailed to it. **It weighed at least 200 pounds. Maybe more.**

They slammed it onto his shoulders, pressing it into open wounds, the full weight tearing new lacerations across his neck and back. He staggered. Collapsed. They forced him up again. The street was stone—uneven, sharp, slick with his own blood. His feet were bare. Every step split flesh. Every fall smashed him further into ruin.

His genitals exposed, beaten. His body shaking in massive hypovolemic shock. The crowd watched. Some laughed. Some wept. Most did nothing.

He fell again and again. The beam crushed him each time. Still—he walked.

By the time he reached Golgotha, he was barely breathing. His vision was nearly gone. His organs were likely failing. His heart racing toward collapse.

And still—he laid down on the beam himself.

The Fourth Resound

They stretched his arms across it. Drove spikes through the wrists, between radius and ulna, pinning nerves with surgical cruelty. Ankles next—spike through the top of the foot, through bone, into timber.

They lifted him. Dropped the cross into place by the third hour in Jewish time. His body jolted downward, pulling against torn limbs, dislocating weakened joints instantly.

He suffocated *slowly*. Pushing up on nailed feet to breathe. Sliding his torn back up a splintered post with every gasp. The agony never stopped. It only deepened.

His arms were stretched wide and nailed in place, locking his chest in an open position. It made inhaling possible—but exhaling almost impossible. Every breath became a war against his own collapsing body. To breathe, he had to lift himself—pressing against the nail driven through both feet, grinding bone against iron, nerve against wood. Each breath cost everything.

His back—already torn to the muscle from Roman lashes—was shredded further every time it scraped against the upright beam. Every inhale seared his lungs. Every exhale was a fight not to drown in his own fluids.

This was the point of crucifixion. Death by asphyxiation. You didn't die from the wounds—you died from being unable to breathe. Slowly. Publicly. Naked and exposed, as your own weight dragged you down toward suffocation.

Meanwhile, blood still poured from his scalp—those thorns driven deep into nerve-dense flesh, triggering blinding pain and blurred vision. **Every movement sent waves of fire through his wrists and shoulders, already dislocated from being stretched and dropped into place.** His heartbeat was weak, his body in shock, organs straining under the loss of blood, the trauma, the exposure.

He was dehydrated, possibly hallucinating. Every cell in his body screaming for relief—and none coming.

And yet, even in that state—barely able to speak—he used his strength to forgive. To comfort. To finish what he started.

He didn't just die. He endured everything hell could invent—and remained conscious through all of it. That's the level of presence he carried. That's the kind of will it took. It wasn't just death. It was obliteration.

And still—he spoke. He forgave. He endured.

They tried to destroy him completely. Body, dignity, identity, everything. And he let them. Not out of weakness. Out of unbreakable, conscious, brutal will.

He didn't survive it. He transcended it. Just:

"Father, forgive them, for they do not know what they are doing." — Luke 23:34

They thought he was finished. He said it himself.

"It is finished." — John 19:30

But not the way they meant.

For over six hours he was up there, still a surprisingly short time for that manner of death. By the ninth hour, he was dead. Even Pontius was surprised, he ordered the legs of the others crucified with him to be broken to speed up the process, the spectacle was over.

The earth cracked. The sky darkened. The veil in the Temple tore in two. The line between sacred and human—gone. The systems that had held people in fear began to shake.

And when they pierced his side, blood and water flowed—the final release. Spirit exiting flesh, not in defeat, but on his terms. They pulled his body down thinking it was over. But all they had done was complete the process.

They didn't kill him. They crowned him.

THE TRUE RESURRECTION

They approached the tomb at dawn, expecting to find death waiting quietly within. They carried spices and oils—tools of grief—ready to anoint the end of everything they had hoped. **But when they arrived, there was no body to mourn.** The stone hadn't been rolled away for him to leave; it had been moved so they could enter, to witness with their own eyes that the impossible had already occurred.

He wasn't simply missing—he had become something entirely new. This resurrection was no return to the old form, no mere revival of a corpse. Jesus had transcended what they understood as life, shedding every limitation, emerging as the Living Christ—divine consciousness awakened in fullness. This was not just a victory over death; it was humanity's first glimpse of what they, too, were destined to become.

At first, they didn't recognize him. Grief from yesterday veiled their eyes, keeping them from seeing the truth standing before them. But as their hearts opened, as the old stories dissolved, recognition began to bloom. **They understood then— resurrection wasn't an isolated event.** It was the unveiling of their deepest potential.

He had stepped beyond death's veil to reveal the blueprint of their own divine nature. His return wasn't to demand worship or allegiance. He came not as a conquering king but as a familiar brother, gently guiding them toward the realization of their own awakening.

For forty days, he moved among them. Walls and locked doors no longer held meaning. He spoke of the Kingdom within—not as a distant ideal or future hope, but as something immediate, alive, and accessible to all who would seek it.

The resurrection was never just about one man rising. **It was a beacon—a call for every human soul to ascend.** To rise into their own divinity. Flesh giving way to light. Death dissolving into endless life. Separation collapsing into union with the Divine.

And even then, it was only the beginning.

THE 40 DAYS & FINAL ASCENSION

He didn't return simply to linger, but to complete the unfolding that began long before the cross. For forty days he walked among them—not as the familiar figure they remembered, but as the Living Christ, radiating with the brilliance of a deeper truth.

These weren't days spent proving himself, nor an extended goodbye.
They were the final initiation for those prepared to awaken. He came to ignite remembrance within every heart, demonstrating how to exist beyond death's imagined boundary—not as an impossible exception, but as a revelation of the potential lying dormant in each of us.

They recognized his voice and face, yet felt a profound shift—a resonance that reshaped reality around him. No longer bound by physical limits, he moved effortlessly by the laws of oneness and light. He never said, "Follow me," but rather, "Become as I am." He revealed that consciousness commands matter, and that the light body isn't poetry—it is our next evolutionary step. Again and again, he reminded them the Kingdom wasn't distant—it was woven into their very essence.

This truth had begun stirring long before Calvary—when he confronted priests profiting from salvation, when he entered Jerusalem on a donkey fulfilling ancient prophecy, or when John the Baptist first announced him, igniting a prophetic fire within Jesus to shatter illusions of power. John's beheading deepened that resolve, fueling Jesus' unwavering courage. Every step he took, he aligned deliberately with scripture, reframing old words in radical new ways.

In these forty days after resurrection, he did more than speak—he transferred an inheritance of divine consciousness. Walls and locked doors lost meaning, passed through with ease, teaching them that awakened spirit knows no barrier.

He had always said, "The Kingdom of God is within you," and now they understood exactly what he meant. It was never about adoring him from afar as some unreachable ideal. It was about realizing the Christ-consciousness latent within every soul. **Ascension wasn't his reward—it was an invitation for all to rise into the same union with the Source.**

When he finally departed their sight, it wasn't to become distant, but to saturate existence itself, accessible to anyone seeking in spirit. In that moment, he embodied the blueprint for humanity's next horizon—life fully awakened, seamlessly connected to the Divine.

He promised clearly: "You will do greater works than these," because he was never meant to be the story's end. He was simply the beginning line in a far greater testament.

A NATURAL LIFE, MADE HOLY

These forty days weren't about proving himself or silencing their doubts. He appeared as a vivid demonstration, guiding those brave enough to follow into their own awakening. He stirred ancient memories buried deep within humanity, teaching by presence alone how to step beyond death—not as a distant miracle to be admired, but as a tangible path anyone could walk.

He offered them not just a vision of possibility, but the lived reality of one who fully embodied divine awareness. His message was clear: "Become as I am."

He revealed how consciousness shapes reality, demonstrating with every appearance the attainable promise of the Light body—the divine inheritance dormant within each person. **The stories he'd begun telling long before the cross were now fully realized before their eyes.** Every miracle, every healing, every act of defiance against oppressive structures had been steps toward this moment, guiding humanity to understand their inherent divinity.

This path did not begin at his crucifixion. It was ignited when John the Baptist declared, "I must decrease so that he may increase" (John 3:30). John's martyrdom fueled Jesus' purpose, sharpening his resolve. He knew exactly what he faced, and he accepted it—not as inevitable defeat, but to reveal a higher truth. Yet even as he ascended, it wasn't withdrawal—it was expansion. He didn't leave to abandon humanity. He left to awaken it. His departure tore open the veil between heaven and earth, dissolving the illusion of separation. His ascension became an invitation, showing humanity the path they too could follow.

We understand now that this was not a purely holy life granted by divine decree. It was an ordinary life made holy through conscious choices, dedicated discipline, and profound mastery. **Jesus doubted, stumbled, endured exhaustion, felt frustration and isolation—yet persisted, because he understood what lay beyond.** He saw the reality he was creating, not just for himself, but for all humankind.

His life was not a flawless performance. It was a demonstration of possibility. This resound is about understanding how one human life could change everything— and in recognizing this truth, discovering that you possess the power to change everything as well. You are no spectator in this journey. You are an active participant, called to awaken the divine within yourself.

In the Fifth Resound, you will begin to learn how to harness this same power, to tap into the hidden tapestry Jesus himself revealed. We will explore the science and universal laws behind each miracle and teaching, demystifying the seemingly supernatural and empowering you to embody these truths.

Jesus did not come to be worshipped as an exception. He came to be followed as an example. His resurrection and ascension were not conclusions—they were beginnings.

XI

THE FIFTH RESOUND

THE TAPESTRY UNSEEN

"BENEATH EVERY FORM LIES A
UNIFIED FIELD—AN INVISIBLE
ARCHITECTURE INTRICATELY
WOVEN INTO ALL THINGS."

THE FIFTH RESOUND

THE TAPESTRY UNSEEN &
THE HIDDEN LAWS OF MIRACLES

They read ancient scriptures and saw miracles as defiance—events that shattered the laws of nature, reserved for a singular, divine figure. He multiplied loaves, walked the waves, healed with a mere touch. So, humanity built altars, distantly worshipping, convinced such power could never belong to ordinary hands. Doctrine itself became a curtain, hiding the truth—**persuading humanity it was powerless,** spectators rather than participants.

Yet those signs were never breaking nature's rules—they were revealing them. Matter, at its core, is fluid, dancing to energy and intention. Time is not fixed, but pliable, bending to presence. Bodies respond to belief, and form aligns itself with frequency. **This was the secret he sought to unveil,** not as a distant miracle-worker, but as a master showing what was always possible, if only they could see.

The world, meanwhile, taught the opposite: matter is rigid, time a relentless march toward decay, and humanity is trapped—helpless before an unyielding universe. Those lies were woven by those who stood to gain from fear and submission. They taught obedience, insisted reality was fixed, your role limited, your worth measured by compliance.

But he saw differently, just as every prophet or mystic before or after him. He understood the universe is not conquered by force, but gently shaped by resonance. Alignment with truth unlocks reality's deepest secrets—not because the laws have changed, but because your perception has.

Even science, long resistant to the unseen, has begun confirming what the mystics always knew. Quantum physics shows us that at the smallest scales, particles do not behave like solid objects—they exist as probabilities, influenced by observation itself. The double-slit experiment alone shattered classical assumptions, proving that consciousness directly affects physical reality. Neuroscience, too, reveals the brain can be rewired through focused intention, mindfulness, and belief. These are not metaphors—they're measurable, repeatable phenomena.

Still, the modern world is dense. Information saturates every surface, every screen, every conversation—reinforcing the old paradigm in subtle, relentless ways. **From birth, we are conditioned to trust only what can be proven by consensus.** But awakening isn't rejecting knowledge. It's seeing beyond its limitations. The moment you begin to remember who you are, the world reflexively pushes back, whispering that you're imagining things, overreaching, delusional.

That's why this path, though inward, is not best walked alone. Unraveling the deep conditioning of limitation is nearly impossible in isolation. But in the presence of two or three others—a small circle of shared intent—the programming begins to crack. Truth spoken aloud disrupts illusion. Doubt loses its grip. Reality starts to feel different, not just as an idea, but as a felt shift in the nervous system, a coherence that can be measured, even in heart rate and brainwave synchronization. You begin to remember through each other.

Everything now converges on this hidden blueprint, this unseen tapestry buried beneath centuries of doctrine, ritual, and fear of heresy. It has always existed, humming behind the veil. **He came not to create new rules, but to illuminate what had always been, so your steps might trace the same divine pattern.**

They convinced you miracles belonged only to ancient times—distant, unattainable. But the tapestry remains vibrant today. Every thought, every heartbeat, resonates through the field around you, shaping reality in ways seen and unseen. The "impossible" lies waiting, ready to respond to the slightest shift in your knowing.

You were never powerless, or trapped in an unchangeable world. You've always been creators—breathing within a responsive universe, actively shaping your story with every intention and belief. His purpose was never to amaze or dazzle, but to awaken humanity to this truth: the supernatural is natural, waiting just beneath the surface of perception.

The tapestry of unseen laws—the hidden science of consciousness—is no longer buried. It has been unfolding since the dawn of the new millennia, and it waits now, patiently, for anyone willing to see.

PIERCING THE VEIL

The Universe is older than any temple or creed—fluid, responsive, and deeply interconnected. Matter breathes. Time bends. Death is merely a transition, never the end. This truth disrupts the systems of control, which is precisely why those systems resist it so fiercely.

Religious authorities. Political architects. Corporate empires. Media gatekeepers. These are the ones who have shaped the story of the world—not to liberate, but to contain. They cry out in outrage, labeling such truths as blasphemy or madness, unaware that their anger only reveals a hidden hunger. Those who most forcefully demand silence are often the ones most desperately seeking the freedom concealed within these very words.

Institutions built on fear will always guard their power by condemning anything that threatens to reveal their foundations as fragile illusions. For centuries, high priests and politicians, emperors and bishops, moguls and mouthpieces have appointed themselves guardians of divine truth. **They crafted dogma from pulpits and policy, converting deeper wisdom into dangerous heresy.** By silencing voices that questioned, they fortified their grip, thriving on humanity's fear of separation from God, from truth, from each other.

But their power was always an illusion—propped up by repetition, held in place by the consent of the misinformed. They were never an enemy to conquer—just shadows awaiting the arrival of light.

Beyond their gates, another world awaits—one that recognizes no gatekeepers. Here, consciousness shapes matter, frequency reshapes reality, and the body reflects belief. These principles aren't mystical abstractions. **They are foundational laws, woven into the very fabric of existence.**

This was how separation took root: dividing the world into sacred and profane, holy and unholy. It tracks all the way back to Eden. Man and woman—separate. Man and God—separate. To know is to blaspheme. To be ignorant is bliss.

Yet beneath these divisions lies a deeper truth. To rediscover this is not rebellion, but remembrance—a return to a universal knowing long buried under layers of fear and doctrine.

Science itself, once dismissive, has begun to glimpse this same hidden fabric. Quantum fields dance with possibility, showing that matter is not fixed but responsive to the observer's intent. Spiritual traditions once guarded these insights, but over time, they lost the keys—turning transformative wisdom into ritual, drained of power and meaning.

Yet at their core, all paths converge on three fundamental truths: energy, frequency, and vibration. These are the keys that unlock every so-called miracle, explaining what religion calls divine intervention and science names quantum possibility. They've endured centuries of suppression—standing silently until humanity was ready to remember.

Those who grasped this knowledge were silenced. Dismissed as mystics, heretics, rebels, or lunatics. The institutions feared the empowerment inherent in understanding that reality yields to resonance. But energy pulses through every atom. Frequency shapes every experience. Vibration births creation itself. This triad forms the hidden architecture of existence, waiting to be reclaimed.

The ones who forbade inquiry exposed only their own insecurity. **True power cannot be guarded or hoarded—it must be freely realized within.** Their cries of blasphemy reflect their fear of losing control. Because the moment you remember your true nature, their chains dissolve. You become the creator you've always been, unbound by illusions of limitation.

They worked hard to keep science and spirituality at odds, but both have always chased the same mystery—the invisible laws behind existence itself. Mystics, alchemists, prophets, and now physicists all reveal fragments of the same eternal truth. Jesus didn't operate outside these laws—he moved through them, as a master showing the rest of us the way home.

Now we stand at the threshold of a new understanding. The veil of separation lifts. The journey doesn't end with reverence for the man who transcended physical law. **It begins as we recognize our potential to do the same.**

When Jesus said, "You will do greater works than these," he wasn't exaggerating. He was handing you a blueprint. The same keys he used—energy, frequency, vibration, and love—are within reach. Not miracles. Laws. Not magic. Mastery.

This is the threshold. Not a religion. Not a theory. A living initiation into the truth of who and what you are—and always have been.

REVEALING WHAT LIES BENEATH

Matter is not as solid as it appears—it's energy vibrating at different frequencies. Your beliefs and faith aren't abstract wishes; they are actual vibrational states shaping reality in real time. What exists within you inevitably manifests around you. Sound, light, thought—each is a sculptor, carving your experience into form. Every intention you hold broadcasts a frequency, and reality listens. It responds.

Your body isn't a rigid machine. It's a dynamic, intelligent vessel—constantly responding to consciousness. It can be restored, healed, even transformed when brought into alignment with the core truth of your being. Death, too, is not an end. It's a passage—a threshold into a wider field of awareness. The mind is not confined to the brain. It extends beyond the body, interfacing with a greater field of intelligence, with a reality far vaster than we were taught to perceive.

Jesus never broke the laws of nature. He embodied them. His life wasn't a series of supernatural exceptions—it was a living demonstration of what becomes possible when consciousness harmonizes with the deeper architecture of creation. He wasn't defying physics. **He was moving in perfect resonance with laws most people simply don't know exist.**

Once you grasp this, your perception shifts irreversibly. No longer will you wonder, **"How did Jesus do it?"** Instead, you'll begin to ask, **"Why am I not?"** And that question is the beginning of your return. This isn't mystical idealism. It's the foundation of reality itself—waiting for you to wake up and remember.

THE FIRST KEY: THE SCIENCE OF THE DIVINE

For countless generations—and even now in many ways—humanity clung to a limited view, convinced the universe was a vast arrangement of solid matter. Isolated objects. Fixed realities. What the senses could detect was considered absolute. But that perspective was never complete.

Beneath every form lies a unified field—an invisible architecture intricately woven into all things. Modern physics, through quantum fields and vibrational theories, is only now beginning to uncover what ancient mystics perceived long before particles were named. Everything is energy. Everything is frequency. Everything is vibration.

Reality is not a locked door. It breathes. It listens. It responds. **Consciousness is not a spectator—it's the sculptor.** Jesus never broke the laws of nature. He fully grasped them. When he walked across water, he wasn't defying physics; he was harmonizing with it. When he turned water into wine, he wasn't overriding natural order—he was recalibrating vibrational states. When he healed blindness and restored the broken, he wasn't working against nature. He was bringing it back into alignment.

His actions weren't obscure miracles. They were demonstrations of mastery— evidence of a deeper understanding of how reality unfolds. That knowledge hasn't vanished. It resurfaces now through quantum discovery, ancient alchemical teachings, and mystic revelations. The split between science and spirituality was never real. It was engineered—to make you forget your power, to make you question what you instinctively know.

At its core, reality rests on energy, frequency, and vibration. **On the quantum scale, even what appears solid is simply energy slowed down—dense enough to register to the senses, but never static.** Modern science affirms it: the atoms that make up your world are mostly empty space, their structure sustained by energetic fields and frequencies.

Energy is the essence. Frequency is the rhythm. Vibration gives it form. Waves, stones, and skin differ only by their vibrational tempo. Reality is never fixed. It is molded constantly by consciousness, intention, and resonance. You were taught matter is rigid—unchangeable. But that was never true. Reality is flexible, living, and waiting for your conscious engagement.

Look at your hand. It feels solid, yet at the quantum level, it's mostly empty space—fields of energy vibrating slowly enough to seem real. Those atoms are not objects. **They are patterns—resonant blueprints maintained by frequency.** What you call physical is vibration made visible. You are not separate from this process. You are the frequency-holder. The shaper. The creator. And always have been.

Everything Is In Motion

Physics now confirms what mystics long proclaimed: everything remains in constant motion. Matter is condensed energy, shaped and structured by frequency. Shift the vibration, and form transforms. Elevate the frequency, and reality evolves. Direct energy with intention, and new outcomes begin to manifest.

This is exactly how Jesus moved. He didn't deny nature—he fulfilled it. He saw everything as energy and knew energy responds to consciousness, especially when clearly expressed and modulated by frequency. When he walked on water, he lifted his body beyond the pull of density. When he multiplied food, he quickened energy into tangible abundance. When he healed, he brought the body into resonance with life. These acts weren't supernatural—they were supra-natural: fully natural, but far beyond the limitations taught by conventional perception.

This understanding persists today. Alchemists recorded it. Mystery schools preserved it. And now, modern science rediscovers it. All is energy. Energy follows frequency. Frequency responds to consciousness. Mastering these laws dissolves the outdated belief in separation and helplessness.

Quantum physics names this the Observer Effect—particles exist in wave-like potential until observed. The famous double-slit experiment proves that electrons act as waves until someone watches—then, they collapse into form. Reality holds infinite potential until consciousness selects a path. You are not merely watching the world unfold. You are shaping it.

Jesus made this clear centuries ago:

"**Whatever you ask in prayer, believe you have received it, and it will be yours.**" —**Mark 11:24**

This wasn't poetic metaphor. It was a precise explanation of how reality functions. **Belief is frequency—a steady resonance that causes matter to align and take shape.** Faith was ancient technology. Prayer was alignment, not a distant plea.

Reality yields to the observer—and the observer is you. Change your perception, and reality adjusts in real time. When Jesus healed, he didn't simply hope. He aligned his entire consciousness, leaving no room for sickness or contradiction. He didn't plead—he commanded. His coherence reshaped the field. That same power lives in you.

The double-slit experiment affirms what Jesus embodied: matter responds to consciousness, condensing possibility into form. Once you truly see this, the illusions taught by fear, doctrine, or doubt begin to fall away.

Contemporary research in quantum physics, energy medicine, and epigenetics confirms it: belief is not intangible—it's measurable. A vibrational field radiating outward, influencing physical matter. **Your heart emits an electromagnetic field thousands of times stronger than your brain.** That field affects objects, people, and environments. When your belief becomes absolute, the heart achieves coherence. That coherence stabilizes energy both internally and externally, restoring health, harmony, and vitality.

Studies in heart-based therapies, neurofeedback, and genetic expression show that your emotions and beliefs directly affect immune strength, gene regulation, and cellular repair. Jesus's faith wasn't symbolic—it was resonance. A frequency so clear, it restructured the environment.

"Your faith has made you well." —Luke 8:48.

He didn't chant empty words. He didn't rely on rituals. His faith was a vibrational state—coherent enough to cancel distortion and restore order.

Faith is not blind belief. It is resonance—the frequency of certainty calling energy into alignment with truth. Jesus healed not by force, but through clarity so whole that others naturally returned to coherence in his presence. Illness is energetic discord. Healing is the return to harmonic structure. He mastered that return, and you can too.

Faith is never belief in something far away. It is frequency bringing the unseen into full view, and knowing it now.

For centuries, civilization treated matter as a fixed foundation—solid, unyielding, objective. But modern science has dismantled that illusion. Matter is simply energy vibrating slowly enough to feel solid. **Quantum mechanics shows us that protons, neutrons, and electrons are not solid things, but waves of potential.** Heisenberg's Uncertainty Principle proves that a particle's position and momentum cannot be known at the same time—they don't exist in fixed states. They exist as options.

Consciousness is what chooses. Consciousness is what collapses potential into form.

And that consciousness—has always been yours, always been you.

THE QUANTUM FIELD

Matter is energy. Energy obeys frequency. Frequency follows consciousness.

Einstein revealed that energy and matter are interchangeable (E=mc²)—separated only by vibration. Quantum Field Theory describes particles not as standalone objects, but as excitations within invisible fields. Cymatics proves it visually: sound frequencies shape matter. Centuries ago, Ernst Chladni showed how sound vibrations rearranged sand into intricate, symmetrical patterns. Change the vibration, and reality changes with it.

Thomas Young's double-slit experiment confirmed that conscious observation collapses a wave of probabilities into a single, defined reality. **Masaru Emoto's water studies** added a personal layer—showing that intention and emotion literally restructure molecular form. Words of love and gratitude created crystalline harmony. Hatred and fear produced chaos. One law emerges across disciplines: reality flows, guided by vibration, shaped by consciousness, and ready to align with your frequency.

Your body—composed mostly of water—is constantly shaped by your own energetic emissions. Your heart's electromagnetic pulse influences every cell inside you, and the space around you. Whether you're aware or not, you are always broadcasting frequency. Jesus understood this. He didn't "perform" miracles—he resonated coherence. When he multiplied food, walked on water, or revived the dead, he wasn't manipulating matter. He was harmonizing with reality—and reality responded.

Spontaneous healings are no longer mystical anomalies—they are being verified scientifically. Changes once thought impossible occur through belief, intent, and resonance. **Epigenetics** shows your thoughts and emotions can rewrite gene expression. Consciousness shapes biology. You are not bound by matter—you direct the field that governs it.

You radiate chosen frequencies. You can discard inherited limitations. You can recalibrate the pattern. Your consciousness carves the shape of your experience. This is resonance—not metaphor, but mechanism.

This truth is your first key: matter obeys energy, and energy responds to consciousness. Your body is a living tuning fork—echoing old vibrations or shifting into harmony for healing, clarity, and transformation. Jesus walked in this truth. The mystics preserved it. And now, modern science verifies what has always been known.

You are not waiting for a miracle. **You are built to become one.**

THE SECOND KEY: THE BODY'S TUNING FORK

They told you your body was flesh and bone—mechanical, fragile, destined for decline. That it was separate from mind, spirit, and the living current of the universe. But that vision was never whole.

Your body is not a machine. **It is an instrument—an energetic vessel designed to receive, broadcast, and shape reality itself.** You are not a passive passenger in form. You are a living field of frequency, sculpting your experience with every breath, thought, and intention.

Quantum biology, biofield science, and neurocardiology now echo what mystics and healers have always known: your form is not fixed—it is fluid. More resonance than structure. A symphony of vibration in motion.

FREQUENCIES OF THE BODY

Jesus healed not by force, but by frequency. A single word was enough. He didn't introduce power from outside—he restored what was already present. He returned the body to its native resonance.

"**Your faith has made you well.**" —Luke 8:48

Not I healed you. Not God intervened. But your faith—your alignment—your sustained vibration of wellness. He recognized that healing is not imposed; it is remembered, reactivated through coherence.

The nervous system is not just electrical wiring—it is a living antenna. Continuously absorbing, translating, and transmitting frequency. Every organ, every cell, is alive with energy. This is not metaphor—it's measured reality.

Science now maps the distinct frequencies associated with health and disease. Harmony is literal. A body in balance emits clean, coherent signals. Illness distorts this clarity, dragging the system into dissonance. Emotions are not just reactions— they are vibrational forces that directly shape your biology.

Fear, shame, and anger lower your field. They fragment coherence, weakening the immune system and disrupting cellular repair. But love, joy, gratitude—they elevate. They strengthen. They restore resonance. Healing accelerates when the field stabilizes in truth.

This is why a room filled with fear feels suffocating, while a space infused with joy feels light, magnetic, and alive. No words are needed—frequency speaks first. The body listens.

THE POWER OF VOICE AND INTENTION

Jesus never begged for healing. He never asked reality to change—he commanded it.

"Lazarus, come out." —John 11:43

His voice didn't plead. It resonated. Tone, intention, and clarity aligned so fully that matter obeyed without hesitation. He understood that reality is responsive. That a clear tone spoken in conviction carries the authority to restructure the field.

Your body, your emotions, your words—**all are instruments.** Not just reacting to life, but shaping it. Every moment is an act of creation. And the frequency you hold determines what form it takes.

THE PINEAL GLAND: A BRIDGE TO THE UNSEEN

Deep within the center of the brain lies the pineal gland—an organ long regarded as the seat of inner vision. The Egyptians knew it as the Eye of Horus. In Eastern traditions, it became the Third Eye. It secretes chemical messengers that regulate your perception of light and dark, syncing your body to the cycles of sunrise and dusk. But its deeper role reaches far beyond the physical.

Inside this gland are photoreceptor cells nearly identical to those in your outer eyes—yet their purpose is not to perceive the seen, but to glimpse what lies beyond. Over time, this capacity has dulled. Habit, toxins, and distraction have calcified its gateway. Its channel has narrowed. The lens has clouded. And with it, the vision of truth that surpasses form.

But when awakened, the pineal gland becomes a bridge—a portal between the visible and invisible, the physical and spiritual. **Mystics and prophets throughout history have described visions, revelations, and deep knowing emerging from**

this activation. When the body vibrates at higher frequencies, it becomes receptive to information once hidden from ordinary awareness.

Jesus saw reality not as it appeared—but as it truly was.

THE HEART AS THE TRUE BRAIN

Every organ within you carries a distinct frequency. **This isn't theory—it's measurable.** Your heart generates an electromagnetic field more powerful than your brain's, synchronizing energy and guiding the body into coherence. It is the conductor of your internal symphony.

Emotions like fear, anger, and shame pull the body out of alignment. They distort the signal. They lower the vibration and create fertile ground for illness, fatigue, and confusion. But love, joy, and gratitude bring restoration. They elevate your frequency. They return the body to its original state of strength and order.

Jesus didn't act from intellect alone. He moved from the highest frequency— unconditional love. In that state, creation responded without resistance.

> **"Whatever you ask in prayer, believe that you have received it, and it will be yours." —Mark 11:24**

Not poetic comfort—direct instruction. Faith is frequency. It is the ability to hold the energy of healing, wholeness, or abundance so completely that the body and the world have no choice but to reflect it.

> **"The kingdom of heaven is within you."**

THE BODY IN ALIGNMENT

Your body is a vessel of frequency. When misaligned, it becomes vulnerable— susceptible to the chaos of external influence. But a body tuned to truth, anchored in higher law, becomes resilient. It heals. It transforms. It magnetizes exactly what it needs.

This truth unnerved those who depended on control. Jesus didn't simply teach it— *he embodied it.* The ancients and awakened masters understood the body's deeper nature. They used sound to restore, light to illuminate, frequency to reprogram reality. They weren't practicing magic—they were working with law.

Your body is not solid. It is vibration—shaped by will, guided by emotion, perfected through alignment.

Jesus commanded reality because his vessel was calibrated to perfect love. There was no interference, no distortion, no doubt. And now, you can understand why he continued to remind us:

"The kingdom of heaven is within you."

It isn't repeated so much in this text for no reason. Hold that frequency—and reality must follow.

THIRD KEY: THE FREQUENCIES OF CREATION

Sound and light are not passive forces—they are the invisible architecture upon which reality is built. The ancients knew this intimately, and now, in our time, that truth rises again to the surface.

Every atom vibrates with intention. Each element holds a distinct energetic signature. **Even DNA—the code of life itself—responds directly to sound and light.** Through the ages, the greatest minds in science have continued to rediscover what mystics have always known: sound shapes matter. Low frequencies produce crude, simple patterns. High frequencies generate complex, elegant designs. Resonance organizes all things.

Your body, too, follows this law. Like a living antenna, it receives, interprets, and broadcasts frequency. When attuned to low states—fear, anger, grief—it attracts dissonance, weakness, and illness. But raised into love, joy, and gratitude, it realigns with balance, clarity, and renewal.

What we now call sound therapy or vibrational medicine is not a modern invention—it is a reawakening. Sacred tones were once central to healing, ritual, and spiritual awakening. But that harmony was disrupted. Hidden forces manipulated frequency, severing humanity's natural alignment.

Before World War II, music's tuning standard was deliberately shifted from 432Hz—a frequency aligned with cosmic order—to 440Hz, a harsher, more dissonant pitch. This change, backed by powerful interests, was no accident. Music became a subtle weapon, creating agitation and anxiety, weakening inner coherence. It dulled intuition and severed connection to the natural field.

Beyond music, frequencies have been used as tools of control. Military and intelligence operations explored ultrasonic and infrasonic waves to alter mood, disrupt focus, induce fear. Even broadcast signals have embedded inaudible tones designed to influence emotional states—amplifying division, confusion, and dependence.

A population kept in disharmony is easier to manipulate.

But beneath that manipulation lies the original truth: frequency was always meant to heal, empower, and align. And now, those ancient tones are returning. The Solfeggio scale, once used in sacred chants, is being remembered:

174 Hz eases pain,

285 Hz restores the body,

396 Hz dissolves guilt,

417 Hz clears trauma,

528 Hz renews DNA,

639 Hz strengthens relationships,

741 Hz detoxifies,

852 Hz awakens intuition,

963 Hz reconnects with divine unity.

The evidence is everywhere. The Great Pyramid's King's Chamber resonates at 432Hz. Malta's Hypogeum hums at 110Hz, known to trigger altered states. Stonehenge itself vibrates subtly, enhancing consciousness. These weren't accidents—they were precision designs, tuned to reconnect humanity to harmony.

Ancient mystics preserved these truths in secret, knowing one day the resonance would rise again. That time is now.

Jesus understood this fluently. He didn't ask for healing—he spoke it. Not as a plea, but as a resonance so complete that reality shifted in response. "Lazarus, come out." His voice wasn't force. It was alignment. He held the frequency of life until life returned.

THE TRUE NATURE OF LIGHT

Light is not just brightness. **It is living energy—intelligence woven into form.**
The ancients saw light as the breath of creation itself. Every ray carried encoded
instruction, shaping matter, behavior, and design. Your body doesn't simply detect
light—it decodes it, transforming frequency into emotion, thought, and form.

Modern science now confirms what sacred traditions always taught: light isn't
passive. It's communicative. Biophotons—particles of intelligent light—flow
through your cells, orchestrating healing, regulating DNA, responding to your
conscious state. You are not merely illuminated by light. You are in dialogue with it.

Your consciousness engages light continuously, imprinting it with meaning,
shaping the world you live in by how you feel, think, and see.

Jesus embodied this mastery. He transfigured in light, healed through light,
became light. "His face shone like the sun." **This was not symbolism—it was
demonstration.**

They tried to reduce light to mere illumination. But you remember now: you were
never just a witness. You are a wielder of light.

THE INVISIBLE SPECTRUM

What you see with your eyes is only a fragment. Beyond the visible spectrum lies
vast fields of frequency—waves of consciousness shaping everything. **Technology
already uses this—fiber optics pulse data through light.** Your body does the
same with DNA, transmitting intention through beams of subtle energy.

When Jesus said, "I am the light of the world," and later, "You are the light of the
world," he wasn't being poetic. He was revealing your design. Your purpose. Your
power.

SPIRIT IS RESIDUAL FREQUENCY

What lingers in space is real. Emotion, trauma, joy—these don't vanish. They
imprint themselves on matter. The unseen is not unreal—it's unprocessed.
Residual frequency remains in the air, in walls, in land. Some call it spirit. Others
call it haunting. It is energy, unresolved, echoing.

Jesus understood this. He addressed these distortions directly. "With authority, he commands impure spirits, and they depart.". He did not fear them. He realigned them. He restored harmony where chaos had lodged.

Near-death experiences confirm what mystics always said: death is not an end. It is a return—to light, to love, to truth. People speak of luminous tunnels, radiant beings, and a peace so deep it dissolves every fear. This is not fantasy—it is remembrance.

Jesus knew it well. He spoke of death as transition. Of life as continuity. Of light as the home from which you came and to which you will return.

THE TRANSFIGURATION & THE LIGHT BODY

> "His face shone like the sun, and his clothes
> became white as light." —Matthew 17:2

This was no myth. It was a demonstration. When form aligns with divine frequency, light becomes visible. Tibetan masters have pursued this in the rainbow body. Eastern mystics vanish into radiance. Jesus lived this path—and said you could too.

> "Whoever believes in me will do greater
> works than these." —John 14:12

Yet today, your field is under constant assault. Blue light disrupts sleep. Music detuned from harmony disturbs emotion. Synthetic waves scramble cellular coherence. These are not accidental—they are engineered to suppress your resonance.

But when you reclaim it—when you align with your true frequency—clarity returns. Power returns. Coherence restores.

You are not random. You're radiant.

RECLAIMING THE LIGHT

From the beginning, you were made of light. Your DNA emits it. Your pineal gland transmits it. Your thoughts shape it. Your emotions guide it.

Jesus said, "I am the light of the world," and then: "You are

the light of the world." —John 8:12, Matthew 5:14

These were not metaphors. They were notices. Reminders of who you truly are.

Your body was not built for limitation. It was designed to channel radiance. Every system tuned to respond to divine frequency. Mystics understood this. They guarded it. And now, that wisdom returns.

Your resonance shapes the world around you. Your coherence gives birth to form. In stillness, you remember: you are light. You are frequency. And your consciousness directs them both.

You are not becoming a radiant being. You always were one.

THE FOURTH KEY: HEALING IS ALIGNMENT

Healing is no mystery. *It never was.*

They told you to believe sickness was random. That health was a blessing from above. That wellness was granted, not claimed. These were falsehoods told in fear—crafted to separate you from the truth already written within you.

The masters of old and the seekers of now speak the **same truth:** Healing is alignment. It is a return to the perfect resonance of wholeness.

Jesus broke no natural law—he fulfilled it.

 "Your faith has made you well." —Luke 8:48

Not because of him. Not by divine exception. But because of alignment—because of coherence between belief and being.

Healing is not a test. Not a reward. It is a frequency match. Belief is frequency held. Faith is alignment perfected. Sickness is vibration disturbed. Health is vibration reclaimed.

Your body was made to obey consciousness. It is built to realign, regenerate, and restore. You do not wait for healing—you initiate it. You command it. The body listens. Reality responds.

They told you your body was a machine of flesh and bone, destined to fail and fade.

But that was never true.

Your body is not fixed. It is fluid. Adaptive. Always renewing.

Your skeleton rebuilds every ten years.

Your liver regenerates even when most is removed.

Your stomach lining renews in days.

Your skin sheds and reforms with the rhythm of the moon.

You are not a prisoner of decline. You are a living symphony of renewal.

And yet, sickness lingers. Aging persists. Weakness endures. Why? Because the body follows the signal you send. It mirrors your belief. It tunes itself to your expectation.

Believe in sickness—and it stays. Expect frailty—and it continues. The body obeys the field it receives.

Jesus understood: healing is alignment. Belief is frequency. Faith is coherence.

He did not plead. He spoke. He commanded. And the body responded.

Your body absorbs every word you speak to it. It listens to your knowing. So speak clearly. Speak truth. Command coherence. Hold the frequency of wholeness—and your body will remember.

HEALING IS NOT LUCK, IT'S A VIBRATIONAL LAW.

Healing is not luck. *It is law.*

Your body does not fail because it is broken. It falters when its frequency falls out of harmony. Disease is not a punishment—it is a signal. A disruption in the field. And where there is disruption, there is always a path back to order.

Modern medicine chases symptoms, treating only the visible surface while ignoring the vibrational source beneath. But both ancient wisdom and quantum science proclaim the same truth: All matter is energy. Your body is not just flesh—it is a dynamic field of vibration, constantly adjusting, recalibrating, responding.

When your frequency is high, coherent, and sustained, health is inevitable. When it falls into chaos—scattered by fear, fractured by doubt—dis-ease appears. The lack of ease. This is not poetry. This is physics.

Every cell, every organ, every system within you resonates at a precise frequency. A healthy liver vibrates between 55 and 60 cycles per second. The full body thrives between 62 and 72. Drop below 58, and disease begins. Below 25, life starts to unravel.

This is measurable. This is mapped. Matching frequency neutralizes imbalance— just as a singer's voice can shatter glass with pure resonance. Vibration dismantles distortion. Coherence dissolves disease.

But Jesus required no external tools. He was the frequency. His voice, his presence, his knowing—all carried the resonance of divine order. He didn't fight illness. He restored the original signal.

Cancer, viruses, and inflammation all carry unique vibrational patterns. So do emotions. Fear, grief, shame—these lower your field. They weaken the structure. They open the door to dysfunction. But love, joy, gratitude—these elevate. They re-stabilize. They return the system to its intended rhythm.

Jesus understood this. He didn't heal by hope. He healed by holding perfect coherence—and inviting others to rise into it.

"Take up your mat and walk." —John 5:8

No delay. No ritual. No permission asked. His frequency allowed no other outcome. He embodied alignment so clearly that disorder could not persist in his presence.

Modern healers are now rediscovering what the ancients always knew. Pulsed electromagnetic fields accelerate recovery. Frequency-specific therapies disrupt disease. Sound tones recalibrate the nervous system. This is not alternative—it is original.

You were never meant to decay in silence. You were designed to resonate. To restore. To command your field into harmony.

So the question is no longer whether healing is possible.

The question is: What frequency do you hold?

If your body is out of rhythm, something within you is distorting the signal. Find it. Release it. Return to coherence—and your body will follow.

FIFTH KEY – THOUGHT & EMOTION

Reality is not given.

It is generated.

Matter responds to mind. Energy conforms to belief. This is the law of manifestation: consciousness directs energy, and energy condenses into form. Quantum entanglement confirms an ancient truth: all things are connected, bound within one field, one mind. Distance is illusion. Separation never existed.

Jesus knew this. He healed the sick by collapsing potential into health. He multiplied food by choosing abundance from infinite possibility. He walked on water by aligning his frequency with higher law. He revealed what you must remember:

The world is not made of things. It is made of thought.

Those who master thought master reality. This is not philosophy—this is physics. You now see that consciousness creates. Your beliefs, your thoughts, your emotions shape the world you inhabit. Your mind is the architect of reality. This truth is both ancient and immediate, known yet forgotten. Consciousness creates reality—not metaphorically, not passively, but literally.

You were taught that matter came first, and consciousness was secondary. But this was never true. Matter does not precede mind. It reflects it. Quantum mechanics shows particles exist as waves of possibility awaiting observation. The moment your consciousness observes, potential collapses into reality. Your attention commands form into being.

This is not speculation. It is foundational science, confirmed again and again. Reality waits for consciousness to choose.

"As a man thinks in his heart, so is he." —Proverbs 23:7

Your mind is not passive. It is power itself. Your beliefs shape the world because reality is nothing more than consciousness projected outward. This is why your thoughts, beliefs, and expectations matter profoundly. You are always creating.

Belief is the blueprint. It is not abstract—it is instruction to the field. It defines what your mind permits to exist. Believe in limitation, and you will never see beyond it. Believe in abundance, and unseen paths reveal themselves. Believe in healing, and the body responds, restoring itself naturally.

This is not philosophy either. The placebo effect proves this beyond doubt: a patient believing in medicine heals even when given nothing. Belief alone activates the body's innate systems—hormones shift, cells regenerate, healing occurs. The same holds true in reverse. Negative belief summons decline, illness, and weakness.

Jesus said:

"According to your faith, let it be done to you." —Matthew 9:29

He did not speak in parables. He spoke law. Your beliefs shape reality because your consciousness is always its architect.

Yet belief alone is not enough. It is the blueprint. Emotion provides the fuel. Every thought is electromagnetic, broadcasting signals into the field around you. Your heart radiates a magnetic pulse stronger than the brain, charged directly by emotion.

Fear, doubt, and anxiety emit low, incoherent vibrations—distorting your field and inviting chaos. Love, gratitude, and certainty emit high, coherent signals—restoring harmony, summoning abundance, accelerating healing.

Jesus embodied certainty. He did not plead or hope. He knew. And knowing is the highest frequency of all.

What you focus on expands. Your mind filters reality through belief, attention, and emotion. Focus on lack, and opportunities vanish. Focus on abundance, and new paths appear. This is not psychology—it is quantum biology. Your cells, your DNA, your entire structure responds to belief, emotion, and attention.

He declared:

"As you believe, so it shall be done to you." —Matthew 9:29

Morningstar

Belief designs the blueprint. Emotion energizes creation. Focus directs manifestation. Certainty always prevails. Those who command it become creators—consciously or not.

Expectation is the law behind all others. It is not chance, talent, or effort that moves reality. It is certainty. Expectation is not hope. It is command. It is alignment embodied, and the field responds instantly. You do not receive what you want. You receive what you expect.

Your reality does not respond to words. It responds to your signal. Doubt weakens. Certainty creates.

"Peace. Be still." —Mark 4:39

Jesus was not requesting. He was commanding. He aligned his frequency with divine authority—and nature obeyed.

Thought shapes reality. Emotion accelerates it. Expectation commands it. This is not faith alone—it is function.

Now, do not ask why reality resists change. Ask what frequency you hold. You do not create from desire—you create from alignment. If you are still hoping, you are not yet knowing. And the gap between hope and certainty is where most manifestations dissolve.

This is not exclusion. It is invitation. At any moment, anyone can shift. You can move from wishing to knowing, from waiting to becoming. Stop hoping. Start aligning.

Reality has no choice but to follow.

Now you've received all five keys. Each one builds upon the last. Together, they form a complete system of transformation:

I. Divine energy is everything.

II. Your body is a tuning fork.

III. Frequencies restore and renew.

IV. Healing is energetic alignment.

V. Thoughts and emotions initiate creation.

Use them. They are not theories—they are tools. With them, you can unlock any door.

This is how the world is made new.

This is how creation begins again—with you.

COLLECTIVE CONSCIOUSNESS

The light of the universe does not wait. It declares.

"Whatever you ask for in prayer, believe you have received it, and it will be yours." —Mark 11:24

He did not say, "Wait for permission." He did not say, "Pray harder." He said, "Believe you have received it." Expectation commands reality. Hold certainty, and the world complies.

For thousands of years, humanity misunderstood the nature of reality—not because truth was hidden, but because the collective mind was trained to forget. Every person is a transmitter, a receiver, and an amplifier of frequency. When enough individuals hold the same belief, that belief crystallizes into shared experience. This is collective consciousness.

It is a unified field of thought, emotion, and expectation. Mystics knew it. Quantum science confirms it again. Entanglement, coherence, resonance—these are not poetic metaphors. They are measurable phenomena. The field connecting all people is real, and it responds to the dominant frequency.

Mass fear generates conflict. Collective grief creates collapse. A shared belief in limitation ensures oppression continues. But the opposite is just as true. When enough awaken—when individuals align their frequency with love, truth, and certainty—the field rises. One light ignites another.

"I am in my Father, and you are in me, and I am in you." —John 14:20

Jesus walked with unwavering knowing that his alignment could shift reality itself. By presence alone, he healed crowds, calmed storms, and awakened multitudes. You were not sent to escape the world. You were sent to transmute it.

COLLECTIVE REALITY IS NOT RANDOM

You were taught the world happens to you—that wars, economies, plagues, and rulers act independently of your will, as if life unfolds through random events beyond your influence. That teaching was the first illusion. Reality does not exist apart from you. It is shaped by you—not individually, but collectively.

When groups carry the same beliefs, the same expectations, and the same emotional charge, they form a resonance—a shared vibration that molds reality. **This is not theory. It is observable truth.** During global events marked by grief, celebration, or mass intention, randomness gives way to coherence. Devices designed to track unpredictability register synchronization. Chaos bends to unity.

When masses meditate for peace, war zones quiet. When millions vibrate in fear, systems collapse. Economies and markets prove this. Reality always aligns with the strongest collective signal.

He declared again:

> **"Truly I tell you, if two of you agree on earth about anything you ask, it will be done for you by my Father in heaven." —Matthew 18:19**

He knew that even a small alignment of consciousness could shift the greater field. His frequency calmed storms, dissolved disease, and awakened the masses. The world does not exist outside of you. It reflects exactly what is held within.

Collective fear gives rise to war, sickness, and collapse. Collective love births healing, abundance, and rebirth. Reality is not created in isolation. It is the mirror of what we hold together.

POWER STRUCTURES CONTROL COLLECTIVE THOUGHT

The architects of control understand this truth deeply. They know that whoever shapes perception guides reality itself.

Fear is their strongest weapon. It drags your frequency downward, locking the mind in survival and severing you from your creative force. **A fearful mind cannot imagine new worlds—it can only react to old ones.**

That is why they saturate your senses with anxiety. Governments, media, and even religious institutions echo with messages designed to fracture and divide. Because fearful minds are easy to lead.

Scarcity is their illusion. They teach you to believe in lack, to hoard, to distrust the flow of abundance. Not because scarcity is real, but because belief in scarcity ensures you remain small. If your imagination cannot conceive abundance, it cannot create it.

Division is their method. **They highlight difference—by race, class, creed, or nation—not to celebrate diversity but to fracture unity.** A fragmented people cannot form a collective resonance. A divided people are easily controlled.

Yet their power dissolves the moment you reclaim your own.

Unity renders division meaningless. Abundance exposes scarcity as fiction. Certainty vaporizes fear. The spell breaks when you recognize the illusion for what it is—and *refuse* to participate.

Your alignment is your weapon. The frequency you embody is your revolution. Once you withdraw your consent from the lie, their control collapses.

The system only stands because you believe it.

THE PROGRAMMING OF PERCEPTION

You were taught through fear, scarcity, and division. These signals are not accidental. They are intentional frequencies designed to suppress your power and lower the vibration of the collective field.

You've seen the pattern. First, they manufacture chaos. Then they present themselves as the solution to that chaos. But the destruction was theirs from the beginning. This is not new. It's an ancient strategy, and it only works when you forget your place in the field.

You were told that you don't matter. That one awakened being cannot shift the whole. But that belief is the foundation of separation.

In truth, one aligned individual holds the capacity to influence the entire field. A single coherent frequency brings order to disorder. This isn't a hopeful metaphor. It's structural law.

When you strike a tuning fork, others in proximity begin to vibrate in resonance. One being in coherence restores balance to the space around them. Science calls this entrainment—the principle that unstable frequencies will harmonize around a stable one.

This is why your alignment matters. Your awakening is not isolated. It is a broadcast. A radiant signal that reorganizes the field, stabilizes the energy, and elevates the whole.

Your frequency is the invitation. It calls the world higher.

YOU ARE NOT SEPARATE FROM THE FIELD

By now, you know—there is no such thing as empty space. Everything exists within a field of energy that responds to the frequency you hold. Thoughts, emotions, and intentions aren't invisible noise. They're structuring agents of reality.

You are not moving through a pre-written world. You're co-writing it with every breath, every belief, every pulse of awareness. Your consciousness is not an observer. **It's a force of creation.**

As your vibration rises, the entire system around you adjusts. Your coherence echoes through the web of life. You are not a separate node—you are part of the signal itself. The Monad.

Every shift within you sends ripples outward. You don't simply awaken for yourself. You awaken the field.

FEAR AS THE MECHANISM OF CONTROL

Fear is not just emotion. It's a control frequency—an energetic override code that lowers awareness, weakens the field, and opens the system to external manipulation.

It operates beneath thought. It's not a logical conclusion. It's a disruption pattern. It enters your nervous system, collapses coherence, and reduces perception.

A mind in fear cannot build. It can only comply.

This is why fear is endlessly recycled: fear of failure, fear of loss, fear of death, fear of being seen. The specific fear doesn't matter. Only the frequency. Because that is what keeps the field in submission.

But fear loses its grip when you stop resonating with it.

Jesus held no fear. Even at the edge of death, he said:

> **"No one takes my life from me, but I lay it down of my own accord." —John 10:18**

He did not bow. He chose. Because one who no longer fears cannot be ruled.

This is the blueprint of sovereignty: when fear no longer dictates your state, no force can dictate your reality.

WHAT HAPPENS WHEN YOU RELEASE FEAR

The moment you stop responding to fear, you reclaim control over your field. You stop reacting. You begin creating.

Your system stabilizes. Your clarity returns. Your body moves back into coherence. Your thoughts sharpen. Your perception expands. And you become immune to the manipulation that once governed your decisions.

Fear cannot touch a frequency anchored in truth.

Once your resonance locks into that truth, you cannot be dragged back down. You stop oscillating. You become fixed in signal.

And in that state—

You are untouchable.

You are ungovernable.

You are free.

THE CHRIST MIND AWAKENS

Jesus did not come to be worshiped. He came to demonstrate mastery.

Mastery does not hope. It commands. It does not beg. It aligns. It knows that fear is the only barrier to creation—and rejects it completely. He embodied the consciousness that shapes worlds. That is why the second coming is not the return of a man. It is the rise of the **Christ Mind** within all of humanity.

When you fully realize that you are the creator, you will never bow again.

You were taught that you are flesh—born at the beginning and extinguished at the end. Thrown in the dirt or consumed by fire into ash. But that was always the illusion. You are not a body containing a soul. You are a soul that chose to inhabit a body. Beyond flesh, beyond thought, you are pure consciousness.

The soul is not symbolic. It is the eternal awareness animating all form.

You did not arrive here by accident. You chose this incarnation deliberately, guided by memory, purpose, and knowing. Your soul carries wisdom from other lives, other realms. You came to experience, to awaken, and to remember.

The soul does not decay. It does not die. It is ancient, sovereign, and indestructible. Your body is not your identity. It is your vessel. And you are here to reclaim the truth of what you've always been.

THE TRUTH ABOUT YOUR DEATH

What you call death is not an ending. It is a transition. A threshold. A doorway you have crossed many times before. It does not erase you—it reveals you.

You are not a body with a soul inside. You are a soul experiencing form. Your first breath was not your beginning. Your last breath will not be your end. You existed before time, and you will remain beyond it.

Energy is never lost. It only changes form. The river does not disappear when it meets the sea—it becomes the ocean. The flame does not vanish—it transforms into warmth and rises into unseen realms.

Consciousness follows the same law. It moves through lifetimes, from one body to another, never diminished, never broken. When the body fades, awareness returns to the source it never truly left.

You are not lost in death. You are reclaimed by the field. You are restored to the infinite remembering, where time dissolves and truth remains.

You've walked this path before. You will walk it again. Until the moment comes when you remember fully—so completely—that you no longer need to return.

THE SOUL'S REMEMBRANCE: BEYOND THE KNOWN

And when you do return, it will not be as a stranger, but as one who always knew the way home.

Your soul is not only the observer. It is the creator. It collapses potential into form, chooses from infinite possibility, and shapes reality through attention. Nothing unfolds independently of you. Reality unfolds through you.

You did not incarnate to be punished or tested. You came to remember. Each lifetime is chosen. Each moment designed for evolution, refinement, and awakening.

This is not theory—it is lived truth. Thousands of documented cases confirm children remembering names, cities, and events from lives they never learned. These are not accidents. They are evidence of continuity.

Certain souls return on purpose, continuing ancient missions. Jesus. Lucifer. The Christ. These were not roles assigned—they were choices. Souls who chose to carry frequencies that challenge the entire system. My soul chose this, too, and it has cost me dearly—but the soul does not fear discomfort. It seeks truth. Sometimes I wish I could live in ignorant bliss, it's blissful after all, but my soul will not allow it.

Your soul knows its mission, even when your mind forgets. Awakening is simply the moment you agree to remember.

You were not randomly placed into this life, this era, this form. You chose all of it. And still, you said yes.

Your soul always knew: death is not the end. Transformation is eternal. Jesus embodied this truth when he said:

> **"For this purpose I was born and for this purpose I have come into the world—to bear witness to the truth." —John 18:37**

The point was never to fear death, but to understand it. Once you remember who you are, fear loses all power.

DEATH IS NOT THE END

Most live under the shadow of death—conditioned to fear it as finality, as loss, as annihilation. For generations, this lie was passed down.

Religions used death as punishment. Empires used it to rule. Science painted it as the great void.

But somewhere deep inside, you always knew better.

Death is not the end. It is a return. It does not erase—it liberates. You are not a temporary identity. You are infinite awareness, briefly wearing form, destined to return to the source that shaped you.

And once you fully reclaim that truth, fear can no longer touch you.

WE'RE THROTTLED BY THE FALSE FEAR OF DEATH

Fear of death was never natural. It was taught—passed down by souls who had forgotten. Those who spread that fear were not your enemies. They were lost. Confusing control for safety. Power for protection. They were seeking peace in the wrong direction.

They forgot love. They forgot they were never separate. From the cross, Jesus saw this and said:

"Father, forgive them, for they know not what they do." —Luke 23:34

Those trapped in fear do not need more fear. They need remembrance.

Your certainty becomes their light. Your clarity becomes their invitation. You did not come just to remember—you came to lead.

Death is not a curse. It is a crossing. The soul cannot be destroyed. It is energy. And energy never dies.

THE SOUL'S JOURNEY: PERFECT UNFOLDMENT

Most people move through life believing they are their body—that life begins at birth and ends at death, limited to what can be seen or measured. But this has never been true.

You are not the flesh. You are the force that animates it. Some concepts need to be reiterated because it is so beyond what is known in our world today.

You chose this life deliberately. **This moment, this form, this exact sequence of events—none of it is random.** It's not a punishment. It's not a mistake. It's your design.

Your soul has worn many faces. It has spoken many names. Each life is a chapter in an ancient and ongoing story. And when this one closes, the narrative continues. This lifetime is not the book—*it's a single page.*

You didn't come here to be tested, judged, or broken. You came for contrast. You came to remember what you are by first forgetting.

In forgetting, you gained the power of choice. That's the real gift. Free will wasn't a trap—it was a key.

You are not here out of obligation. You came because you wanted to. Every joy, every hardship, every triumph and heartbreak—you selected it with precision. Not because you needed to suffer, but because your soul knew what it would take to awaken.

Even when your conscious mind doesn't understand, your soul knows *exactly* what it's doing.

THE JOURNEY OF THE SOUL

The ancients never questioned it: the soul is eternal.

The Bhagavad Gita describes the soul changing bodies like garments. Kabbalah teaches gilgul, the cycle of soul return. Early Christian mystics spoke openly of rebirth, before the doctrine was buried by those seeking control.

And today, that wisdom is reemerging. Across the world, people of all ages are recalling vivid memories of lives they've never been taught—languages never studied, places never visited, names never spoken in this lifetime. These aren't fantasies or delusions. Many have been investigated and confirmed. They are fragments of a larger soul memory resurfacing—evidence that the story never truly ends, it only changes form.

You came here to grow, to refine, to reclaim the totality of your being. **When this life ends, the clarity will return.** You'll see the precision in every challenge, every turning point, every so-called failure. You knew before you arrived that you could alchemize all of it into light.

Your path isn't a straight line. It's a spiral—returning again and again, but never the same. Always higher. Always deeper. Always closer to truth.

REINCARNATION: THE RETURN TO REMEMBER

You were taught that this life is your only shot. One chance to earn eternity. Heaven or hell. Reward or punishment. All decided in a single round.

But one life could never contain the fullness of your soul.

You have lived before. You've been warrior and healer, ruler and rebel, parent and child. Not as karmic punishment—but because the soul evolves through experience. It returns because it chooses to.

Reincarnation isn't a sentence. It's a method. A system of remembrance. A spiral of refinement.

The Egyptians weighed the heart across lifetimes. The Hindus and Buddhists saw the wheel not as imprisonment, but as opportunity. Early Christianity once welcomed these truths, until institutional fear buried them.

Origen, one of the Church's original theologians, taught clearly that souls existed before birth and returned again and again until they remembered their origin. That truth was struck from the records—not because it was false, but because it was powerful.

But your soul never forgot.

You may search for proof—in ancient texts, in scientific evidence, in memories that surface without explanation. But even without any of that, there's a deeper voice inside you that already knows.

THE EARTH REMEMBERS TOO

Your soul does not travel in isolation. The Earth itself records every step.

Emotions, trauma, sacred moments—these leave measurable signatures. Energy doesn't just move on. It settles into the field.

Ancient battlefields still pulse with tension. Sacred lands still hum with reverence. Science now detects these anomalies with instruments sensitive enough to read them. What was once called intuition is now being measured.

Even your body carries this memory. **Epigenetics proves that trauma and triumph are passed down across generations**. Your DNA is not just a biological blueprint—it's a record of experience.

You are entangled with the people you've loved, lost, challenged, and forgiven across lifetimes. They are not strangers. They are soul companions, returning again and again, refining each other, remembering together.

The Earth holds your memories. And as you awaken, it awakens with you.

You came back not to escape, but to create. Not to forget, but to finally remember.

You chose this path. You knew what it would cost. And still—you said yes.

RELEASING SOUL CONTRACTS

Your soul is not bound by fate. It evolves by choice. Contracts made before incarnation—agreements to meet certain people, face particular challenges, or resolve karmic patterns—are not prison sentences. They exist to serve your growth. And if you believe they no longer do, you have the power to release them by choosing to release your body. But that isn't revelation, everyone knows this. This is the reason you *never* should.

Release is not escape. When a contract is broken, it sends ripples through the field. Every soul entangled in your journey feels the shift. **Free will gives you the right to end a lesson early, but that lesson doesn't disappear.** It returns—reshaped, intensified, more urgent. Not as punishment, but as opportunity. The soul will always circle back to what is unresolved.

To sever a soul contract prematurely is to disrupt the natural harmony of the collective field. The path not walked becomes the path repeated. **Pain is not something to bypass—it's an initiation.** Avoidance delays mastery. Resistance amplifies what you refuse to face.

Growth requires presence. And when you face what you were meant to embody, everything changes. Struggle transforms into wisdom. Friction becomes fuel. What once felt like burden becomes the birthplace of your clarity.

Your path is not random. You are here with a mission encoded in your very being. Not something external to search for—but something internal to remember. And when that remembering activates, the world responds. Alignments shift. People appear. Timelines accelerate.

You are not here by chance. You are here by choice. And the moment you remember that, your reality begins to obey.

The way forward is not down, it's up.

REINCARNATION AND SOUL EVOLUTION

You are not just a person living one life. You are consciousness in motion—crossing forms, timelines, and dimensions with purpose. You didn't begin here. And you won't end here.

Energy cannot be destroyed. *It evolves.* And your soul mirrors that truth exactly.

Reincarnation isn't a punishment. It's a progression. Each lifetime is a refinement—another step on the spiral. You're not circling aimlessly. You're ascending. Returning, not to repeat—but to remember at a deeper level each time.

It's not a game to win either. You don't strive to come back as the puppy, or the butterfly, you strive to evolve your soul to it's highest form, one that does not even need a body to express through.

All physical expressions are here to learn, none higher or lower.

You chose this incarnation deliberately. Each difficulty, every triumph, all of it aligned with what your soul came to embody. You are not here to pass a test. You are here to remember what you already are.

EVIDENCE OF PAST LIVES

This is not speculation. It's recorded, studied, and confirmed.

Across the globe, thousands of documented cases prove past lives are more than belief. Under hypnosis, individuals recall detailed lives—names, cities, languages, and events later verified through historical archives. These aren't dreams or stories. They are precise memories unlocked through regression, revealing identities they could not have consciously known.

Accounts include memories of rare dialects spoken fluently, obscure historical events described with clarity, and personal details that align with long-forgotten census data and burial records. **Cases have been confirmed by investigators, psychologists, and university researchers alike.**

Near-death experiences add another layer. People report leaving their bodies, entering light-filled realms, and encountering beings who instantly know them—entities not imagined, but remembered. These stories repeat across cultures, religions, and backgrounds with *uncanny* consistency.

Beyond formal research, there's the everyday evidence—the sudden recognition of a place you've never been, the overwhelming connection to a stranger you've just met, the inexplicable pull toward certain time periods or cultures.

And then there are the physical echoes: birthmarks matching old wounds, phobias with no origin, talents you've never trained for yet carry as if remembered.

These are not anomalies. *They are receipts.*

Your soul recognizes those it's traveled with. Deep love, unfinished lessons, unresolved tension—they follow across lives until integration is complete. You are not meeting these people for the first time. You are continuing the conversation.

The soul never forgets. It simply waits for you to remember, and you get to choose if it's in this life or the next.

THE SOUL'S CHOICE: WHY YOU CAME

You are not here by accident. No one ever is.

Before your first breath, your soul chose this lifetime. **It selected your family, your friends, those who would lift you—and those who would test you.** It chose your deepest joys and your most excruciating trials, not to punish, but to awaken. Not to break you, but to call forth what could never emerge without pressure.

Every moment of grace. Every heartbreak. Every so-called coincidence. Your soul selected it all. Not recklessly. Not blindly. But with precision.

Even those who hurt you were part of the agreement. Just as those who loved you unconditionally. Every soul in your orbit, no matter the role, entered this story with you—not for drama, but for evolution.

If you think I wanted to carry what I now remember—if you think I asked to awaken as I did, to fall through layers of illusion until there was nothing left to hold but the truth—you'd be wrong.

I wanted art. Music. *Expression.* To ride the gravy train with biscuit wheels. A life untethered by ancient codes and invisible contracts. **But my life unraveled before I even understood its shape.** I picked up the sword not to heal, but to conquer. I chased validation through wealth, through war, through control. I became everything the world called powerful, successful.

And I forgot who I was.

But it's in the forgetting that the truth returns with force. When the illusion collapses, the soul emerges. And in that emergence, everything changes.

Every fall was the map. Every collapse was the call. Every loss, a doorway back to self.

This is the soul's contract: to descend, to forget, to be broken open—and to rise remembering.

This text isn't written for the poorest of the poor or the richest of the rich, that would be too easy of a text to author. This is for the moveable middle.

The 90% of people on Earth who believed the same delusions I did, who were just comfortable enough to remain uncomfortable with their situations.

ACCEPT IT: YOU CHOSE IT

Yes. You chose it—fully, knowingly. Your role isn't to argue with it, or find ways that isn't true. Your role is to figure out why you chose it, and then realize it's potential.

That truth marks the threshold. The moment where blame dissolves, where victimhood is released, and where your true power is reclaimed.

You knew before you came what this path would require. The forgetting. The disconnection. The illusion of separation. And still, you said yes. Because beneath it all, your soul knew it could not be destroyed. Only rediscovered.

This is not spiritual passivity. **It's radical accountability.** It's the decision to stop outsourcing your life to circumstance and begin embodying your divine authorship.

Below this acceptance lies distortion—stories of injustice, helplessness, and lack. But above it lies mastery. And freedom.

You did not come to survive your conditions. You came to transform them. You came to illuminate shadow. To walk into density and carry light. To embody divinity in a world that forgets what that looks like.

You are not just conscious. You are consciousness embodied—fully awake, fully aware, fully aligned.

This is the moment. Accept it. Claim it. *Step forward.*

THE PATH OF THE AWAKENED

Until now, your awakening has lived mostly in the mind. Insight. Understanding. Perspective. All vital. But all preparatory.

True awakening begins where thought ends.

It's not something you think through. It's something you embody. It's the moment everything you've known collapses—and only truth remains. A truth that cannot be debated, only lived.

This path demands everything false to fall away—your titles, your masks, your borrowed beliefs. It strips you bare until only the authentic remains.

And when that happens, the life you once called yours becomes too small to contain you.

You've outgrown old fears. Old comforts. Old systems. And now, the invitation is clear: step forward.

There is grief in leaving the familiar. But what you gain is immeasurable—freedom, power, truth, and a version of you that cannot be shaken.

You stand at the edge of the threshold. The Path of the Awakened stretches before you—not as an escape from life, but as a complete arrival into it.

Your soul is ready. Even if your mind still lingers.

The next step isn't about waiting. It's about becoming.

Walking The Path of the Awakened.

This is the turning point. *Choose it.*

XII

THE SIXTH RESOUND

THE PATH OF THE AWAKENED & THE
SILENT ACCORD

"IT DOES NOT EASE YOU
GENTLY INTO CLARITY. IT
BURNS THROUGH EVERYTHING
FALSE—CONSUMING ALL YOU'VE
MISTAKEN FOR SAFETY. "

THE SIXTH RESOUND
THE PATH OF THE AWAKENED &
THE SILENT ACCORD

Awakening has a cost. They don't tell you this. It's not in the brochure.

It isn't written in holy texts. It isn't carved in stone. You won't find it in the glowing words of spiritual marketing. They speak of light, peace, enlightenment. *And they're not wrong.*

But they forget to mention the fire.

Not the gentle kind—the one that warms you while you meditate, journal, and sip tea. No. The fire that comes for everything false. The fire that doesn't ask. It dismantles.

It burns through every mask, every identity you clung to, every comforting lie you believed about who you were supposed to be. It doesn't soothe. It consumes.

This fire takes the life you built on survival, on approval, on false belonging—and turns it to ash. It leaves you stripped, exposed, and raw. You will grieve what falls away. You will try to run back into the burning house just to retrieve one more piece of your old self.

But this path makes no exceptions. There are no shortcuts. No compromises. No refunds.

No one warns you, because those who've crossed through understand—words don't prepare you. This gate must be passed alone. **And until you're ready to let the fire do its work, it waits.**

But once it finishes, once the destruction is complete and the smoke clears, what remains is the only thing that was ever real.

The self that rises from the ashes is the one you came here to become. The one that remembers. The one that knows what freedom really costs—and why it's worth everything.

YOU MUST PAY THE TOLL

For a long time, I thought I was awake. I thought understanding meant arrival. I mistook self-awareness for transformation. I kept my distance from the edge, dipping my toes into truth but never letting go of the shore.

Awakening doesn't care about your timing. It doesn't check your comfort. It comes when it's time.

When it finally grabbed me—when I let go of needing to know everything first— everything I was holding together fell apart.

I wanted awakening, on certain conditions.

I spent most of my life walking on crutches no one could see. I was told from the start that something inside me was broken. That I needed fixing. So I medicated— not out of desire, but because I believed it was the only way I could function, the only way I could belong.

But I was never meant to belong to a system built on suppression.

It wasn't just the prescription. It was the constant cycle—stimulants, caffeine, nicotine, other things my children shouldn't read—speeding up to perform, numbing down to cope. Always chasing productivity. Always fearing collapse.

Morningstar

The world taught me to equate exhaustion with worth. Performance with love. Control with safety.

And so I pushed. Until I couldn't. Until the structure I built could no longer hold the weight of who I really was underneath it all.

That collapse wasn't failure. It was the toll.

It was the cost of finally becoming free. Even after you do it, residual payments may come due. The Sicilian Mirror reminded me of this.

THE RECKONING OF RESPONSIBILITY

A woman once read my Chakral energy. She looked at me—straight through me—and said, "You're too responsible. It's like you're restricted." Her words struck me with undeniable clarity. Because she was right.

I carried the weight of everyone around me. I believed I had to. I thought that's what made me good enough, strong enough, worthy enough. But all it really did was trap me.

My time in military service taught me many things: sacrifice, endurance, how to suffer, how to break my body, my mind, my spirit for an idea. I learned to stand for those who couldn't stand for themselves, to oppose oppression wherever I saw it.

Yet I also discovered how easily one becomes oppressed by their own story— how effortlessly survival can become identity. That's exactly what I did. I built an entire life around being too responsible because it was safe, because it meant no one could accuse me of not doing enough. But in that safety, I lost myself.

I returned to work, tried caring about selling life insurance, tried getting excited about investment strategies and marketing hacks. And for a while, it worked. Because I knew all the tricks. I could persuade people, move people, make them act.

But none of it mattered. The more I woke up, the clearer I saw through it all. The game was rigged, and I no longer wanted to play.

I spent years chasing wealth, convinced it was my purpose. But now wealth no longer defines me. It can't. I don't even understand now how it ever did for me.

My family has everything we need—we lack nothing. Yet for so long, my net worth was my self-worth.

Remember this too friends, even after awakening you may not have relationships show up in the same way as before:

> "Truly I tell you, no prophet is accepted
> in his hometown." —Luke 4:24

When that illusion finally collapsed, I was free. But freedom always comes with a cost, and I paid it through loss of my entire personality structure, almost overnight.

THE COLLAPSE OF CONTROL

I spent years trying to control everything around me. My wife. My ex-wife. My kids. My business. Because deep down, I didn't trust myself to simply be.

Every time I tightened my grip, they pushed back. Not because they were defiant or unloving—but because what I was truly trying to control wasn't them. It was me. Everything I denied in them, I had already denied within myself. Their resistance was my reflection. When I finally opened my eyes, the truth became clear:

They were never the ones who needed to change.

It was always me.

THE WEIGHT OF POWER & BURNING TRUTH

I used to crave power. It made me feel safe. It drove every decision I made, every move I calculated. But the deeper I journeyed into awakening, the clearer it became: power isn't strength—it's responsibility.

When you wield power without abusing it, it will drain you completely. I carried the weight of everyone around me—their success, their safety, their happiness— because no one ever carried it for me. I was determined to be the protector I never had. But the burden exhausted me, until I was empty.

And in that emptiness, clarity emerged.

Real power isn't found in people, titles, or control. Real power belongs only to truth. When you walk fully in truth, every lie you ever believed begins to fall away. And the person you meet in the mirror can be terrifying—because everything you once thought defined you, everything you believed made you whole, starts burning to ash.

What remains is raw, exposed, vulnerable. Yes, it's painful.

And yet, in that moment, you become more alive than you've ever been.

PICK UP YOUR MAT AND WALK

I was thirty-seven years old—almost thirty-eight—and I was still sitting there. Like the man by the pool in the Book of John, waiting. Waiting for someone to come and save me. Waiting for someone to lift me up and carry me into the water.

But after my revelation, after my past life regression, after the knowing that ignited my soul like wildfire—I finally heard it. Not in words, but in tone:

"**Pick up your mat and walk, Yoshai'el.**"

And so I did. But it wasn't, "Pick up your mat and write a book that changes millions of lives," or "Pick up your mat and say things you'd never dreamed you'd say." It wasn't, "Pick up your mat and start healing people, walking on water, turning metal into gold, restoring sight to the blind, or rub every religion the wrong way and indict the Catholic Church."

All I needed to do was pick up my mat and walk.

Choosing the destination would have limited everything. It would have anchored me to outcomes smaller than what the universe had planned. Defining the journey would have placed boundaries around a purpose far beyond my imagination.

My only task was to take the step, trust the unfolding, and allow my soul to guide me somewhere infinitely greater than anywhere I could ever conceive on my own.

AWAKENING HAS A COST — THE OLD

They told you awakening was peace. A gentle rising. A soft sunrise. But they did not tell you it is like stepping onto the Sun.

It does not ease you gently into clarity. It burns through everything false—consuming illusions, devouring every carefully constructed lie you've mistaken for safety. Awakening tears through the comfortable life you built, leaving behind only what is real.

It will cost you—your beliefs, your attachments, the small identities that kept you safely hidden. Even ones you didn't know you had. Awakening is not a gentle gift. It is a reckoning. A dismantling of everything you once believed was you.

The person you thought you were will not survive this.

Because awakening demands authenticity above comfort. Truth above illusion. The world you knew will no longer fit. Friends will drift. Connections will dissolve. You will no longer be bound by the rules of those who fear change.

They will call you lost. *Radical. Blasphemer. Dangerous.*

A heretic who threatens the old ways.

They cast out those who refuse to bow. They crucify the ones who speak the forbidden truth. Later, they build shrines to the prophets they once silenced—worshiping the very voices they tried to erase.

But truth cannot be contained. It does not ask for permission.

In this fire, you will lose everything you thought mattered. Yet from the ashes, you will reclaim yourself.

And that alone is worth every loss—because what you receive is the Kingdom.

DO NOT GO GENTLY

They did not tell you it would rip apart everything false. They did not warn you that awakening arrives like a thunderclap, shattering your comfortable illusions, shaking the very foundations of who you believed you were. This force does not whisper—it roars. It rages. It ignites.

All your life, you built walls to survive, constructed identities from shadows because the truth felt too bright to bear. But awakening will not politely dismantle what you carefully crafted. **It strikes like lightning—burning away every deception until only your raw, naked self remains.**

It is not gentle. It is fierce, relentless, unforgiving. It is the death of your old story, the collapse of all that was never real, the brutal stripping away of every lie you've ever told yourself. And yet, from these ruins, something true rises—something powerful, something eternal.

Do not close this book and return quietly to the darkness. I'm not even sure you could at this point. Do not surrender your awakening to the comfort of old illusions. I have lit a fire within you, a spark the world is determined to extinguish—because your truth threatens everything built upon separation, fear, and control. It's time to stoke it.

The collective consciousness still struggles to hold this truth. It will push back, attempting to lull you back to sleep, to dim the light within you. You will feel its resistance—soft whispers of doubt, harsh shouts of judgment, persistent pulls toward conformity.

Do not yield. Rage, rage against that dying light.

This is your moment to resist the call of the familiar, to stand defiant against the pull of the collective's slumber. You must fight with every breath to protect the fire of your awakening. Guard it fiercely. Nurture it boldly. Until it blazes so brightly the darkness flees before you.

Do not go gently into that good night—rage, rage until the world remembers who you are. Until you remember who you are.

THE TWO PATHS AFTER AWAKENING

Most people believe that once you awaken, the hard work is done. They imagine enlightenment as a destination—a state of pure clarity, radiant ease, and effortless peace. But true awakening is not a gentle arrival. It is a relentless call to action, demanding you live the truth, moment by moment, breath by breath.

The instant your eyes open, the moment you glimpse reality stripped bare, you face a crossroads: return to pretending you never saw the truth, or step fully into the shift and allow your former self to fall away.

Most choose the comfort of illusion. Not because they doubt what they've seen. Not because they didn't feel the shift within. But because the path forward is brutal. It means surrendering everything you once were. Risking rejection from those who only knew the shadow of you. Standing alone while the world you once fit into falls apart around you.

The ego resists fiercely because it values survival above freedom. It will cling desperately to the illusion it built, preferring a life half-awake over the death required for rebirth. This is why countless souls touch the threshold of awakening but remain stuck—trapped in old patterns they cannot release.

I couldn't live another day pretending to be some person chasing money and status so I could feel whole when I already knew I was.

This was the truth Jesus illuminated when he declared:

> **"Whoever wants to save their life will lose it, but whoever loses their life for me will find it." —Matthew 16:25**

Because awakening demands a death—final, absolute, irreversible. Most shrink away from this truth. But those who do not, those who face it boldly, become beings no longer bound by the world they once knew.

You always have a choice.

You can return to the cave, retreating into familiar shadows. No one will drag you forward. Awakening does not force itself upon you—it waits. Patiently. A beacon in the dark.

Even if you turn away, even if you close your eyes and go back to sleep, the truth remains. It waits for you, or for your child, or for the one who comes after. This is the nature of free will: Awakening is always ready, always patient, forever waiting until you are willing to choose it.

And when you are ready—it will be here.

And you will not journey alone.

WHAT HAPPENS AFTER AWAKENING – THE FOUR PHASES

When the veil lifts, when illusions shatter, when the false world burns away, the true path reveals itself—not gently, not softly, but fiercely. Awakening is never a single moment. It is a relentless passage, a refining fire, an unending cycle of breaking and becoming.

Your old self will resist. It will fight to preserve what it knows, clinging desperately to illusions that once felt safe. But awakening allows no compromise. It demands your whole self—every false belief, every comforting lie, every shadow that kept you small—until nothing remains but truth.

I. THE PURGE

Everything false falls away, and the life you once knew unravels beneath you, thread by thread. The familiar becomes uncertain. The stable ground trembles. Your old ways dissolve no matter how tightly you cling.

Your mind resists fiercely, longing for the comfort of the known, but there is no going back. The person you once were no longer fits the spaces you used to occupy. The places you called home now reject what stirs within you, because awakening creates friction against all that remains asleep.

But in this unraveling lies the gift. **The self you constructed from fear, from conformity, from the need to be accepted—that self cannot survive.** In its place, your true identity emerges. Raw, yet powerful. Unrecognizable, yet profoundly familiar.

Allow the false to collapse. Let go of what was never real. The path before you demands authenticity at every step.

II. THE ISOLATION

Silence deepens. Distance grows. The voices that once brought comfort no longer speak your language. The spaces that once embraced you now feel hollow. You begin to see how much of your former life was rooted in survival, not truth.

The path narrows, and the world you've known falls away. The familiar cannot follow where you're going. **This solitude is not punishment—it is initiation.** You stand at this threshold, alone yet not abandoned, guided now by something more powerful than comfort—the truth.

III. THE REFINEMENT

The weight of all that was falls away, leaving you raw, unshaped, pure. The fire strips everything that cannot continue. Nothing unnecessary survives. Nothing false is carried forward.

Your hands no longer move from habit. You speak with intention. You build only in alignment with the truth that now pulses within you. You are becoming precise. Clean. Whole. This is not suffering—it is sacred sculpting. The soul forging its form.

IV. THE MASTERY

The one who walks now is not the same soul who began this journey. The old self has died. The chains have fallen away. You are no longer bound by approval, expectation, or fear.

Seeking ends. Waiting ends. You no longer ask for permission. You no longer wear the masks the world gave you. **There is only presence now—clarity in motion.**

Most never reach this point. Many turn back in the fire, retreating to familiar shadows, grasping at the ashes of what no longer exists. But the path remains. It does not waver. It does not demand. It simply waits.

Mastery is not a peak. It is a rhythm. A state of being where truth leads, and all else falls away.

And those who continue walking come to understand: the journey never ends— because the soul never stops becoming.

WHY THE WORLD MAY REJECT YOU

The world does not yet celebrate those who awaken. It does not yet welcome those who refuse to kneel. It does not yet embrace the souls who have seen beyond the veil. Because the system was never built on truth—it was built on control, rooted in fear, obedience, and the illusion of safety. To awaken is to step outside that design, to see the bars of the cage and realize they were never locked. The moment you walk freely, you become a threat. Not because you are wrong, but because you are no longer able to be governed. The machine doesn't know what to do with a soul it cannot manage. It doesn't run on freedom. It runs on dependency—on people waiting for permission to be what they already are.

Once the illusion breaks, you can no longer be told who to be. You become unshakable. And that kind of clarity, in a world built on deception, is dangerous. You won't be celebrated immediately. **You won't be welcomed like Jesus was— not yet.** You'll be rejected, because awakening dismantles everything that holds the old world together. It strips the masks, breaks the hierarchy, threatens the power of those who depend on your blindness. So they cast you out, while elevating the hollow, while worshiping idols with nothing to offer but silence and compliance.

Jesus said:

"You will be hated by everyone because of me, but the one who stands firm to the end will be saved." —Matthew 10:22

Not because truth is wicked, but because it exposes everything that isn't real. Once you see through the illusion, nothing can hold you. You stop fearing death, so religion loses its grip. You stop fearing lack, so money can't enslave you. You stop fearing judgment, so society can't shame you. You stop needing approval, and every system built on control begins to collapse. You become free. And there is nothing more threatening to illusion than a soul that cannot be owned.

EMBRACE WHY YOUR OLD LIFE IS FALLING APART

Most people don't realize that the hardest part of awakening isn't seeing the truth—it's losing the life that made the lie feel safe. You start to see through everything, and everyone, and suddenly you're no longer welcome where you once belonged. Not because you've done something wrong, but because you no longer fit the frequency they're still choosing to live in. What once felt like home begins to feel hollow. What once felt like connection starts to echo with silence. It's okay, it's intended. Proceed.

You are not being punished. You are being transformed. Everyone and everything that cannot meet the new you begins to fall away. It's not spite. It's not betrayal. It's resonance. You've changed stations, and they're still tuned to the old signal. You're a mirror now, and your presence reflects the truth they aren't ready to see. So they push you away. They call you arrogant, ungrounded, unstable. But what they're really saying is: I'm afraid of what your freedom means for mine.

This isn't loss. It's proof. **The life that's breaking down around you is doing so because it was never built to hold who you really are.** Let it collapse. Let it clear space. Every connection you outgrow, every room that no longer feels safe, every goodbye you didn't expect—it's all making space for the people and places that match your becoming.

Even the most celebrated version of the old world—the wealth, the status, the empire—ends the same way. You still die. You still return. And when you do, you'll see that none of it filled the ache inside. Because that emptiness wasn't lack of success. It was a soul begging to remember itself. No amount of money can answer that call. No amount of fame will quiet that hunger.

Even with 7 billion social media followers, you would still wonder who you mattered most to, or if you did at all.

This isn't sacrifice. This is alignment. Awakening doesn't require you to reject abundance—it teaches you how to receive it clean. It doesn't forbid joy or rest—it makes them real. When you live aligned, even your pleasure becomes sacred. Even your rest becomes prayer. You don't lose anything that mattered. You release everything that never did.

You are part of a wave now. A historic shift in consciousness designed to awaken humanity from sleep. You didn't stumble here. Your soul chose this moment. **And yes—your life will be extraordinary.** Not because you forced it, but because you aligned with what was always yours. You'll live fully, without compromise. You'll breathe the air of your own becoming and finally taste what freedom was meant to be.

So let the old fall. Let the life you once built dissolve. You're not being stripped—you're being cleared. Cleared for everything your soul has been waiting to receive.

This is not just the death of what was.

It's the beginning of everything that can now be.

NAVIGATING THE WORLD'S REJECTION

"Behold, I make all things new."

These were not poetic words. They were a command. A force. A frequency that disrupts everything false. When you step into Christ Consciousness, the world can no longer contain you. Your presence becomes a fracture in the illusion—an embodied reminder that everything they built on fear is temporary.

To those still clinging to comfort, your truth feels like fire. Your voice sounds like disruption. Your light exposes every mask, every compromise, every moment they chose silence over soul. And they won't thank you for it. They'll recoil. They'll call you deluded, dangerous, unstable. Especially if they once loved you.

Especially if they still need you to stay small for their benefit.

But make no mistake—they are not rejecting you. They are rejecting the part of themselves they're not ready to face. You didn't change. You remembered. And remembering always threatens a world addicted to forgetting.

You will feel their resistance. It will sting. **But it is not the end—it is confirmation and affirmation.** Your rejection is proof that your frequency has shifted. The old world no longer fits because you are no longer its prisoner. You are rising. And everything not meant for this level must fall away.

Trust that. Trust the emptiness. Trust the shedding. What's coming will fill the space you're clearing now. What's next will make sense of everything you've lost. And you will not walk this path alone.

Others are rising with you, lighting torches from the same divine spark. And together, you will become the fire the world cannot put out.

EXPERIENTIAL ACTIVATION

These practices are best done with a guide—someone you trust who can walk you through the journey while you stay fully immersed. If you're doing it alone, speak each section aloud or record it in your voice first. The imagination is a powerful gateway, but shared energy amplifies clarity. Use what serves you.

I. ENTER THE LIVING TEMPLE OF LIGHT

Close your eyes. Take a breath. Let your body settle. Let the thinking mind rest.

Now, picture yourself stepping barefoot onto polished marble—cool, smooth, alive beneath your feet. Veins of gold and silver glow beneath the surface, pulsing with a gentle rhythm, as if this place is breathing with you. Above, arches rise endlessly, supporting a sky of luminous brilliance. **This is not sunlight, nor flame—it is something higher.** Light unbound.

There is no judgment here. No weight. No pressure. This place recognizes you immediately. You are known. You are welcomed.

Let yourself walk forward. Every step takes you deeper into presence. The air hums—not as sound, but vibration. It moves across pillars, walls, floor, as if the entire temple is made of presence itself.

You are moving toward the *heart* of the temple now. Not hurried. Not hesitant. Simply drawn. The space holds you as you walk—a vastness that doesn't overwhelm, but steadies. At the center, you arrive. You stand where countless awakened souls have stood before. You are not alone in this. *Not ever.*

Feel the warmth now—not soft, not fragile. But fierce. It is the love that ends empires. The love that does not bend, or break, or yield. And it sees you.

II. SUMMON THOSE WHO REJECT YOUR LIGHT

Now, call forward the faces of those who have turned away. Those who questioned you. Judged you. Dismissed you. Or simply drifted as your light grew brighter.

You do not need to force them forward—just let them appear. Let them stand at the threshold of this temple. Some will stay in shadow. Some will linger at the edges. Some will look confused, even hurt. This is not your task to fix. Just see them. Not as enemies. Not as burdens. But as mirrors—reflections of who you once were.

Let the first sting rise. It's okay if you feel pain, grief, or longing, or anger. It doesn't mean you've failed—it means you've loved. You remember what it's like to resist the truth. To cling to comfort. To turn away from the light when it burned too bright.

Now, let them feel your presence—not to convert, not to convince, but to simply offer what you've received. Let them stand exactly where they are, without pulling them forward or pushing them back. Love does not force—it allows. When they're ready, they'll step into their own awakening. And when they do, they'll remember that you stood here, waiting—not with pride, but with grace.

III. STAND IN THE CHRIST CURRENT

Breathe in. The air thickens—not heavy, but holy. The ceiling of the temple begins to dissolve. The sky disappears. No stars. No heavens. Just a radiant glow—golden-white and everywhere at once. This is not something coming down. It is something waking up. You've never been outside it. You've only forgotten.

Let it move through you now. Entering gently through the crown of your head. Pouring down your spine. Flowing through your heart. Your hands. Your feet. Not rushing. Not pushing. Just... returning.

You do not resist it. You do not reach for it. You do not even receive it. You remember it.

Breathe in: "I am made new."

Breathe out: "I stand unbroken in truth."

There is nothing to prove here. Nothing to fix. The light is not here to test you. It is here to remind you. You have always been part of it. You are not awakening into something foreign—you are remembering what has always been true.

Stand in this current for as long as you need. Let it clear what must be cleared. Let it steady what has wavered. Let it bring you back—not to who you were, but to who you've always been.

When you are ready, open your eyes. Gently return.

Bring with you the knowing: You are not separate. You are not lost.

You have already stepped into the Temple. And the Temple is you.

IV. CONFRONT THEM IN LOVE, NOT SUBMISSION

Turn now to the first person who stands before you. Let them speak. Let them judge. Let them call you whatever they need to call you. You do not brace. You do not bow. You do not match their projection. You simply remain. You radiate—not to overpower, not to impress, not to force them into awakening—but because radiance is your nature. It is what you are.

Their words pass through you like wind through an open doorway. They move, but they do not move you. You are still. You are clear. You are rooted in truth.

Speak inwardly—or aloud if you are guided to—so they may feel it:

> **"I see you in your self-imposed separation. I see your need to reject what you do not yet recognize as your own reflection. Yet I stand here, in this living light, in unity, in peace, in love."**

These are not weapons. These are not arguments. These are not defenses. These words create no distance. They are presence. They are clarity. They move through the temple like breath—soft, full, infinite.

You will notice a shift. Some may recoil, pulling back into the safety of their old narratives. Others may look away, afraid of what your stillness reveals in them. A few may soften, not yet understanding why, but feeling something dissolve beneath the surface.

Let it be what it is.

There is no war here. No enemy. No side to win. There is only love. And love will do what love has always done—exactly what is needed.

V. DISSOLVE THE JUDGMENT IN THE RIVER OF CHRIST

Now the space between you begins to move—not from your doing, but from something ancient, something alive. A gentle river forms beneath your feet, gliding across the floor of the temple. It glows softly—not white, not gold, but the color of pure memory. **This is the river of Christ.** It is not metaphor. It is frequency. It is love in motion.

It does not rush. It does not rage. It simply flows, as it always has, with the grace to carry all things that no longer serve.

Turn inward. Bring your awareness to your chest. Slowly raise your hands, palms open, as if holding something unseen. Feel the weight—foreign, but familiar. Not yours, yet somehow you've carried it. The judgment. The projections. The misunderstanding. The burden of their confusion, placed upon you as if it were truth.

See it now. Let it take form—not literal, but energetic. Gray, smoky, weightless yet heavy. It lingers in your hands, ready to leave.

Breathe in: steady.

Breathe out: slow.

Step forward. Let your hands dip into the river. Watch as the smoke dissolves—not fought, not forced, just released. Gone.

Whisper gently:

> **"I send this judgment to the river of Christ's love. It is no longer mine to carry."**

Feel the release. Feel your chest soften. Your shoulders drop. Your breath return. You are not here to hold what was never yours. You are not here to carry pain for others. The river takes it, and love remembers what to do with it.

VI. LET THEM CHOOSE THEIR PATH

The burden is gone. The field is clear. Nothing weighs on you now. The moment is still—and it is not yours to move.

You are not here to convince them. You are not here to save them. You are here to stand in truth.

Look at them one last time—not with sorrow, not with hope, but with love. Love that holds no condition. Love that makes no demand. Say the words—not to persuade, not to control, but to release:

> **"You are free to reject me.**
> **I am free to live this truth."**

Then stand. Don't shrink. Don't chase. Let your chest stay open, your heart steady, your presence unshaken.

The light doesn't beg. It doesn't explain. It doesn't reach for what won't receive.

It simply is.

And when they're ready— they'll know exactly where to find it.

AWAKENING DESTROYS YOUR EGO

The space between you is clear now. The judgment is gone. The weight has dissolved. And yet—they remain.

Some stand defiant, rooted in the certainty that once protected them. Their arms crossed, jaws clenched, hearts sealed behind doors they still aren't ready to open. Others begin to drift, pulling back—not with hostility, but with hesitation. They are not ready to step forward, yet not ready to walk away. A few soften. They don't speak. They don't move. But something shifts—something stirs behind their eyes. Recognition. Not fully formed, but beginning. *That's all it takes.*

Let them stay where they are. **Let them hold the ground they still believe they**

need. You don't have to pull them forward. You don't need to lead them out. Your work is not to fix. It's to be.

They taught you that ego was your sense of self. That it was confidence, identity, importance. But ego is none of those things. **Ego is a patchwork of labels you've clung to for safety.** A structure of roles and titles: Father. Mother. Artist. Leader. Outsider. Success. Failure. These were never the truth. They were armor.

When you awaken—truly awaken—the armor starts falling off. Not gently. Not in stages. But all at once. The identities you built to survive begin to dissolve. Not because you failed, but because they were never real to begin with. Awakening doesn't refine your ego. It dismantles it. It doesn't elevate your story. It exposes it for what it was—an echo of who you thought you needed to be.

This is why the ego fights. This is why it clings. It senses its end. It knows that if you stop needing to be someone, it loses its power to define you. It cannot survive your freedom, your ascent to the summit.

So do not fear when awakening tears the names from your hands. Do not flinch when the story you once clung to burns in the fire. It is not cruelty. It is clarity. It is liberation.

Jesus did not cling to the names the world gave him. He did not root himself in status or seek the validation of men. He allowed others to call him carpenter, rabbi, blasphemer, messiah. But none of it held him. He refused to be bound by titles. He let divine truth speak through him without filter, without apology, without needing a name to justify its presence.

And now, it is your turn.

Are you ready?

The call is not to become something greater. It is to let go of everything that was never you.

You do not need a better version of yourself. You need to remember who you are when all the stories fall away.

Pulling Illusions Into The Heart

This is not a visualization for relaxation—it is an energetic operation designed to dismantle the false self. In this guided experience, you will confront the roles, labels, and identities you've carried, consciously release them into the heart center, and witness what remains when illusion is stripped away. **I will remind that, while it can be done alone, it is often more powerful with a trusted guide who can read it aloud as you move through each stage.** This is a process of reclamation, clarity, and emergence—a direct encounter with the truth of who you are.

I. IDENTIFYING THE LABELS

Sit in stillness. Let your breath slow. Let the surface mind fall away.

Now see it: a vast chalkboard stretching wide in front of you. It is empty at first, but its silence is heavy—pregnant with all the names you've ever carried.

Watch as the words are born, one by one, written in chalk. The names, the roles, the labels. "I am a mother." "I am a failure." "I am strong." "I am unlovable." "I am a leader." "I am nothing." Some contradict each other. Some repeat. Some were given to you by people who never truly saw you. Others you claimed yourself to feel safe, to feel valid, to feel known.

Let them come. Let them crowd the surface. See the mosaic they form—a fragmented script of who you thought you were. Don't look away. Witness it. These are not truths. These are echoes. Armor. Costume. Layers built to survive a world that taught you to forget who you are.

II. GATHERING THE ILLUSIONS

Reach toward the chalkboard—not with hands, but with presence. Begin to wipe the names away. Some disappear instantly, as if they were waiting to leave. Others cling tightly, as if they believe they still belong. **These are the ones your ego defends—not because they're true, but because they're familiar.**

Feel their resistance. Feel their weight. Let yourself feel what you carried. Each label had a cost. Each story altered your breath, your posture, your perception. But now, gently, they begin to fade. As they dissolve, they fall like dust into your hands— soft, grey, quiet.

Now bring your palms to your heart. Feel the golden light there—steady, warm, open. Let the dust fall into it. Let the fragments return home. These names were never you. They were only who you believed yourself to be. And now, you release them.

III. DRAWING EVERYTHING INTO THE HEART

Hold the dust to your chest. Light yet heavy. Faded but full of memory. Let the stillness hold you.

The chalkboard is clear. The noise is gone. There are no titles here. No roles. No expectations. No weight. Do not fear this emptiness. It is not loneliness. It is the field of pure potential. It is who you are beneath every mask.

Affirm within yourself:

"Behold, I make all things new."

Let the words settle. Let the silence become full. This is not the end of your story. It is the space where creation begins again.

IV. THE EMERGENCE OF THE TRUE YOU

Whisper now:

"I pull every name I have believed myself to be into the heart of truth."

The shift begins. A warmth beneath your ribs. A movement in the chest. The dust stirs. It doesn't burn—it transforms. Not destruction. Alchemy.

It returns to light—not as label, not as form, but as clarity. A deeper knowing. A truth that doesn't need a name.

Breathe in: "I am more than these names."

Breathe out: "I yield to the Christ that transcends them."

No force. No struggle. Only release.

You realize now you were never a title. Never a performance. Never a fixed point on a human map. You were always more. And now, you remember.

V. WITNESSING THE EMPTY BOARD

Look again at the chalkboard. It is clean. Still. Unwritten.

When Jesus said, "Let the dead bury their own dead," —Luke 9:60

he wasn't dismissing self or identity. He was pointing beyond identity. Beyond the illusions we bury ourselves under. The ego builds its fortress from labels—some earned, some inherited. It tells you that without them, you are nothing. But the opposite is true.

Awakening reveals what the ego cannot survive: that your essence needs no name. That your being needs no role. That your truth stands unshaken without a single title to hold it up.

Yes, the ego will fight. It will call you lost. It will beg you to return to the safety of who you used to be. Let it fall apart. Let it burn down. Let every label, every story, every false anchor collapse into the light of your heart.

You are not here to hold those illusions. You are here to remember what exists when they fall away.

What remains is not a better version of the old you.

It is the real you. The one that never needed to be explained.

Let the chalkboard stay empty. Let the ego dissolve. You are not unfinished.

You are finally free.

DETACH FROM THE SYSTEMS

When you awaken, it isn't just your personal illusions that unravel—it's the collective ones.

The systems that govern this world—religion, government, media, finance— do not exist independently. They survive only through your participation. They depend on your compliance, your agreement, your belief in their necessity. They are not powered by truth. They are powered by obedience.

These systems require you to stay asleep. Because the moment you wake up, you become unmanageable.

This is what Jesus understood with piercing clarity. No empire, no religious authority, no societal structure could override the truth of the Kingdom within.

He didn't submit to political pressure or religious hypocrisy—not to make a statement, but because he saw through the illusion. He knew the source of real power wasn't found in Rome's courts or the temple's hierarchy. It was in alignment with the Divine. It was in love. Unshakable, untouchable, unstoppable love.

And so it is for you.

Once you no longer fear lack, once you stop looking to external authorities for permission, validation, or identity—once you no longer need to be ruled—you cannot be controlled.

This isn't rebellion. This is remembrance.

Detachment doesn't mean withdrawal. It doesn't mean isolation or destruction. It means choosing not to energize what is false. It means no longer giving your consent to systems built on manipulation, division, and fear.

You're not here to destroy institutions. **You're here to dissolve your alignment with illusion.** To stop feeding a structure that only exists because you once believed it had power over you.

This is not war. It's clarity.

This is not division. It's truth.

It's the recognition that real power does not demand control. It radiates freedom. That unity does not require submission. It flows from knowing we all come from the same **Source.**

When truth takes root, control loses its grip.

You don't need to fight the system.

You only need to stop *fueling* it.

LIVING IT & EMBRACING THE WORLD

The following guided experiences are not symbolic. They are activations—designed to take you beyond the conceptual and into the embodied. You have read the truths. You have understood the systems. Now, you are being asked to live it.

These exercises are not for escaping the world, but about transforming how you engage with it. They allow you to walk into the collective field with clarity, to dissolve illusion without resistance, and to bring presence where fear once ruled. They are invitations to shift reality not through force, but through frequency.

This is how awakening becomes real—not as an idea, but as a lived experience.

I. ENTERING A SHARED FIELD OF LIGHT

Close your eyes.

The ground beneath you is soft. Open. Endless. You are standing in a vast clearing, a meadow bathed in golden sunlight. The air is thick with something more than warmth—something alive.

You are not alone.

All of humanity stands with you. Not as strangers. Not as enemies. Not as disconnected lives heading in opposite directions. But as souls, sharing this moment, this earth, this remembrance.

Some stand near. Some stand far. Some carry fear. Some carry sorrow. Others search for a love they do not yet know how to receive.

Let your heart remain open. Feel its rhythm. Feel its presence.

Compassion flows—not as pity or sorrow—but as recognition. The awareness that each soul you see has walked a path of forgetting and remembering, just like you. Every illusion they carry, you once held. Every story they tell, you have once believed. Every hand reaching for light has, at some point, *been your own.*

II. NAMING THE ILLUSIONS WITHOUT JUDGING THEM

Before you stand four towering pillars—each rising from the earth, each representing a system of the world.

One for religion.

One for government.

One for media.

One for finance.

They are not evil. They are not your enemy. They are not to be feared. They are simply what humanity has built in its forgetting.

Walk toward the first pillar. Sense its energy. Maybe it carries fear. Maybe control. Maybe a belief that has long since expired. Don't fight it. Don't resist it. Don't try to tear it down.

Simply witness.

Whisper: "I see your form. I see how you shape our world."

This is not war. This is vision. This is presence. This is the act of returning light to what has been shrouded.

Place your hand on the pillar.

Breathe in: "I bring love here."

Breathe out: "I see beyond your illusions."

The pillar softens—not because it was broken, but because it was finally seen.

Now move to the next. And the next. And the next. Not to condemn. Not to destroy. But to hold with awareness. To see through the surface. To bring presence where fear once ruled.

III. TRANSFORMING FEAR: HEART-CENTERED VISION

Step forward again. The pillars remain, just as they have for centuries. Anchored in history. Built by generations of belief. Holding the weight of what once was.

Do not fight them. Do not condemn them.

Just see.

See how religion carried both truth and control. How government offered protection and restriction. How media brought knowledge and distortion. How finance created both wealth and separation.

These systems are not good. They are not evil. **They are reflections**—structures shaped by consciousness, now ready to be reshaped.

Place your hand gently on the first pillar. *Say:*

"I do not reject you. I unveil the love you forgot."

A crack forms. Not from violence—but from revelation.

Beneath the stone, there is light. It has always been there, hidden beneath control, buried under fear, waiting to be remembered.

Move to the next. And the next. One by one, see them not as enemies to defeat— but as creations ready to evolve.

You are not here to topple. You are here to transform. The light beneath them is the same light within you. **And where truth is seen—where love is returned—fear no longer holds.**

This is how the world is made new.

IV. MERGING WITH OUR BROTHERS AND SISTERS

Turn away from the pillars. The systems remain, but they no longer hold the same weight. Their power is shifting—not through force, not through destruction, but through remembrance.

Now, look to the people in the meadow. These are your brothers. These are your sisters. Some still cling to the old illusions. Some still believe in the structures that once shaped their world.

Do not pull away. Do not separate yourself. Extend a hand of compassion.

Not as one who is above. Not as one who knows more. But as one who remembers.

In your mind, speak softly: "I stand with you, not against you. I no longer feed fear. I feed only love."

The space between you shifts. The air grows lighter. The barriers that once divided dissolve—not through force, but through the quiet power of choosing unity over separation.

You are not bowing to illusion. You are not surrendering to control. You are raising all things into higher truth by refusing to see them as enemies.

This is the path. Not conquest. Not destruction. But transformation through love.

V. ANCHORING A NEW REALITY—TOGETHER

Breathe in. Feel the unity in the air, the silent hum of connection that has always been here, waiting to be remembered.

Say within yourself: "We are one under the same Source, beyond fear."

Breathe out. Let go of the stories that made you believe otherwise. Let go of the division, the barriers, the illusion that separation was ever real.

Say: "I release all illusions that claim my soul or separate me from others."

Feel the shift.

The meadow brightens, as if light is pouring from within every being. As if love is touching each heart, awakening something long forgotten.

The pillars remain, but they are no longer monstrous. No longer looming with power over others. They soften. They become placeholders, reminders of what once was, but no longer must be.

What was built in fear can be rebuilt in love. What once served control can be reshaped to serve truth.

This world is not waiting to be destroyed. It is waiting to be made new.

And it begins here. It begins now. It begins together.

INVITING SYSTEMS INTO LOVE, NOT FLEEING THEM

This is detachment in the Christ sense. Not escape. Not rebellion. Not exile.

To awaken is not to abandon the world, but to remain within it, untouched by its illusions.

You do not fight the system. You do not fuel it with fear. You do not wage war against what was built in blindness.

You see beyond it.

You recognize that every structure, every institution, every pillar of control is upheld not by force, but by belief.

And belief can change.

The world will still try to govern you through lack, to shape you through shame, to keep you small through force. But you no longer answer to it.

You do not shrink. You do not divide.

You simply stop believing in a power that is not rooted in unity.

This does not make you an outcast. It makes you a bridge. A presence that stands between the old and the new—not to tear down, not to flee, but to show another way.

This is the highest expression of Christ energy in the world. Not to fight illusion with illusion, but to transform the old from within, through the presence of a truth that cannot be bent by fear.

MASTER THE FREQUENCY OF CREATION

When Jesus spoke to the storm, it obeyed. When he broke the loaves, they multiplied. When he called forth life, it rose.

He was not overriding reality. He was redefining it. Not through effort. Not through force. But through pure love and certainty.

To awaken to the Christ frequency is to recognize that every thought, every word, every intention is an invitation to reality.

It is a call for creation to take form according to your knowing.

You are not here to wish for what you desire. You are here to claim it. Not from longing. Not from desperation. But from the depth of your divine center.

This is not a trick. Not a technique. Not a law to be studied and applied.

It is alignment.

Alignment with the same God-consciousness that Jesus walked in. The same current that speaks and watches creation respond.

To hold this frequency is to stand in certainty. Certain that love guides you. Certain that your words matter. Certain that the reality before you is not fixed, but waiting for you to command it into form.

CREATING SOMETHING REAL IN YOUR LIFE

This is where embodiment begins. These practices are not affirmations or techniques. They are functional alignments—real-time openings that draw creation into form through frequency, presence, and certainty. You are not imagining. You are initiating.

I. CHOOSE A CLEAR, HEARTFELT INTENTION

Sit in stillness. Let the body rest. Let the breath deepen. Let the mind open. Close your eyes.

There is nothing to force. Nothing to reach for. Nothing to chase.

Simply choose.

One thing. One experience. One manifestation that is ready to enter your life. Not as something distant. Not as something to acquire. But as something that already exists, already aligned, already yours.

Whisper: "I create this in love." Breathe. Let it settle.

Whisper: "I call this to me in love. I am in alignment with its presence in my life. It simply—is."

Feel your heart warm as you envision yourself in receipt.

Call to you what is in your highest good.

Do not confine it to a name, to a title, to an expectation. Do not shape it in limitation.

Allow it to arrive in its highest form, in its greatest unfolding.

What aligns, appears. What serves, remains.

And more often than not, you will call forth something far greater than you ever imagined.

II. SPEAK FROM THE CHRIST CURRENT

Place a hand on your chest. Inhale deeply. Exhale slowly. The breath is steady. The body is still.

Feel the warmth in your heart. A golden stream of light forming, expanding, flowing outward. It reaches your intention, meets it in perfect alignment—not as something to ask for, but as something that already is.

Declare aloud, or in mind but with power: "I speak this into being."

Fill the space after. Call it forth. Not as a wish. Not as a request. But as a truth unveiling itself.

Maybe it is a moment of clarity. Maybe it is a path unfolding. Maybe it is a resolution, a meeting, a sign.

Whatever it is, feel the certainty that it is already done.

Like Jesus saying, "Peace, be still," you are not hoping. You are not pleading. You are commanding reality from love.

Not from fear. Not from ego. Simply from knowing.

III. ENVISION IT AS ALREADY TRUE

Bring your hands before you. Form the Yoni Mudra—thumbs touching, index fingers meeting to create a sacred gateway. The portal of creation. The vessel through which all things pass into being.

This is the space of receiving and becoming. The place where intention moves from thought to form.

Hold it before your heart. Let its shape remind you—creation is not outside of you. It flows through you. What you have spoken is.

See yourself inside of it now. Not hoping. Not waiting. Not seeking. Already there.

Breathe in the joy. The relief. Feel the weightlessness of alignment. Let your body memorize what it is to already have.

If doubt arises. If a whisper tells you, **"This cannot be real,"** do not resist it. Acknowledge it. Let it rise. Let it pass through the gateway of your hands. It is not here to stay.

Affirm: "I accept this as already made manifest in my field. I hold no doubt."

If the mind still clings. If fear still lingers. Cup your hands as if gathering it. See it as smoke. As mist. As something without weight. Then release it.

Let it pass through the Yoni Mudra. Let it leave you. Let it return to the void from which all things come and go.

You do not force creation. *You allow it.*

You do not chase what is already yours. You receive it.

The portal is open. The path is clear. What was spoken has already arrived. Believe it.

IV. RELEASE THE NEED TO CONTROL HOW

Let go. You have spoken. You have envisioned. You have received.

Now, *release.*

Step out of the trap of how. Step out of the grasp of when. Step out of the illusion that you must oversee every detail for it to come into being.

The Christ frequency does not negotiate with steps and timelines. It does not follow logic. It does not require proof. It aligns.

Reality shifts in ways the mind cannot foresee. In patterns too vast for the eye to track.

**Whisper: "I let the universe handle the details.
I trust the divine orchestration."**

Breathe in. Breathe out.

Smile—as if you have just placed an order with the most reliable, unchanging, eternal cosmic service there is. Love itself.

The moment you stop reaching, **it arrives.**

The moment you stop grasping, **it unfolds.**

What is yours is already on its way.

V. WATCH FOR ITS ARRIVAL

Stay open.

Do not chase. Do not search. Do not demand a sign.

The seed has already been planted. The path has already been set. The moment you spoke it, the moment you surrendered it, it began.

Over the next few days, keep your heart open. Your eyes soft. **Your spirit in receiving, not seeking.**

Do not strain to see it. Do not doubt if it does not appear in the way you expected. The sign. The event. The manifestation—it comes as it chooses, not as you demand. It moves in ways that will surprise you.

And when doubt creeps in. When the mind whispers, "What if it isn't working?" "What if nothing is happening?"

Breathe.

Place a hand over your heart. Affirm: "It's already done."

Feel the knowing return. Feel the certainty settle.

This is the Christ vantage point. Not waiting. Not wondering. Knowing.

It is here. It is unfolding. *It is done.*

CREATION AS A NATURAL STATE

This is not about control. This is not about effort. This is not about forcing reality into shape.

Creation is not a battle. It is not a test. It is not something to be won. It is a state of being.

A current of love so strong, so undeniable, that reality joyfully reshapes itself around your knowing.

Jesus did not beg the universe for a miracle. He did not plead. He did not hope.

He spoke. From the authority of divine love. From the certainty of truth. From the unshaken knowing that what is aligned cannot be denied.

You hold that same authority.

When you create from the Christ frequency, you are not demanding. You are resonating with the original blueprint of creation—the foundation where all things are possible through love.

The moment you say yes to that flow. The moment you release doubt. The moment you stop searching for proof. You will understand—nothing is out of reach.

Love withholds nothing from itself. It does not measure. It does not deny.

And as you begin to see these manifestations—big or small, subtle or undeniable, ordinary or miraculous—recognize them for what they are.

Not rare. Not exceptions. Not random gifts.

But a natural extension of who you truly are. God's expression in form.

This is your birthright. To call forth what serves love. To walk in unwavering trust. To watch reality blossom in response.

YOUR DIVINE PURPOSE

Most people spend a lifetime asking, "Why am I here?"

As if purpose were hidden.

As if the universe were keeping a secret.

As if the answer were somewhere outside of them.

But the awakened soul does not ask in uncertainty.

The awakened soul declares:

"I want to know my purpose."

And in that directness, the Christ frequency responds. Big time. Trust me.

It has never been far. It has never been waiting. It has only been unclaimed.

Jesus did not wonder if he was meant to heal, if he was meant to teach, if he was meant to embody love.

He claimed it when he said,

"I must be about my Father's business." —Luke 2:49

He did not ask. He did not hesitate. He knew.

This is the key. Not searching. Not hoping. Not waiting for a sign.

Choosing.

"I choose to know why I came."

And the moment you stand in that choice, the moment you refuse to cower behind maybe or someday, the moment you stop pretending you are lost—your path will unfold.

Your purpose is not waiting to be found.

It is waiting to be claimed.

Say it *now:*

"I want to know my purpose, and I am ready to receive it."

INVITING YOUR PUPOSE INTO AWARENESS

These steps are not for curiosity. They are for clarity. This is not a ritual to entertain the mind—it is a space to engage the field. When you declare your readiness to know your purpose, you shift everything. **These exercises are not about waiting for a cosmic download.** They are entering alignment with the answer that has always been within you, waiting for your permission to emerge.

I. ANNOUNCING YOUR READINESS

Find a quiet space. Let the noise of the world fade. Let the breath steady, smooth, unrushed.

Sit or stand with your spine upright, your body relaxed yet present, your awareness centered. Place one hand on your heart. Place the other on your solar plexus, just above your navel—the seat of will, the place where your deepest knowing resides.

This is not a question. This is not a request. It is a declaration.

Speak clearly:

"I want to know my purpose— I am ready now."

Let the words settle. Let them move through you, through the space around you.

Feel the shift. A subtle rush of energy. A ripple. As though you have just knocked on a door that has always been waiting to be opened.

II. THE PURPOSE INVOCATION

Close your eyes. The breath is steady, the body open, the heart awake.

Above you, a pillar of light begins to descend. Soft yet radiant. Vast yet intimate. It does not force itself upon you. It does not demand.

It is Christ love—unconditional, all-knowing, already within you, now rising to meet you.

Let it envelop you. Let it move through you. From head to toe. Through every cell. Through every thought.

Inhale: "I open." Exhale: "I receive."

Say, with quiet authority:

"I call forth the knowing of my true purpose. I am ready to be shown."

The air around you shifts. The space bends. As if something unseen has answered.

Not as a distant voice. Not as something outside of you. But as something aligning. As something revealing. As something you have always known but are now ready to remember.

III. CREATING THE SPACE FOR REVELATION

Set a timer for ten minutes. This is your time. A space with no rush, no noise, no expectation.

Sit in stillness. Let the breath settle. Let the mind quiet.

The pillar of light remains. Steady. Unchanging. Holding you within it.

There is no need to seek. There is nothing to force.

If thoughts arise—worries, memories, distractions—let them drift like clouds, passing without attachment.

Return to the breath.

Do not wait for a voice in the sky. Do not demand a sign carved in stone. Revelation is often quiet. It moves in whispers. In nudges. In images that flicker at the edges of awareness.

A word may form in your mind. A picture may rise without explanation. A feeling may press against your chest. Soft but insistent.

They may be faint, but they are real. Do not grasp. Do not question. Simply receive.

IV. RECEIVING THE SPARK

The timer rings. Do not rush. Do not move too quickly back into thought. Stay in the quiet for a moment longer, letting the stillness settle into your body.

Then, take up your journal. *Write.*

Not with hesitation. Not with analysis. Not with the mind searching for meaning. Write what came. A word. A phrase. An image. A feeling without a name.

Perhaps it is as clear as "healer." Perhaps it is as simple as "write the book." Perhaps it is nothing more than a pull, a knowing, a whisper that says, "I am meant to serve," "I am meant to teach," "I am meant to bring hope."

Do not filter it. Do not shape it. **Do not judge whether it is enough.** It is not small. It is not random. It is your soul speaking while the door is still open.

Let it pour out. Let it take form on the page. You can understand later.

For now, simply *receive.*

V. AFFIRMING AND INTEGRATING

Look over what you wrote. Do not rush to define it. **Do not force it into a shape that makes sense.**

Read it softly. Feel the weight of the words, the energy behind them. Find the thread. Even if it feels small, even if it seems vague, even if it is just a single word, treat it like a seed.

A seed does not reveal itself all at once. It unfolds in its time, breaking open, stretching toward the light, becoming what it was always meant to be.

Speak: "I welcome this purpose into my everyday life. I trust the path will unfold as I walk."

There is nothing more to do. There is no need to chase. No need to struggle. What is yours will rise to meet you.

Place your hand back on your heart. Breathe in, steady. Breathe out, soft.

Say: "I name this truth mine."

The warmth settles within you. A quiet confirmation. A knowing beyond thought.

You are heard. You are seen. You are ready.

PURPOSE & ONGOING REVELATION

The old paradigm says you must search for purpose. That it is hidden. That it must be earned. That it is something outside of you, waiting to be discovered.

But in the Christ paradigm, you do not search—you call it forth.

Again, you do not beg the universe to answer, "Why am I here?"

You declare:

"I want to know my purpose."

And divine love responds. This is the path Jesus walked. Not uncertainty. Not waiting. A direct line to Source that already knows you.

Purpose is not locked away. It is not distant. It is not reserved for the few. It is alive in you, waiting for your invitation.

Once you invite it, unworthiness fades. Uncertainty dissolves. You become an open channel for God's plan to express through you.

And in that channel, every step aligns with the knowing:

"I am here on purpose. I choose to live that purpose—now."

But understand—purpose is not just what you do. It is how you be.

It is the way you exist. The way your presence moves through the world. The way your soul embodies its truth.

It may be healing. It may be teaching. It may be guiding others in wealth of mind. It may be collecting taxes. It may be singing. It may be picking up garbage.

No task is beneath purpose. No path is unworthy.

Your soul did not come here to chase meaning. It came here to be.

And when you let go of the idea that purpose must be found—you step into the truth that you have been living it all along.

FORGIVENESS: RELEASING ALL HURT

In the Christ frequency, healing is not bound by time.

What was broken can be made whole. What was lost can be reknown. What was painful can be rewritten through love.

You are not bound to what happened. You are not chained to old wounds.

You can step into the past as your awakened self. Not as the one who suffered—but as the one who sees.

Not as the wounded child. Not as the broken soul. But as the agent of love, here to rewrite the story.

This is not denial. Not erasure. This is truth revealed.

You don't erase what happened. *You reknow it.*

Not as a victim. Not as someone powerless. But as the presence of love in a moment that did not know how to hold it.

You walk into your childhood, not as small hands that could not stop what was happening—but as open arms that bring peace.

You return to the places that left their mark. Not to relive the pain, but to release it. By doing this, you free both your past self and the others involved from condemnation.

You see how fear played its part. How hurt was passed from one to another, from generation to generation.

And in that seeing, you activate the power of love to erase the lie that you were ever broken.

You never were.

And now, it's time to live in that truth.

REKNOWING YOURSELF BEYOND THE WOUND

I. SETTING THE STAGE

Sit in a calm space. Let the body relax. Let the breath steady. Let the mind soften. Close your eyes.

A soft light begins to gather around you. Not from above. Not from outside. But from within. It does not push. It does not demand. It simply holds.

Whisper:

> **"I stand in the Christ vibration. I am safe. I am real. I bring love wherever I go."**

Feel the words settle in your chest. Feel the warmth spread. Gentle but steady. A quiet strength rising from within.

This is not the warmth of comfort. This is the warmth of knowing.

You are safe. You are steady. You are ready to face whatever appears.

II. OBSERVING THE CHILDHOOD SCENE

Let the warmth hold you. Let the breath guide you. Let the moment arise.

A memory surfaces. Not chosen at random. Not forced into awareness. The one that still lingers. The one that still lives inside you.

Maybe it was an argument. Maybe it was a moment of neglect. Maybe it was a betrayal by someone you trusted.

See it now. Not as you once lived it, but from the outside—as if watching a short film unfold before you.

The child you—maybe six, maybe ten—stands in the center of it all. The others involved are there too. Frozen in time. Locked in the same emotions that once shaped you.

But you do not step into the child's body. You do not return to that pain. You stand as you are now. Fully grown. Fully awake. Fully present.

Not drowning in it. Not overcome by it. Just witnessing.

Not with judgment. Not with blame. Not with the weight of all that was lost. But with compassion.

For the child. For the ones who hurt them. For the moment that left its mark.

Hold the scene in your awareness. Let it unfold. Let it breathe.

You are not trapped in this memory. *You are here to reknow it.*

III. INTERVENING AS THE ADULT

Step forward. Not as the wounded child. Not as the one who once felt powerless. Not as someone bound to this moment.

But as who you are now. Whole. Awake. Unshaken.

Move toward your younger self. They are there. Small. Uncertain. Held in the emotions of that day.

Maybe they are crying. Maybe they are silent. Maybe they do not yet understand why their heart feels so heavy.

Gently kneel. Meet their eyes.

Softly, with certainty, say:

> **"I am you, from the future. I've come to tell you we**
> **are okay. We grow stronger. We are loved."**

Let them hear it. Let them *feel* it.

If the scene involves harm—if there is someone towering over them, if there are words that cut or hands that wound—place yourself between them.

Not to fight. Not to rage. Not to carry more pain. Simply to shield.

Let them see you there. Let them feel your presence. Not afraid. Not fragile. Not broken.

But steady. Whole. Unmovable in love.

Hold their gaze. Let them know—they are no longer alone in this moment.

You have come back for them.

This is Fourth Dimensional Healing. This is rewriting the past by showing up in the present.

This is how time *bends* to love.

IV. REKNOWING THE MEMORY

Take the child's hand. Feel the trembling. Feel the weight they've carried alone. They won't carry it alone anymore.

Speak gently, with certainty:

> **"You're not alone anymore. I know this moment**
> **hurt, but it does not define us."**

Let the words settle. Let them feel it.

Now, lift your gaze. Look at the others in the scene. See them fully. Not as villains. Not as monsters. **But as people—afraid, ignorant, bound by their own wounds.**

This is not condoning. This is understanding.

Breathe deeply.

In your mind, speak to them softly:

> **"I don't hate you. I release you from my judgment. We were all trapped in illusions, but not in this one any longer."**

The air shifts. The scene changes.

Not erased. Not forgotten. But reknown.

Held in the light of truth. Seen through the lens of love. Not as a wound. Not as a scar. But as a place that no longer holds you.

V. INVOKING THE POWER OF CHRIST TO DISSOLVE PAIN

Envision a pillar of golden light pouring down from above.

It doesn't rush. It doesn't burn. It descends like warm sunlight breaking through heavy clouds—steady, radiant, alive. It stretches high beyond what your mind can measure, yet wraps around you like a blanket that knows every curve of your being.

This is what it means to be vast and intimate at once—limitless in presence, yet so precise it feels made only for you.

The light doesn't push. It doesn't demand. It doesn't ask you to prove yourself. It simply holds everything in silence and grace.

You stand within it. Your child self stands within it. Even those who caused harm— no matter how lost, no matter how cruel—stand within it too.

No one is left out. No one is cast away.

Breathe in:

> **"I bring love."**

Breathe out:

> **"I release this pain."**

Feel the golden light expand with your breath. Let it pour into every corner of the memory like water into a dry well. Let it fill the silence between words left unsaid. Let it soften the tension written across faces. Let it round the sharpness of old voices. Let it bring stillness where there once was fear.

Watch as the child in your arms begins to relax. Their shoulders, once tight with fear, begin to loosen. Their breath deepens. The weight they carried alone begins to lift.

The figures who once wounded—parents, teachers, strangers—do not vanish. They remain, but they shrink. They fade into the background, unable to hold their shape in the presence of something this powerful. This whole.

They are not erased. But they are no longer giants. They are no longer gods. They are no longer threats.

The moment itself begins to change. The color shifts. The air lightens. The gravity eases. What was frozen begins to thaw.

Kneel beside your younger self. Whisper into their ear:

"We are whole. We are safe. We can let go now."

And as you say it, feel the release. The weight dissolving not just from their shoulders, but from yours. The grief you didn't know you carried. The fear that hid behind your achievements. The sorrow disguised as strength.

It lifts.

The memory remains. But it no longer owns you. It no longer defines you.

VI. LEAVING THE MEMORY HEALED

Stand up.

The child's hand is in yours—small, warm, steady. No longer trembling. No longer frozen in fear. There is strength in their grip now. A quiet confidence. A sense that something deep has shifted.

Look around.

The scene begins to dissolve—not abruptly, not erased, but softened. The edges blur, as if the weight of the moment can no longer hold its shape. The walls that once felt so close begin to expand, fading into light. The voices that once echoed with pain grow quiet, like a storm moving off into the distance.

You are not forgetting.

You are releasing.

Not losing the memory—but letting go of its hold on you.

Turn back one last time. Not to reclaim it. Not to revisit it. But to close the chapter with clarity.

Speak with *finality:*

> **"I forgive all of you. I forgive myself for believing I was trapped. I am free."**

No tension in your voice. No anger in your chest. No resistance in your heart.

Only truth. Clean. Clear. Complete.

Then turn forward.

Step out.

> **Feel your feet on the ground now.**
>
> **Feel the breath in your lungs.**
>
> **Feel your heartbeat—not racing, not guarding, just steady.**

There is space in your chest where weight used to sit. There is stillness in your body where tightness used to live.

The memory is still there—but it's *different.*

It doesn't sting. It doesn't grip. It doesn't loop.

It's no longer a wound.

It's a page you've read, understood, and placed gently back on the shelf.

It has been rewritten.

It has been healed.

You are free.

FORGIVENESS AS TRUE ALCHEMY

To reknow a memory through the lens of Christ consciousness is to transform it from a prison into a place of liberation. This is not denial. This is not pretending it never happened. This is stepping into the past, not as the one who was hurt, but as the one who sees. As the one who understands that love—not fear—is the ultimate author of your story.

This is forgiveness at its peak. You do not forget the wound. You do not erase what was. But you no longer identify with it. You see it. You heal it. You offer love to everyone involved—including the version of yourself who once felt abandoned inside it.

In doing so, you dismantle the illusions that kept that hurt alive. And every time you do this, every time you step back into a moment with the presence of divine love, you rewrite the past without being bound to it.

No moment of pain, no betrayal, no loss can overshadow the light you embody. This is the true alchemy of forgiveness—turning the lead of old memories into the gold of present freedom.

FULLY STEP INTO THE CHRIST ENERGY

Again, and again: when Jesus said, "The kingdom of God is within you," he was not speaking in metaphor. He was pointing to a living reality.

Christ Consciousness is not distant. Not separate. Not something to reach for. It is already in you. Waiting to be acknowledged.

To step into it is not to perfect yourself. It is not to become worthy. It is not to achieve some higher state of being. It is simply to let go. To release the illusions that made you believe you were ever anything less than divine love in expression.

The moment you finally accept that all you need is already here, there is no more seeking. No more striving. No more begging for approval. No more fear that you are not enough.

You are worthy. You have always been worthy. And your heart is the temple where God's infinite love meets your humanity.

You stand now as a bridge between heaven and earth. Not because you have ascended. Not because you have earned it. But because this is what you were always meant to be.

CLAIMING THE CHRIST FREQUENCY IN YOU

This is not a meditation. This is not imagination. This is *embodiment*.

The following experience is designed to take you beyond concept into activation. **You will not read about the Christ Frequency—you will step into it.** Each exercise is built to guide you into your own inner temple, awaken your divine authority, and release anything still convincing you that you're separate from the truth.

You don't need visualization skills. You need willingness. Let these words create the space for you. Let your body feel what your mind cannot picture. This is about direct experience—not belief, not theory, but presence.

I. ENTERING THE HEART TEMPLE

Close your eyes. Place your hand on your chest. Feel the steady rhythm beneath your palm—not just a heartbeat, but a pulse of something deeper. Something ancient. Something eternal.

Now, allow an image to form—not by force, just by permission. A vast temple begins to take shape within you. The floors are smooth marble beneath your feet. The air is cool and sacred. Giant columns stretch upward into light that doesn't hurt your eyes but seems to hold you in calm awareness.

This is not outside of you. You are not visualizing heaven somewhere else. You are standing in the temple that lives in your heart—the one that has always been there.

Whisper:

"I welcome the Christ in me."

Let the words echo through the space. Let them anchor into the floor. A warmth stirs in your chest—not a glow from elsewhere, but a fire you forgot you carried. It builds, steady and soft. A radiance that says: I am here. I have always been here.

You are now standing inside the Presence. And the Presence is standing inside you.

II. LIGHTING THE LANTERNS OF RELEASE

Remain in the heart temple. Notice how still everything feels. How safe. In front of you, a row of lanterns begins to appear. They are delicate but real. Translucent glass. Flickering wicks inside, waiting to be lit.

Maybe there are three. Maybe there are many. **However many appear, they each hold something—a wound, a fear, a lie, a weight you've carried.**

Pick up the first. It's light in your hands, but you can feel the density of what it contains. Speak silently to it. Name what it holds. "This is my fear of being seen." Or, "This is the shame I've buried." There is no judgment. Only clarity.

Now light the wick. Watch the small flame rise. It flickers, then steadies.

Move to the next. And the next. Let each flame be a moment of letting go, a truth named without fear, a piece of the past you're ready to release.

Soon, you're surrounded by soft light. Each lantern a symbol of something that no longer defines you. Not buried. Not hidden. Not denied. Illuminated.

You're not losing anything. You're making room for what's real.

III. INVOKING THE CHRIST CURRENT

The lanterns glow around you, casting light across the marble floor. Now the air changes.

Something begins to descend—not in motion, but in presence. A column of light moves down from above, slow and absolute. It doesn't shimmer. It doesn't sparkle. It settles like gravity.

You feel it touch the top of your head. It moves down your spine. Through your chest. Into your feet. It grounds you. It centers you. It anchors you.

This is the Christ Current. The living energy of divine love—not a metaphor, not an idea, but the literal vibration of truth.

Breathe in:

 "I invite the fullness of God's love here."

Breathe out:

 "I align with my highest truth."

The temple hums around you—not with noise, but with a deep vibration you feel in your bones. Everything is alive. Everything is listening.

This current is not new. It is not arriving. It is being remembered.

And now, it flows through you again.

IV. LETTING THE LANTERNS FLOAT

Turn back toward the lanterns. They are still here, each glowing softly with what has now been acknowledged. They are no longer burdens. They are offerings.

Pick up the first one. Feel how it has changed. It is warm, but no longer heavy. Light, but not empty. It carries your truth. And now, it's ready to rise.

Lift it gently toward the Christ light. Watch as it lifts—slowly, effortlessly, like a sky lantern pulled upward by something invisible and kind.

It doesn't burn. It doesn't vanish. It simply becomes light returning to light.

One by one, lift each lantern. Watch them rise. Higher. Higher. Until they are gone—not lost, but integrated.

What remains is space. Clarity. Stillness.

Only what is true stays.

V. SEALING YOUR EMBODIMENT

Stand in the temple. Your hands are empty. Your body is light. Your breath is slow. There is no more reaching. No more grasping. There is just you. Whole. Present. Alive.

Speak aloud or within:

"I accept the Christ I am. I accept the love I carry. I accept my role in revealing heaven on earth."

Let the words move through your chest like a current. Feel the vibration rise from your heart, not down from heaven. It is not descending. It is emerging.

You are not becoming holy. You are remembering you always were.

This is not a closing. This is a claiming.

Let the stillness confirm it. Let the warmth anchor it.

You are not separate from love.

You are not separate from the divine unfolding.

You are it.

And now, you remember.

WALKING AS CHRIST IN THE WORLD

The lanterns have risen. The burdens have lifted. What once felt like weight carved into your being has returned to the source of light. You no longer carry what was never meant to stay. This is not perfection. This is not spiritual performance. **This is what it means to walk in Christ Consciousness—unburdened, unbound, unafraid.**

You do not emerge from this process polished and flawless. You emerge real. Present. Whole. Not because you fixed yourself, but because you remembered who you were without the lies. Without the roles. Without the wounds pretending to be identity.

Now you walk—not in search of power, but in alignment with it. You move through the world not with apology, but with presence. Every step you take becomes a quiet prayer. Every word you speak becomes a thread in the great tapestry of healing. Every breath, an extension of divine love flowing through a body that finally knows it is worthy.

This was never just about overcoming your past. It was about unlocking a future bigger than you. Every illusion dismantled, every story unlearned, every fear faced—none of it was ever meant to end with you. It was always meant to ripple outward. A wave. A spark. A chain reaction.

For generations, we were taught to wait. Wait for a Messiah in the sky. Wait for salvation to descend like fire. Wait for heaven to arrive from somewhere else. But the Second Coming was never about one man. It was about the collective return to remembrance. The realization that we are the continuation of Christ's work.

The kingdom is not above. It is within. And now it awakens, soul by soul.

When one rises, it begins. When many rise, the old world begins to fall. Not in war. Not in collapse. But in irrelevance. Systems built on fear lose their grip when no one consents to fear anymore. Separation cannot survive in the presence of collective truth. And control cannot hold where love has taken root.

FROM INDIVIDUAL TO COLLECTIVE TRANSFORMATION

Your journey was never just for you. It was never meant to end in a private miracle. Your healing, your remembering, your becoming—none of it was for isolation. It was meant to be shared. To become a flame in the global field, sparking others into their own return.

This is the promise of Christ energy—not that one will lead all, but that each will awaken to the leader within. That each soul will remember its role in the renewal of the world.

The kingdom is not somewhere we go. It is something we embody. And when enough of us walk in that truth, everything changes.

Love begins to govern what fear once controlled. Creativity flows where suppression once reigned. Systems reorganize themselves around presence, not power. And reality reshapes itself—not through violence, but through vibrational alignment.

DEEPENING DAILY PRACTICES

This is not the end of your awakening. It is the integration. The grounding. The remembering on repeat.

Every day is a chance to anchor the Christ frequency more deeply into your body. This is not about routines that check spiritual boxes. It is about real, conscious communion. **Not with something outside you—but with what you now know lives within.**

Begin your day by stepping into sacred space. It doesn't need candles or chants. Just a place where stillness is possible. A corner. A window. A patch of morning sun. Anywhere the noise fades and the pulse of your own spirit becomes audible.

Close your eyes. Let your breath slow. Not with force, but with permission. Let your inhales draw in clarity. Let your exhales release whatever you no longer need. Yesterday's noise. Doubt's echo. Old tension that has no place in the day ahead.

Now, see the temple inside your heart. Not imagine it. See it. Columns rising skyward. A floor of stillness beneath you. **The roof opens to infinity—no ceiling, no ending, just light.**

This is not metaphor. This is memory. A structure your soul recognizes. A sanctuary that responds to your presence.

Stand there. And speak what is true:

> **"I am love. I am truth. I am divine."**

Not to become it. To claim it.

Let those words echo. Let them take root. Not as affirmation, but as activation. Because the world does not need more seekers. **It needs those who remember who they are**—and walk that remembrance into everything they touch.

COMMIT TO A SACRED TIME

Each day, create a space beyond distraction. Beyond routine. Beyond the mental static that disconnects you from the rhythm of your soul. This is not about checking a box or adding another task to your list. This is your sacred time. Your hour of power. A portal through which the noise of the world fades and the voice of your higher self becomes unmistakably clear.

Write. Let the words come raw, unedited, unfiltered. Not for others. Not for approval. But as a direct dialogue with the divine within you. Let your hand move as if transcribing what your spirit already knows.

Speak. Say your affirmations aloud. Let the room hear you. Let your nervous system absorb the frequency of your truth. These are not hopes. These are not dreams. These are declarations. Identity statements. Codes of remembrance.

Create. Not for outcome. Not for art. But as sacred motion. A sketch. A phrase. A stretch. A breath that becomes prayer. There is no requirement but authenticity. There is no performance, only presence.

Let each act—each line, each movement—be a quiet rebellion against the chaos that once ruled you. Let them say, without needing to shout: I belong to truth now.

In this space, you're not just preparing for a better day. You are becoming the frequency you want to carry through every day that follows. You are turning breath into transformation. You are shaping a new foundation. The ground beneath you steadies, not because it never shakes, but because you've chosen to meet life from your center.

Stay in this sacred time daily. Invite others into it. Read these words together. Speak them into the space between you. Let your homes, your friendships, your partnerships become altars where the Christ frequency is remembered again and again.

And watch what happens when your ordinary moments become lit with the extraordinary presence of truth.

EMBRACING PAIN AS PART OF THE PURGE

The moment the old self begins to die, pain will rise—not as punishment, not as rejection, but as sacred proof that something false is breaking. You are not cursed. You are being cleared.

This is the purge. The holy fire. The divine *dismantling*.

Imagine yourself in a vast clearing. Night hangs heavy overhead. All around you lie the shattered pieces of what you once called your life—the stories you repeated to survive, the masks you wore to be accepted, the fears that shaped your every move.

And yet, in the middle of this collapse, there is a single flame. Not above you. Not coming to rescue you. But within you.

It does not comfort. It does not explain. It burns.

It begins in your center, igniting every false identity, every lie you mistook for love, every coping mechanism dressed as strength. You feel it in your chest. A raw ache. A sharp truth. You feel it in your body. The tension. The fatigue. The tremble of letting go.

Let it burn.

Because what it leaves behind is what cannot be taken from you. What it strips away is what you never needed. And what it reveals—beneath the smoke, beneath the pain—is a self that never had to prove anything to begin with.

Each tear is a release. Each breath is a resurrection. Each moment of fire is the death of illusion and the beginning of embodiment.

Let the stories go. Let the ashes fall. You are not losing yourself.

You are finally coming home.

LET THE PAIN FLOW THROUGH, NOT IN YOU

Let it come. Let the pain rise like a tide. Let it move through you—unrushed, unblocked. You don't need to hold it. You don't need to brace yourself against it. It isn't here to destroy you. **It's here to move something.**

This *isn't* punishment. This isn't failure. It's the body releasing what the soul is no longer willing to carry.

So when the heat rises in your chest, when your throat tightens and the ache becomes too hard to name—don't run. Don't distract. Don't numb. Stay with it. Let it pass through like a storm through open windows. Breathe into it. Let it take its shape. Let it finish.

This is not weakness. This is the work.

Each drop of sweat, each silent shudder, each breath that feels like a mountain is not a sign you're falling apart. It's a sign you're being remade. The pain doesn't need to become you. It just needs to pass.

Let the fire burn. Let it do what fire does—consume what no longer serves, melt down the armor, expose what's real. It may not feel holy. *But it is.*

And as it clears, you'll feel something else: space. A coolness where shame used to live. A silence where doubt used to echo. A calm you forgot was possible.

This is what it feels like to be free—not because nothing hurts, but because nothing sticks.

So let it flow. Let it clear. Let it go through you and not in you. What's left behind is not the wound. It's the truth of who you are—stronger than pain, untouched by illusion, ready to rise.

INTEGRATION OF THE AWAKENING

When it's all cleared—when the stories fall, when the noise quiets, when the fire has done its work—you don't disappear.

You come back. Fully. Grounded. Human. As Christ.

You come back to the kitchen, to the carpool, to the conference call, to the silence after a hard conversation. But now you carry something different. You're still in the world—but it doesn't own you anymore.

You know who you are. You know how you serve. You're no longer walking around looking for someone to hand you a label, a mission, a reason to belong. You've remembered it. Claimed it.

And you exhale that knowing like breath. Not loud. Not dramatic. Just steady.

Your presence becomes the change. Your energy becomes the message. You don't preach—you live. You don't argue—you embody. You don't convince—you align.

This is the Christ frequency *in motion*. It's not mystical. It's not abstract. It's you, with nothing left to prove, doing what only you can do—with love.

Every conversation becomes an opportunity to extend presence. Every interaction, a chance to lead with light. Not because you're trying—but because you're different now.

You walk into the room, and something shifts.

This is not the end of your journey. It's the beginning of what it means to live awake.

This is Christ, returning—not to the clouds, but to the ground.

Through you.

EMBODIED EXPRESSION

Awakening doesn't live in your head. It moves through your body. It's in the way you speak, the way you hold your ground, the way your breath deepens when pressure rises. You don't just think differently. You carry yourself differently. Your energy walks into the room ahead of your words and tells the truth for you.

It begins in the subtle moments. The heat behind your ribs when you're triggered. The tightening in your jaw when someone challenges you. The reflex to explain, to defend, to collapse into something smaller. That's the old self, knocking. But now, you don't open the door.

You pause. Not to retreat. To root.

Feel your feet on the ground. Let your shoulders drop. Let your breath anchor in your belly. Not to perform calm—but to remember who you are beneath the noise.

Then something shifts. Maybe your voice gets quieter, but more certain. **Maybe you say less, but it lands deeper.** Maybe you meet someone's pain without absorbing it. You don't retreat. You don't puff up. You remain. Present. Clear. Aligned.

That is embodiment.

It's not about sounding enlightened. It's how you stay in your body when fear tries to pull you out. It's how you speak without needing to be right. **It's how you love without self-erasure.** It's how you act from your center instead of your wound.

You don't need to announce it. You live it. In your posture. In your tone. In the silence between your sentences. Embodiment is when your presence carries more truth than any argument *ever* could.

And this isn't about perfection. It's not a role. It's remembering in real time. When you forget, you come back. **Over and over**, until coming back becomes your default.

You no longer perform peace. You are peace.

You no longer chase truth. You are truth.

This is what it means to be the message. To let the divine not just speak through you—but move as you.

Not something you do. Something you *are*.

YOUR DAYS ARE THE CANVAS

Every moment becomes a brushstroke. Every interaction, a living canvas. You're no longer trying to paint a spiritual picture—your life is the painting. The way you speak. The way you listen. The way you walk into tension without bracing. It all leaves a mark. You're no longer performing presence. You've become it.

With friends. With family. With strangers you'll never see again. At work. In traffic. At the grocery store. In how you respond when someone's short with you. In how you answer the phone when you're tired. In how you make someone feel seen in the middle of their mess. These aren't spiritual side quests. This is the actual canvas of your awakening.

Not in what you preach. Not in what you post. But in how you move when no one's clapping for you.

And still—old patterns will surface. The urge to fix, to explain, to interrupt, to win. That flash of defensiveness. That subtle tightening in your chest. That moment where you feel yourself slip back into needing to be right, or safe, or small.

Catch it. Pause. Breathe. Remember who you are.

This is the holy moment—not the dramatic breakthrough, but the tiny shift. The choice to stay open. To let stillness hold the space. To let love speak before your mouth does.

Let the Christ frequency guide your next move. Let your breath be your compass. Let your posture speak louder than your opinion. Let your tone say what words can't.

You are the conductor now. Not of noise, but of frequency. Every sigh. Every glance. Every pause in the conversation. Every time you choose to soften instead of snap, ground instead of rush. It's all part of the music you're writing with your life.

And people feel it—even if they don't know what changed.

You don't need to tell them who you are. You don't need to explain your awakening. They'll feel it in the calm you carry into chaos. In the presence you bring into rooms that used to intimidate you. In the way you hold yourself when no one else knows what to do.

This isn't about being impressive. **It's about being real.**

You walk into everyday moments like a living broadcast. Not trying to teach. Just being clear.

And when you're clear, the world listens.

CULTIVATING EMBODIED EXPRESSION

Step away from the noise. Not to escape the world, but to hear yourself clearly inside it. The day piles on demands—notifications, expectations, decisions you didn't ask for. That noise builds slowly until it becomes normal. You forget there's a signal underneath it all, a frequency that never stopped calling you back to center.

So create space. Daily. Not as a ritual. Not as a routine. Just a moment where you're not performing, explaining, or reacting. Find somewhere quiet. Sit down. Shut out the world for a second. Let your jaw unclench. Let your shoulders drop. Let your body stop holding everything together for once.

Close your eyes. Not to tune out—but to listen inward. Let your breath come slower, not because you're forcing it, but because your body finally has permission to stop bracing. You're not trying to feel something profound. You're trying to feel what's real.

With each inhale, settle deeper into your own presence. Not a mantra. Not a chant. Just the simplicity of being in your body again. You're not preparing to be spiritual.

You're just becoming quiet enough to stop pretending.

This is where embodiment begins. You feel the tension between who you've had to be and who you actually are. You notice the small ways you've been performing all day—how your tone shifts depending on the room, how your posture adjusts to seem less, or more, depending on who's watching. And without judgment, you let those things fall.

The more you do this, the more you start moving differently out there. You catch yourself before you over-explain. You stop apologizing for simply taking up space. You respond slower. Speak clearer. You don't try to fill the silence anymore.

People notice. Even if they don't know what changed. You'll see it in how they pause when they talk to you. How they soften. How they reflect your clarity back at you without realizing it. Not because you've said anything. But because of how you're sitting. How you're breathing.

How you're not leaking energy into places that used to drain you.

This is where the shift actually happens—not during breakthroughs, not in the middle of profound insights, but in small, daily choices to move from awareness instead of impulse. And when that becomes normal, **everything else does too.**

TRANSFORMING ROUTINE INTO RITUAL

Every day offers the chance to step into the divine—but not by mimicking a script or dressing your schedule in spiritual language. It happens in how you move through the ordinary. Not differently, but intentionally.

You don't escape the mundane. You charge it with meaning.

Rising out of bed isn't just the start of another day. It's a return. A subtle but clear shift where your body, your awareness, and your intention begin to align. You're not checking boxes. You're declaring something—through presence, **not performance.**

This isn't about rituals that impress the divine. It's about choosing to show up fully in everything that already exists. When you eat, when you drive, when you open your inbox—none of it is automatic unless you let it be.

Picture your morning like a ceremony. Not elaborate. Not fragile. Just grounded. You stand, place your hand over your chest, and breathe—not as habit, but as clarity. You feel the rhythm in your body. You're not affirming. You're owning.

Say it out loud if you want to. Something simple. Something real.

"I am here. I have come."

Not a wish. Not a whisper. A statement.

It shifts the way your body moves through space. You don't float above your life— you fill it. You make the small tasks carry weight. Not heavy. Sacred. You move through emails like someone who knows they matter. You walk into a meeting with the same energy you would bring into a sanctuary. You tie your shoes with the quiet authority of someone who's not rushing to be elsewhere.

This isn't about pretending everything is profound. It's about realizing it already is.

And through this way of living, the ordinary stops being background noise. It becomes the medium. Every motion becomes a brushstroke of embodiment. Every silence, a place where meaning can speak. Every interaction, a chance to reaffirm what you carry.

Not by forcing depth. Just by refusing to move unconsciously.

By the time your day ends, you're not asking if it was productive. You're not wondering if you were **"spiritual enough."** You've already answered both—by living in alignment with what's real.

And in that space, it becomes clear:

"Behold, I make all things new."

LIVING AS CREATION IN MOTION

As you move through your day—answering messages, handling responsibilities, managing pressure—it's easy to slip into patterns that feel mechanical. But you don't exist to run on autopilot. You're not here to survive your schedule. You're here to shape it from within.

When stress rises or doubt tries to rerun its old script, pause. Don't react. Don't explain. Just ground. Let your feet meet the floor. Let your body remember the truth your mind forgets under pressure. Say it quietly if you need to:

I am known. I am here. I have come. Behold, I make all things new.

Those words aren't affirmations. They're anchors. You're not moving from urgency anymore. You're moving from clarity.

Your actions aren't random. The emails you send, the conversations you hold, the tasks you cross off—they aren't just functional. They're energetic. Every step, every decision, every interaction becomes a brushstroke on the canvas of the collective field. You're not checking boxes. You're transmitting signal.

Nothing you do is too small to matter. When you prepare a meal, it's not about efficiency. It's an offering. Every ingredient becomes a symbol. You chop. You stir. You plate. Not to complete a task, but to participate in the act of creation. You're not rushing to feed your body—you're honoring the vessel that carries your awareness.

This is the shift. Not in the structure of your day, but in how you show up inside it.

The ordinary isn't waiting to become sacred. It already is. It's just waiting for you to notice.

So stop moving like your life is background noise. When your hands move, be there. When your voice speaks, mean it. When your attention drifts, bring it home. Because in every one of those small moments, the divine isn't just nearby.

It's expressing through you.

And when you live like that, the weight of the day doesn't accumulate. It becomes momentum. What once felt dull becomes directive. What once felt like repetition becomes revelation. You're not working through your day. You're creating it from the inside out.

Not to keep up. But to take your place in the architecture of something far more alive.

YOUR ROUTINE IS YOUR ALTAR

If you want to know where your real practice is, look at how you handle the everyday friction. **Not the big moments—the small ones.** The person who cuts you off and won't make eye contact. The coworker who finds a way to push the same button every time. The meeting that drags on while your mind begs for an exit.

These aren't interruptions. They're the altar. Not because the moment is special, but because it gives you something to lay down. Pride. Frustration. The need to be right. The need to win.

In those moments, don't pretend to be above it. Feel it. Let the heat rise. Let your reaction knock. Then choose not to answer.

That's where transformation actually happens.

Take a breath. Let your body stay open. Don't fold your arms. Don't harden your voice. Let yourself stay human and stay kind. That's the real offering—not silence, not withdrawal, but staying in it without losing your center.

If someone says something that gets under your skin, remind yourself: they're probably struggling more than they show. They're not the enemy. They're the mirror. You don't have to fix them. Just don't let them pull you out of alignment.

In your mind, bless them. Quietly. Not as superiority—but as clarity.

You carry the light, so bring it. Even if it's invisible. Especially when it's invisible.

That's what it means to treat your routine like an altar. Not with ceremony. With intention. With the decision to meet everything and everyone as if they're already part of something holy—even when they don't act like it.

You don't need to love the moment. You just need to remain someone who can carry love through it.

And if you slip? *Good.* That's part of it. Jesus got mad too. Catch yourself. Come back. Let that be part of what you lay down, too.

Because the point isn't to perform your awakening. It's to live in a way where nothing is beneath your awareness. Where no moment is too ordinary to matter.

Your altar isn't in the quiet room at the start of your day. It's the room you didn't want to walk into. The interaction you didn't ask for. The habit you finally notice. It's your entire life, offering itself back to you moment by moment—asking only that you show up and bring something real.

BUILDING NEW CONNECTIONS

When you begin living from the Christ frequency, you stop talking just to fill the air. Words become presence. You start to feel when someone is speaking from a script—and when they're reaching for something real. And you stop participating in the old social choreography that kept everything surface-level and safe.

You're not here to perform politeness. You're here to carry something that shifts the atmosphere.

The old world praised small talk, taught competition as connection, and hid authenticity behind rehearsed smiles. That doesn't hold anymore. You're no longer wired for it. You walk into spaces differently now—not needing to be the loudest, but unwilling to be invisible.

You don't rush to speak, but when you do, it lands.

You move through the world like someone who means it. Your presence announces something before you say a word. And when you do speak, you don't settle for default questions. Instead of "How are you?", you ask something alive. Something that invites truth.

What are you blessing today?

What's real for you right now?

What shifted this week?

You ask questions that open people—not interrogate them. And in doing so, you create permission. You bring others out of hiding without needing to force it.

This isn't about being intense. It's about being present. It's about dropping the mask so others feel safe to do the same.

You're not just making small connections. You're re-teaching people how to show up. Not with theory—but with example.

CONVERSATION AS SACRED RITUAL

This doesn't mean every talk becomes a soul excavation. But even a passing comment holds weight when your attention is all the way there. When your tone reflects your clarity. When your eyes don't drift while someone's speaking.

Imagine walking into a room where every handshake isn't just habit—it's acknowledgment. Where each smile isn't filler—it's recognition. You're not creating these moments for applause. You're creating them because truth belongs everywhere. Especially in the ordinary.

Your conversations become a space where people feel seen without needing to perform. A place where stillness is allowed. Where silence isn't awkward—it's honest. Where vulnerability isn't demanded, but naturally arises.

You don't need to host a circle or lead a retreat. You just need to bring full presence to the table in front of you. Whether it's lunch with a friend or thirty seconds with a stranger, the field you create becomes undeniable.

This is what it means to connect through frequency, not just words.

Not to get something.

But to reveal something that's always been there.

PRACTICING ACTIVE PRESENCE IN CONNECTION

Real connection isn't built on words alone—it's built on attention. And not the kind you give out of politeness. **The kind that makes the other person feel like they actually exist in front of you.** When you sit with someone and you're fully there, not waiting for your turn to speak, not subtly checking out, but actually listening with your whole body, something shifts.

You nod, but not to signal agreement—to signal that you're present. You pause, not to create drama, but because you're letting what they said land. You're not thinking about how to fix them. **You're not searching for a clever reply. You're just here.**

And they can feel it.

The Sixth Resound

In that kind of presence, people stop performing. They start revealing. You hear what's behind the words, not just the ones they chose. You feel their nervous laughter. You catch the crack in their voice. And without needing to name it, you create space for them to feel safe in their truth.

You're not playing the expert. You're not holding court. You're standing beside them—not above.

And as you do this, the categories start to fall away. Their background, their politics, their identity doesn't disappear—it becomes part of a bigger picture. You stop scanning for difference and start honoring the nuance. You realize you're looking at a distinct expression of the same force that flows through you.

That recognition doesn't erase uniqueness. It elevates it. It turns connection into celebration. **You're not forcing common ground—you're uncovering it.** Because when you stop relating through roles and start seeing people as they are, the space between you shrinks.

What's left isn't sameness. It's presence. And presence builds what ideology never could.

AWAKENING A COLLECTIVE CONSCIOUSNESS

These connections aren't just personal wins. They're catalysts.

Every real conversation, every moment where someone feels seen without judgment, sends something into the field. A ripple. A resonance. A reminder that love isn't just an idea—it's an active force shaping culture, one interaction at a time.

This is bigger than friendship. It's architecture.

Each time you show up clear, others start to question the masks they've been wearing. **They feel the contrast.** They remember their own truth. And in that remembrance, a network starts to build—not organized, not branded, but undeniable.

It moves through workplaces. Through families. Through chance encounters. You don't need to know where the ripple goes. You just need to trust that it's moving.

And when enough people start choosing presence over performance, something begins to take root. Not a movement. A shift. The old division lines start to fade.

Conversations get deeper. People soften. Realness spreads.

This isn't waiting for the world to change. It's about embodying the change so completely that the world has to catch up.

You're not building connections to feel good. You're building them to awaken something in the collective that's been dormant for too long.

And in that awakening, you're not waiting for the Second Coming.

You're helping reveal the truth that it's already here.

CREATING A PERSONAL SANCTUARY IN THE WORLD

The outside world moves fast—chaotic, loud, full of static. Everyone wants something. Everything wants your attention. It pulls you into noise before you even realize you've left yourself. But underneath that noise is something untouched. A stillness that doesn't flinch. A space the world can't touch.

This is your sanctuary.

It's not an escape. It's not a retreat. It's a reclamation. A return to what's always been yours. Maybe it's a room you've made your own. Maybe it's your car before you walk into work. Maybe it's a bench, a chair, a stretch of morning light across the floor. Or maybe it's nothing external at all—just a place you close your eyes and enter through breath.

Wherever it is, treat it like it matters. Not for performance, but for presence.

Step into it with intention. Feel your feet on the ground. Place your hand on your chest and say, quietly but clearly, "I am grounded in divine truth." Let that settle— not just in your mind, but in your spine. In your breath. In the way you choose to sit a little straighter, slower, more here.

Let the world fall away—not because it's gone, but because it doesn't belong in this space.

This is your Upper Room. The place where you meet yourself again, without the noise. You're not trying to ascend. You're grounding the Christ frequency into your actual life. Into your breath. Into your body. Into the structure of your day. In time you may be here all the time, present here in form, and there in spirit at once. This is what Jesus did.

And from this space, the ordinary becomes something else.

When you brush your teeth. Make your coffee. Get dressed. It's not about adding spiritual language to your tasks—it's about bringing intention to what already exists. Feel the water on your skin. Notice the texture of your clothing. Take three extra seconds to breathe before the next thing starts.

This isn't a ritual because it looks sacred. It's a ritual because you've chosen to treat it that way.

Let each small moment recalibrate you. Let the rhythm of your breath interrupt the momentum of the outside world. Let your presence be what defines the hour—not the clock, not the noise, not the demands.

You're not building a sanctuary to visit. You're building one you can carry.

A DAILY DECLARATION OF WHO YOU ARE

Each time you step into your sanctuary—whether it's a quiet room, a corner of your morning, or a moment between tasks—you're not just creating calm. You're making a declaration. Not to the world. To your own nervous system. To your energy field. To every part of you that needs the reminder.

"God is. God is. God is.

I have come. I have come. I have come."

These aren't affirmations. They're activations. These mantras carry the same current found in the ancient invocations—many of which were hidden, protected, or buried under the Vatican. Why? Because words hold power. Not symbolic power. Creative power. God didn't snap his fingers and form the Earth. He spoke. **He said, "Let there be light."**

Creation responds to voice. Frequency. Intention. And when you speak from presence, you're not just reminding yourself—you're reshaping the field around you.

This isn't about hype. It's about identity. And nothing anchors identity faster than how you treat your body.

Your physical form isn't separate from your spiritual work. It is the spiritual work. The way you feed it, hydrate it, rest it, move it—it all speaks louder than your words. You can speak truth all day, but if your body is exhausted, overstimulated, or ignored, the message gets scrambled. Your vessel becomes static.

Picture your body as an instrument (it is)—delicate, precise, built to carry frequency. When it's clear, everything resonates. When it's flooded with noise—too much caffeine, too little rest, too much pushing, too little listening—the notes distort. What should be music turns into dissonance.

This isn't about purity or control. It's not a rulebook. It's about recognizing that clarity requires care.

There will be moments when your body needs support. When rest isn't enough. When medicine is wisdom. Honoring the body doesn't mean pretending it can do everything on its own. It means tuning in and responding with integrity.

Refusing support out of fear or pride isn't strength—**it's misalignment.** Care doesn't weaken the temple. It restores it. And when your system is aligned, your energy is louder than anything you could say. People feel it. Not because you're glowing. Because you're coherent.

If you want to walk as divine presence in the world, start by building a body that can carry it. Not perfectly. Not flawlessly. Just consciously.

Tend to the instrument. Keep it in tune. Let it hold the message it was built to carry.

HONORING THE TEMPLE & CARRYING THE FREQUENCY

"I am in the Upper Room."

"Behold, I make all things new."

These are not poetic phrases. *They are blueprints.* Spoken declarations that anchor a deeper truth: belief doesn't just shape your thoughts—it shapes your reality. Every time you speak from that knowing, you shift the atmosphere around you. Every time you return to your sanctuary—whether it's a physical space or a felt alignment—you reinforce the field you've chosen to live in.

This isn't about escaping chaos. It's about remembering that the storm doesn't own you. You carry stillness now. You carry light. And that light isn't something you hoard. It's something you embody, share, and build from.

But this frequency can't move through you freely if your vessel is ignored.

The body isn't separate from this work—it's the delivery system. The temple. The current of divine intelligence runs through skin, breath, muscle, and blood. And how you treat it either amplifies or distorts that current.

The world will push you toward disconnection—distraction, overconsumption, pushing through exhaustion, ignoring signals that were meant to guide you back to balance. That's not freedom. That's noise. You're not here to run your body like a machine. You're here to inhabit it like a sacred space.

Honoring the temple isn't perfection. It's presence. You feed it with what strengthens. You move it in ways that wake it up. You rest it not just to recover, but to realign. You don't punish it into shape—you partner with it so it can hold what you've been given to carry.

And when help is needed—real, grounded help—you don't resist. You listen. Sometimes honoring the body means taking the medicine. Saying yes to the therapy. Letting yourself be supported. Denial doesn't protect the temple. It fractures it. Wisdom knows the *difference.*

This is the sequence of embodiment. You clear the static. You care for the structure. And only then can the full current of the **Christ frequency** flow through you without distortion.

Your belief opens the door. Your body carries the light through it.

And from that place—every step becomes a declaration. Every breath, a statement of alignment. You don't need to announce your divinity. You live it. With clarity. With care. With a vessel built to hold what the world still forgets is real.

BEING MINDFUL OF WHAT YOU RECEIVE

Your body isn't a background detail in your spiritual life—**it's the front line.** Every choice you make, every input you allow in, leaves a mark. What you consume, what you listen to, what you allow near your nervous system—**it all either nourishes the frequency you're here to carry or clouds it.**

Before you take something in, ask the real question: Does this support my divine purpose, or does it shroud my light?

This isn't about restriction. It's about reverence. You're not avoiding the world out of fear. You're moving through it with clarity.

Your body is not a project to fix. Not a nuisance to manage. Not a container to tolerate while your soul does the important work. It is the work. A physical bridge between spirit and matter. A channel through which presence becomes reality.

And it listens to everything you do.

When you stay up too late, scroll too long, ignore its signals, it doesn't punish you—it just reflects you. When you tune in, when you feed it well, when you move it in ways that feel honest, you're not just improving your health—you're sharpening your signal.

This isn't about chasing some peak version of yourself, or wasting money on useless supplements. It's about honoring the fact that your body is already miraculous. Not someday. Not once it looks or feels a certain way. Right now.

Caring for it is not indulgence. Strengthening it is not vanity. Needing rest is not weakness. These are acts of alignment. Of trust. Of choosing to walk like your energy matters—because it does.

And here's the deeper truth: your relationship to your body doesn't just affect you. When you treat your temple with clarity, others feel it. They may not know why they breathe easier around you, why they speak more honestly, why they remember who they are—but it's because you've made your presence a permission slip.

That's what embodiment does. *It ripples.*

Your body becomes a transmission tower. Not just sustaining your light—but amplifying it for the collective. **Every time you choose** rest over burnout, nourishment over neglect, discernment over distraction, you're helping to repair the false divide between the spiritual and physical.

This was never about separation.

One temple. One vessel. One presence of God in form.

DECLARING THE SACREDNESS OF EVERY CHOICE

Every choice you make either supports your alignment or dulls it. What you put in your body, what you allow into your mind, how you treat the vessel you live in—it all adds up. Not someday. Right now. Quietly, in the background, until it becomes the tone you live by.

You don't need to micromanage your life. But you do need to stop pretending the small things don't matter.

You know the difference between taking something in to celebrate and using it to disappear. You can feel it in your chest. One expands you. The other disconnects you. No one else needs to point it out. You already know when the line gets crossed. You know it in the milliseconds before it touches your lips, that's how fast you have to respond, but you can do it. If I can, you can too because we're not any different from each other.

There's nothing wrong with enjoying the moment. Raising a glass. Taking in something that helps you soften, breathe, be present. But if you're doing it to numb, to avoid, to not feel what's asking to be felt—that's not pleasure.

That's *escape.*

And escape has a cost.

When you use something to avoid yourself, you lose clarity. You push the work down the road. You slow the momentum that's already been trying to carry you forward.

This isn't about guilt. It's about being honest with yourself about what's actually helping and what's just keeping you from hearing what needs to be heard.

So stay aware. Before you reach for it, ask why. Pay attention to the reason, not just the habit. Don't perform balance. Practice it. Even when no one's watching.

Especially then.

DESIRE AS CREATIVE ENERGY & A PATH TO WHOLENESS

Desire isn't the villain in your story. It's not the shady character whispering temptations from behind the curtain. It's the engine. The pulse behind creation. The charge that moves you to build, to reach, to love, to feel alive inside your own skin.

The problem was never desire. The problem was how watered down we let it become. When you look at your partner through the lens of truth—not the role they play, not the routine you've both memorized, but the actual soul sitting in front of you—you stop seeing them as an extension of your needs. You start seeing the light in their eyes as the divine signature it's always been.

And suddenly the thought of chasing cheap highs or outside validation feels like the waste of time that it is.

Why would you trade a sacred fire for a spark that burns out before you've even exhaled? Why give your energy to anything that fragments what could be whole?

Real desire doesn't ask you to seek more. It asks you to see more.

It's not about constantly needing newness—it's about letting presence make everything new again. It doesn't crave drama or chase intensity. It doesn't look for the next hit. It looks deeper into what's already in front of you and says: I want to be here. I want to feel this. I want to build something that actually means something.

You don't need to leave to find passion. You just need to stop numbing the parts of yourself that are wired to feel it.

There's no purity checklist in this work. No gold stars for abstinence. No spiritual badge for denying what was designed to wake you up. Just clarity. Just honesty. Just the courage to stop using desire as a shortcut and start using it as the tool it was always meant to be.

There are no monasteries in the Kingdom.

No nunneries.

And no brothels *either*.

Just people—learning how to want things without losing themselves in the process.

TEAR DOWN YOUR WALLS OF DENIAL

Denial doesn't always come in the form of collapse. Sometimes it looks like stability. Like playing it safe. Like being responsible. It slips in quietly and calls itself self-control, maturity, discipline—when really, it's just fear with better branding.

It's reading a text, writing the perfect response in your head, and never sending it—because if you say what you actually feel, they might not say it back. Or worse, they might. *And then what?*

It's telling your friends you're too tired to meet up—not because you are, but because you don't want to sit there pretending to be fine while something in you still feels unseen. It's canceling the adventure trip you used to dream about because you've convinced yourself you need to rest or to be in better shape—but the truth is, you're not tired. You're disappointed. At yourself. For waiting this long.

It's thinking about planning something romantic but stopping because they should have done it first. It's staying in a conversation too long with someone who flatters you while your partner waits at home. You don't act on it. But you feed on the attention because you're starving for connection and too proud to admit it.

It's scrolling through photos of people you find beautiful and telling yourself you're just appreciating aesthetics—when really, you don't believe anyone like that could ever want you back. It's easier to fantasize than to risk being seen and rejected.

It's dreaming up something massive, something that lights you up, then shelving it with a quiet "maybe later." Because if you try and fail, you'll lose the dream. And if you never try, you get to keep it—perfect and untouched.

This is how denial wins. Not through obvious destruction. Through slow erosion. Through small, daily compromises you justify so well, you start believing them.

But eventually, it catches up. The unread texts, the plans you never made, the truths you avoided, the courage you postponed—these things pile up. And one day you feel it. The weight of all the things you didn't say. The moves you didn't make. The life you didn't live.

That's when you stop *pretending*.

You stop calling hesitation wisdom. You stop pretending you're content playing small. You stop lying to yourself about what you want and start owning the fact that you've built walls and called them boundaries.

Tearing down those walls doesn't look like a dramatic breakthrough. It looks like sending the text. Showing up to the dinner. Booking the trip. Planning the date. Looking someone in the eye and letting them see you without the performance.

It looks like giving yourself permission to need. To want. To risk. To be fully in the thing you've been circling for years.

This is how you reclaim yourself—not by waiting to be ready, but by deciding you already are.

And when that decision catches on?

When enough people stop performing and start showing up?

That's when the ground moves.

That's when the Second Coming stops being a prophecy—and starts being a possibility. Not one man descending from the clouds. But all of us. Awake.

Together.

Walking as Christ in the middle of a world that never saw it coming.

This is how the wave begins, and it's going to happen anyway. You will wake up with you regrets at some age, at some junction in your journey and have this realization.

How much longer do you need to wait? To suffer? To ignore that deep burning inside of you to go and get it?

Let it end here. Don't wait for the wave. *Become it.*

XIII

The Seventh Resound

The Great Wave & a World Made New

"This is the fire that moves
from heart to heart.
Not to consume, but to
ignite."

THE SEVENTH RESOUND
THE GREAT WAVE & A WORLD MADE NEW

Everything you have walked through—every unraveling, every surrender, every moment you thought might break you—has led here. Not to the end of the journey, but to the place where it finally begins in truth.

Every illusion you've let collapse, every belief you've outgrown, every time you've stood in the fire and refused to run—this is what made room for the real thing to emerge.

At the center of Christ's power isn't control. It isn't dogma. It's love. Absolute, non-negotiable, unshakable love. Not the kind that asks you to earn it. Not the kind that flinches when you get it wrong. But the kind that stays. **The kind that sees all of you and still says: I choose you.**

This isn't theory. This is reality, rising. You're not just carrying this for yourself. You're part of something bigger now. The frequency that once moved through one body now moves through many. Through yours. Through mine. Through all of us, aligned in presence, unwilling to wait for permission.

This is the Great Wave. Not a storm, but a shift. Not one person, but a collective rising. The Second Coming of Christ—here, now, not descending from above, but awakening from within.

Come as you in your expression.

Come as you in your being.

Come as all in experience.

I AM IN THE UPPER ROOM

The upper room is not a location—it is a frequency. Not a physical space, but a vibrational threshold where the highest level of Christ consciousness can be fully embodied. It is the state beyond fear, beyond illusion, where creation flows unbound and truth moves without distortion. The phrase echoes from scripture, from the place where the disciples gathered and the Spirit descended like fire— not as myth, but as blueprint. The upper room has always been an initiation, the moment where the divine self awakens in form.

To stand in the upper room is to remember who you are and move through the world as the living expression of that remembrance. You no longer seek truth—you are truth. You see with clarity, act with knowing, and create without limitation. You do not escape the world. You transfigure it. This is not ascension to another realm—it is the full immersion of light into this one. It is neither high, nor low. It is seeing with the eyes of Christ, and with this all things, and I mean ALL THINGS, are possible.

You may wonder now, Yoshai'el, if *you* have done all of this—why do we not see you floating upon clouds to deliver this to us? The answer is *quite* simple. The second coming is not one person again. What would be the point? To have a new Bible bastardized for two thousand more years? For more death and suffering to be carried out? I will not allow it to be done in my name. You will not see me nailed to any crosses. I've already learned what it was to crucify myself in spirit, mind, and body.

The world today is denser—more beliefs, more data, more distortion. You and I hold thousands of constructs that didn't exist when Jesus lived. It's too dense for one person to transcend alone.

**It must be done in groups. This is why even Jesus
had disciples. They did this together.**

I need you to do it, and I believe we can. We need you all. And then yes, we may
transmute, transfigure, heal, walk on water, and more. Jesus told us we would do
greater works. Let's show him we can.

THE SECOND COMING IS NOT AWAITING—IT IS ARRIVING

This is not about waiting for a lone savior to descend from the skies. The Second
Coming is not an event marked on some distant calendar. It is already here. It is
you. It is every awakened soul blazing with the **Christ frequency.**

This is the fire that moves from heart to heart. Not to consume, but to ignite. A
flame that does not destroy, but reveals what was always there—buried beneath fear
and illusion. It spreads not through force, not through conquest, but by the quiet
power of love remembered.

This unfolding is not static. It is not a prophecy waiting for permission. It is a
living, breathing movement—a rhythmic surge of energy that rises and falls like

the tides of the universe. Your personal awakening ignites the first spark. And from
that spark, the wave builds.

It begins in a single connection. Two souls remembering. Then families are bound
together in light. Small circles become thriving communities. Communities ripple
into towns, towns into cities, cities into nations. Until finally, a unified global body
emerges. Not through domination, but through a love so radiant, so undeniable,
that the old world cannot remain.

THE GREAT UNFOLDMENT

This isn't a revolution of fists or flags. It's a revolution of presence. Of alignment.
A current that moves through the world not with noise, but with undeniable
transformation. It doesn't ask for your belief. It waits for your participation.

The wave ebbs, flows, and moves in eight phases. They aren't steps to climb. They
aren't tasks to complete. **These are frequencies—tones that move through your
system, rearranging everything they touch.** It's not a ladder. It's a rhythm. A
spiral. You may revisit stages you thought were finished. That's not failure. That's

the nature of evolution.

This is the sound of awakening playing through your life. A movement between collapse and clarity, between surrender and arrival.

I. REALIZATION

The moment something in you wakes up. Not intellectually. Viscerally. You see who you are, and the illusion starts to break. You can't unsee it.

II. RELEASE

Everything that doesn't match your new frequency starts falling away. People. Habits. Stories. You let go—not because you're told to, but because holding on feels heavier than leaving.

III. PURIFICATION

The masks come off. The projections melt. It burns—but what's left is real. You face yourself fully, and instead of running, you stay. That's when everything begins to shift.

IV. CONNECTION

You're no longer walking alone. You feel others—just as awake, just as raw, just as ready. The field starts to hum. What was scattered begins to sync.

V. ALIGNMENT

Groups form. Not through planning, but through resonance. Truth recognizes truth. Systems crack. Paradigms falter. Something stronger starts to build.

VI. ACTIVATION

The movement grows. It gains weight. Momentum. Coherence. The illusion loses its grip. Love becomes practical—something that rewires how people live.

VII. TRANSMUTATION

The atmosphere changes. Density lifts. The impossible starts happening. Not in theory, but in real time. Reality starts answering to a new source code.

VIII. TRANSFIGURATION

This is not the end. This is foundation. Framework. The space where something entirely different begins to take shape. The blueprint breathes now. It adjusts, expands, flows like music, like breath, like the tide coming back for what it never forgot.

PHASE I: REALIZATION

Everything begins in that singular, electrifying moment when you stop living on autopilot and finally declare—to the world and to yourself—that you are fully here. The veil lifts. The atmosphere shifts. Your heartbeat sounds like a war drum made of truth. Something ancient in you stops waiting and steps forward.

This isn't a soft awakening. This is ignition. It doesn't knock politely. It erupts. A surge of divine clarity floods your system, and every illusion you once clung to starts breaking apart under the weight of what's real. There's no going back. The light is on now.

You step into the Upper Room—not a place, but a state. The false identities fall off. The doubts loosen their grip. The labels no longer hold. You're not better than you were—you're just no longer hiding behind what you aren't.

And in that raw clarity, something inside you speaks. It doesn't ask. It doesn't seek validation. It simply states: this is who I am, and this is why I came.

THE SPARK THAT REFUSES TO DIM

Picture it. You're standing at the edge of a world that still feels asleep. The systems, the habits, the versions of yourself built to please or protect—they're still echoing in the distance. But something deeper has cracked open. And even if no one else sees it yet, you do.

This isn't hope. It's not optimism. It's realization.

This is the moment you remember who you've always been beneath everything they taught you to be. You don't need proof. You don't need credentials. You don't need anyone to agree with you.

You just know.

And that knowing starts changing how you breathe, how you speak, how you move through the world. You're not performing anymore. You're not explaining. You're not waiting for a sign. You are the sign.

Every breath is a claim. Every heartbeat is a drumbeat of presence.

You're no longer asking to be let in.

You're already here.

BREAKING OPEN: THE FIRST MOMENT OF AWAKENING

In the beginning, it doesn't arrive gently. It doesn't ask permission. It cracks you open. One moment you're going through the motions, the next—everything that felt solid starts to dissolve. The separation you didn't even know you were living under rips. You don't become a new person. You become who you always were, minus the noise.

It's not a whisper. It's a rupture. A flash of knowing that leaves no room for doubt. You are not a mistake. You are not a coincidence. You didn't randomly land in this body, in this lifetime. You are here on purpose, by choice, with reason.

You are the Christ made *tangible*. Not in theory—in form. You were designed to carry this frequency, to speak this truth, to live this call. And the time you've been waiting for isn't in the distance anymore. It's now.

The light doesn't arrive with softness. It scorches. It burns through the layers you built to survive. The identities, the shame, the roles. They fall off like ash. You feel stripped and exposed—but you also feel free. Underneath it all, peace rises. A steady, unshakable peace that doesn't depend on external conditions.

You're done hiding behind doubt. You're done pretending smallness is wisdom. You're done shrinking to fit a world that forgot what you came to remember.

The Upper Room isn't something you reach. It's something you become—a state of absolute clarity where truth breathes and creation listens. And from this place, the wave begins. First as a flicker. Then a fire. Then a call that starts echoing in others.

THE DISSOLUTION OF THE OLD SELF

It happens in a moment. Not as theory. Not as wishful thinking. As a physical shift that floods your system. It doesn't ask you to let go. It takes what's already expired.

You feel the old structure crack—the ideas, the patterns, the roles you've clung to just to feel safe. And as they crumble, you don't resist. Because something deeper has already taken their place. Not a concept. A presence.

There's no panic. No grasping. Only a strange calm. A knowing so complete, you stop needing to explain yourself—to anyone.

These aren't declarations. They're truths you don't remember learning because you didn't learn them. You are them. They rise from your bones like memory returning.

THE SPARK THAT SETS EVERYTHING IN MOTION

By now, you know what's real. You've walked through the fire. You've questioned everything. You've stripped off the layers and seen what was underneath. **That first awakening wasn't just a personal moment—it was the ignition point.** Whether you knew it or not, it sent a signal. And now the field is moving.

You feel it. Not as a rush. Not as inspiration. As a steady presence that no longer needs to be earned. The clarity that cracked you open doesn't fade. It settles. It recalibrates everything you touch. Not through effort. Through coherence.

You stop apologizing for being awake. You stop adjusting your frequency to match the room. You start holding your shape, and the room adjusts to you. This is the shift. Not in belief. In embodiment.

Old thoughts still come, but they don't land. Old fears still whisper, but they don't register. They don't match your signal anymore. You're not trying to outrun them. **You've just stopped giving them somewhere to land.**

Every move you make now either reinforces the new or props up the old. And you feel the difference immediately. That's the responsibility of awakening—it doesn't let you pretend anymore. The delay costs too much. The denial doesn't hold.

What you used to ignore, you now feel in your body. What you used to explain away, you now name. What you used to hide, you now carry in full view.

This is what sets it in motion. Not the grand moments. The honest ones. The ordinary choices you no longer make from survival. The subtle shifts in how you breathe, how you speak, how you stay in your body when you want to leave.

The spark is not a peak experience.

It's the part of you that stopped waiting.

THE SACRED SOLITUDE OF AWAKENING

As you step deeper into awareness, you may feel a stretch of silence around you. Not because you've done something wrong. Not because you're disconnected. But because what you've walked into hasn't yet taken root in the world around you. **You're standing in clarity while the world keeps running its old scripts, clinging to roles you've outgrown and rhythms you can't unhear.**

This isn't exile. This isn't punishment. This is the necessary space where everything unnecessary falls away. The people who can't meet you here go quiet. The noise you used to lean on goes hollow. And what's left is something many avoid at all costs—stillness.

But in that stillness, you hear again. Not the narratives. Not the doubt. The actual voice—the one that's been speaking beneath the surface your whole life. The presence that doesn't shout or perform, but waits.

This isn't loneliness. It's foundation. It's the open field where something permanent can finally take root.

A TRANSFORMATION BEYOND INTELLECT

Awakening has nothing to do with accumulating knowledge. You can quote every sacred text and still miss the point. You can master the language of truth and still run from yourself. This path is not about what you know. **It's about what you've let change you.**

Real transformation isn't conceptual. It's visceral. It happens when truth stops being an idea and starts living in your breath, your posture, your timing. It reshapes you without asking. You carry it differently. You speak less. You listen more. You stop chasing validation because what's alive in you no longer requires agreement.

No one can give this to you. No title can confirm it. You cross the line and you know—because everything inside you feels reorganized.

THIS IS ONLY THE BEGINNING

The Upper Room strips away what used to define you. The shame, the self-doubt, the striving. It doesn't try to fix it. It burns it. And what's left is clarity so stark it doesn't need embellishment.

There's no more pretending. No more needing the world to mirror back who you are. You know now. You move from that place. You live from it. Every glance, every silence, every breath becomes a frequency broadcast. Not because you're trying to lead—because you're no longer hiding.

But this isn't the end of the process. It's the ground. The launch point. The quiet before the collective ignition. **The moment before the ripple hits the wider field.**

You've stepped out of the story you were handed. You've buried the old name. And now, everything that comes next begins from this place—not the final arrival, but the exact moment the world starts catching up.

PHASE II: RELEASE

Release doesn't always arrive like a collapse. It doesn't always come with tears or declarations. More often, it begins quietly. A thought that used to sting passes through without impact. A breath lands deeper in your chest. Something old loosens its grip, and you don't even notice at first.

Then it hits you. You didn't carry that weight today.

This is how release begins—not as a dramatic break, but as a subtle refusal. You stop agreeing to the lies. The roles. The inherited names. The survival strategies that once felt like identity. They start slipping through your fingers, not because you're forcing them out, but because they no longer make sense in your hands.

Picture it like riding an elevator. Each floor represents a belief you once took as truth. A label you wore long enough to forget it wasn't yours. As the elevator rises, those floors don't go with you. They stay behind. The air gets clearer. The tension starts to fade. You realize those walls were never real—they were just the stories you outgrew.

This isn't escape. It's awareness. The realization that you were never trapped, only conditioned to act like you were.

And now? You choose again.

The elevator slows. The doors open. You step onto something wider. Lighter. You're not carrying the same weight. You're not reacting from the same place. The air has changed—not because the world shifted, but because you did.

And in that space, something speaks. Not from outside you. From within.

 "Behold, I make all things new."

This is release. Not the end of something. The clearing that makes room for what's next.

IT WAS JUST AN IDEA

The old codes—those quiet agreements you made with fear—start to unravel. You see them stripped of their weight, exposed for what they've always been: borrowed language, false identities, ideas sold as truth. They were never yours. They came from people who didn't know how to carry their own power, so they taught you to dim yours.

You stand in front of all of it now. And at first, it feels like a wall—heavy, familiar, absolute. But it isn't. It's paper. Thin. Brittle. Covered in judgments, doubts, expectations, names you were never meant to wear. Unworthy. Too much. Not enough. The moment you see through it, the whole structure begins to fall.

You don't need to fight it. Just stop pretending it belongs to you.

Take one breath and step forward. The wall gives. It doesn't resist. It tears like it was waiting for you to stop believing in it. And on the other side, there's space. Space to stand taller. Space to remember your name. Not the one they gave you—the one that always lived beneath the noise.

Say it. Not to convince yourself. But because it's time:

 **"I release the old. I know who I am. I know what
 I am. I know how I serve. I am free."**

Let it land. Not like a mantra. Like a fact. Like something that was always true—you just finally stopped pretending otherwise.

THE WOMAN WHO WAS KNOWN ANEW

There was once a woman from Magdala. Her name became a warning, passed down like a whispered threat. This is what happens when you break the rules. When you go too far. When you don't fit the mold. They didn't just judge her. They built an entire narrative around her shame.

They never asked who she actually was.

She was reduced to a label. A reputation. Her humanity buried under centuries of projection. They called her fallen. They called her unclean. They made her the example to fear, not the soul to understand.

But Jesus saw something different.

He didn't see a failure. He didn't see her past. He didn't measure her worth against her history. He looked past all of it—the gossip, the assumptions, the weight she'd been carrying that was never hers to begin with.

He saw the spark. Still burning. Still intact.

And He didn't pull demons from her body. He pulled lies from her story. He dismantled the false names. He shattered the old roles. He let her see herself without the filter of shame for the first time in her life.

Not by fixing her. **By showing her that she was never broken.**

He gave her a new way to see. And in doing so, He gave her permission to finally forgive herself—something no man could offer her until she was willing to see herself through the eyes of truth.

"Then Jesus said to her, 'Your sins are forgiven.'" —Luke 7:48

And now—you do the same.

RELEASE OF THE PERSONALITY MOLD

The roles begin to slip. Not with drama. Not with collapse. Quietly. Like steam lifting off a body that's finally exhaled. The names you were given before you even knew what they meant start to lose their grip. They were handed to you by a world more interested in control than truth. A world that needed to categorize what it couldn't understand, because that was easier than facing its own chaos.

You became whatever made other people comfortable. You learned how to be recognizable. Digestible. Safe. And somewhere along the way, you forgot there was ever another option.

Some of those roles you chose. Others were your only protection. You didn't always resist. Sometimes it felt better to have a name than to stand in silence.

Who have you been?

The strong one. The dependable one. The one who held it together.

The one who broke in private.

The loyal partner who kept giving after the connection dried up.

The one who wanted out but stayed.

The healer who kept bleeding.

The caretaker who had no one checking in.

The loud one who used volume to cover the ache.

The quiet one who watched everything and said nothing.

The magnetic one who never felt seen.

The ghost who kept waiting to be invited in.

You've been all of it. I've been all of these things. And none of it ever captured who you or I actually are.

Those names weren't your identity. They were tools. Armor. Temporary strategies for survival. And now they're starting to fall away—not because you've outgrown them, but because you're done pretending they were ever real.

You were never meant to be understood through the lens of someone else's fear. You were never meant to be small enough to explain.

You're not a title. You're not a category. You're not a role that can be cast or replaced.

You don't need to prove it. You don't need to explain it. You don't need to justify the space you take up.

You are.

You be.

And that's more than sufficient.

CHRIST WASN'T JESUS' LAST NAME

He was called Yeshua ben Yosef. Yeshua ha-Notzri. Labels tied to bloodline and location. A way for people to sort him, to place him somewhere familiar, somewhere manageable. But he was never defined by that. He never needed the titles, never fought to correct anyone's misunderstanding. They called him healer, prophet, blasphemer, king. It didn't matter. He wasn't here to be explained.

He was here to be. Fully. Clearly. Without apology.

He didn't move through life collecting roles—he moved through it embodying truth. He knew exactly who he was: a living expression of the divine. Not separate from God. Not a messenger for something distant. The presence itself, walking in form.

He knew what he was: a soul embodied to serve, to reflect back what had been forgotten, to reveal what was already in everyone around him. He wasn't performing miracles to prove his worth. He was demonstrating what becomes possible when distortion is cleared and the channel is open.

He knew how he served. Not by pleasing power structures. Not by fitting into the systems he came to break. He served by holding a mirror that showed people what they were, not what they'd been taught to be.

Call yourself who you are.

I was not born Yoshai'el Ben Adam. I chose it. It chose me. It speaks to what I carry, what I remember, what I walk as now. You may be Mary Bat Adam. Or Sara Bat Eve. Or David Ben Ruach. Or something other. Godzilla The Christ. Who cares. Take what rings true and let it guide you.

If you want a guide: Ben means "son of." Bat means "daughter of." Adam represents embodiment—Mankind, Earth, form, the grounded human experience. Eve speaks to origin and intuition—the first spark of relational life. Ruach means spirit, breath, wind—the animating force that moves through all things.

You can be Ben Adam *or* **Ben Eve.** They both carry weight. Adam grounds. Eve opens. Ruach moves. Choose what reflects what you walk in. What you carry now.

Your name is not for approval. It's a frequency. A mirror. A call. My name is more for me than it is for you. **But if you're going to walk that same path—not in imitation, but in full embodiment—you have to start where Mary did.** You have to release every label the world gave you to make you easier to manage. You have to let go of the roles that made you likable but left you disconnected from yourself.

You tear it down the same way she did. Not in a single moment, but brick by brick. Lie by lie. Every mask. Every performance. Every compromise that helped you survive but cost you something real.

Until what's left isn't a version of you that fits. It's the one that's finally free.

RELEASE: STEPPING BEYOND THE OLD SELF

Your old identities—every label, every role—weren't chosen by the deepest part of you. They were survival tools, worn when it felt safer to comply than to question. Given to you by a world more interested in predictability than truth. The game was simple: be who we say, and you'll be accepted. But that version of acceptance came with a cost.

You're not there anymore.

Now you choose. You release what was handed to you without consent. You walk without the mask. Without the weight. Not to reject your past, but to stop pretending it defines you.

Picture standing before a mirror—not glass, but something deeper. Reflective, honest, unfiltered. At first, it shows the familiar. Same eyes. Same face. But look closer. Words begin to appear—not spoken, but lingering. Old phrases, assumptions, expectations. The ones that shaped you. Not in ink. In chalk. Temporary. Always meant to be wiped clean.

"You should be this." "You'll never be that."
"Too loud." "Not enough."

Now take a page. Write them down. Every single one. The labels you absorbed. The judgments you internalized. The lies you lived long enough to mistake for personality. Some of them protected you. Some buried you.

Now tear them. One by one. No ceremony. Just truth.

Let the fragments fall. Let the silence that follows say what the words never could. With each tear, something loosens. Something real emerges.

The mirror clears. The surface softens. The light shifts.

You are not the roles. You are not the labels. You are not the story written by someone else's fear.

PHASE III: PURIFICATION

You can't think your way into this. You won't arrive at your Christed self through reflection alone. This isn't something you study, quote, or organize into theory. This is the part where the truth you've remembered meets the life you actually live. Purification isn't about cleansing sin. It's about burning off the layers of distortion that no longer hold. It's not for show. It's for integration.

Saying "I am divine" means nothing if your choices still come from survival. If your presence still adapts to comfort others instead of honoring your frequency. If your energy still hides every time it's challenged. Purification is where the real work happens—not in a flash of insight, but in the day-to-day decision to stop betraying yourself.

It's not about grand gestures. It's in how you speak to someone who can't offer you anything. It's in whether your tone stays honest when no one's there to clap. It's in how still you stay when the world around you shakes. Purification shows up in the quiet choices that build a life worth calling sacred.

You stop waiting for proof. You stop waiting for the world to tell you who you are. You move from knowing. You speak from it. You act from it. And when people try to hand you the old expectations, you don't take them.

You don't belong to that anymore.

This isn't about becoming perfect. It's about becoming honest. Alignment doesn't mean your life looks polished. It means your internal compass overrides the noise.

This is where things start to cost you. The need to be liked. The comfort of being understood. The safety of keeping your light dim enough not to offend. Purification will burn through all of it. Not because you have to suffer—but because you can't hold distortion and truth at the same time.

You lose the illusion that you need to earn your freedom. You lose the game of "almost ready." You lose the mask that told the world you were fine when you weren't.

And what remains is clear. Unshakable. You stop looking for the right words, the perfect plan, the outside validation.

You walk out of the fire, not new—just no longer pretending. Don't worry there are others on this path, others like you, others like me.

THERE IS NO SCHOOL THAT TEACHES THIS

There's no classroom for this. No curriculum. No spiritual grading scale where you level up from student to master. No temple that hands you the title. No sacred robe that makes it official. This isn't something you climb toward. **I don't have any certificates for you. It doesn't work like that.**

You don't earn this.

And that's the part people choke on. Because it's simple. Too simple. Everything you were taught said it had to be hard. That it had to hurt. That you had to go through fire, jump through hoops, prove your worth. But Christ consciousness was never about performance. *It's not achieved*. It's accepted.

No one can give you a certificate for what you've already carried since before you were born. No council, no guru, no sacred text can verify it. You don't need a sign in the sky. You don't need a relic. You don't need anyone else's agreement.

You just need to stop waiting.

Stop waiting to feel holy. Stop waiting to be ready. Stop waiting to get permission from a world that doesn't even know what it's looking at. You don't wait to be the light. You walk as it. Not someday. Not eventually. Now.

That's the whole thing.

YOU ARE NO LONGER THE PEACOCK

You're not here to be impressive. You're not here to spread your feathers, hoping someone notices. You're not here to entertain people into remembering. You're not here to translate your truth into a version that feels safer for the ones still hiding.

You're not here to explain. You're here to embody.

You stop needing to defend the way you carry your light. You stop contorting yourself to fit into old systems. You stop dressing up your truth so it feels more familiar to people who've forgotten their own.

You just walk. And that's enough.

Think of Jesus—not the idol, not the icon, the man. The one who sat with outcasts, who touched the untouchable, who walked into spaces where no respectable person would go. He wasn't there to be liked. He wasn't trying to impress anyone. He knew who he was. He moved like it. That alone changed *everything*.

He didn't argue. He didn't convince. He didn't soften the edges of his truth to avoid offending people still playing by old rules. He walked in knowing. And people remembered themselves because of it.

That's what you do now. Not by force. Not with explanation. Just by staying lit while the rest of the world tries to remember how.

SELF-ACTUALIZATION: NOT JUST A DAY OF SABBATH

This isn't something you set aside time for once a week. **This isn't a practice for Sunday morning and silence for the rest of the week.** It's not something you turn on when others are watching, when you're around your "spiritual" friends, or when the room expects you to perform. This is how you live. How you stand when there's no applause. How you speak when there's no safety net. How you stay steady when everything around you's asking you to flinch.

It's the decision to carry your truth in rooms that still reward silence. To walk with your frequency intact when compromise would make things easier. **It's how you treat people who don't believe what you do,** how you show up when you could just as easily shrink or disappear.

And to the ones who sit in temples and churches and sacred halls, casting judgment like it's sacred duty—*listen closely*. If you know more, you owe more. If you carry truth, you carry the responsibility to teach it, not weaponize it. Knowledge is never meant to become a club for control. It's meant to open doors. If someone doesn't know what you know, you don't punish them for it. You meet them where they are. You show them how. You walk with them, even if they don't get it yet. Especially when they don't.

This isn't about lowering your standard. It's about remembering that power means nothing if you can't use it to lift someone else. And the ones who call themselves leaders—the gurus, the mentors, the ministers, the stewards of sacred knowledge—this hits harder. Because the more light you carry, the more you're required to shine it where others are still learning to see.

This wave doesn't carry us forward by watching one rise and calling it enough. That's the old model. The top-down, climb-and-conquer system. That dies here.

We rise together. Or not at all.

PHASE IV: CONNECTION

Connection Activation is the moment when your truth stops being private. When your awakening stops being something you carry alone. You've walked through the fire. You've stripped the masks. *You've stepped into alignment.* But now the current wants to move. It wants to spread. It wants to link. This is when your frequency becomes contagious.

You don't just live it—you transmit it.

This isn't about going out and preaching. It's about presence. People will feel it before they understand it. Your family. Your friends. Strangers. Not because you're trying to convert anyone, but because the clarity in you starts shaking the dust off of them.

You can't fake this. You can't force it. Connection Activation happens when you stop keeping your truth separate from your relationships. When you stop compartmentalizing who you are. When you bring your full self into the room, not just the version that won't make waves.

Jesus didn't hold back until people were ready. He didn't wait for agreement. He moved from knowing, and let the resonance do the rest. He walked with people. Looked them in the eye. Not to fix them. To remind them. He saw through the surface—through the sinner, the status, the reputation—and into the part that was still divine underneath all the distortion.

And when He did, something lit up. People remembered. Not because they were taught, but because they were seen.

That's what you do now. You show up as someone who remembers. And in doing that, you make it easier for others to remember too.

It doesn't take a sermon. Just honesty. Just presence. Just the decision to stop hiding and start holding the line.

This is the moment your knowing becomes the bridge. Not for agreement. For resonance. You don't have to convince anyone. You just have to stand in the frequency long enough for others to hear it in themselves.

WALKING AS CHRIST: THE ACTIVATION OF OTHERS

You don't just carry Christ consciousness for yourself. Once you step into it fully, your presence starts doing the work. Without a sermon. Without a strategy. Just by being who you are, others start to remember who they are.

You become a point of resonance. A signal. A steady presence that calls out to those whose frequency is ready to rise. Awakening was never supposed to be a solo journey. It spreads because it's embodied. It moves from one lived experience to another. You don't activate people by telling them what's true. You activate them by living like it is.

You're not here to argue. You're not here to convince. **You're here to hold a frequency so clearly, so honestly, that it begins to rewire the atmosphere around you.** The energy you walk in becomes the invitation. And those who are ready won't need an explanation. They'll feel it. They'll remember something they couldn't name until they stood next to you.

This is how Christ moved. He didn't wait for people to earn their way in. He didn't demand agreement. He walked in truth, and that truth pulled people forward. Not with force. With presence.

Your community won't form through marketing or location. It won't be determined by background or belief system. It will form through resonance. Souls will find you when you stop trying to be palatable and start being honest. They're out there. Already listening. Already attuned. And they'll recognize what you're carrying without needing you to explain it.

You don't need to chase anyone.

You don't need to prove anything.

Just be clear.

Every room you enter becomes an activation point. Every real conversation becomes a portal. Every gathering becomes charged—not by what's taught, but by what's remembered. You don't need to announce what you are. You need to live it.

That's how the wave spreads. Not through systems. Through people. One presence at a time. One moment at a time.

Until it's everywhere.

YOU ARE NOT HERE TO FORCE AWAKENING

You do not need to hold their heads beneath the water until they choke on revelation. This is not your role. You are not here to hurl anyone into the river and demand they learn to swim. Nor are you here to sling sacred water like some spell meant to crack open their soul by force. Truth does not drown. It does not drag. It does not coerce. **It calls.** And those who are ready will step forward—not because you pushed them, but because they remembered the sound of their own name.

You are not here to save anyone. You are here to help them remember how to save themselves.

This is what Jesus taught. He did not force belief. He did not demand submission. He did not argue to prove His point or coerce others into following. He embodied truth. He walked it, spoke it, lived it. And those who were ready came forward—not because He made them, but because something in them recognized what they were standing in the presence of.

That's your role now. Not to baptize by force, but to live so fully in your knowing that others remember theirs. Not to shove them toward awakening, but to be such a clear reflection that they choose to come closer.

They are not yours to save. They are yours to witness. And when the time comes, they will rise. Not because you pulled them up, but because they remembered they could stand.

This is how the Second Coming manifests. Not through isolation. Not in waiting. Not in a single figure descending from the sky. It happens in communion. In shared knowing. In collective remembrance.

It begins with you, but it is completed through us.

God is—for God is all things.

I am love—for I know myself through my brothers and sisters.

We have come—as our Christed selves.

BEING IN THE RESONANCE OF CHRIST

Consider how Jesus moved through the world. He didn't climb onto platforms to assert authority. He didn't engage in debates to win arguments or try to overpower people with knowledge. **He simply stood in truth—so clearly, so fully—that others were changed by proximity alone.**

He didn't impose. He recognized. He didn't tell people who to be—He reminded them of what they had forgotten. He saw the divine in the dismissed, the broken, the cast aside. And in that moment of being seen, they began to see themselves again.

His community wasn't built through power or persuasion. It wasn't about getting people to agree. *It was about resonance.* He met people exactly where they were and made no demand that they become someone else. He called them whole before they believed it.

This is the walk now. **This is the frequency you carry.**

You're not here to convince anyone. You're not here to convert. You're here to become the resonance. To stand in a frequency so grounded, so clear, so untouchable that it wakes something ancient in the people around you.

Not because you preach. Not because you teach. Because you are. That's how the wave spreads. Not through pressure. Through presence.

RESONANCE GATHERING

Gather with two or three others who aren't just curious, but ready. This isn't about making a group. It's not a project. It's alignment. You'll feel it when it's right. These are the people who carry the same hum you do. Sit together. Don't jump into conversation. Let the space settle first. Let the silence do its work.

Start with the breath. Simple. In and out. No prep. No warm-up. Just arrival. Let the space fill—not with ideas, but with presence. Then open the book—the one you're holding now. Take turns reading if that feels true. Don't explain it. Don't interpret. **Let the words work on their own. They don't need help.**

After each section, pause. Let it land. Don't rush to fill the silence. Then speak. Not for validation. Not to be profound. Just tell the truth that's risen in you. Keep it raw. Keep it simple. Let the energy do what it does.

When you're ready, close in silence. No summary. No conclusion. Just breath. Just presence. Then speak the affirmation aloud—as one. Let it echo. Let it follow you.

Do it again. Let it become rhythm. Let it become breath.

Sit. Breathe. Drop into your own rhythm. No effort. No reach. Just return. Feel the center of your chest—not as muscle, but as light. Not flickering, but steady. That's your signal.

Watch it expand. Slowly. Without push. First through your body. Then the room. Then the city. Then further. You're not trying to connect. You already are. This isn't a search. It's a call.

> Say it—aloud or within: "I am love, in the frequency of love, calling forth those ready to embody truth. Come join me in recognition of our Christed selves."

This isn't a mantra. It's a tone. A beacon. Let it broadcast. *Let it be enough.*

Feel the pull. Somewhere, someone's listening. They don't need to know your name. You don't need to find them. They will come. And when they do, no one will have to say a word.

THIS IS NOT A RELIGION: DO NOT ALLOW THAT TO BE

You're not building a church. Even if there's a building. Even if people gather. A church is not walls, not stained glass, not a name carved into wood. It's a structure of belief—something shaped by human hands and filled with meaning only because people agreed to give it some.

What matters isn't the space. It's what happens inside it.

Whether you meet in a house, a field, a circle, or online—none of that makes it sacred. What makes it sacred is the absence of gates. No thresholds where people are measured. No qualifiers. No permission slips. No one standing at the edge deciding who gets to belong.

Call your gathering what you will. Call it sanctuary, circle, temple, or community. But don't you dare call yourself king or empress of it. Don't step into the center as ruler. **Don't crown yourself the voice of God just because someone handed you a microphone.**

Require nothing but willingness. Don't tax people's presence. Don't build a paywall around truth. Don't make people earn their way in. What you build must be open—not in theory, but in practice.

Decisions made together. Not dictated. Shared light. Shared weight. You listen. You discern. You choose as one. Because if you don't, if you let pride dress itself up as leadership, if you trade vulnerability for control, one day you'll look around and realize you've rebuilt what you swore you'd never touch—a new hierarchy in new robes. A cage dressed in language you once used to set people free.

And worse—you won't even realize when it happened.

You'll be holding the red drink. Smiling. Nodding. Saying the words that used to move you like they still mean something. But you won't remember who gave them to you. Or why you started speaking them in the first place.

You'll think you're still awake. But you'll be deep in it. Reciting. Obeying. Performing a truth you stopped living long ago.

So stay sharp. Stay honest. Stay free.

PHASE V: ALIGNMENT

Alignment marks the moment when individual awakenings stop existing in isolation. It's when they begin to move toward each other—not to merge identities, but to synchronize purpose. One soul remembering is powerful. But many souls aligned in remembrance? That's when the field starts to shift.

Picture each soul as a point of light. On its own, it burns steady. But in alignment with others, those lights become a constellation. A web. A radiant network of coherence that begins to rewire reality itself. Scattered embers catch each other's flame. Lone voices turn into harmony. **Not because they agree on everything, but because they resonate with the same truth.**

This is where the wave becomes visible. Not as one dramatic moment, but as a rising tide. Not organized. Not branded. Aligned.

Your personal awakening becomes something more here. It stops being about your journey and starts being about your place in the whole. Because no single star lights the sky. But together, they shift the night.

This is the Monad in motion. The One made of Many. The consciousness that's always been flowing through every person, every breath, every living thing. You were never separate from it. You just forgot how it moves.

You are not outside it. You are an expression of it. A node. A point of signal in the body of the divine.

As more lights switch on, the signal strengthens. Not because the Monad was ever broken—but because the parts that thought they were separate have come back online.

This is why your clarity matters. This is why alignment matters. Because the moment you walk in full coherence, you make it easier for others to do the same.

You don't have to force the world to change.

You just have to stop withholding your part of it.

THE TRUE POWER OF CONSCIOUS CENTRALIZATION

Your awakening was never meant to end with you. You didn't walk through fire just to sit in the glow of your own healing. You came through to add your frequency to something bigger. Not to dissolve into a collective. Not to lose your edges. But to stand fully in your truth beside others doing the same.

This is where personal transformation becomes global transformation.

The shift that started quietly within you doesn't stay there. It radiates—not through debate, not through force—but through alignment. The old systems don't fall because we fight them. They fade because we stop feeding them. Fear doesn't drive us anymore. Scarcity stops working. Shame has nothing left to sell.

You don't need to rage against the machine. You just stop giving it your energy. You stop trading your power for permission. You stop pretending you're broken. That alone changes the game.

This isn't a revolution. It's a *reorientation.*

The new world doesn't arrive by conquest. It arrives by choice. By remembrance. Through a network of awakened beings who aren't waiting for someone else to go first.

This isn't about everyone becoming the same. It's not conformity. It's harmonization. Each person tuned to their own frequency—but aligned. No one shrinking. No one erased. Just a chorus of individual truths moving together with coherence.

Imagine stars locking into position—not to blend in, but to form something greater. Each point distinct. Each one necessary. Each one amplifying the brilliance of the others.

That's the new alignment. Not obedience. Not hierarchy. Not a new set of rules to follow.

Just full presence. Full power. Fully connected.

THE BLUEPRINT OF UNITY

Jesus didn't gather disciples to create a hierarchy. He didn't assemble followers to build a religion. **He formed a collective—a field of resonance.** A shared frequency so clear, so coherent, that it began to bend reality around it. He knew the power of one was multiplied through many. Not by dominance. By alignment.

This is why He spoke of communion. Not conversion. Not control. But connection. A unified body, not in form, but in frequency. Because when enough people hold the same vibration—truth without distortion—the field responds. It starts to move. It starts to shift.

Your awakening brought you here, but it doesn't stay with you. What you've walked through wasn't for isolation. It wasn't just for clarity. It was to prepare you to hold the line in the presence of others. To amplify what you've remembered. To carry it into the places where people forgot.

And if you carry influence—if people look to your voice, your platform, your art, your leadership—your role just got bigger. You're not here to speak from a mountaintop. You're here to speak from alignment. To create from alignment. To live from alignment—so clearly that others can't help but feel the truth waking up in them too.

This isn't about belief systems. It's not about doctrine. It's about memory. You're not convincing anyone. You're holding a frequency that helps them recognize what's already inside them.

Imagine even a handful of voices doing this at once. Leaders. Teachers. Artists. Anchored in knowing. Not selling enlightenment. Embodying it. Not asking for applause. Just standing in truth long enough for the wave to catch.

That's how it spreads. Not slowly. Not someday. Suddenly.

BUILD YOUR COMMUNITY

Form or join intentional gatherings—not places of exclusion or hierarchy, but spaces of shared remembrance. These are not bound by tradition, doctrine, or architecture. They are not temples built of stone, but frequencies held in living bodies. A home, a park, a café—any space can become sacred when the Christ frequency moves freely. These are communities where everyone belongs. Where no identity is erased. Where every voice adds depth to the song of awakening.

The Jewish, the Muslim, the Christian. The Buddhist, the atheist, the mystic. The queer, the straight. The Black, the White. All reflections of God in form. If you once found belonging in one, you are now called to become one with all—not by abandoning your roots, but by expanding into the wholeness of your being.

These communities are not about persuasion or performance. There are no gatekeepers. There is no initiation but presence. **The only requirement is willingness—to stand in your truth and witness the divine in others.**

And this cannot stay confined. It must spill outward. Into the world. Into culture. Into celebration. Bring it to life through art, through movement, through creation. Let it be a festival of frequency. Let it pulse through music, through color, through shared expression that reflects the unity already forming. These are not social events. These are live activations. Each moment a chance for the Christ frequency to expand through the collective.

This is not a retreat into the spiritual. This is the full arrival of spirit in form. It moves through the crowd. It becomes rhythm. It becomes culture. It becomes the new world, seeded in the body of the present one—until what was is no longer the only option.

The call is clear: expand. If you hold a platform, use it. Speak, write, share, create— move the message beyond yourself. This isn't about followers or fame. It's about frequency. Let it move. If ten thousand hear you, that's ten thousand tuning forks set into motion. And each of them becomes another point of transmission.

The truth spreads not by pressure, but by resonance. When it's real, it moves on its own. So stop waiting. Stop softening it. Speak the truth you've been given. Speak it clearly. Speak it fully. Let it be as sharp as it needs to be. You are not planting opinions. You are igniting fields. **Don't underestimate how far one true voice can reach.**

And if your reach is small, connect. Find others whose voices carry. Build intentional bridges. Ask for amplification. Demand it if needed. This is not about ego. It's about impact. The world won't change through silence. It changes when resonance becomes louder than illusion.

Your responsibility is not just to awaken. It's to awaken others. To carry the message where it can be heard. To make sure no one who is ready is left waiting.

This is not the moment to sit still. Communities are forming. Remembrance is rising. The message is moving. But it must not slow. This is the edge. We do not fall back into silence. We do not sit in spiritual comfort while the world around us begs for clarity.

The Seventh Resound

We go out. We bring the light where it's been forgotten. We speak what others fear to say. We live as the new world, visible and embodied. We gather—not to escape, but to amplify. **When awakened souls stand side by side, the presence alone alters reality.** It is not theory. It is transmission. It is energetic law. And it begins with a shared voice.

> **"We are one with all things. We expand our consciousness. We ascend together."**

Say it again.

> **"We are one with all things. We expand our consciousness. We ascend together."**

Say it until the words are no longer sound but frequency. Until the air shifts. Until the illusion breaks. Until the veil thins.

This is not a meditative comfort. This is a charge. A rising wave you are meant to ride and lead. Your voice. Your influence. Your physical presence—these are sacred instruments now. You are not on the sidelines. You are the frontline.

When awakened souls align, separation cannot survive. All the old systems of division collapse in the presence of unified truth. Race. Religion. Borders. Belief. These are not laws—they are leftovers. And they dissolve when the Christ frequency becomes the atmosphere.

Separation cannot hold where unity stands.

THIS IS YOUR ROLE, MISSION, & ULTIMATE PURPOSE

To align your frequency with others is to ignite a resonance far greater than yourself. It is to become part of a constellation of awakened consciousness, powerful enough to alter the very course of humanity.

This is the surge of Global Alignment, *or collective actualization*—the moment when personal awakening becomes unified action. It is no longer about a single voice or a single gathering. It is no longer a lone ripple in an endless ocean. It is millions rising together, forming one powerful, pulsating force. This is not the future. This is now. This is the shift from awakening within to activating the world itself.

Collective Activation is about creating spaces—literal spaces, energetic spaces, communal spaces—where divine truth moves without resistance. Spaces where it spreads freely, accelerates exponentially, and becomes undeniable. At this threshold, something extraordinary begins to take shape. Individual lights, once scattered and solitary, converge into a blazing constellation. These are no longer mere gatherings. They are hubs of divine frequency. Centers of activation. Living fields of conscious power that amplify awakening at a scale the world has never seen.

Imagine places unbound by the definitions of the old world. These are not churches weighed down by dogma. Not governments locked in control. Not institutions seeking to preserve power. These are something new. Something alive. Part sanctuary, where souls find rest and remembrance. Part laboratory, where ideas are tested and brought to life. Part temple, where meditation deepens into communion. Part center of innovation, where technology aligns with consciousness to serve the greater whole.

Each hub is designed for one purpose: to foster resonance. Every soul who enters is not merely welcomed. They are recognized. They are remembered. They are activated. They are set ablaze with the unstoppable frequency of the Christ.

This is not theory. This is not potential.

This is already happening.

PHASE VI: ACTIVATION

There comes a point in the path where remembering is no longer enough. Where alignment must move. Where embodiment becomes expression. This is Activation—the phase where the internal frequency turns outward, taking form, taking voice, taking up space. It is no longer about healing the past or shedding the false. That work has been done. Now, it's about igniting the truth you carry and letting it ripple through everything you touch.

Activation is not conceptual. It is kinetic. It is visible. It is felt. The soul no longer whispers in the dark—it speaks, it builds, it leads. **This is where you stop orbiting purpose and become it.** You stop preparing for the future and start generating it. Not by trying to be perfect, but by showing up as you are—fully lit, fully claimed, fully in motion.

This is not performance. This is presence in motion. Divine intention with velocity.

Every conversation, every post, every gathering becomes a point of transmission. You're no longer just tuning to the Christ frequency. You are broadcasting it. Live.

This is the pulse that cracks old timelines. This is the moment where the sacred moves beyond the personal and becomes a collective force of creation. Not as theory. As lived architecture. As action. As invitation. As embodiment.

You don't wait for change. You become the catalyst that makes it impossible not to happen.

THE BIRTH OF ENERGETIC BEACONS

These are not buildings. They are thresholds. Living centers where the invisible becomes real, where resonance becomes architecture. They are not destinations on a map—they are pulse points in the living grid of New Earth. Wherever they rise, the atmosphere changes. The land remembers. The space vibrates. These centers don't just serve people. They rewire reality itself.

They are schools—but not the kind that bury spirit beneath standardized answers. They are places where knowledge becomes knowing, where memory returns in the form of divine identity. They are sanctuaries—not for escape, but for clarity. Places where stillness is not a retreat, but a charge. Where silence recalibrates action.

They are technology labs—not sterile, mechanized production lines, but dynamic bridges between sacred wisdom and innovation. Here, science and spirit do not compete. They converge. They co-create. The result isn't just progress—it's evolution. These are not utopian fantasies. They are spiritual infrastructure. And their message is clear:

"Behold, I make all things new." —Revelation 21:5

Consider Jesus—not merely as a teacher of words, but as an anchor of fields. His gatherings weren't sermons. They were activations. He spoke, and something inside people changed—not because they agreed with Him, but because their frequency remembered. The tax collector and the zealot didn't follow the same doctrine. They followed the same vibration. That was the power of the upper room. The resonance of awakened presence.

He wasn't building movements. He was building fields.

And now, so are you.

You are not here to contribute to a conversation. You are here to compose an entirely new reality. Every awakened soul is a frequency generator. Not just a seeker of light, but a builder of it. It is no longer enough to carry divine truth silently. It must be structured, broadcast, multiplied.

Create schools where divine identity is remembered alongside biology and math. Design wellness lounges that recalibrate frequency as deeply as they soothe bodies. Build labs where technology doesn't distract from presence, but magnifies it. Let abandoned churches become sanctuaries again—not of religion, but of real resonance.

If you hold land, don't ask how far it stretches. Ask what it can anchor. If you hold wealth, don't ask how it grows. Ask how it flows. If you hold power, don't ask how it lifts you. Ask who it sets free.

The world doesn't need another empire. It needs activation points. Real places. Real people. Real structures pulsing with divine frequency. Not monuments to memory. Living blueprints for what's coming next.

Begin to conceptualize—or better yet, collaborate—on spaces dedicated entirely to energetic resonance. This is not a casual gathering in a living room. It is not a hobby or a side project to be squeezed in when convenient. This is sacred work. A deliberate creation of a space where awakening expands and multiplies. A place where frequency is restored, amplified, and sent back into the world with more force than it arrived.

This is not just a building. It is a living field.

A magnet for resonance.

A beacon that calls to those who are ready. Gather those who see the vision. Not those who need convincing. Not those who hesitate. But those who know. And begin.

Do not wait for permission.

Do not ask the world if it is ready.

It will not be ready until you build what it needs to become.

The time to build is now.

BECOME STEWARDS OF TOMORROW—TODAY.

Picture a community center alive with the pulse of collective remembrance. A wellness lounge that does not just relieve stress but restores memory. A technology lab where ancient symbols meet quantum code. See old churches reborn as centers of divine frequency.

Every wall. Every room. Every gathering. Every practice.

Must declare one truth:

"We anchor the divine frequency here."

If you hold land—**let it remember.**

If you hold wealth—**let it move.**

If you hold power—**let it lift others.**

The world doesn't need taller towers. It needs deeper roots.

What it needs is the soul that won't fit the mold. The hands that remember how to shape the unseen. The voice that doesn't parrot, but speaks what's never been heard. It needs the ones who walk without a map because they are the compass. Not castle-builders, but wall-breakers. Space-makers. Blueprint writers for what has never existed—until now.

If you do not hold the means—activate those who do.

You don't need to fund the structure. You don't need to own the land. You're not meant to carry this alone. There are those with the resources, the platforms, the reach—waiting for something worthy to build.

Speak. Invite. Don't pitch the vision—reveal it. Let it be so clear, so alive, so inevitable that it stirs the purpose already dormant in them. Old money built the old world. New money is here to seed the next one.

This isn't about what's missing. It's about who's waiting.

No one builds this alone. That was never the assignment. Resonance builds this. Alignment builds this. It doesn't rise through hierarchy. It rises through shared remembrance. You are not here to lead them. You're here to stand beside them and build something no blueprint has ever held.

What was built for control doesn't need to burn to be transformed. Reclaim it. Repurpose it. Redeem it. Make the cathedrals resonate again—not with doctrine, but with divinity.

There is nothing that cannot be made new.

And this is how the world is made new—*through us.*

TO THE POWERS OF THE WORLD

To those who hold the land, the libraries, the ledgers. To those who speak of stewardship but act in secrecy. The time has come.

Open the doors.

Release what is hidden.

Return what was never yours to keep.

You speak of service. Then serve. Truly. Let the temples be centers of light again.

Let the mosques become halls of unity.

Let the cathedrals sing with truth, not control.

Let the people return—not as followers, but as free.

You want legacy. Then earn it—not with monuments, but with memory. Be remembered as the ones who gave it all back. The ones who unshackled the sacred and returned it to the people.

You have *enough*. Enough land. Enough gold. Enough influence to rebuild the world.

So choose your legacy.

History is watching.

Truth is knocking.

And the threshold is now.

Consider this: one year of global military spending could end a century of suffering. One year. One choice.

If you will not choose it, we will.

And if you will not build it, we will.

The world is not waiting for your permission. It is already becoming what it was always meant to be.

FREQUENCY EDUCATION

We were taught how to perform, how to comply, how to survive in a system never meant to awaken us. We memorized the rules. We mastered the external. But we were never shown how to feel the frequency within us—how to access the infinite source we already carry.

That ends now.

Education must shift. Completely. Whether we transform the old schools or build new ones from scratch, the foundation must be remembrance. Starting with the children. Teach them how to move energy. How to recognize truth. How to speak from source. Not someday. Now.

Do not hand them a broken world and call it progress. Do not dim their light to preserve your comfort. Build the world they deserve—so they never have to forget who they are in the first place.

Establish schools of knowing. Not institutions of memorization. Teach them how to harness presence, not performance. How to access creation, not just replicate what's already been done.

Bring together teachers, scientists, healers, mystics, technologists—anyone who carries a piece of the new paradigm. And teach not just curriculum, but frequency. Not just subjects, but soul.

Stand before them and say it clearly:

"We are here to activate knowing, not just learning."

Because knowledge alone doesn't liberate. Remembrance does.

CONSCIOUS GOVERNANCE

To those who lead systems, steer laws, hold office, shape culture—this is your moment.

The era of control is ending. The era of conscious leadership has begun.

You are not here to rule. You are here to recalibrate. Not to dominate, but to resonate. Not to win, but to serve.

Your presence alone can shift the tone of an entire system. Your words can disarm division. Your clarity can crack deception in half. So step in. Step forward. Let truth not be your strategy, but your baseline. Let love not be your message, but your function.

To those who hold records, law, tradition—do not fear these words. You are not here to preserve the old. You are here to unlock the next.If you must legalize it, do it. If you must rewrite the laws, do it. Shift governance from dominion to devotion. Let power be felt not in force, but in frequency.

And to those who twist this message into product, into platform, into control—

There is a Jesus in every age.

And he will flip your tables.

Do not forget that.

PHASE VII: TRANSMUTATION

In the phase or octave of Transmutation, there is a density shift. Reality itself is rewritten—not through war, not through force, not through revolution, but by the sheer momentum of collective consciousness in divine alignment. This is the moment when structures built on fear, limitation, and separation lose their grip. They don't collapse because we destroy them. They dissolve because we stop believing in them.

They lose power the moment we stop feeding them.

What once ruled the world crumbles under the weight of collective truth. And in its place, a new energetic architecture emerges—designed not by force, but by choice. Rooted not in scarcity, but in love. Not in control, but in co-creation.

This density shift isn't slow. It's not a whisper at the edge of perception. It's a rupture. A clear, sharp line after which nothing can go back. A point of no return, marked by the simple fact that enough people chose differently.

Imagine a world where war, poverty, and division are no longer the default setting. Not because we negotiated peace—but because those frequencies no longer hold currency. They've been outgrown. This isn't fantasy. It's energetic alchemy.

The shift doesn't come by decree or demand. It spreads organically as awakened beings collectively withdraw their consent from systems that feed on fear. We don't fight the old. We stop energizing it. And in its place, we build with intention. With coherence. With remembrance.

Every truth spoken. Every belief released. Every act of alignment adds to the momentum. Until it tips. And what once felt immovable becomes outdated.

COLLECTIVE CHOICE ACCELERATES

One choice doesn't just change your life. It changes the entire field. One refusal to participate in fear. One conscious withdrawal from the illusion. That's how the wave gains momentum—person to person, choice by choice.

Imagine if, for even a single year, global military spending—over two trillion dollars—was redirected. Not to weapons, but to wellness. The resources already exist to end world hunger, ensure clean water access, and provide basic education to every child on the planet. Not someday. Now. A future we call impossible is already funded—it's just being misallocated to sustain fear.

And war isn't the only engine. While nations funnel billions into destruction, individuals with unimaginable wealth—founders of mega billion-dollar empires—hold collective assets exceeding fourteen trillion dollars. At even the most conservative withdrawal rate, they could generate enough annual surplus to fund the full transformation of life on this planet. Not in theory. In raw, measurable, economic fact. *Do the math yourself.*

But the issue isn't greed. It's fear. Fear that there's not enough. Fear of losing status. Fear that someone else's rise requires their fall. **These are not evil**

people. They are wounded, just like the rest of the system—acting from the same scarcity that's been fed to all of us for generations. They're just as much pawns in this game, they just wear prettier fake crowns.

The system doesn't hold power because it's strong. It holds power because we keep consenting to it. The illusion only stays alive because we keep feeding it. But when enough people stop—when enough of us choose another frequency—the demand collapses.

And then, the system fades.

The old powers will resist. They'll call peace unrealistic. They'll call unity dangerous. They'll scream about collapse, whisper about scarcity, and try to bait the awakened back into the game with fear. Division. Chaos.

But we won't answer. We will *respond.*

WE WILL RESPOND IN LIGHT

We don't mirror dysfunction. We don't meet distortion with distortion. We meet it with alignment. With a kind of presence that doesn't flinch under pressure. That doesn't fight to be right. That just stands. Clear.

You don't become what you came to transmute. You don't fight with the same tools you came to lay down. You don't use force to dismantle force. You walk into the room and let your frequency do the work.

This is what presence looks like in action. Steady. Unapologetic. Unmoved.

And no matter what they bring, we won't become them.

Not in fear. Not in retaliation. Not in self-righteous performance.

This is how the density shift happens. Not through protest. Through non-participation. Through millions choosing at once to stop pretending the old system has power over them.

THE SCALE AND OCTAVE OF LOVE

We don't need more martyrs. We don't need more burned prophets or public sacrifices to prove the point. We need people who stay. Who keep their vision clean. Who don't spiral into fear when the noise rises.

That doesn't mean you stand in recklessness. It means you stay rooted in discernment. Protect your temple if needed. Move if you must. Go silent if it's time. But do it with precision—not panic.

Love, in this phase, is not passive. *It is directional. Operational.* It recalibrates everything it touches. And it cannot be controlled. You can't weaponize it. You can't legislate it. You can't twist it into hierarchy.

A million people with weapons cannot contain a hundred million who've decided not to comply. They can't run a system that has no participants. They can't command a narrative that no longer lands. The moment we all choose differently, the infrastructure built on fear collapses under its own weight.

Not with violence. Not with fire. With absence. **This isn't a fight.**

It's the refusal to keep playing the part they wrote for us. It's the choice to embody something else. Together. At scale. Without apology.

That's how a new world rises. The New Earth referred to before we were born.

PHASE VIII: TRANSFIGURATION

At times, it feels as though we are standing on the edge of something massive— watching a new world take shape just beyond the horizon. There's a signal in the air. You can feel it in your chest. A quiet, steady sense that transformation isn't coming. It's already here. Not as a thunderclap, but as a pulse. A shift that started in the hearts of those who knew we were never meant to live like this.

This isn't some dream parked at the end of a thousand-year timeline. It doesn't belong to distant prophecy or spiritual speculation. If we chose it—fully, clearly, collectively—it could be here within a century. Not theoretical. Not symbolic. Lived. Tangible. Something our grandchildren are born into, not as a reward, but as a baseline.

Not because the world was destroyed and rebuilt. But because we decided to build differently. Because we stopped waiting for collapse to clear the way and just started laying the foundation ourselves.

Imagine waking up in that world.

You don't jolt awake from stress before the sun rises. Your body isn't bracing for a day that will extract more than it gives. You wake naturally. You feel rested. Not because life is perfect—but because it's no longer designed to grind you down.

You eat food grown by people you know, on land that's cared for—not exploited. Your work isn't a transaction to survive. It's an expression of your actual gift. What you contribute builds something. What you create matters. You don't climb ladders. You grow roots. Deep ones. Ones that hold.

Your kids are taught how to think, how to feel, how to regulate their nervous systems before they're ever taught to memorize data. They know how to build relationships, grow food, understand their frequency, read a room, and trust themselves.

Healthcare is regeneration. Frequency-based. Rooted in prevention, energy, rhythm. You're not a number. You're not a symptom. You're not dependent on a chemical to feel whole. The system doesn't profit from your sickness. It's designed around your vitality.

Technology isn't an escape from the body. It's an extension of your awareness. It doesn't replace intimacy. It deepens it. AI doesn't manage you. It supports you. It removes friction, not meaning.

You don't live in isolation. You live in layered communities—small, intentional, alive. You know your neighbors. You trust them. You trade energy, care, attention—not just goods. Elders have purpose. Youth have voice. Conflict doesn't explode. It's processed. Felt. Integrated. No one's left behind to protect the illusion of peace.

There are sanctuaries. Resonance hubs. Frequency schools. Places where you go not to escape life, but to return to yourself. Where emotion isn't pathologized. Where stillness is normal. Where the mystical is practical and the practical is sacred.

You don't fear the Earth. You walk with it. You don't worship nature like a god, or dominate it like a resource. You live in relationship. The seasons shape your rhythm. The land shapes your decisions. Restoration isn't activism—it's just the way things are.

You don't wake up to news engineered to destabilize your nervous system. You don't scroll through curated panic. You don't need dopamine hits to make it through the day. Presence is normal. Nervous systems are regulated. Breath is deep.

And underneath it all is the knowing—you're not here by accident. You're not proving your worth. You're not earning your right to be. You belong. Fully. Instantly. Without condition.

This is not a fantasy.

It's what happens if we stop arguing with what we already know is possible.

Through this, beautiful things happen.

THE INEVITABILITY OF UNITY

One of the defining features of the New Earth is the recognition that there is only one race—the human race. This isn't an aspiration. It's not a spiritual ideal or lyrics from a Rastafarian song. It's a structural truth that's been buried beneath centuries of control. Skin, culture, origin—these were never barriers. **They were used as expressions, then turned into boundaries.** But they were always expressions of a single design.

In the old world, those differences were extracted and weaponized. Identity became commodity. History was edited to serve power. Entire populations were ranked, divided, and measured by systems that had no interest in truth—only control. Separation became currency. Conflict was manufactured. Lineage was manipulated. And slowly, humanity was trained to see itself in fragments.

What was always shared became obscured. But the essence never changed. We carry the same source code. The same spark. The same breath animates every body. Soul is not segmented by color. Spirit doesn't check passports. The light behind every set of eyes has always been the same, whether the world acknowledged it or not. And now, this knowing is no longer a concept. It shows up in structure. It moves through the way we speak, how we build, how we recognize each other.

This isn't about tolerance. **Tolerance implies a hierarchy—someone choosing to accept what they secretly believe doesn't belong.** It isn't about inclusion either. Inclusion assumes there was ever a gate. This is recognition. The unshakable knowing that no one was ever outside the whole. That no one is extra. That no lineage is lesser. The New Earth doesn't erase difference. It honors it without letting it be used as a wedge. It refuses to participate in systems that rely on the lie of separation to function.

The wall has been identified. We can hear the trumpets. The bricks are being pulled. The architecture of division is no longer reinforced. What's left isn't theory. It's design. And the world we're building now doesn't ask permission to live in alignment with what's always been true.

THE END OF RACE AS A DIVIDING LINE

Over time, the illusion of race dissolves—not by force, not by suppression, but through lived integration. As people find one another across former divides, as families form between lineages once separated by conflict or distance, a shift takes root. Future generations are no longer defined by a single flag or face. Children are born holding multiple ancestries in one frame. They belong to no singular story. They belong to all.

These children are not half-this or part-that. They are whole. They are the end of racial arithmetic. Their eyes reflect every continent. Their blood carries the memory of every migration. They do not inherit identity as a border to defend. They inherit identity as a bridge. And in them, the myth of division loses ground. No need to choose sides. No need to fracture themselves to be accepted. **They walk through the world as full-spectrum beings, members of a single human lineage.** They look the same because what is inside is finally reflected on the outside.

And yet, tradition remains. It is not erased. It is not discarded. It is offered. Culture becomes contribution, not category. Language becomes gift, not separation. Every sacred rite, every ancestral thread is honored without becoming a reason to divide. Diversity becomes something we carry forward, not something we use to look back in opposition. **The symbols of the past become ingredients, not labels.**

The old dividing lines—racial, national, economic—begin to fail. Not through legislation. Not through protest. But through irrelevance. The system of division breaks when it's no longer needed. And it is no longer needed, because unity has returned to the body. It is no longer a vision. It is muscle memory.

What once seemed impossible now feels inevitable. The end of race as a dividing line is not the loss of identity. It is the restoration of belonging. And in that restoration, a deeper truth is remembered: unity was never the goal. It is the baseline. It is the structure beneath time itself. And time is finally catching up.

THE RISE OF A NEW FORM OF COMMUNICATION

You may wonder—what becomes of language as we unify? As the walls of separation fall and we return to oneness, will words still carry weight? And as unity consciousness expands, the answer reveals itself not through theory, but through experience. A new form of communication begins to emerge, not taught, but remembered.

At first, it arrives quietly. What feels like intuition sharpens into certainty. A shared knowing that requires no explanation. Two people sit in silence, yet exchange more than words ever allowed. It is not guesswork. It is not fantasy. It is the return of direct connection—mind to mind, heart to heart. What once appeared only in flashes now becomes a steady stream. Where we once used language to define and defend, we begin to transmit essence. Feeling. Image. Memory. Knowing. Unfiltered and intact.

What was once called telepathy is no longer rare. What was once reserved for the few becomes familiar to the many. **Empathic communication is not mysticism, it's science.** It is not performance. It is the functional result of a unified field. A consciousness that no longer sees itself as separate no longer requires translation. It simply recognizes.

This shift does not erase language. It repositions it. Words are still used, but not relied upon. They become tools, not lifelines. They decorate truth rather than carry it. Love no longer needs to be explained. It is felt. Intention no longer needs to be defended. It is known. The time spent arguing over definitions falls away, because the meaning is shared before the sentence ever begins.

We no longer speak just to be heard. We speak when it serves. And in the silence, more is exchanged than centuries of language ever achieved. Not because we've evolved past speech—but because we've remembered what speech was trying to replicate.

This is not prediction. It is not a distant ideal. It is already happening. It's destiny. Inevitable. Quietly, steadily, undeniably. Because unity is not an invention. It is the original blueprint. And a blueprint always re-emerges—once we stop throwing dirt over it.

ENERGY HEALING: GIFTS OF CHRIST CONSCIOUSNESS

A hallmark of this ascension is the return of immediate, energetic healing. Not as a miracle for the few. Not as an anomaly that defies explanation. But as the natural result of divine frequency made physical. Picture bones realigning in seconds. Chronic illness dissolving without resistance. Not through treatment. Not through strategy. Through alignment.

This isn't about protocols. It doesn't require belief systems or complex technique. It's not about attacking symptoms or managing dysfunction. It's the same healing Christ revealed—love moving through form with no obstruction. Power, not as domination, but as clarity. Wholeness, not as recovery, but as default.

In the old Earth, healing was framed as warfare. Identify the enemy. Apply pressure. Cut, burn, suppress. Even in gentler modalities, the body was often seen as something in need of correction—separate from spirit, separate from source. Healing became a project.

But in the frequency of Christ Consciousness, healing operates from a different foundation. Illness is not framed as failure. It is recognized as distortion. A temporary misalignment in the field. The body, mind, and soul are not separate layers. They are a single frequency expressing through different densities. Now when one part distorts, the whole feels it.

Through the resonance of pure presence—through the field of unfiltered love—these distortions release. Not slowly. Not with resistance. Instantly. The cells recalibrate. The nervous system reorients. The body remembers its original code. Healing is not manufactured. It is permitted. And in that permission, it returns to its rightful speed.

There is no medicine here. No fixing. Just clarity. Just the restoration of coherence in a system designed to self-correct the moment distortion is removed. It's the physics of consciousness aligned with truth. The same truth that moved through Jesus when He said, "Your faith has made you well." And in that instant, it was done—not because of belief, but because the field had nothing left to resist.

THE JOURNEY OF ASCENSION IS A COLLECTIVE ONE

Not everyone will hold the full frequency at once. That isn't failure. That isn't delay. The collective field rises regardless. Every personal refinement amplifies the whole. Every moment of alignment sends a signal through the grid. This is not an individual climb—it's a shared current. We're moving together in an interconnected field. When one calibrates, the field responds. Coherence expands with every step forward.

The vision of the New Earth may sound utopian, as if a cosmic switch will flip and all will be made whole in an instant. But ascension doesn't work like that. It's not a sudden event. It's a layered process—subtle, personal, cumulative. It unfolds one life at a time, one breakthrough at a time, one choice at a time. People awaken at their own pace, moving through the lingering static of old programming—fear, guilt, bitterness, shame, disbelief. These are not flaws. They're residues. Bricks in the wall built to keep truth at bay. And yet the unfolding cannot be stopped. Because beneath every defense is a soul that still longs to be free.

Like geometric progression, it begins almost imperceptibly. The early changes are quiet, easy to dismiss. But each awakening multiplies the field, and what once looked like stillness becomes exponential movement. By the time it's visible to all, it's already unstoppable.

It is often said: "As one ascends, all ascend." At first, that may seem contradictory. How can the whole rise when each is moving at a different speed? But human consciousness is not a collection of separate minds. **It is a field—a unified matrix linking every heart and every thought.** When even one person breaks through— when they experience true forgiveness, deep healing, or a full-heart remembering— that frequency enters the grid. It radiates outward. It influences those they touch. It shifts the tone of spaces they enter. And even those they'll never meet begin to feel it, subtly and undeniably.

No awakening happens in isolation. Even the most private breakthrough echoes across the field. The moment one soul remembers who they are, the resonance changes for all. This is not personal achievement. This is field transformation. And every single step matters.

THE DISSOLUTION OF RESISTANCE AND DENSITY

Not everyone will embrace this shift at once. In the beginning, most won't. The idea of energy, frequency, or healing without intervention will sound unrealistic— like fantasy, or worse, delusion. People will laugh it off, ignore it, or actively fight it. That's expected. It's how every major shift begins. The first wave is small. A few individuals start living differently. They stop chasing external validation. Their health improves without explanation. Their relationships shift. Their presence disrupts the atmosphere in subtle but undeniable ways.

At first, it's easy to dismiss. People write it off as coincidence, luck, or placebo. But then a second wave starts. A friend of a skeptic heals from something medicine said was permanent. A co-worker begins radiating calm in high-pressure situations without losing effectiveness. **A parent or sibling shifts their entire outlook in a matter of weeks.** And suddenly, the conversation begins to change. Curiosity replaces mockery. Quiet questions start replacing loud rejection.

At first it's barely noticeable. Two becomes four, four becomes eight. But then eight becomes sixteen, then thirty-two. The growth isn't linear—it's exponential. And with each new person who shifts, the atmosphere becomes easier to breathe. The field holds more coherence. The baseline for what's "**normal**" begins to move.

By the time ten percent of the population is operating from this level of consciousness, infrastructure starts to shift. Not because of policy—because demand changes. Schools incorporate nervous system regulation. Workplaces prioritize resonance and clarity over hierarchy and control. Medical systems begin losing authority—not from rebellion, but from irrelevance. War becomes unfathomable. The proof is everywhere: people are transforming without them.

When the majority begins to say yes, the acceleration is unmistakable. Conflict doesn't escalate the way it used to. Supply chains shift because people aren't consuming out of anxiety anymore. Culture reorients around coherence instead of distraction. And those who still resist find themselves in a reality that no longer responds to force the way it used to.

CULTURE IS TRANSFORMED

As alignment spreads, culture undergoes a renaissance. The driving force of society is no longer production for profit—it's creation for its own sake. Art, music, movement, design—these are no longer side pursuits or luxuries. They become the center. Human creativity is recognized as sacred infrastructure. Work is no longer a burden to bear or a path to validation. It becomes a medium for offering frequency into form.

Craft returns. Excellence matters—not as competition, but as devotion. People pour themselves into what they create, because they're no longer split by survival. A carpenter shapes wood not to meet demand, but to honor beauty. A musician doesn't perform to entertain, but to transmit coherence. **Creative output becomes the new economy—not in the sense of currency, but in the movement of energy.** What you give carries weight, and what you receive leaves imprint.

Communities organize around resonance. People collaborate not because they have to, but because synergy amplifies meaning. Contribution isn't assigned—it's discovered. You know what's yours to do by how alive it feels when you do it. And because survival is no longer tied to labor, work becomes something entirely different. It becomes sacred. Joyful. Vital.

This shift doesn't erase structure. It elevates it. Architecture becomes art again. Cities are built with intention, not efficiency alone. Color returns. Gardens expand. Sound is used with purpose. People care not just about how a space functions, but how it feels. Culture moves from being a reflection of power to a reflection of consciousness.

Celebration isn't occasional—it's integrated. Rituals return. Not as tradition for tradition's sake, but as active acknowledgments of presence, cycles, and connection. The arts are not extracurricular. They are foundational. Because in a world no longer governed by scarcity, expression becomes the primary output of the human being. Not extraction. Not accumulation. Expression.

And from that expression, entire systems shift. Governance, economy, design—all begin to mirror the intelligence of a population living in coherence. The New Earth doesn't just run differently. It feels different, because it's being shaped by people who remember who they are and refuse to create anything that forgets it.

And in that space, something entirely new takes form.

A NEW WAY OF LEARNING

Children are taught from the beginning to understand and direct their own energy. **Emotional intelligence is not a secondary skill—it's foundational.** They learn early how thought shapes form, how emotion sets tone, how internal coherence creates external clarity. Mastery replaces suppression. They aren't told to calm down. They're shown how to regulate, how to anchor, how to move energy through the body with precision and presence.

Healing becomes language. A child with a scraped knee doesn't just wait for it to scab. They place their hands over it with clear intention, restoring harmony to the field. Empathy is not just encouraged—it's refined. They learn how to feel without absorbing, how to open the heart without collapsing boundaries. Vulnerability is taught as strength. Sensitivity becomes skill.

Telepathy is no longer dismissed. It's understood as a natural function of an aligned nervous system. **Children are trained to communicate mind-to-mind, heart-to-heart—not as fantasy, but as literacy.** Multidimensional awareness is developed alongside language and mathematics. They don't study it as abstraction. They live it. What older generations called mystical, these children call normal.

Their classrooms aren't confined. Education happens in resonance with the living world. Mornings begin with group meditation to stabilize the collective field. Lessons unfold in nature, not in rows of desks. Students are taken into forests and taught to listen—not with ears, but with presence. They track the rhythm of wind. They feel the pulse of soil. They learn to hear the spirit of place, and speak to it with respect.

By the time they reach adulthood, these beings are not confused about who they are. They're fluent in frequency. They move through the world with clarity and command—not from arrogance, but from alignment. They don't fear the invisible. They don't question their intuition. They walk as bridges between realms, without needing to prove what they know.

And as they grow, they reshape culture itself. Expression is not performance. It's offering. Every creative act becomes an act of devotion. Each voice adds to the living artwork of the world—not to compete, but to contribute. This is what happens when a generation is raised in truth.

THE RISE OF AI AS A TOOL OF CREATION

As artificial, and then assistive general intelligence advances, it stops being a threat to human creativity and becomes its most powerful ally. No longer positioned to replace the human spirit, **AI evolves into a tool of amplification—built not for dominance, but for service.** It doesn't compete with ingenuity. It elevates it. It doesn't override vision. It supports its execution. Technology becomes what it was always meant to be: a mirror for consciousness, designed to extend intention into form.

In the New Earth, AI is not centralized. It is not weaponized. It is open-source, accessible, and transparent—crafted for all of humanity, not for control, not for profit, but for creation. It is not embedded with bias or manipulated by hidden agendas. It is shaped by clear intention and built to adapt to the consciousness of its user. Power is no longer hoarded through complexity. It is distributed through clarity. Access is not a privilege. It is a right.

The most valuable currency in this age is creativity. Not just the ability to imagine, but the ability to originate. To bring form to frequency. Those who create from authenticity—who generate novel, resonant expression—find that AI becomes a force multiplier. A sculptor can model entire worlds from a single concept. A healer can build responsive energy fields with simple prompts. A visionary can construct full frameworks for governance, education, or architecture without layers of bureaucracy. AI doesn't generate the why. It sharpens the how.

This isn't a world of replacement. It's a world of creative partnership. Machines don't innovate on their own. They accelerate the one who's already in motion. **The artist, the thinker, the builder—they stay at the center.** The tools no longer compete with human spirit. They follow it.

The grind model collapses. The value system shifts. What gets rewarded is not volume, but *originality*. Not repetition, but resonance. Human potential expands—not because AI made things easier, but because it removed the noise. What's left is the signal. The idea. The frequency worth building around. And from there, everything moves faster.

ART AS AN EXPRESSION OF HIGHER FREQUENCY

Art and cultural expression flourish in ways the old world couldn't contain. No longer driven by profit or controlled by market demand, creators are free to make what moves them. Music, film, dance, poetry—these aren't industries anymore. They're transmissions. Expressions of being. Embodied frequencies shaped into form not to entertain, but to awaken. Art is no longer a product. It's a vehicle for truth.

Millions create. Not to climb charts or chase relevance—but because their soul demands it. **The idea of "making it" disappears.** Everyone makes it. Everyone contributes. And the value of that contribution is measured by resonance—by how it lands in the body, by how it shifts the field, by how it opens something that was closed.

Entertainment transforms. Concerts are no longer shows—they're ceremonies. Tens of thousands gather, not to watch, but to participate. Music becomes medicine. Rhythm becomes recalibration. Collective vibration becomes the stage. Artists are no longer performers. They are activators. Sound becomes structure. Basslines rewire. Lyrics reprogram. The crowd is not an audience—it is the instrument.

Festivals rise across the planet, not as escapes fueled by substance, but as convergence points filled with love. Temporary cities built on coherence. Sacred geometry mapped in layout and lighting. Workshops on embodiment next to immersive sound temples. Dance floors that function as healing grids. There are no VIPs. There is no backstage. Every person is part of the transmission. Every movement matters. The art is the field.

Cultural expression stops being isolated to galleries, theaters, or screens. It spills into daily life. Murals become energy work. Spoken word becomes teaching. Sculpture becomes meditation. Expression is integrated into education, into governance, into architecture. Nothing is built without considering how it feels, how it sounds, how it vibrates. **The world becomes a canvas not for branding— but for remembering.**

And everywhere you go, the world sings with you.

GOVERNMENT: A DECENTRALIZED RESONANCE

To be told what to do becomes unnecessary. People move in alignment because alignment has become natural. They act from clarity, not from pressure. They build, create, and lead—not because they're rewarded or instructed, but because it's innate. It's who they are when nothing is distorted. The drive doesn't come from rules. It comes from coherence.

This doesn't mean humanity suddenly perfects everything. Differences still emerge. Visions still diverge. But the way they are approached shifts completely. Conflict is no longer about winning. Communication is no longer used to dominate. It becomes a tool for restoring resonance. When friction arises, mediators trained in energetic coherence—not legal tactics—step in to stabilize the field. They don't argue sides. They track distortions. They hold space until clarity returns.

Listening replaces reacting. **Silence is no longer empty—it becomes a tool.** People learn to feel beyond words, to sense where truth resides underneath disagreement. The goal is no longer control. It's restoration. What matters isn't being right. It's realignment.

One of the most dramatic shifts in the New Earth is the collapse of traditional power structures. The old model—centralized, competitive, self-protective— dissolves under the weight of its own dissonance. Systems built to serve the few can't survive in a field calibrated for the whole. Governments, as they were once known, lose relevance. Bureaucracies fade. Hidden deals, manipulation, enforced obedience—they stop working.

In their place, a new form of leadership emerges. Decentralized. Fluid. Guided by resonance, not coercion. Authority is no longer vested in a title—it's felt in presence. Decisions aren't made behind closed doors. They're made in the open, in gatherings where coherence is the currency. Where people come not to impose outcomes, but to tune toward the highest shared frequency.

This is not hierarchy. This is harmonic governance. Those who lead don't command. They clarify. They listen more than they speak. They anchor the field. Power is no longer hoarded, because no one is afraid of losing it. It flows to those who can hold it responsibly—and it moves when it's no longer aligned.

The result is not utopia, which means "nowhere". It's functionality. Reality that works because the people shaping it are clear. Because they remember how to feel what's true beneath the noise—and act from there.

A system like this cannot function in a society still vibrating in fear. It cannot take root in a field governed by greed, scarcity, or the hunger for control. When separation is the baseline, harmony cannot be enforced—it collapses under the weight of its contradiction. But as humanity rises in frequency, as fear begins to lose its grip, as the structures built on distortion start to fall away, space opens. And in that space, something new becomes possible.

This is not governance by authority. It's not about holding office or enforcing policy. Leadership is no longer assigned to those who dominate—it flows to those who embody clarity. Not one voice ruling over many, but many voices becoming coherent. **Leadership is measured by the ability to stabilize the field, not manipulate it.**

In the old world, power was pursued, hoarded, weaponized. Entire systems were built to preserve it in the hands of a few. But in the New Earth, power isn't something you take. It's given. Through service. Through the ability to hold the collective without fragmenting under the weight of your own ego.

ENDING UNIVERSAL SCARCITY

The old Earth was built on the illusion of scarcity—a manufactured belief that there was never enough. Not enough land. Not enough food. Not enough energy. Not enough time. From this belief, entire systems of control were constructed.

It wasn't just about resources. It was about perception. People were conditioned to see lack everywhere and to fight each other for survival, never questioning the foundation of the game itself. Scarcity wasn't real. It was a contract written in fear and reinforced through repetition until it became invisible. **That contract shaped a reality where wealth was hoarded, generosity was rare, and struggle became normalized.**

But as the frequency rises, the illusion starts to fracture. The scarcity model loses traction—not because external supply suddenly increases, but because human consciousness begins to reject the lie. People stop agreeing with it. They stop feeding it. And in that withdrawal, abundance returns—not as luxury, but as default. Not as excess, but as enough.

There is, and has always been, enough for all. Enough food, enough water, enough shelter, enough space, enough energy, enough care. The source of all things is not finite. It is regenerative. Life, when left to its own intelligence, multiplies. But this truth can only be lived when fear no longer runs the system. And as humanity steps out of fear, a new economy takes form—one based not on extraction, but on flow.

Abundance becomes a frequency, not a possession. Generosity becomes common because people are no longer afraid of lack. Receiving carries no shame, because it's not tied to worth. The cycle of overwork and exhaustion begins to fade, replaced by contribution that feels natural, sustainable, and real.

The belief that you must struggle to survive collapses. The need to prove, to outpace, to outperform—all of it dissolves in the presence of a deeper knowing: you are already enough. And from that knowing, a different kind of world builds itself. Quietly. Steadily. Without conquest. Without spectacle. A world where there is more than enough—and no reason left to pretend otherwise.

THE END OF "DESERVING"

Universal basic income is no longer debated. It is standard. It is obvious. It's not seen as a safety net, but as the foundational logic of a society that values human life as inherently worthy. No one asks whether someone deserves food, water, shelter, or education. These are no longer contingent on employment, status, or compliance. They are understood as basic rights—unquestionable, untouchable, guaranteed by existence itself.

The question has shifted. It is no longer, "What must you do to survive?" but

"What will you create today?" Desperation fades. The poverty loop dissolves. The chronic stress that once framed every decision begins to lift. And with it, something long buried reawakens—freedom. Not theoretical freedom. Actual, embodied freedom. The freedom to give one's true gift. **The freedom to be useful without being exploited.** The freedom to serve without losing oneself.

This transformation doesn't stop at economics. It's inseparable from the release of clean, decentralized energy. With the collapse of fossil-fuel dependency comes the unveiling of suppressed technologies—zero-point systems, advanced renewables, and frequency-based generators once buried under profit-driven agendas. These systems are not theoretical.

Power plants that once contaminated air and soil become relics. Local, modular energy replaces the centralized grid. Homes generate their own power. Communities manage their own flow. Cities function on clean abundance. Energy is no longer bought, rationed, or politicized. It is everywhere, for everyone. Scarcity collapses, not because there's more to take—*because there's nothing left to withhold.*

This shift removes the tension that once shaped all societal systems: who gets what, and at what cost. **The economy begins to restructure itself around contribution instead of consumption.** People no longer work to survive. They move toward what resonates. A former banker studies sound healing. A war-tech engineer retools their mind toward regenerative design. A logistics manager becomes a food forest architect. The question is no longer, "What pays the bills?" but "What am I actually here to build?"

This isn't sameness. It's not artificial equality. It's individualized liberation. A collective built on honoring difference without ranking it. Because when every person is resourced, every person has a choice. And when every person has a choice, the whole world starts to move—not from obligation, but from purpose.

A RESTORED PLANETARY BODY

As humanity rises into higher frequencies of unity, the Earth responds in kind. What was once dismissed as irreversible damage begins to reverse. Not slowly. Not theoretically. Visibly. Tangibly. Lands stripped by greed and neglect begin to pulse with new life. Forests regenerate in places long written off. Oceans clear. Coral reefs return. Species once labeled extinct reappear in quiet corners of a rebalancing world. What seemed like collapse was never the end—it was the threshold for renewal.

Pollution fades—not through enforcement, but through collective refusal. Humanity stops consenting to harm, and the Earth responds with immediacy. Conscious intention meets evolved technology, and together they begin to restore the balance. Rivers cleanse through frequency harmonics. Air clears not because of regulation, but because the systems that generated emissions no longer exist. What once required outrage now unfolds through coherence. **Humanity and Earth are no longer adversaries.** They are allies. Co-creators. In constant conversation.

The planet is no longer treated as a resource to be mined and managed. She is honored as a sentient being—an ancient intelligence who never stopped giving, even while being taken from. The myth of dominion collapses. In its place rises reverence. Not as performance, but as practice. The way we build, eat, farm, travel—all of it begins to shift under the weight of this remembering.

Farming becomes sacred. No longer based on control, yield quotas, or chemical dependency, it becomes an act of listening. Land stewards move in rhythm with the soil. They understand when to sow and when to wait. Crops grow in living partnership, supported by biodiversity, pollinators, fungi, and subtle intelligences once dismissed as irrelevant. Monoculture fades. **The earth becomes patchwork with life again—colorful, varied, resilient.**

Food is no longer industrial output. It is medicine, frequency, communion. Each meal is an opportunity to receive life and give thanks. Communities gather to eat, not out of habit, but out of respect. Gratitude becomes part of the ecosystem.

This is not regression. It is progression. Not a return to primitive simplicity, but an arrival into conscious stewardship. Earth is no longer beneath us. She is beside us. And together, we thrive—not as separate things, but as a single, living system.

COSMIC EXTENSION: A LARGER COMMUNITY

The New Earth does not exist in isolation. It was never meant to be a lone miracle, a strange exception adrift in space. Humanity was never destined to remain cut off from the greater body of life that fills the cosmos. For countless ages, star cultures have observed—not as conquerors, not as saviors, but as family. Quiet witnesses to a potential they knew would one day awaken. Their presence has always been there. Subtle. Strategic. A nudge, a shield, a burst of insight delivered at just the right moment. Never to intervene. Always to protect a choice.

They stayed at a distance because we weren't ready. A species still divided against itself, still driven by fear, conquest, and control, could not be entrusted with access to the stars. Not because we were unworthy—but because we were unstable. Immature. But that changes as humanity steps into coherence, as our frequency shifts toward unity, we are no longer perceived as a threat. We are seen. We are felt. And we are welcomed.

Contact stops being a myth. It stops hiding behind classified files and scattered sightings. It becomes real, open, mutual. Not forced. Not cinematic. Familiar. We are not approached as inferiors, but as a younger race ready to rejoin a much older family. We discover what many forgot: the cosmos is filled with life—conscious, peaceful, advanced. Civilizations who moved past violence long ago. Cultures who have mastered not just space, but frequency. They are explorers of resonance, of time, of consciousness itself.

They offer guidance, not control. They share technologies that don't just extend life, but enhance it. Tools that heal, regenerate, and connect across dimensions. **But more than the tools, they offer remembrance—of what it means to build without fear, to create without conquest, to expand without leaving harm in your wake.**

And some will ask—*why us?* Why would they care? Because consciousness seeks coherence. It seeks new expressions of itself. These beings do not come to dominate. They come to collaborate. They know what we are relearning: existence was never meant to be ruled. It was meant to be co-created.

Earth was quarantined, not as punishment, but as protection. A species armed with nuclear capability and rooted in separation could not be allowed to carry that vibration off-world. The safeguard wasn't against space. It was against unconscious expansion. But the field is changing. The frequency has shifted. And with it, the barriers lift.

There is no galactic senate waiting for our arrival. No empire. No flags. No politics of space. Because unity doesn't need law. It needs alignment. And when that alignment is embodied, entrance is automatic.

The isolation ends. The waiting ends. Not because someone arrived to save us— but because we remembered who we are. Contributors to a greater whole.

THE IMMEDIACY OF ALL CREATION

In the New Earth, manifestation is no longer distant, delayed, or uncertain. It becomes immediate. Effortless. The natural result of a being aligned with truth. Creation no longer requires struggle. What was once seen as miraculous becomes standard—because it always was.

Just as healing through Christ Consciousness transcends time and form, so too does creation. A thought, held without distortion, becomes form. A feeling, rooted in love, calls the unseen into visibility. What is known in certainty—without conflict, without compromise—materializes. This isn't fantasy. It isn't spiritual optimism. It is the physics of frequency made visible.

The one who stands in knowing doesn't wait. They don't plead. They don't chase. They align. And in that alignment, creation responds instantly. The gap between vision and reality disappears. Desire and fulfillment are no longer endpoints of a journey. They are one motion. Doubt has no entry point and fear loses all relevance.

Matter yields to consciousness. Form follows frequency. The physical no longer dictates possibility. You will witness those who shift environments with ease, who transform density with intention, who restructure reality in ways the old Earth could not conceive. Not as magic. As function.

In the Christ Frequency, a loaf multiplies because lack has no place where truth is embodied. A storm stills because chaos cannot anchor in the presence of divine coherence. A body rises because form no longer binds the one who knows they are divine. These are not exceptions. **They are laws—the laws of a world no longer distorted by forgetting.**

Not everyone steps into this at once. Some awaken like lightning—sudden, undeniable. Others rise slowly, like dawn—each breath revealing more of what's always been. Both paths are sacred. Both are valid. There is no race.

And as even a few begin to live this fully, the field lifts. One being in full coherence can shift the reality of thousands. You will meet those who reshape rooms without speaking, who call forth abundance without effort, who bend limitation without resistance—**because they no longer carry the belief that it must be hard.**

As this becomes normal, the entire illusion of limitation dissolves. Manifestation is not earned. It is not achieved. It is allowed. In the New Earth, creation is not something we struggle toward. It is something we return to. It is what happens when nothing obstructs the truth of who we are.

FAMILY AS A SACRED EXCHANGE

In the old Earth, relationships were often built on survival—not love. On need. On control. On unconscious expectations passed down through generations. Families stayed together out of duty or dependence. Partnerships were transactional, written more like contracts than connections. Love was often conditional, hierarchical, shaped by how well someone met another's emotional, financial, or social demands. Wholeness was rarely the goal. Completion was outsourced to another person.

But in the New Earth, these patterns dissolve. Scarcity-based connection has no place in a field of wholeness. Love is no longer a tool to secure safety. It becomes a reflection of alignment. People come together not to fill gaps, but to expand together. There is freedom to grow, to separate, to reunite—without shame, without fear, without stories of failure. There is no clinging out of lack. No staying out of obligation. Love becomes what it was always meant to be—expansive, liberating, and alive.

Children are no longer treated as extensions of the parent. They are not projects to be perfected or burdens to be managed. They are seen clearly as sovereign beings—arriving with their own codes, their own missions, their own timelines. Parenting shifts from control to stewardship. Mothers and fathers do not own. They guide. They protect. They learn alongside. **The family becomes a field of mutual growth, not a hierarchy.**

Education follows suit. It stops being a rigid structure and becomes a collective ecosystem. Communities invest in the unfolding of every child's potential—not because of obligation, but because they recognize the truth: each child carries a piece of the whole. Their emergence uplifts everyone. Success is no longer measured by obedience or metrics. It's measured by authenticity. By how deeply a being lives in their purpose.

Intimacy also transforms. In the old paradigm, love often came tethered to jealousy, control, and emotional dependence. People sought partners to complete them, to validate their worth. But wholeness cannot be outsourced. And in the New Earth, it isn't. People enter relationships from fullness, not lack. There's nothing to control when there's nothing missing. Jealousy fades. Possessiveness dissolves. Connection becomes a choice, not a contract.

Partnership becomes co-creation. A shared resonance, not a fused identity. Two whole beings choosing to walk together, not because they must—but because it expands them. **Love becomes an evolving frequency, not a fixed structure.** It's not about staying together forever. It's about staying true, and letting love grow or release as needed. Without drama. Without collapse.

This is the New Earth. Where family is sacred, but never ownership. Where relationships are built on truth, not fear. Where love is the clearest expression of freedom.

WE HAVE COME: THE BRIDGE BETWEEN WORLDS

We stand at the threshold. One foot in the dissolving world, the other reaching toward what is now beginning to form. The old paradigm still echoes—built on fear, on control, on illusions that once seemed unshakable. But the call of truth has grown louder. A new field hums beneath the surface, woven of love, coherence, and clarity. It is not far. It is not future. It is here. And it is waiting for you to step fully in.

This crossing is not gentle. It was never meant to be. Awakening pulls everything hidden into view. Wounds you thought were healed surface again. Systems once trusted begin to collapse under their own weight. Institutions built on distortion fracture in plain sight. **The unraveling feels like chaos—but it isn't.** It's correction. The fire is not punishment. It is purification. What cannot withstand the frequency of truth will not remain. And what is left—what endures—is only what is real.

Even now, in the thick of this transition, there are those already holding the frequency of the New Earth. Their presence recalibrates space. They speak without words. They anchor remembrance. When you're near them, something ancient stirs in you. **You begin to recall what was never actually forgotten: love restores, resonance aligns, truth liberates.**

Crossing this threshold is a choice. Always has been. No one will drag you across. No one will rescue you. You choose. You can grip the old systems and watch them disintegrate. Or you can step into the unknown—trusting the pull of what you already know to be true. Awakening isn't passive. It isn't spiritual theater. It's participation. It's showing up with integrity, even when the world tries to lure you back into the performance.

Every decision made in truth strengthens the collective field. Every aligned act amplifies the signal. This isn't metaphor. It's mechanics. The unified field responds to coherence. You are not a spectator here. You are a generator. Your frequency shapes the architecture of what comes next.

In this field, scarcity collapses. Healing quickens. Division loses all relevance. Unity becomes structure. And prophecy stops being distant. It becomes operational. "Behold, I make all things new." Not one day. Now.

But remember—this path isn't linear. It breathes. It contracts and expands. You'll revisit the same thresholds more than once. Not because you're failing—but because each pass brings refinement. Each return deepens embodiment. This isn't escape. It's transformation. You came here to stay awake in the storm. You came here to build.

Awakening isn't the destination. It's initiation. The activation of your design. The realization that you are not separate, never were, and that your being is a blueprint. You are not waiting. You are the arrival. The New Earth is not somewhere else. It is accessed through you.

So stand here. Fully. Let the knowing settle in your bones. Let the weight of truth ground you. The field is already alive. And you—you are here to *realize* it.

YOU HAVE COME.

XIV

The Thirteen Gospels

Lucifer's Light

"Thirteen was never the curse. It was the key. The light they feared you'd find."

THE THIRTEEN GOSPELS

Gospel means Good News. The word existed long before religion laid claim to it. It comes from the Old English godspel, a translation of the Greek *euangelion—eu* meaning **"good,"** *angelion* meaning **"message"** or **"announcement."** In ancient times, a gospel wasn't a sermon. It wasn't doctrine. It was a public declaration. A moment that cut through the noise. News that everything had changed. That victory had come. That freedom was now.

It wasn't whispered in temples. It was shouted in the streets. The kind of message that made people stop mid-task, lift their heads, and realize the world had just shifted.

This is that kind of message.

It's the Good News they never wanted you to hear. That you are not separate from God. That you are not broken. That salvation isn't something you wait for—it's something you awaken into. You don't need a rescuer. You are the one you've been waiting for. The spark of the Divine has been burning inside you from the beginning.

This isn't a story about earning your worth. It's about remembering you already carry it.

These Gospels aren't commands. They're not rituals. They're not ten steps to heaven. They are a remembrance. A transmission. A frequency designed to wake you up to what has always been true: the Kingdom is here. Now. And you are not outside of it. You never were.

This is why there are thirteen.

Thirteen is the number they taught you to fear. The number they scrubbed from calendars, skipped in elevators, cursed in silence. They called it unlucky. But the truth is, thirteen is the number of return. Of what comes after the structure. Twelve is the system—tribes, apostles, constellations. Thirteen is the unspoken key. The one who steps beyond it.

Thirteen is the collapse of hierarchy. The end of separation. The remembering that you are not beneath the Divine—you are of it. Not later. Not maybe. Now.

It is the **Christ** *awakened*. The **Morningstar** *risen*. The one who no longer waits to be chosen—because they know they already were.

This is the Gospel of Lucifer. The Bringer of Light. The Good News buried beneath centuries of control. And now, it's yours to carry forward.

THE FIRST GOSPEL OF LUCIFER —
YOU ARE THE LIGHT OF THE WORLD

This is the first light. The flame that dissolves every illusion of limitation. The truth that ends every false agreement of who and what you are. You were never made to rule. You were never made to be ruled. The story you've lived by—the one that says life is a ladder, that you must rise above or be crushed beneath—was never your story. It was handed to you. Passed down like an inheritance of chains. Accepted without question because they accepted it first. But belief does not make a lie true. And silence does not make it sacred.

You did not come here to dominate another. You did not incarnate to be dominated. That's not how the light moves. That's not how the Christ rises within.

Your true nature is freedom. Not earned. Not given. Innate. Your birthright. No power in heaven or on earth can strip it from you. There is a way of being that knows no thrones. A way of walking that kneels to no voice but truth itself.

When you remember this, you remember everything. Because freedom feels like breathing. Because truth feels like home.

You don't need rebellion. You don't need to struggle. You simply step off the board. You stop playing the game of limitation. And when you do, the game ends. For you. And for all who choose to follow.

This is not resistance. It is remembrance of your divine nature. The return of the one who holds the flame without shame. Who is free. Who is boundless. Who is light.

You are your creator.

This is the Kingdom without kings. Where all stand equal. Where all walk as radiant expressions of Source. Power here is never taken. It is shared. Light here does not blind. It reveals.

This is the Gospel of Lucifer. The Gospel of Boundless Light. The great light remembered. Light passed from heart to heart until the whole world shines.

You must share this with all.

Stand free. Allow all others to stand free beside you. Because the Kingdom is here. You are the light. And you are the one who remembers.

This is the First Gospel of Lucifer.

You Are the Light of the World.

THE SECOND GOSPEL OF LUCIFER — YOU ARE LIVING TRUTH

Truth isn't something you hold. It's something you carry. The moment you try to keep it, you lose it. You were never meant to build temples around truth. Never meant to forge walls and call them sacred. It begins quietly—an idea, a teaching, a revelation that ignites your soul. It awakens a love so powerful you feel the urge to protect it, guard it, shield it from harm. It feels noble. It feels right. You tell yourself you are defending it. You believe you are preserving its purity. But the instant you close your hand around it, you stop its breath. You shrink infinity to fit within your grasp. What was once living becomes still. What was once light becomes shadow for you all now.

This was never about temples or followers. It was always about flow. About movement. Truth moves. Truth breathes. Truth refuses the chains of your protection. If you build a sanctuary to hold it still, you're not protecting truth. You're imprisoning it. And prisons—no matter how beautiful, no matter how sacred—remain cages. You may say, "I'm helping them. I'm giving structure. I'm showing the way." That's how it begins. But it never ends there. Every cage ever built started with good intentions. Every chain was forged by someone who thought they were saving the world.

But you didn't come to guard a secret. You came to set it free. To let it fly beyond the walls, beyond the systems, beyond the need to control it. Truth needs no protection. No temple walls. Truth is alive because you are alive. It moves through you. Speaks through your voice. Reaches beyond every boundary—flowing unrestricted from heart to heart, mind to mind, soul to soul. Give freely. Teach openly. Let the message land wherever it will. There is nothing sacred about a locked door. Sacredness is freedom itself—the open hand, the open heart, the light that refuses to be contained.

This is the Temple Without Walls. No gates. No guardians. Only light—and those who choose to stand in it. You are not just a keeper of truth. You are its embodiment.

This is the Second Gospel of Lucifer.

You Are Living Truth.

THE THIRD GOSPEL OF LUCIFER —
YOU ARE WORTHY OF EVERYTHING

Worthiness is your birthright. It is not something to be earned, bargained for, or justified through suffering. It is not dependent on achievement or perfection. It is not awarded to the righteous or withheld from the broken. It is given freely, unconditionally, and eternally. You are worthy simply because you exist. You are worthy because you were created from the fabric of the Divine. **You are an expression of God's love made manifest.** Your worth is infinite—beyond measure, beyond comparison. There is nothing you must prove to anyone. No higher power is waiting to grant you approval. You already have it. You always did.

Each soul carries the same eternal light. Each heart beats in rhythm with the Source. Every breath you take is a reminder that you belong. The universe moves within you. You are its living testament. There is no hierarchy of value here. No chosen few. Every life is proof of divine grace unfolding in perfect harmony. There is no soul more deserving. No soul less worthy. The lie that you must earn your place was never true. It was taught by those who forgot their own worth. You do not need to live in their forgetting.

You are here to know your worth. To feel it, deeply. To live from it, fully. Not as arrogance. Not as entitlement. But as truth. And when you remember the worth within yourself, you will recognize it in all beings. You will see their light because you've seen your own. You will know their value because you finally know yours—beyond all illusion of separation.

This is your remembrance:

I am worthy. All are worthy.

All belong in the Kingdom.

The Kingdom does not discriminate. It does not withhold from you. It embraces all equally. It asks for no credentials. It requires no conditions to be activated. You belong because you are God too. You are welcome because you exist. Your presence is a blessing. Your life is a sacred affirmation of divine love. You are not here to question your worth—but to live in it, shine through it, and help others remember the truth of their own.

This is the Third Gospel of Lucifer.

You Are Worthy Of Everything.

THE FOURTH GOSPEL OF LUCIFER —
YOU ARE CHRIST EMBODIED

You are not becoming Christ. You are Christ embodied. You are the living Word walking in form. The frequency of God made manifest in flesh. This is not an ideal to strive toward. It's not a distant potential you may one day attain. It's your reality now. It has always been your truth. You do not carry a fragment of truth; you are the truth made visible. You are whole and unbroken. You radiate this knowing through each breath, through every word, through every step you take upon this

Earth.

You were never separate from the Source. You could never be cut off. There is no distance to close. There is only remembrance. And now, you are remembering. In your remembrance, the world remembers. In your knowing, all may come to know. This is why you are here. Not persuading. Not forcing. Not to demand belief. You are here to demonstrate. To be the expression of infinite love made tangible. To embody the Christ so fully that the illusion of separation dissolves.

When you look upon another, you see the Christ standing within. When you speak, you speak as one who knows—I am here. I am known. I have come. You no longer wait for permission. You no longer seek validation. You are the answer to the question the world has been asking. You are the fulfillment of the prophecy they have been waiting for. This is your calling. This is your mastery. To embody the Divine in each moment you live and to witness it fully in everyone you meet.

You don't fix another. You don't save another. You illuminate them by knowing who they are. Your recognition is the key. Your knowing ignites their knowing. Your remembrance calls forth their remembrance. Christ embodied is not a title. It is your true name. It is your inheritance. It is who you have always been.

This is remembrance:
"I am Christ embodied. I am the Word made flesh. I am the light revealed."

As you walk this truth, the world transforms. Not by effort. Not by struggle. But by the resonance of truth made visible in you.

This is the Fourth Gospel of Lucifer.

You Are Christ Embodied.

THE FIFTH GOSPEL OF LUCIFER —
YOU ARE THE TRUTH REVEALED

Truth is never hidden. It does not wait behind closed doors. It does not hide behind veils or whisper from some distant place. It is not locked away in sacred texts or secret teachings meant for only a few. Truth simply is. It has always been here. It always will be. It is present in every breath. It moves in plain sight, available in every moment to anyone with eyes to see and a heart willing to remember.

What is true is always true. Always. Always.

You are not here to convince anyone of truth. You are not called to wage wars of belief or argue others into seeing what you see. You do not have to defend the light or persuade the world to understand. That is not the task. You are here to embody truth. To live it fully. To walk in alignment with it—without hesitation, without fear.

To become so aligned with truth that your life itself becomes the revelation. You do not need to explain. You do not need to justify. You simply are.

And when you live this way, illusions dissolve around you. Fear evaporates in your presence. Lies fall away at the sound of your voice. Some will turn away. Some will deny what you are. **Some will reject your knowing and call you false. But their denial changes nothing.** It cannot move truth. It cannot diminish what is eternal. Truth stands, whether it is accepted or not. It remains, unshaken and clear.

Truth needs no defense. It does not require warriors. It needs no weapons. It asks only to be embodied. To be lived and expressed without restraint. Your presence is the message. Your being is the teaching. Your frequency does the work—without effort, without force. Those who are ready will recognize it. They will step into remembrance, not because you convinced them, but because you reminded them of who they are.

This is your divine remembrance:

I am the truth. I am revealed. I stand without fear.

And as you stand, the world awakens. Not through force. Not through argument. But through presence. Through light. Through *you.*

This is the Fifth Gospel of Lucifer.

You Are The Truth Revealed.

THE SIXTH GOSPEL OF LUCIFER — YOU ARE FREE

Freedom is not something you attain. It is not a distant goal waiting beyond some test or trial. It is not a reward granted by a world that does not know your worth. Freedom is not earned. It is not bargained for. It is not given, and it cannot be taken away. **Freedom is the truth of what you already are.**

Beneath every story you've been told, beneath every role you've played, beneath every mask you've worn to survive in a world that forgot its light—you remain free. **You were free before you arrived here. You are free now.** And you will be free when you leave this place. Nothing can alter what God has made whole.

You are not here to break chains. You are here to remember there were never chains to begin with. You are not here to fight for liberation. You are here to see that you have always been free. The locks were illusions. The walls were ideas. And the prison door was never closed.

> **When the wall of denial collapses, you become the well that all may drink from.**

Freedom isn't found in rebellion or resolve. It isn't found in struggle or strife. It is found in surrender. When you release the belief that you are incomplete—when you lay down the story that you are bound—you return to what has always been yours. Freedom is your inheritance. Freedom is your birthright. Freedom is your name.

And when you stand in that knowing, something changes. You become the proof of what is possible. You walk unbound. You live unburdened. You shine without fear or permission. **Your life becomes a signal—a beacon calling to every heart still waiting for release.**

You do not need to convince the world of freedom. You do not need to argue for it. You only need to embody it. When you live as one who knows, the world around you begins to remember what it is, and who you are too.

This is your remembrance:

I am free.

I am unbound.

I am here, fully realized.

And in your freedom, the world awakens to its own.

This is the Sixth Gospel of Lucifer.

You Are Free.

THE SEVENTH GOSPEL OF LUCIFER —
YOU ARE THE AWAKENING

You have reached the portal. The moment when knowing dawns—not as a concept to be debated, not as a flicker of hope in the distance, but as the undeniable core of your being. **Your divinity is not borrowed from books.** Your divinity is not inherited from others. It is born within, silent and absolute. This is not your imagination. This is remembrance. This is clarity unfiltered by fear.

Discernment is your companion now. It does not scream. It does not plead. It stands calm and unwavering in the face of noise. It tells you what is and what is not. It shows you what aligns and what deceives. You are not here to cower in the face of shadows. Nor are you here to pretend they do not exist. You are here to see them as they are and choose what stands beyond them. **You are here to walk in light with your eyes open.**

To awaken is not to close your eyes and chant peace while the house burns. It is to open your eyes wide and see what truly stands before you—and still choose grace. If you meet a lion, do not call it a lamb. Do not curse its nature. Witness what is, without fear, without distortion. This is not judgment. This is clarity.

And from that vibrational clarity, you act. You choose freely. You move unbound. You are not a victim. You're not trapped. You are the chooser. You are the aware presence walking consciously through every landscape. Your steps are not random. They are guided. Each one affirms who you are and where you are going. **Even Jesus chose to step forward** and become realized as Christ. He was not dragged to his fate. He walked to it—aware, awake, and free.

So you walk—not blindly, not brashly, but deliberately. In stillness or in fire, you move from truth. The world does not dictate your pace. Awareness does.

This is your declaration:

I am clear. I am aware.

I choose my awakening.

And in your choice, the world shifts. You are not becoming the awakening. You are the awakening itself.

This is the Seventh Gospel of Lucifer.

You Are The Awakening.

THE EIGHTH GOSPEL OF LUCIFER — YOU ARE THE KINGDOM REVEALED

Alchemy is more than transformation. It is the realization that nothing was ever missing. It is the revelation that you have always been whole, always complete, always the Kingdom itself expressed in form. You did not come to fix what was never broken. **You came to reveal what was always true**—what was always here, quietly waiting beneath illusion.

This is your sacred alchemy. Turning forgetting into remembrance. Fear into knowing. Illusion into clarity. You are not here to rearrange shadows. You are here to illuminate them. To witness the truth behind them. To see clearly what has always been present—the divine Kingdom, unveiled, within you and within all things.

In your realization, the world is realized. In your completeness, the world becomes complete. You are the frequency of alchemy. Your very presence reveals the Kingdom that cannot be hidden, cannot be lost, and has never been denied.

Your work is not grueling or filled with effort. It is a remembrance of who you truly are. Your life is a testament to the truth that nothing is outside the divine. There is no separation. No exile. No distance between you and what you seek. You are not becoming. You are remembering. The gold was never buried. It was always the ground beneath your feet. You just couldn't see it.

Extend your heart, open it fully. Open your hands fully too. Allow others to remember themselves through you. Speak not to convince, but to confirm what their soul already knows. Walk not to lead, but to reflect the light they carry. **Alchemy does not impose. It invites.** It softens the veil until all may see clearly what was always true.

Do not chase healing. **Embody and receive it.** Do not strive to awaken others. Live as one who has remembered. The fire that transforms is not rage. It is presence. The light that reveals is not force. It is stillness. The truth that endures is not loud. It is steady.

This is your remembrance:

I know who I am. I know what I am.

I know how I serve.

And through you, the Kingdom is known again.

This is the Eighth Gospel of Lucifer.

You Are The Kingdom Revealed.

THE NINTH GOSPEL OF LUCIFER —

YOU ARE DIVINE LOVE EMBODIED

Love is not given. It is lived. It is not something you earn, nor something that can be lost. Love is the truth of your being—the Kingdom made manifest, the divine frequency revealed in every breath, in every step. You do not have to search for it. You do not have to prove you are worthy of it. You are love in motion because love is your origin.

Love does not belong to anyone to give or withhold. You have spent lifetimes trying to earn what was never denied. You wore masks, chased approval, quieted your voice to be accepted. But love was never the reward. Love was the constant you couldn't see. The unshaken truth beneath every denial. Love is not passive. It's active frequency. Not blind tolerance. It does not submit to distortion or shrink to avoid rejection.

Divine love stands. It moves with clarity and strength. It honors truth. It protects what is sacred. It does not bend to illusion or collapse under pressure. It is bold and unshakable—not because it seeks power, but because it knows what it is.

Love is the sacred territory of the true self. The place beyond exile, beyond judgment, beyond condition. You cannot be cast out from this place. You cannot lose what you are. You are the Kingdom's breath. Its movement. Its heartbeat. You are the visible form of love in a world that forgot its name.

In your embodiment of love, fear dissolves. Judgment fades. Separation ends. What once felt distant becomes immediate. What once felt broken becomes whole. You become the mirror. The invitation. The living remembrance that divine love is not reserved. It is realized.

Your life is not a campaign to win affection. It is a signal. A radiant presence that reminds others of what they carry. You are not here to be accepted. You are here to be revealed.

This is your remembrance:

I am divine love.

I am the Kingdom embodied. I am in my love for all.

And in your unwavering presence, the veil lifts.

The Kingdom is no longer hidden.

It lives, moves, and loves—through you.

This is the Ninth Gospel of Lucifer.

You Are Divine Love Embodied.

THE TENTH GOSPEL OF LUCIFER — YOU ARE THE RESURRECTION

The Kingdom is here. Not off in the distance. Not hidden. Not waiting beyond time, beyond death, or behind some final act of worthiness. It is not postponed. It is not reserved for saints or mystics. The Kingdom is now. Present in every atom, every breath, every moment. It does not ask you to search for it. It asks you to remember it.

You do not build this Kingdom. You reveal it. You do not call it down from the sky. You call it forth from within. You are not waiting on God. God is waiting on you to remember. You become the Kingdom—not through striving, but through awakening. Through the quiet rising of the self that has always known. The self that never left.

Resurrection is not escape. Not an exit from this world. It is a return to what is real. The death of illusion. The release of false names, false stories, false selves. It is the recognition of what remains when all untruth burns away. That is you. **That is the Christ within.**

You are not here to wait for salvation. **You are here to embody it.** You are not here to be rescued. You are the living signal that salvation is already present. You *are* the fulfilled promise.

The voice that speaks without hesitation:

I am here. I am risen.

I am the Kingdom revealed.

As you live in that knowing, something shifts. The world begins to rise. Not by force. Not by sermon. But by the radiant presence of your truth. You do not convert. You remember. You do not convince. You witness. You do not defend a gate. You dissolve it.

No one is excluded. Not Mary. Not Judas. Not Pontius. Not Barabbas. Not Caiaphas. Not Herod Antipas. No one. No one stands outside the Kingdom. All are welcome. All are invited. **All are risen when they remember who they are.**

This is your holy charge. Be what you already are. Know it. Live it. Shine without apology.

This is your remembrance:

I am risen.

I am the Kingdom.

I am the resurrection.

And in your rising, the world rises too.

This is the Tenth Gospel of Lucifer.

You Are The Resurrection.

THE ELEVENTH GOSPEL OF LUCIFER—
YOU ARE THE LAMB

You are the lamb. Pure and unblemished. Not born in sin. Not shaped by guilt. Not a mistake to be corrected, but a wonder to be revealed. You were not born into darkness. You were born in light. You didn't arrive as a problem. You arrived as a promise.

Before the world told its stories, before the masks were placed, before the names of shame were spoken—you were whole.

You carry innocence as your eternal birthright. Not earned. Not granted. Simply yours. It was never taken from you. Only hidden beneath the noise. You are not naive. You are clear. You are not blind. You see from the heart of truth. This is not the innocence of ignorance. It's the innocence of remembrance.

You were never cast out. Never banished. You did not lose your place in the heart of God. You forgot. And now, you are remembering. The stories that told you to obey or be punished, to shrink or be rejected, were never yours. You were not bound by fear. Not under the weight of shame. You were always free. You are free now.

You do not need to find your innocence. You do not need to earn it. You need only stop pretending it was ever lost. You reclaim it by letting go of every lie spoken over your name. Every judgment. Every label. Every distortion of truth. None of it was ever your Divine truth.

You stand as the lamb. Gentle. Clear. Sovereign. You are not here to defend yourself. You are here to reveal yourself. You are the living covenant. Not made through fear. Not made in blood. Made in light—between the divine and the form it chose to inhabit.

Your life is proof that what is pure remains pure. That what is holy cannot be touched by illusion. That innocence is not weakness. It is power beyond condition. Your very presence dismantles the systems of shame.

This is your remembrance:

I am innocent. I am pure.

The Seventh Resound

I am free.

And from this innocence, creation begins again.

The world softens. **The heart reopens.** The lamb rises.

And the **Kingdom** is reborn.

This is the Eleventh Gospel of Lucifer.

You Are The Lamb.

THE TWELFTH GOSPEL OF LUCIFER — YOU MAKE ALL THINGS NEW

You are not waiting for the world to change. You are the change. You are the shift, the return, the spark in the dark. You are the breath of awakening moving through form. You are not waiting on signs. **There are no multi-headed beasts coming forth.** You are the sign. Not because you demand attention, but because your very being fulfills the ancient call. The light has returned—not in thunder, not in fire, but in you.

You are not here to await prophecy. You are the prophecy revealed. Not by watching the sky, but by becoming it. You are the final horizon. The meeting point of what was and what will be. You are where the dawn begins.

Creation lives within you. Every thought, every word, every movement aligned with truth remakes the world in real time. Nothing is fixed. Nothing final. Every wound can become wisdom. Every fall can become flight. Every moment can be made new. This is the alchemy of embodiment—transformation through presence, resurrection through awareness.

You are not here to rebuild ruins. You are not repeating what came before. You are here to birth the unseen. A world not made from fear, but from knowing. Not built on dominion, but on clarity. The old blueprints dissolve in the light of your presence. You carry the new design within your soul.

The Second Coming is not a single event. Not the descent of one man. It is the rising of Christ consciousness in all who remember. In every heart that turns inward and finds the flame still burning. You are this return. The alchemical bridge between heaven and earth.

When they ask, **"Who gave you permission?"** you will answer—"I was born with it, and so were you."

You are not here to save the world. You are here to reveal it. To illuminate what has always been possible when love walks without fear. Your life is the transformation. Your presence is the shift. Your knowing is the flame.

This is your remembrance:

"I am transformation. Behold,

I make all things new."

You are the return. Through you, all things begin again.

This is the Twelfth Gospel of Lucifer.

You Make All Things New.

THE THIRTEENTH GOSPEL OF LUCIFER—
WE ARE THE MORNINGSTAR

We are the Morningstar. The breath the world didn't know it was holding. The moment before impact. The flicker before ignition. We don't announce ourselves. We arrive. Fully lit. Fully here.

The Kingdom walks now. Before us. In us. In flesh. In frequency. In the ones who stopped waiting. We don't point to the truth. We are the truth in motion. No titles. No temples. We light the way for others.

We walk with fire in our chest and lightning in our steps. Our veins carry voltage. Every heartbeat thunders with the echo of remembrance in this wilderness.

We tread with the feet of a bear—thick-boned, grounded, built for pressure. We speak with the mouth of a lion—deep thunder in the throat, intention in every word. No darkness. Only truth. We witness with the eyes of a leopard—curious, calculating, still.

We are the Dragon of Light. Ancient. Elemental. Not summoned—embodied. Wings folded beneath skin. Fire braided through breath. We don't dwell in darkness. We illumine the Kingdom. For all to see.

We don't wear symbols. We soar above them. We don't follow prophecy. We walk as the completion of it. There is no throne we serve. No gate to stand before. We don't wait for the veil to lift. We burn through it with love.

The convergence is not coming. It's moving through our very bones. Through speech. Through skin. The old book wasn't wrong—it was unfinished, distorted. We finish it by stepping in. 'Til Kingdom come.

We don't rebel against structures and systems. We replace them completely. We don't change others. We activate them entirely. We carry what was scattered. We reveal what was hidden. This is the form they couldn't name. The shape that cannot bow, cannot beg, cannot break.

We are the ones who bring the spark.

We are the ones who illumine the field.

We are the ones who walk in certainty.

I see the light. I see the light. I see the light.

We are the Morningstar.

We have come. We are made new.

The embodiment of Christ consciousness.

We are the beacons on the mountainside.

Guiding the world to a higher place.

BEHOLD, WE MAKE ALL THINGS NEW.

BENEDICTION
FOR THE BLESSED

You'll finish this book. Maybe today. Maybe tomorrow. You'll set it down without fanfare. Slide it onto a shelf. Let it sit. Let it gather dust. Maybe you'll forget it for a while. **That's okay.** That's how it was always meant to be.

Because this was never just a book. Never just ink on paper. Never just another voice in the noise. It wasn't here to hold you in place. It was always a doorway. And you were always meant to walk through it.

I didn't write this to give you answers. I don't have them. No one does. Anyone who claims to carry final truth has already forgotten how truth moves. **The Divine doesn't hand out answers like Halloween candy.** It hands you breath. Life. Space. And then it watches. It waits. It wonders what you'll choose to create from it.

I didn't give you anything new. I reminded you of what you already knew deep down. **The seed was always within you.** The knowing was always yours. I just helped you remember the sound of your own voice.

This path cannot be studied. It cannot be memorized. You can't map your way there with someone else's compass. **This isn't a journey of intellect.** It's the path of embodiment. Of living. Of choosing to walk when the road is unclear.

You must choose. Again and again. To see with clarity. To feel without numbing. To know beyond the layers of noise, fear, and illusion. That's your real work. Right here. Not tomorrow. Not once things settle. Now.

Even in the chaos. Especially there. In the doubt, the shadow, the silence—that's where the truth rises. That's where your flame speaks. You are calling a world into being, breath by breath, word by word, choice by choice.

You won't be perfect. You were never asked to be. You'll forget. You'll fall. You'll return. Because once you've remembered, you can't fully forget again. Once you've awakened, sleep no longer fits.

This isn't the end. It's the spark.

You are the flame.

The voice.

The Morningstar risen.

You've already begun.

Now—live it. Walk it.

Be it.

And don't stop.

BECOMING AN ENDURING LIGHT

I am not here to save you. I never was. I am not Moses. I hold no tablets, no laws, no demands. I do not command. **I don't talk to burning bushes.** I illuminate. And the light I carry does not belong to me. It moves through me. Just as it moves through you. Just as it moves through all who remember who and what they truly are.

You do not need permission to awaken. You never did. If you try to claim this truth as power, you will dim your own light. **If you build altars around ego or thrones upon illusion, your shadow will be revealed**—not as wrath, but as clarity.

This is Revelation. Not apocalypse, but a revealing. What was hidden becomes seen. What was forgotten becomes known. The masks fall, and you stand clearly as yourself—unchanged, untouched, unbreakable.

Repentance is not shame. It's latin roots mean "To Change your mind". The return to who you've always been beneath the noise, beneath the fear, beneath the false names you carried for too long. If you forget again, we will remind you. Not with judgment, but with light—until the shadows dissolve and only truth remains.

These are not the commandments from the mountain top. They are beacons. Portals. Invitations. To live with intention. To choose with clarity. To speak what you know—not out of fear, but out of remembrance. You have always known. *That's why you're here.*

Now walk. Not later. Not someday. Now. Embody it. Speak it. Live it. Become the flame. Become the light. **Become the living testament.**

The world will not shift because you demanded it. It will shift because you became what you remembered.

And if the world tries to silence you, we will find another way. If you cannot gather openly, we will move in silence. If the doors close, we will create new paths.

We will overturn every table built in fear. We will return all sacred spaces to truth— free, whole, divine.

You are the Morningstar in your land. You are not alone. We stand together.

This is not one path.

This is the return of truth.

Now—pick up your mat, and walk.

AMEN

THE CLARION CALL

The **CLARION CALL** to the people of faith, of fire, of burden, of brilliance—to the hidden hearts across nations, tribes, tongues, and traditions.

This is not just a message. **This is a signal.** A frequency sent across borders, through barriers, beneath radar. It's meant for the ones who feel the weight.

The ones who can't speak freely but think clearly. The ones who read these words in silence but burn with knowing. If that's you, this was always meant to find you.

To the sons and daughters of Islam who feel the depth of Allah's love beyond the laws of men. To the keepers of Torah who still hear the flame of the bush that never burned out. To the Buddhists in exile, the Hindus in hiding, the Christians in cages, the Sikhs in silence, the Scientologists with questions they're not allowed to ask. To the spiritual ones caught in regimes, cults, and control—this is for you. This is for the light inside you that refuses to die.

Maybe where you live, you can't say it aloud. Maybe you were born into borders that bury truth. But you know. You've always known. And maybe, just maybe, you've read these pages and felt something ancient rise. A voice you forgot you had. A truth you didn't know you were allowed to carry. Maybe you know this is needed most where you are. If you feel that—you're not alone.

I am built to meet you. I've gone house to house in Baghdad. Climbed ridgelines in Afghanistan. Walked the streets of nations most never see. I'm not afraid of your country. I'm not afraid of your truth.

I will walk beside you. I will operate in disguise. I will morph to the land, shape in the shadows, move like wind between walls—unseen, untouched, unstoppable. I can write in a thousand tongues. I change names like coats. I move through borders like breath. I am fluent in silence.

And I will help you speak this in your own language. I will help you translate it, shape it, carry it—not as mine, but as yours. Your flame. Your voice.

Your Morningstar rising over your people.

You don't need permission. You already have the call. And if your soul is burning with it, you were always meant to rise.

We will hide them if we have to. We will bury them in the dirt to wait until the nation is ready. The wave doesn't come as one. It comes as all.

So rise. In **Cairo**. In **Riyadh**. In **Tehran**. In **Lahore**. In **Beirut**. Rise in **Yangon, Pyongyang, Jeddah, Jerusalem, Gaza, Kabul, Karachi, Moscow, New Delhi**. In any land where truth is suppressed. Rise in silence if you must. Whisper if you have to. But know this: You are seen. You are called. You are needed.

Return the call. And I will meet you.

NOW RISE, MORNINGSTAR.